THE YEAR THAT TRIED MEN'S SOULS

THE YEAR
THAT TRIED
MEN'S SOULS

A Journalistic Reconstruction
of the World of 1776

MERRITT IERLEY

South Brunswick and New York: A. S. Barnes and Company
London: Thomas Yoseloff Ltd

6 8110

A. S. Barnes and Co., Inc.
Cranbury, New Jersey 08512

Thomas Yoseloff Ltd
108 New Bond Street
London W1Y OQX, England

Library of Congress Cataloging in Publication Data

Ierley, Merritt.
     The year that tried men's souls.

     Includes bibliographical references and index.
     1. United States—History—Revolution, 1775–1783.
I. Title.
E208.I3   973.3   75-29699
ISBN 0-498-01849-0

End paper illustration:
THE WORLD (Thomas Kitchin, London, c. 1776).

Map Division—New York Public Library—
Astor, Lenox and Tilden Foundations

PRINTED IN THE UNITED STATES OF AMERICA

To my alma mater,
the College of William and Mary,
whose earlier sons made much of this news

MAPS AND ILLUSTRATIONS

THE WORLD (Thomas Kitchin, London, c. 1776)   End papers

THE AMERICAN COLONIES (Thomas Jefferys, London, 1775)   p.   24–25

THE MOON (Samuel Dunn, London, 1772)   31

LONDON (John Rocque, London, 1746)   68–69

BOSTON AND ENVIRONS (William Faden, London, 1777)   81

THE NORTH POLE (John Gibson, London, 1775)   131

THE BATTLE OF SULLIVAN'S ISLAND
(William Faden, London, 1776)   179

PENNSYLVANIA EVENING POST, July 2, 1776   198–199

SOUTH AMERICA (Thomas Jefferys, London, 1775)   242

THE BATTLE OF LONG ISLAND
(William Faden, London, 1776)   253

THE CITY OF NEW YORK (Thomas Jefferys, London, 1776)   273

THE BATTLE OF VALCOUR ISLAND
(William Faden, London, 1776)   294

MILITARY OPERATIONS NORTH OF NEW YORK
(William Faden, London, 1777)   302

THE BATTLE OF WHITE PLAINS
(William Faden, London, 1777)   314

EUROPE (Thomas & Andrews, Boston, c. 1780)   347

THE BATTLE OF TRENTON (William Faden, London, 1777)   374

PREFACE

The Year That Tried Men's Souls is a frankly different approach to history—different in what it seeks to do, and different in how it goes about it.

What it seeks to do, within the limits of a reasonable amount of space, is to recall one year in as broad detail as we record the year in which we are living. To put it another way, its mission is to recapture the totality of that year, the world over, and to do so by restructuring it in the same essential way that we chronicle our own history-in-the-making.

What we record about our own times we call first of all news; and it is routinely news of man in all his diversity—as much about science, law, commerce, medicine, religion, art, music, sports, and so on, as it is the politico-military events which are the grist of traditional history-telling. And just as that is so now, so was it then. The newspapers, books, and magazines of 1776 (albeit a little less so in America than in Britain) reveal an appetite for news about murders and other crimes, new books, fashions, the weather, fluctuations of the stock market, art, theater openings, and so on, that is strikingly like our own times. If all this were merely peripheral, it would be merely interesting. But as one digs into this so-called periphery, while at the same time digging afresh into the essential events, one inevitably comes away with a broader perspective. This can be true with something as simple as the weather (the winter of 1776 was one of the severest on record in Britain, leading one to suspect that George III really did have a cold heart); it can be more revealing when an increase in crime and an apparent decrease in industrial productivity in Britain are claimed to be linked to discontent over the war in America; when reports of the latest Paris fashions, and particularly a new fad in jeweled shoes, appear in curious contrast to accounts of shoeless Continental soldiers.

How this book approaches its mission will also strike the reader as different. It will be immediately obvious in that it is not written as a continuous narrative. There are no extended themes, and no chapters (unless the month of January as a whole can be considered the first of twelve "chapters"). The presentation is purely chronological. Events unfold as they did at the time, in a news format not very unlike that by which they first became known. There are no conclusions—the reader being free to draw them for himself from the interrelation of events.

The "news" approach is in keeping with the use of newspapers as the principal basis of research. And because this work is based primarily on what was in print in 1776, it provides a fair guide to what was known at the time, in the sequence that such news became public; and by omission, what was clearly not yet public knowledge at the time (as for example, the debates on the Declaration of Independence).

Research included a general review of virtually all the American and European newspapers, magazines, and books printed in 1776 and still available in libraries in the United States. More than 130 of these titles (mostly newspapers, published anywhere from one to six times a week) then were selected as the primary source material. There was also extensive research into secondary sources to test validity and to incorporate into each story such additional material (provided it would have been known at the time) as to make it more interesting and more meaningful. All writing, except of course that which is in quotes, is the author's own.

There has been a conscious effort throughout this work to find analogy with the present—to find those everyday events which are strikingly like today's news, and against which whoever chooses to do so may ponder the progress of mankind over the intervening two centuries and consider anew the cyclical nature of history. Thus will the reader come across all these: the tribulations of a rising cost of living, a price freeze, a troublesome stock market, extortion of the nations of western Europe by Middle East potentates, crime in the streets, air pollution, peace talks, debates over secrecy in government, the problem of Ireland, a threatened carpenters' strike, a significant civil rights decision, controversy over a new form of medical treatment, bad reviews of new plays, the latest Paris fashions, an exciting boxing match.

At the same time that there has been an attempt to find analogy with the present, and to offer the whole in a way modern readers will find familiar, there has been an intent to do so in a way that is faithful to the source material and to the fundamental test of whatever appears here: that it could have been written the same way at the time. There are thus a number of technical considerations which require some explaining.

Format

The manner of presentation is suggestive of some modern publications, but in many ways is equally representative of eighteenth-century journalism: the use, for example, of category headings ("Foreign Affairs," "Law Intelligence," and "Parliament" being a few in regular use then), as well as introductory quotations, footnotes, italics for emphasis, and the story form that opens, "DIED: January 2nd, in London: John Smith . . ."

The only real exception is the use of short headlines, a journalistic development that came in the next century.

Timing

The reader should always bear in mind the slowness of communication in that day, some idea of which is evident in this from the *London Packet* of November 20, 1776: "The west and northwest winds having continued to blow for many days past, a vessel [and thus, news] from New York may therefore very reasonably be expected daily to arrive." Communication between America and Europe required at least four and a half weeks, and in many cases it might have been months before a story originating on one continent appeared in the press of the other. To avoid confusion, events in this book are reported the week they happened, whether in Europe or America. If a particular date has significance, it is given; otherwise "this week" or "has happened" is used for easier reading.

Language and Terminology

There has been a determined effort throughout this project to use only that language (except in quotation or in a technical context) which is demonstrably common to both the eighteenth and twentieth centuries. Curiously acceptable, therefore, are such expressions as "mince words," "get one's brains knocked out," "jailbird" and "chick" meaning a young girl. The determination of acceptability was based on evident usage in 1776 as well as on the standard of that time, Samuel Johnson's *Dictionary of the English Language,* then in its twenty-first year, and the standard of the present day, the *Oxford English Dictionary,* to which a few contributions are being made from the research on this book. Where there were variations of form or spelling of place names in source material, the modern form is used. For example, the official name of that state was then "Massachusetts-Bay," but the present form of "Massachusetts" was also used (as by the newspaper, the *Massachusetts Spy*) and is used here. The term "correspondent" is used frequently and legitimately. Many newspaper stories in 1776 were headed, "From a correspondent," and meant just that. As opposed to common modern usage, however, such a person was not in the employ of the newspaper, except in rare cases.

Congress

The official record of the Continental Congress, published in 1776, was called the *Journals of Congress;* hence the simple term "Congress" (rather than "the Congress" or "Continental Congress") is used here. It has the merit of being the term we use today. Congress, unlike the British Parliament, met in complete secrecy; but it regularly published an abridged record (what was left after a screening committee went to work on the whole) of its activities, and also released the same periodically to newspapers. These published records actually constituted by far the most of its business, and provided the basis for what is included in this book. Carefully omitted here is whatever is known to have been withheld at the time.

Parliament

Both the House of Commons and the House of Lords of Great Britain were regularly and extensively covered in the press (American as well as British), even though the galleries were sometimes closed to the public. Accordingly, coverage of Parliament in this book includes detailed accounts of debates, whereas that for Congress cannot.

Sources

With only a very few exceptions, each story that appears in this book has been written on the basis of something in print (a newspaper article, a new book, and so on) in 1776. Such primary sources are all listed at the end of the book. Occasionally will there be a story based on some other source (private correspondence, later historical writings) where there is reason to think such information was public knowledge at the time. These few exceptions will be clear from the source notes.

Further on the matter of sources should there be a brief comment on eighteenth-century newspapers. Generally speaking, the British papers were the most advanced in the world at that time. What particularly distinguished them was a newly developing notion that a newspaper should go out and get the news, rather than merely publish official promulgations and other forms of editorial contributions delivered to the door. The term "newspaper reporter" was just coming into use, and a mention of it in the *London Packet* of November 11, 1776, is one of the first uses of the term, if not in fact the first, on record.

American newspapers, on the other hand, were sometimes little more than printed bulletin boards. They generally lacked the wherewithal to do much more than print official notices, military communiqués, contributions from readers, and a few local goings-on that constituted the hard news. A good deal of space was given to reprinting the same sort of thing from newspapers in other cities. Inaccuracies and misspellings were not uncommon, although proofreading was surprisingly good and would put many a modern newspaper to shame.

As sources for historical research, eighteenth-century American newspapers—there were thirty-one published at the time of the Declaration of Independence—must be read carefully, and indeed it would be difficult to do otherwise considering the very small type that was used. Care must be taken to sort out the verifiable from the unfounded. What is usable from any given issue is often little, but it can just as often be eloquent. An example is this description of the Battle of White Plains in the *Connecticut Journal* of November 6, 1776:

> The scene was grand and solemn; all the adjacent hills smoked as tho' on fire, and bellowed and trembled with a perpetual cannonade and fire

of field pieces, hobits and mortars. The air groaned with streams of cannon and musket shot; the hills smoked and echoed terribly with the bursting of shells; the fences and walls were knocked down and torn to pieces, and men's legs, arms and bodies mangled with cannon and grape shot [fell] all around us.

This book makes use of many such firsthand accounts, quoting them directly, and of hundreds of other less dramatic but equally important contemporary reports as the basis of this unique look at a year long past but eagerly recalled.

M. I.

October, 1975

ACKNOWLEDGMENTS

My principal acknowledgment is to J. Mark Reifer, of Honington, near Shipston-on-Stour, Warwickshire, England (M.A., history, Trinity College, Oxford; formerly assistant dean and tutor in politics and economics, Wroxton College, Wroxton, England; at present, supervising research associate, the New Jersey Legislature). His thorough and thoroughly capable critique of this manuscript, reflecting a practical understanding of both British and American history, was uniquely appropriate and is deeply appreciated.

The Index—a laborious task—was the work of Edna Ierley, Madison (New Jersey) Public Library.

Among the many others who have, in some way or another, provided assistance I wish in particular to acknowledge John F. Bullough, Virginia Chuchra, Lois Ely, Robert Ierley, Florence Melville, Betty Pellet and Maureen Petrosky.

The list of research libraries consulted is too long to be appropriate in its entirety. These, however, ought to be mentioned as having been used the most: American Antiquarian Society, Beinecke Rare Book Library (Yale University), Historical Society of Pennsylvania, Library Company of Philadelphia, Library of Congress, New York Historical Society, and especially—because of its convenience to home and its abundance of material—the Rare Book Division of New York Public Library (Maud D. Cole, Keeper of Books).

AN INTRODUCTORY COMMENT

A history professor, as deceptive as he was brilliant, began his first lecture to freshmen:

"History teaches us that history teaches us nothing!"

Like the mule who was clubbed before he was spoken to, the students responded with immediate attention. But the professor was wrong. Author Ierley so proves as he marshals the newspapers of 1776 to tell the story of that year, often in their own words. His history teaches us that history does indeed teach us—and it teaches us fundamental lessons.

One such lesson is that freedom shrinks again. Across three quarters of the globe, embracing perhaps eighty per cent of the earth's people, no man is free to speak his mind, or write or broadcast the truth, without the fear of a knock on the door in the middle of the night, disappearance, prison, torment, and perhaps even death.

For the extreme, read Solzhenitsyn's reporting.

For the more recent past and the present, consider the Philippines, where newspapermen are in jail and the press is censored.

For the future, ponder India, where critics of government are imprisoned without charges and the press is censored.

What has 1976 got to do with 1776?

One lesson is that it is the passionate few who make freedom live. There was not in 1776, nor is there in 1976, much visible public support for or even understanding of a free press.

With gracious respect for his readers, Author Ierley lets us draw our own parallels. He teaches by comparisons, but you must draw your own. Here are a few:

Then: In Colonial Massachusetts, Editor Fowle is jailed for printing his opinions on taxes. Now: Three American reporters are jailed for protecting news sources—sources without which there would be none of that news which leads to reform of government.

Then: *New York Packet* Publisher Loudon's copies of a tract rebutting *Common Sense* are burned by people who had not even read it. Now: In Charleston, West Virginia, mobs demand destruction of textbooks they have not read.

Then: The British government shackles newspapers with punitive taxes, saying "some people think they [newspapers] do more harm than good." Now: Somewhere, many times each year, a governmental body weighs new laws to tax newspaper advertising, to suppress certain kinds of advertising, and to conduct the public's business secretly.

History teaches us fundamentals, and one of them is the inter-relationship of a free press and a free society. We have in America today a journalistic heritage unequaled by any country on earth. But it is not a self-perpetuating heritage. It must be continually guarded—preserved from any and all who would try to turn it to their own ends.

Society recognizing that and acting accordingly; the newspaper profession recognizing that and acting accordingly—therein is the surest hope of America remaining in the free quarter of the globe.

J. Montgomery Curtis
Director, 1947–1967
American Press Institute
Columbia University

September, 1975

THE YEAR
THAT TRIED
MEN'S SOULS

PART I

1776

January
S	M	T	W	T	F	S
	1	2	3	4	5	6
7	8	9	10	11	12	13
14	15	16	17	18	19	20
21	22	23	24	25	26	27
28	29	30	31			

February
S	M	T	W	T	F	S
				1	2	3
4	5	6	7	8	9	10
11	12	13	14	15	16	17
18	19	20	21	22	23	24
25	26	27	28	29		

March
S	M	T	W	T	F	S
					1	2
3	4	5	6	7	8	9
10	11	12	13	14	15	16
17	18	19	20	21	22	23
24	25	26	27	28	29	30
31						

April
S	M	T	W	T	F	S
	1	2	3	4	5	6
7	8	9	10	11	12	13
14	15	16	17	18	19	20
21	22	23	24	25	26	27
28	29	30				

May
S	M	T	W	T	F	S
			1	2	3	4
5	6	7	8	9	10	11
12	13	14	15	16	17	18
19	20	21	22	23	24	25
26	27	28	29	30	31	

June
S	M	T	W	T	F	S
						1
2	3	4	5	6	7	8
9	10	11	12	13	14	15
16	17	18	19	20	21	22
23	24	25	26	27	28	29
30						

July
S	M	T	W	T	F	S
	1	2	3	4	5	6
7	8	9	10	11	12	13
14	15	16	17	18	19	20
21	22	23	24	25	26	27
28	29	30	31			

August
S	M	T	W	T	F	S
				1	2	3
4	5	6	7	8	9	10
11	12	13	14	15	16	17
18	19	20	21	22	23	24
25	26	27	28	29	30	31

September
S	M	T	W	T	F	S
1	2	3	4	5	6	7
8	9	10	11	12	13	14
15	16	17	18	19	20	21
22	23	24	25	26	27	28
29	30					

October
S	M	T	W	T	F	S
		1	2	3	4	5
6	7	8	9	10	11	12
13	14	15	16	17	18	19
20	21	22	23	24	25	26
27	28	29	30	31		

November
S	M	T	W	T	F	S
					1	2
3	4	5	6	7	8	9
10	11	12	13	14	15	16
17	18	19	20	21	22	23
24	25	26	27	28	29	30

December
S	M	T	W	T	F	S
1	2	3	4	5	6	7
8	9	10	11	12	13	14
15	16	17	18	19	20	21
22	23	24	25	26	27	28
29	30	31				

JANUARY

SEE how the naked trees their leaves have lost?
The earth is covered with hail, snow or frost,
Is now disrob'd of all the Summer's pride,
That not a flower i'th' fields can be espied.

The Virginia Almanack
January, 1776

THE WEEK OF JANUARY 1st

The World

New Year, New Flag

As the old year ended, so did the Continental army, all enlistments expiring with the stroke of midnight the 31st.

But the army of the thirteen American colonies, something under 20,000-strong, is still there—still encamped at Cambridge, Massachusetts, as it has been for the last half-year. And there are mostly the same old faces. Faces that winced to the first sight of blood at Lexington and Concord last April; faces that brightened to a short-lived taste of victory in the first assault at Bunker's Hill last June; and still other faces that are new, faces tightened into masks of bewilderment and pride.

By and large, the ranks of the Continental army are staying with it and renewing enlistments for another year, even knowing better now the fear, the uncertainty, the unspeakable hardship that will be theirs with it.

Hardship is already felt in the biting New England cold. The Charles River between Cambridge and Boston is nearly frozen over, nature there-

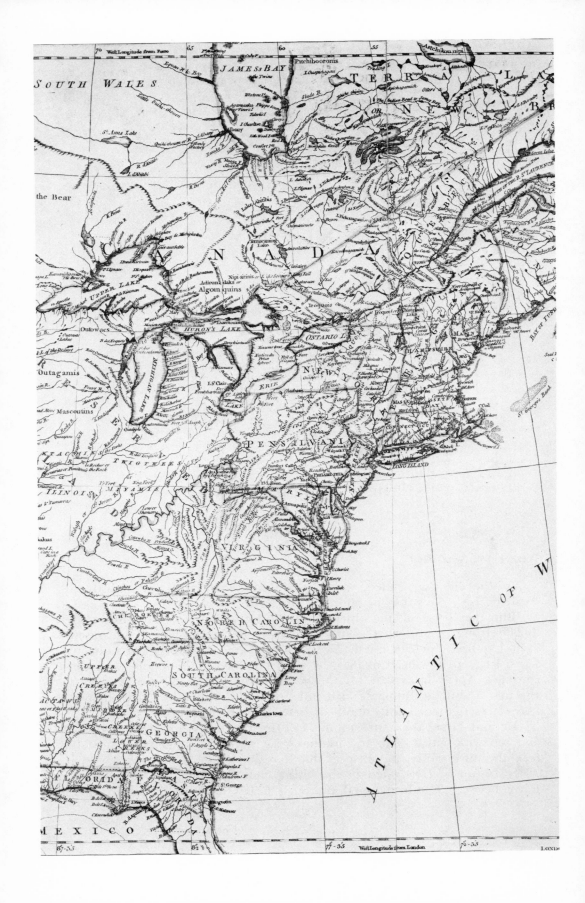

THE AMERICAN COLONIES (Thomas Jefferys, London, 1775). Shown here:
the thirteen United Colonies, with East and West Florida to the south, Canada
to the north, and Indian lands to the west. (Maine was a part of Massachusetts.)
The United Colonies and their populations (with capitals in parentheses—there
being two in some cases, the seat of government shifting): Massachusetts, 400,000
(Boston); New Hampshire, 150,000 (Portsmouth); Rhode Island, 59,678 (Providence and Newport); Connecticut, 192,000 (Hartford and New Haven); New
York, 250,000 (New York); New Jersey, 130,000 (Burlington and Perth Amboy);
Pennsylvania, 350,000 including Delaware (Philadelphia); Delaware, population
included with Pennsylvania's (New Castle); Maryland, 320,000 (Annapolis);
Virginia, 650,000 (Williamsburg); North Carolina, 300,000 (New Bern and Halifax); South Carolina, 225,000 (Charleston), and Georgia, no population estimate
(Savannah). The population figures are those of a census made by the Continental
Congress in 1774—and are likely on the high side. Georgia was not then represented in Congress; Delaware's population was figured in with Pennsylvania's. On
this map, the word "of" following "Atlantic" is a misprint for "or." The complete
terminology is "Atlantic of [or] Western Ocean." "Ilinois," at left, is a reference
to the Indians of the region, not the future state.

Map Division—New York Public Library—
Astor, Lenox and Tilden Foundations

by building a bridge of ice between the camps of the American and British armies.

With the new year has come a new flag—of thirteen red and white stripes—raised in military use for the first time on New Year's Day by General Washington's men on Prospect Hill in Cambridge, from which vantage they continue to hold the British army at Boston in siege. The flag is basically the British red ensign, with six horizontal white stripes sewn across its field of red. In the canton in the upper left remain the ensign's crosses of St. George and St. Andrew.

On the British ensign, the two crosses symbolize the union of England and Scotland that created Great Britain sixty-nine years ago. In this new flag the two crosses call to mind the unity that legally obtains between the American colonies and the mother country, despite the enmity of the past years. The thirteen stripes, meanwhile, represent the ties among the colonies, once altogether separate in government, economy, religion and culture but now acting more and more as one.

As this new year of 1776 begins, there are those who argue that a flag symbolizing both unity with Britain and unity within the colonies will not long endure such disparate elements. Either the crosses of St. George and St. Andrew will prevail, which is to say union with the mother country restored by force; or the thirteen red and white stripes, which is to say union of the colonies and independence from Great Britain. No few are beginning to think the latter—perhaps before another new year has dawned.[1]

New Year, Old Message

In London, while the rest of the city marked the occasion much as usual, his Majesty King George III also observed New Year's Day at St. James's Palace with a custom: the reading of an "Ode for the New Year" by Britain's poet laureate, William Whitehead.

It was less a paean than a plaint; less a eulogium to the new year than a message for America. Surveying the state of the world at the threshhold of 1776, poet Whitehead found Britannia casting a pensive eye across the sea, scarcely to check a rising sigh or a trembling tear at what she sees. Dismayed, Britannia pleads:

> Sheathe, sheathe the sword which thirsts for blood
> (She cried) deceived, mistaken men!
> Nor let your parent, o'er the flood,
> Send forth her voice in vain!
> Alas! no tyrant she,
> She courts you to be free:
> Submissive hear her soft command,
> Nor force unwilling vengeance from a parent's hand.[2]

New Year, New Chance

In Paris, the French government kept New Year's Day by announcing a general pardon for all deserters from the armed services. Anticipated result: the return of as many as 20,000 men to the ranks.[3]

The War

The Destruction of Norfolk

As the old year ended Norfolk was Virginia's largest city and its principal seaport. A bustling community of 6,000 people, many made affluent by its commerce, it carried on extensive trade with the other colonies and the world.

Hours into the new year, reeling under a brutal attack by the British, its citizens could only wonder whether there would continue to be a Norfolk at all; days later, they no longer wondered.

Mid-afternoon on Monday, the 1st, Lord Dunmore, the royal governor now in exile with a small British fleet off the Virginia coast, made good a threat to turn his cannon on the town—his request for critically needed supplies denied by the city. And turn them he did, in a cannonade that seemed never to end. But that was not enough for the royal emissary whose relations with his colony grew so bad that, six months ago, he abandoned his palace in Williamsburg and sought safety at sea. Able at last to vent his anger, he did so to the limit. Under cover of his thunderous attack, Dunmore sent marines ashore to do with the torch whatever might be left undone by the cannon. Since the buildings nearest the shore were all made of wood, and since the wind was blowing inland, a holocaust was assured. With the first few houses and wharves set aflame, the wind took up the British cause, from timber house to timber shop, spreading flame and destruction throughout the day and into the night.

On Tuesday, the 2nd, Colonel Robert Howe, commander of the patriot forces, sent off a dispatch to the capital, Williamsburg, warning that the fire had spread with amazing speed. "It is now become general, and the whole town will, I doubt not, be consumed in a day or two," he predicted.

At week's end, Norfolk is nine-tenths a smoldering ruin. Gone are nearly all the houses and churches, the mills at Tucker's Point, even the Scotch distillery at Gosport. What few houses remain are occupied by patriot troops, who, while powerless to deal with the greater form of destruction, have had success in beating back British raiding parties that have advanced upon the dying city from time to time.

Despite the awesome loss in property, loss of life has been remarkably low, most of Norfolk's citizens escaping inland. There are reports of only three killed and seven injured.[4]

Uncertainty In Boston

The British garrison at Boston remains in a state of siege as it has for half a year. But the confidence of the past has begun to give way to uncertainty and despair. The troops and the Tories remaining with them in the city have been particularly dispirited since a storeship bound for Boston was captured by an American privateer.

Fuel and provisions are scarce. Each soldier has rations of four pounds of pork and two loaves of bread a week. To offset the fuel shortage, thirty men from each company were ordered recently to take axes and cut up wharves and a church. Smallpox is prevalent, along with dysentery and black jaundice. The sick are being separated to prevent the spread of illness.[5]

Keeping Warm

Continental troops stationed at Cambridge are having a somewhat easier time than might otherwise be the case in fighting off the bitter New England winter. Since the Battle of Lexington last April, the people of Massachusetts have reportedly completed 13,000 suits of soldiers' clothes entirely of their own wool and flax.[6]

Congress

Background note appears on Page 51.

"The Unmanly Designers"

Congress opened the year by taking a hard and firm position on that notorious hotbed of Tory resistance, Queens County, New York. Observing that Queens citizens recently refused to elect delegates to the Convention of the Colony of New York, Congress reacted with a charge of desertion to the American cause, accusing Queens citizens in general of "an unmanly design of remaining inactive spectators of the present contest." If Britain prevails, they can purchase favor at an easy rate; if the United Colonies win, the people of Queens will be in a position, said Congress, to "enjoy, without the expense of blood or treasure, all the blessing resulting from that liberty."

Thus did Congress make known its contempt, and go on by resolution to declare that: all who voted against sending deputies to the Convention be named in a list of delinquents; that all trade and association with them cease; that no inhabitant of Queens be permitted to travel to any other part of the United Colonies without a certificate from the Committee of Safety or Convention of New York, upon penalty of three months' imprisonment; that no lawyer prosecute or defend any action at law by a citizen of Queens upon penalty of being treated as one himself.

All this—if it can be enforced—may help to put down Tory resistance. But Congress went one step further to make sure. It ordered troops to round up and arrest Tory leaders in Jamaica, Newtown, Flushing, Hampstead, Cowneck, Rockaway and Oyster Bay.

But enemies to the patriot cause are by no means unique to New York. Congress therefore also resolved to recommend to all the Assemblies, Conventions, and Committees or Councils of Safety in all the colonies that the "mischievous machinations" of such enemies be frustrated by disarming them all and by keeping in custody, or under surety bonds, the most dangerous among them.

In other action this week, Congress ordered an issue of 10,000 new dollars to replace ragged and torn bills from the 1775 issue of Continental currency.[7]

The Colonies

"Throwing off Dependence"

Without a governor and without any effectual machinery of government since Loyalist John Wentworth left the colony last June rather than join what looked like revolution, New Hampshire now has taken the boldest political step of any colony: it has set up its own form of government under its own constitution.

In so doing the northernmost colony followed a recommendation of the Continental Congress of last November: that it "establish such a form of government as, in their judgment, will best produce the happiness of the people, and most effectually secure peace and order in the province during the continuance of the present dispute between Great Britain and the colonies."

Taking that admonition to heart, New Hampshire's Provincial Congress on January 5th adopted a constitution that gives the colony a House of Representatives, elected by the eligible voters of the colony, with the sole power to originate legislation for raising, levying and collecting money; and a separate legislative body of twelve persons, called the Council, whose members for now will be selected by the House and later elected by the people. All acts must be approved by both branches of the Legislature to become law. Likewise will the appointment of all officers of the militia and the army require the approval of both houses, along with most civil officers of the colony.

Such a form of government is hardly radical in its own right; what makes it significant is that it is the form of government devised by the colony for itself, and not that which was instituted for it in London. But whether it will remain in effect permanently is still to be seen. New Hampshire's representatives, in adopting their constitution, made it clear that they acted only out of necessity and only as a temporary expedient. They cited the departure of Governor Wentworth as leaving the colony "destitute of legislation" and lacking of any machinery of justice; there

have been no courts to punish criminal offenders, thus risking the lives
and property of honest people to the mercy of wicked men. Said the colony's representatives, gathered at Exeter: "We consider ourselves reduced
to the necessity of establishing a form of government, to continue during
the present unhappy and unnatural contest with Great Britain; protesting
and declaring that we never sought to throw off our dependence upon
Great Britain, but felt ourselves happy under her protection while we
could enjoy our constitutional rights and privileges; and that we shall rejoice if such a reconciliation between us and our parent state can be
effected as shall be approved by Continental Congress, in whose prudence
and wisdom we confide."[8]

Never Too Old

In the Borough of Westchester, New York, the day after New Year's,
Alderman Leggett took as his bride Mrs. Catherine Everits, a widow, age
39. Alderman Leggett is 77.[9]

Holidays

By order of the Honorable Commissioners of his Majesty's Customs
in North America, the following days are to be kept and observed as holidays during 1776: January 1, New Year's Day; January 18, Queen's Birthday; January 30, Anniversary of King Charles's Martyrdom; February 20,
Shrove Tuesday; February 21, Ash Wednesday; March 25, Lady Day;
April 5, Good Friday; April 8 & 9, Easter Monday and Tuesday; April 23,
St. George's Day; May 16, Ascension Day; May 27 & 28, Whitsun Monday
and Tuesday; May 29, Anniversary of King Charles's Restoration; June 4,
King's Birthday; August 12, Prince of Wales's Birthday; September 18,
Anniversary of Landing of George I in Great Britain; September 22, Anniversary of Coronation of George III and Queen Charlotte; October 25,
Anniversary of Ascension of George III to the Throne; November 1, All
Saints Day; November 5, Powder Plot Day; December 25, Christmas; December 26, 27 & 28, Christmas Holidays.[10]

Foreign News

Quiet Quays

With trade between Britain and the Colonies at a standstill, custom
house quays in London are considerably neater and cleaner, no longer
piled high with tobacco, oil, timber, potash, pelts, whalebone, rice, indigo
and other commodities from North America. Nor with innumerable trunks,
bales, casks and cases of diverse products bound for the colonies. Porters
and other workers, having considerably more time with nothing to do,
stand about idly. For a penny or two, they will gladly post a letter or
fetch a hackney cab.[11]

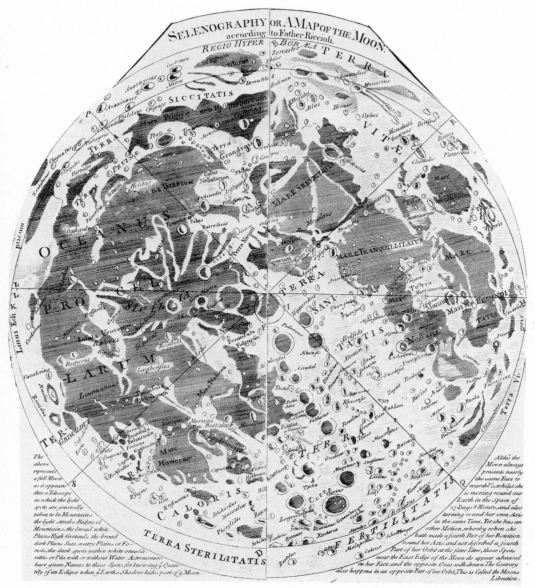

THE MOON (Samuel Dunn, London, 1772; in Thomas Kitchin, A General Atlas, London, 1777). It had already been more than a century and a half since Galileo first produced a detailed drawing of the moon based on telescopic viewing. In the meantime, a Jesuit astronomer by the name of G. B. Riccioli had supplied (in 1651) the nomenclature—Sea of Tranquility, Sea of Serenity, and so forth—that we still use today. Here then is the moon in the detail by which it was known in 1776.

Better Bounties

The British Admiralty has announced that able-bodied seamen will now get forty shillings, and ordinary seamen twenty shillings in bounty for enlisting in his Majesty's fleet. Not sure of enough volunteers, however, the Navy is reported to be considering a draft at Greenwich Naval Hospital, picking the most healthy, or least ill, men for ships bound for America.[12]

Science

One Eclipse This Year

Americans interested in astronomy will find 1776 a disappointing year. Of five eclipses predicted, only one will be visible in the colonies. That will be Tuesday, July 30th, a total eclipse of the moon. Eclipses of the sun on January 20th, February 19th and July 15th as well as of the moon on February 4th will not be visible to Americans. There will, however, be a transit of the planet Mercury. Based on Halley's Tables and on observation of the last such transit November 9th, 1769, by the Philosophical Society of Philadelphia, Mercury will appear just to touch the lower circumference of the sun on the afternoon of Saturday, November 2nd.[13]

Law

A Binding Force

> *"From the same original of the King's being the Fountain of Justice, we may deduce the prerogative of issuing proclamations, which is vested in the King alone. These proclamations have then a binding force, when they are grounded upon and enforce the law of the realm."*
>
> —Blackstone

Quoting that extract of the eminent English jurist's recent *Commentaries on the Law of England* (1765–69), Boston's loyalist-published *Massachusetts Gazette* this week reminded inhabitants of the recent proclamation of his Majesty, King George III, supressing rebellion and sedition in the colonies. The *Gazette* said it offered the reminder "in order that no fellow citizen may be ignorant of the judgment of the law."

The proclamation to which the newspaper referred requires all obedient and loyal subjects, as well as British military and civil officers, to transmit to the proper authorities "due and full information on all persons who shall be found carrying on correspondence with, or in any manner or degree aiding or abetting the persons now in open arms or rebellion against our government within any of our colonies or plantations in North America."

Such conduct is high treason, and the *Gazette* added this reminder, quoting the law of the province: "If any person shall levy war against our Lord the King, or be adherent to the King's enemies, giving them aid or comfort in the realm or elsewhere, he shall suffer pains of death."[14]

And The Governor, Too

In a court of law it is customary for the defendant, after sentencing, to conclude the proceeding by humbly intoning, "God save the King."

A recent proceeding in Lancaster County, Virginia, concluded differently. A man tried and convicted of stealing sheep listened impassively as the sentence was read: "Have him burned on the hands." All remained quiet for the concluding formality. At once, with what struck an observer as "the greatest seeming intensity," the prisoner looked up and roared, "God d--m the King . . . and the governor, too."[15]

THE WEEK OF JANUARY 8TH

The War

All The King's Horses

From Brunswick, Germany, there is a report of a treaty between his Majesty, King George III of Great Britain, and the Duke of Brunswick and Lunenburg for German troops to support British military operations in the American colonies.

How good a bargain the king struck may be debated. The treaty provides for 350 light cavalry—but not their horses. If his Majesty wants them mounted, he will have to supply the horses himself. Otherwise the cavalrymen will act as infantry.[16]

Furloughs Terminated

All men of the Continental Army off on furlough or out on recruiting duty have the word from Adjutant General Horatio Gates: return to their units by February 1st. Any officer failing to meet the deadline will be immediately cashiered; any non-commissioned officer or soldier will be tried and punished as a deserter. Gates's order suggests there may be plans for an assault on the British army in Boston, where it has been held under siege since the middle of last year.[17]

Congress

Canada and Currency

Supporting the war effort in Canada and the value of Continental currency in the colonies dominated the activities of Congress this week.

The colonies' delegates in Philadelphia undertook a new effort to maintain the value of Continental paper dollars, which are often considered less valuable than their equivalent in coin. In a resolution Thursday, Congress showed its concern with those "evil disposed persons" who have attempted to depreciate the bills of credit emitted by order of Congress.

Therefore, declared Congress, "if any person . . . refuse to receive said bills in payment, or obstruct or discourage the currency or circulation thereof and shall be duly convicted by the committee [of safety] of the city, county or district, or in case of an appeal from their decision, by the assembly, convention, council or committee of safety of the colony where he shall reside, such person shall be deemed, published and treated as an enemy to this country and precluded from all trade or intercourse with the inhabitants of these colonies."

As for the war effort in Canada, Congress:

—Directed that shipwrights from New York and Philadelphia be sent immediately to General Philip Schuyler, the commander of Continental forces in the Province of New York, at Fort Ticonderoga, to build up to one hundred small, flat-bottomed boats for transporting troops and their baggage from there to Canada when the appropriate time comes;

—Sent two shipwrights to Albany to build scows for passage across Hudson's River;

—Ordered that a large supply of provisions and stores be sent to Fort George, on Lake George in the Province of New York;

—Directed that officers of the Northern Army be responsible for stores issued their units, and that the value be deducted from the pay of those who have embezzled or wasted the same;

—Ordered that one additional battalion each be raised by New Hampshire, Connecticut, New York and Pennsylvania for deployment in Canada.

Congress this week also approved an appropriation of 500,000 dollars for the continued maintenance of the Continental Army under General Washington in Cambridge. And it approved a modest bonus for army privates. Henceforth each will be entitled to free mail—letters received as well as sent—during time of service. Such letters will be franked by the private's commanding officer, or some other person authorized by him. Those at the bottom of the Continental army now have the same privilege as the man at the top. Last November 10th, Congress accorded the franking privilege to the commander-in-chief, and two days earlier approved the same prerogative for itself, applicable to each member of Congress while it is in session.[18]

The Colonies

Aid for Norfolk

The Convention of Virginia, assembled in Williamsburg, this week appropriated 1,000 *l* for the immediate relief of the citizens of Norfolk and directed the Committee of Safety to see to their removal further into the interior of the Colony and away from the destruction of the once prosperous seaport, attacked by the British on New Year's Day.[19]

As then, so here: pound sterling is shown as a small l *after the amount.*

Foreign News

Shivering In Britain

Seven days into the new year, Britons were finding that of 1776 already rivaling the worst winters on record. An intense snowstorm on Sunday the 7th, ushered in by a high easterly wind, piled snow higher than almost anyone could remember. To make matters worse, the snow was followed by an intense cold that dropped temperatures lower than almost anyone could remember.[20]

Preliminary Budget

In London, his Majesty's government is reported to have approved a preliminary budget of 3,300,000 *l* for military operations for the year, mostly in America. The Royal Navy will get 1,800,000 *l* to maintain a force of fifty-six ships ranging in size from sixteen to fifty guns. They will be manned by 16,000 seamen and 3,000 marines. The army, meanwhile, will total about 34,000 men with a budget of 1,500,000 *l*. The final budget for all operations of government will not be submitted to the House of Commons until April.[21]

Reassignment In Ireland

Despite the continued rumblings of discontented Irishmen, the number of British troops on assignment in Ireland will consist of about 5,000 men in nine regiments of Horse Dragoons and eleven regiments of foot soldiers. The new total will be 3,000 fewer than at any time in recent memory, and perhaps the smallest number since the reign of Elizabeth, two centuries ago.[22]

Prices In Paris

Although butchers and bakers in Paris have been under the express orders of the police to adhere to the established prices for meat and bread, some have been taking a chance selling at higher rates. Those caught are being fined and ordered to close up their shops for three months.[23]

DIED: January 14th, at Bird Place, Hertfordshire, England: the Honorable Edward Cornwallis, lieutenant general of his Majesty's forces and Governor of Gibraltar. He was brother of the Honorable and Most Reverend Dr. Frederick Cornwallis, the Archbishop of Canterbury, and uncle of Charles, Earl of Cornwallis who, though a Whig, is a rising major general in his Majesty's service.[24]

Law

On Freeing Slaves

Acts of the New Jersey Legislature dating back to the reign of Queen Anne prescribe the manner in which a slave may be given liberty, and, equally important, the reason why a fixed procedure is deemed to be necessary at all. The reasoning: "Negroes are idle . . . and prove very often a charge to the place where they are."

To make certain a freed slave turning to an idle life would not become an encumbrance to the citizenry, the law prescribes: "Any master or mistress, setting at liberty any slave, shall enter into sufficient security to her Majesty, her heirs and successors, to pay yearly to such slave Twenty Pounds during life, and if such slave shall be made free by any will, the executors shall enter into the security, which, if refused to be given, the said manumission to be void and of none effect."

In New Jersey, about 1756, a landowner named Caleb Haines, of Burlington, provided in his will that his two Negro slaves, David and Dinah, would have their freedom upon his death. When he died, the two went free. Subsequently they had several children.

Last year Haines's daughter, Esther Barber, seized one of the children of David and Dinah on the contention that the manumission was void; Haines's will had provided no security. Through a writ of habeas corpus, the Negro girl, Beulah, was taken into New Jersey Supreme Court last May and the case was heard. But the court made no decision, concluding it was a case of considerable importance, thus requiring further reflection.

Finally the court has announced its verdict: young Beulah is to have her freedom. The court ordered her set free from the "illegal detention" of Esther Barber, and it declared the manumission of 1756 valid even though no security was provided.

For the court it was clearly a case of liberal rather than literal construction. The justices declared that the evident intention of the legislation was not to prevent Negroes from becoming free, but to prevent their freedom from becoming a burden to the community. In this particular case, David and Dinah and their children supported themselves and posed no burden for others. Thus was the spirit of the manumission law satisfied. To decide otherwise, said a report in the *Pennsylvania Gazette* this week, in announcing the decision, "would be to prefer a literal construction to the clear intention of the Legislature, and nothing [is] more common than for judges to construe an act according to the spirit of it where the letter and the spirit . . . disagree."[25]

The decision was actually handed down during the November, 1775, term of the New Jersey Supreme Court, but was apprently first reported in the press January 17, 1776.

Books

Uncommonly To The Point

The notion of independence from Great Britain has crossed no few minds in America. Many reject it outright; most have reservations ranging from mild to serious; some are convinced it is the inevitable course.

Among the last, few have dared to express themselves at all, and none to the degree of an anonymous author of a book just published in Philadelphia—a document so forthright, so outspoken, so certain of its own conclusions that it cannot help but attract attention and perhaps even influence many in that vast middle ground of uncertainty and indecision.

Loyalists will condemn it, and point to it as a confession of what they have argued all along to be the erring ways of thought of a rebellious rabble; advocates of liberty will point to it and say it is a manifestation of a gathering force sweeping toward a new and independent nation. Thus what for one side will be a recitation of the common sins of treasonous thinkers will, to the other, be that which only makes *Common Sense.*

So titled, and totaling seventy-nine pages, with an introduction signed only, "AUTHOR," the book published January 9th by R. Bell of Philadelphia offers—as it says—"nothing more than simple facts, plain arguments and common sense" in support of its clear call for independence from Great Britain.

Not only in its message but in its commitment to expressing that message in a "plain and simple" way does *Common Sense* have the potential for swaying minds. Often emotional, always unequivocal, it is obviously a tract for common people and not a treatise for the learned elite.

Some samples:

On independence: "Everything that is right or reasonable pleads for separation. The blood of the slain, the weeping voice of nature cries, 'Tis time to part."

On George III: "the Royal Brute."

On kings in general: "In the early ages of the world, according to the Scripture chronology, there were no kings; the consequence of which was that there were no wars; it is the pride of kings which throws mankind into confusion. Holland without a king hath enjoyed more peace for this last century than any of the monarchial governments in Europe."

On the freedom of British citizens: "The will of the king is as much the law of the land in Britain as in France, with this difference, that instead of proceeding directly from his mouth, it is handed to the people under the more formidable shape of an act of Parliament. For the fate of Charles the first hath only made kings more subtile—not more just."

On British support of her American colonies: "America would have flourished as much, and probably more, had no European power taken any notice of her."

On the argument America should be governed by Britain because her citizens first came from Britain: "The first king of England of the present line (William the Conqueror) was a Frenchman, and half the peers of England are descendants from the same country; wherefore by the same method of reasoning, England ought to be governed by France."

On the cause of liberty: " 'Tis not the affair of a city, a county, a province, or a kingdom, but of a continent—of at least one-eighth part of the habitable globe."

And its rightness: "The Sun never shined on a cause of greater worth."[26]

THE WEEK OF JANUARY 15TH

The War

Better Days

In 1771, as commandant of the Green Mountain Boys in the New Hampshire Grants, he was worth a reward of twenty *l* from the royal governor of New York, then in a territorial dispute with the Colony of New Hampshire. Three years later he was good for 100 *l*. By the time he led the American raid that resulted in the capture of Fort Ticonderoga last May, the price on his head was immaterial. Even though voted out of command by the Green Mountain Boys, his impulsive and daring exploits had marked Colonel Ethan Allen as a prime target for the British.

A target he ceased to be last September when American forces under his command made a foolhardy and unsuccessful move against Montreal. Captured, handcuffed and chained, Allen was sent off to Britain with no ascertainable future except an indefinite and likely barbarous imprisonment. Now from Cork, Ireland, comes a report that somewhat better days may be ahead. Colonel Allen is reported confined aboard the 28-gun British warship *Solebay* along with about fifty other American prisoners— and finding life a little more tolerable than it has been these past months. With the obvious approval of a more lenient British command, the citizens of Cork have taken up a collection—nearly fifty guineas so far—to buy food and clothing for Allen and the other prisoners. The first result of the collection was made evident last week as a hamper full of wine, sugar, fruit, chocolate and other food went aboard the *Solebay*.

Touched by their generosity, Colonel Ethan Allen replied with a note: "I received your generous present this day with a joyful heart. Thanks to God, there are still the feelings of humanity in the worthy citizens of Cork towards those of your bone and flesh who, through misfortune from the present broils in the empire, are needy prisoners."[27]

The Congress

Fighting Power

Strengthening the United Colonies' military capacity had the most attention of Congress this week.

Among other things, it:

—Resolved to use all possible dispatch in reinforcing the army in Canada, not only for military advantage to the colonies but for the "security and relief of our friends there";

—Directed Pennsylvania, New Jersey, New Hampshire, Connecticut and New York to hasten the embarkation of troops scheduled for northern duty;

—Requested General Washington to make available one of his battalions at Cambridge for service in Canada;

—Ordered four more battalions raised in New York for the protection of that Colony and for securing Long Island from its Tory dissidents;

—Pledged, as an incentive to recruiting, a bounty of six and two-thirds dollars for each new enlistee properly clothed and armed with a good firelock and bayonet, and four dollars for every new soldier lacking such equipment (which will be supplied to him by the army, the cost deducted from his pay). Further enlistment bonuses will include a free blanket and haversack plus one month's pay in advance.

In order to assist the individual colonies in raising the battalions required of them, Congress appropriated 12,500 dollars in aid to each of the colonies sending battalions for service in the north.

Congress also approved one other directive of possible significance. Henceforth, no indentured servant may be employed aboard the fleet or within the army of the United Colonies unless he gives his consent.[28]

The Colonies

Dunmore's Secret

Virginia's royal governor, Lord Dunmore, for whom the contempt of Virginians is unmatched by any living man except perhaps King George himself, would like nothing more than to have at his disposal the British force that was sent to restore order in Massachusetts—the more soundly to put down his own rebellious subjects.

Just how much so was revealed in a secret document from Dunmore to General Howe in Boston. The message fell into American hands when a British ship was intercepted off the New England coast by the more-and-more famous privateer, Captain John Manly. In his message Dunmore begged Howe to send 5,000 *l* and 3,000 men. In return he promised to furnish the besieged garrison at Boston with fresh provisions by plundering—with the help of those 3,000 men—the inhabitants of the Colony of Virginia.[29]

Foreign News

Background note on Page 52.

Lord North Resigning?

Britain's beleaguered First Minister, Lord North, is rumored to be more determined than ever to resign his post and be free of the responsibility of executing the King's policies—not always to his liking—against the American colonies. More and more faced with the likelihood of a military settlement, he appears to be concluding, said London's *St. James's Chronicle,* "that some invisible agent overrules every plan of reconciliation he has been able to devise."

Most likely successor, if Lord North does resign: Lord George Germaine, Secretary of State for the Colonies. Germaine is known to approve the propriety of military action in the colonies, but is said to differ on two points: 1) he condemns the conduct of it thus far; 2) he would have the colonies retain those constitutional rights to which they have a just claim—when, of course, they are defeated.[30]

Absolute (Nothing) Monarch

Can the King do no wrong? An anonymous writer in the *New England*

Chronicle of Cambridge, Massachusetts, thinks so, but hardly in a way that would please his Majesty.

"It has been answered by some to this effect," said the anonymous wit, "that the King does nothing as King but by his ministers; and therefore whatever wrong is done by the administration of the King must be attributed to his ministers—not to him. But according to this, what does the King do, as King? Why, nothing—neither right or wrong! And what is the King, but an absolute nothing!"[31]

The argument that "The King can do no wrong" was a device characteristically used by the Whigs in Britain for attacking the King without attacking the King. They sought to place the onus on the King's ministers to achieve their ends.

No Record

Reports from Russia say her Imperial Majesty, Catherine II, recently made the trip from the former capital of Moscow to the present one of St. Petersburg in four days. The journey by sled included a brief stopover at Tulle, where the Tsarina observed the manufacture of arms.

Her Imperial Majesty's time of four days for the journey of more than 400 miles is no record, however. Peter the Great, in the early days of the century, is said to have covered the same distance in forty-eight hours. The difference: his Imperial Majesty commanded the use of twenty-four horses to pull his sled, and traveled all night while peasantfolk lighted the roads with lanterns.[32]

Missing Persons

Authorities in France are looking for the sub-cashier of the Treasury of the Village of Poissy, near Paris. He has been missing for several days, and they surmise there is a connection between the disappearance of the seventy-year-old official and a deficiency of 80,000 livres in the treasury. Meanwhile, the clerk of the Company of French Comedians is also reported missing—with 60,000 livres.[33]

Religion

The Pursuit of Peace

Even though amicable measures have not yet proved effectual in reconciling differences between the colonies and Great Britain, the search for a peaceful settlement must go on. So said the Quakers of Pennsylvania and New Jersey, gathered this week in Philadelphia for their yearly meeting.

In a document entitled *The Ancient Testimony and Principles of the People Called Quakers, Renewed*, the representatives of the society made clear their position. Basically, it is this:

"A religious concern for our friends and fellow subjects of every denomination, and more especially for those of all ranks, who in the present commotions, are engaged in public employments and stations, induces us earnestly to beseech every individual in the most solemn manner, to consider the end and tendency of the measures they are promoting and on the most impartial enquiry into the state of their minds, carefully to examine whether they are acting in the fear of God, and in conformity with the precepts and doctrine of our Lord Jesus Christ, whom we profess to believe in, and that by whom alone we expect to be saved from our sins. . . .

"The scenes lately presented to our view, and the prospects before us, we are sensible, are very disturbing and discouraging; and though we lament that such amicable measures as we have proposed both here and in England, for the adjustment of the unhappy contests subsisting, have not yet been effectual; nevertheless, we should rejoice to observe continuance of mutual peaceable endeavours for effecting a reconciliation; having grounds to hope that the divine favor and blessing will attend them."[34]

Theatre

Not an Epic One

A new production of Ben Jonson's comedy, *"Epicoene, or the Silent Woman,"* at London's Drury-Lane Theatre, is no delight to the critics. "The public will soon tire of it," said one.

This version of the play has had a good deal of editing from the original, but remains a little morose for a comedy, particularly in the roles of Truewit and Otter. Sir Amorous la Fool and Sir John Daw are better drawn, but a scene in which they get into a rumpus, and are finally locked in a closet, becomes childish from its length. On the whole, *Epicoene* has some merit in its depiction of the people and manners of the times in which it was written (1609), but as good theater it is too artificial to be a success.

As for the acting, commented London's *St. James's Chronicle*: "All the actors, except Mr. King and Mr. Parsons, performed indifferently. Bensley is the worst old man we ever saw. . . . The uniform goggle of his eye, by which he means to express infirmity and distress, is more the look of a man in anguish from the colic."[35]

Press

Calling Fowle

Independence has "homely, ugly features."

"It is monster of so horrid mien
As to be hated, needs but to be seen."

"Oppose it, Gentlemen, in the
beginning; a little delay may be fatal;
and like a neglected wound, it may
mortify, and corrupt the whole body."

With such epithets as those did a first-page article in Daniel Fowle's *New Hampshire Gazette* take on the subject of independence for the American colonies. But worse than what it said was the fact that the article in Fowle's January 9th issue was addressed to the "Congress at Exeter."

This week in Exeter, the New Hampshire House of Representatives (as it is called) took note of the article, decided it was "injurious to the cause of liberty" and called Fowle to appear and explain how such an "ignominious, scurrilous and scandalous piece" came to appear in his newspaper.

It won't be the first such appearance for the Portsmouth printer. In 1754, while still in his native Massachusetts, Fowle was called before the General Court on suspicion of printing an anti-Excise Act pamphlet entitled *Monster of Monsters;* for that, he spent three days in jail.[36]

There is no record of what happened to Fowle before the House of Representatives; but it would appear that he was exonerated. The Journal of the New Hampshire House of Representatives, in March, June and September, 1776, records that he was given a total of £ 56:7:0 in state printing business.

THE WEEK OF JANUARY 22ND

Congress

Indian Relations

"We have now a full proof that the Ministerial servants have attempted to engage the savages against us."

What Congress had feared—that the British Ministry would try to incite the Indians, and especially the warlike Iroquois, to rise up against the colonies—was thus confirmed from Albany, December 14th, in a letter to Congress from General Philip Schuyler, Commander of Continental forces in the Province of New York. The letter reached Congress in Philadelphia just before Christmas, and was published, at the order of Congress, the first of the year.

Such an attempt to stir up the Indians, whether successful or not, comes as no surprise to many Americans. British Indian policy in general has been mistrusted since the Proclamation of 1763 forbade settlement by American colonists west of the Appalachian Mountains. Following the outbreak of hostilities last year, Congress advised the individual colonies to establish alliances with the Indians if the British entered into offensive alliances or encouraged hostilities on the part of the Indians. Then, on July 13th of last year, taking initiative into its own hands, Congress began to entreat the Mohawks, Oneidas, Tuscaroras, Cayugas and Senecas —missing only the Onondagas among the Six Nations of the Iroquois—to seek friendly relations with the United Colonies. At the same time it appointed a number of commissioners to represent the United Colonies in their dealings with Indians throughout the land.

Now, obviously alarmed by General Schuyler's report, Congress is stepping up its efforts to win the allegiance of the Indians. This week it approved a major importation agreement that will encourage the flow of 40,000 *l*'s worth of Indian goods into the colonies in the coming months. And the reason why is clear enough in the resolution: "to preserve (their) confidence and friendship, and to prevent their suffering for want of the necessaries of life."

Under this act, goods will be sent into the colonies through the Indian commissioners, who will fix prices and license traders. For such work they will receive a commission of two and one-half per cent.

The commissioners are directed to allow the Indians reasonable and fair prices for their skins, furs and other goods, and not to take advantage of them. The traders, in turn, are to dispose of such goods only at established prices.

Should any commissioner also happen to be a member of Congress, the act presumes his legislative duties will preclude his participation in the trade arrangement; but in any event, it prohibits him from sharing in the remuneration.

Congress this week also received and acted upon a report of a special committee on a memorial to General Richard Montgomery, the widely popular American commander who fell at Quebec last December 31st. The memorial will be a statue carved in France by arrangement of Dr. Benjamin Franklin. The act carries an appropriation of 300 *l* and declares that the memorial is to "express veneration . . . of that gallant officer who, after a series of successes, amidst the most discouraging difficulties, fell at length in a gallant attack upon Quebec."

In other action this week, Congress:

—Agreed to requests that soldiers who are married may have a portion of their monthly pay forwarded directly to their wives:

—Directed that the Articles of War be translated into French, and that 500 copies be sent to Canada;

—Approved the hiring of a private secretary for President [of Congress] Hancock.[37]

Foreign News

Royal Lineage

It may be that kings and commoners, rich and poor, this race and that race all trace their lineage back to Adam. But along the way, diversity has developed; and even royal bloodlines have been known to take a common turn or two.

Anything but hiding its scorn for the present embodiment of British royal blood, *Freebetter's New England Almanack* for 1776, published in New London, Connecticut, gives this "genealogical account of the Kings of England:"

"George the Third, grandson of George the Second, the son of George the First, who was cousin to Queen Anne, the daughter to King James the Second, who was son to Charles the First, the son of James the First, who was third cousin to Elizabeth . . . (and so on) . . . Henry the Third, the son of King John, who was son to Henry the Second, the cousin of Stephen. who was nephew to Henry the First, the son of William the Conqueror, who was a son of a whore."[38]

Books

Less Anonymous

The identity of the author of the fast-selling *Common Sense* remains a mystery—but a little less so. In an advertisement in the *Pennsylvania Evening Post* announcing the sale of a second edition, Publisher Robert Bell has added something new: "Written by an Englishman." Thus eliminated from the guessing game are such names as Thomas Jefferson, Samuel Adams, John Adams, Benjamin Rush and a host of other native-born Americans.[39]

Religion

Extending the Jubilee

"Open me the gates of righteousness, that I may go into them, and give thanks unto the Lord." —Psalm cxviii. 19

As did his predecessors before him, Pope Pius VI last February 26th went to the Holy Door at St. Peter's in Rome, knocked three times, waited as workmen pried loose a covering of bricks and masonry, then entered the basilica to begin the Roman Church's eighteenth Holy Year of Jubilee.

As did his predecessors, Pope Pius last Christmas Eve left St. Peter's by the same *porta santa*, closed it, took a golden trowel and set the first brick in place, waited as workmen completed the sealing of the door for another twenty-five years, then declared the Holy Year of Jubilee officially closed.

In between, pilgrims flocked to Rome from all over the world in numbers that apparently established a record. During Holy Week alone, more than 95,000 persons were reported lodged at the Hospice of the Holy Trinity in Rome. The reason for the mass pilgrimage: to offer special acts of worship (confession and visitation on consecutive days to the major basilicas of Rome) and receive a plenary indulgence granted only during a jubilee.

The designation of a holy year is centuries old. Pope Boniface VIII established the custom with the bull *Antiquorum habet* in the year 1300, apparently intending that such a celebration take place every 100 years. But so great was the demand for another one sooner, that Pope Clement VI proclaimed 1350 as the second year of jubilee. By 1475 the interval was changed to twenty-five years so that each generation of Christians might easily expect to see one, and that custom has continued to the present day. At other times there have been so-called "extraordinary" jubilees on fifty-nine occasions, these being chiefly upon the accession of a new pope; the most recent was in 1724 when Benedict XIII became pontiff.

As old as is this custom in the Roman Church, it is far older in its antecedents. In the days of ancient Judaism, every fiftieth year was begun with the sounding of the *shofar,* or ram's horn; then following the instructions of Leviticus, liberty was proclaimed throughout the land. Debts were forgiven, and slaves set free.

Despite the fact that more of the faithful went to Rome last year than in any preceding holy year, many could not; sickness, feebleness, poverty, distance all conspired to make it impossible for some. Following therefore a custom dating back nearly three centuries to the pontificate of Alexander VI, Pope Pius has declared an extension of the jubilee in all countries of the Christian world beyond Italy. It provides a similar indulgence for special acts of worship that can be carried out at home. Unlike any other extension in the past, all of which have been at most a fortnight, this one will last for six months from the time the papal bull is first published in each country.

One reason for the longer extension is that the jubilee was late starting last year. It would ordinarily have begun on Christmas eve, 1774, but was delayed because a successor to the late Pope Clement XIV had not yet been elected.[40]

Medicine

Medicinal Uses of Coffee

In *Philosophical, Medical and Experimental Essays,* recently published, British physician Thomas Percival tells of a doctor who suffered a severe headache and took eighteen drops of laudanum, an opiate, followed by three dishes of very strong coffee, then lay down to rest. In half an hour, the pain had subsided, but he was unable to sleep despite the fact he was accustomed to taking a nap at that hour.

A few weeks later, for a similar headache, he repeated the same remedy, with the same effects. Still a few weeks later, he again took eighteen drops of laudanum, but this time did not follow it with coffee. In a short time the opiate had put him to sleep, but did not entirely remove the pain.

By this account, coffee appears to change the effects of the opiate, and that conclusion would confirm an earlier writing in which Dr. Percival took note of the large quantities of coffee consumed by the Turks and Arabians "because it counteracts the narcotic effects of opium, to the use of which these nations are much addicted."

As for a better use of coffee, Dr. Percival suggests an ounce, freshly roasted and brewed immediately after grinding, taken in a dish without milk or sugar, as the best antidote for asthma.[41]

THE WEEK OF JANUARY 29TH

The War

Close Escape

One of America's more formidable weapons is turning out to be the privateer—a privately owned vessel fitted out with light armament and commissioned by Congress to take on enemy shipping and capture anything and everything of value. A privateer is thus more or less a licensed pirate, except that the booty, minus a percentage for the captain and crew, goes to the government.

Among America's privateer captains, there is perhaps none who has acquired booty—and fame—as fast as Massachusetts' Captain John Manly, whose cruiser, the *Lee,* sailing under his colony's green-and-white Pine-tree Flag, is the scourge of British supply ships in the waters off New England. Last year, when General Washington pleaded with Congress, "I am in very great want of powder, lead, mortars, indeed most sorts of military stores," knowing full well he could not expect fulfillment of his request, Captain Manly arrived with powder, lead, mortars and other sorts of military stores captured from his British prey. Among the artillery was a particularly large mortar, since named "The Congress," which is now in use against the British in Boston.

Although not heavily armed, privateers have sufficient firepower to cow a merchant vessel, all the while evading British warships for whom they are no match. One day this week, Manly failed the evading.

When Captain Manly's privateer left Plymouth for the high seas, it had gone perhaps twelve miles before it was spotted by an armed British brig out of Boston. Outclassed by British armament, Manly turned back to the west and toward shore. Just below the North River in Scituate, he ran aground. The brig moved in for the kill, anchored, and began firing . . . ten times, twenty-five times, fifty times, two hundred times, and kept it up. No fewer than 400 shots were heaved at the helpless American vessel. But the accuracy of the British fire was dismal. Shot after shot dropped harmlessly in the water. A number did hit the privateer, one passing six inches from Captain Manly, who was confined to his cabin by illness. But not a single American was wounded.

The British later set out in small boats to put a torch to Manly's vessel, but on seeing the approach of townspeople, some of them armed militia, the British sailors changed their minds, returned to the brig, and set sail.

While much of the British cannonade fell short of the mark, landing in the water, much also missed the target by going long. Next day, Scituate residents counted at least 130 cannon balls that landed on the shore, doing no damage whatever to man or vessel.

As for Manly, he made repairs, awaited higher tide, and sailed off for the high seas—his green-and-white Pinetree Flag flapping in the breeze, his lookout scanning the seas for powder, lead, mortars, and most sorts of military stores.[42]

> *The Continental Congress on November 25, 1775 established rules and procedures for privateers. For example: The master of the ship had to have a commission from Congress; he was authorized only to seize ships employed in the war against the Colonies (for trans-portation of troops, armaments, supplies); if the master bore the full cost of outfitting his ship, he could keep all he captured as a prize; if Congress or one of the Colonies paid for outfitting the ship, the master could keep only one-third.*

Congress

Saying "I Don't"

Young men with ideas of valor and glory who say "I do" to the recruiter sometimes wake up the next morning a great deal less convinced in the wisdom of their enlistment in the Continental Army. In view of their age, their still developing maturity, their proclivity for seeing life in the black-or-white of exciting deeds and derring-do, and their lesser judgment of the harsh realities of military life, should they be bound irrevocably to their often hasty acquiescence to the resourceful recruiter?

Not so, said Congress this week. It decreed that any person under twenty-one who enlists in the army or navy may henceforth, within twenty-four hours of enlistment, obtain a discharge by refunding to the recruiter whatever money or other forms of bounty were paid.

In other action this week, Congress:

—Requested creditors to defer arrest of any soldier who is a debtor of thirty-five dollars or less until his enlistment concludes;

—Determined that any soldier who loses his firearm, except through carelessness or misbehavior, will be issued a new one at no cost;

—Welcomed back for another term John Hancock, Samuel Adams, John Adams and Robert Treat Paine and welcomed for the first time Elbridge Gerry as the delegates to Congress from Massachusetts;

—Took Saturday off, for the first time this year.[43]

The Colonies

Mission Completed

Early in January, as part of a plan to rout Tory resistence in Queens County, New York, Congress ordered troops to seize the leaders. This week, 700 New Jersey militiamen and 300 regulars did the job—with little difficulty. Sample newspaper comment: "Such is the badness of their cause, which no doubt rendered them cowards, that they were disarmed without opposition."[44]

Foreign News

The Cost of War

The year 1704 was a glorious one for England. The pick of his Majesty's army plus troops of augmentation from allied powers—66,000 in all—campaigned brilliantly throughout Spain, Portugal and the Low Countries, along the Rhine and the Danube, and, under the Duke of Marlborough, consummated the fighting in that immortal victory over the French and Bavarians at Blenheim in Bavaria. English fleets, manned by 40,000 seamen, were equally victorious in the West Indies and on the high seas. For that glorious record, the Exchequer paid out 4,647,140 *l*.

The year 1775 was not a glorious one for England. The pick of his Majesty's army campaigned with generally little distinction at Boston, Charlestown, Bunker's Hill, Lexington and Concord, ending up the year besieged back in Boston. For that not-so-glorious record, Lord North had a budget of 4,886,651 *l*.[45]

Books

Uncommon Controversy

When *Common Sense* went into second printing this week—its first edition having sold out—it also entered into its first controversy. There will be two second editions by two separate publishers.

The anonymously authored book was first published January 9th by
Robert Bell of Philadelphia. It turns out now that the author, through
two intermediaries, had an arrangement with Bell whereby all of the
author's profits would be used for the purchase of mittens for Continental troops fighting in Canada. When the intermediaries went to Bell and
asked for an accounting, the publisher claimed there had been no profits,
and hence no money for mittens.

Apparently unbelieving, the author then decided to get a new publisher, and completed the necessary arrangements with Bell's competitors,
William and Thomas Bradford. Notwithstanding the presumed legal complications, and apparently without authorization, Bell went right ahead
with his second edition on January 25th. In advertising it, he derided his
competitors' "smallness of print and scantiness of paper" which he said
would make the Bradford edition resemble his own "in figure and utility
as much as a British shilling in size and value resembleth a British half-
crown."

The Bradfords, in the same issue of the *Pennsylvania Evening Post,*
decided to make public the story about the mittens for the troops in Canada, obviously hoping to provoke public interest on behalf of their own
version of *Common Sense,* to go on sale February 14th at half the cost of
Bell's two-shilling edition. Moreover, they threatened suit against Bell.

That only infuriated Bell. In Thursday's paper, still insisting there had
been no profits, Bell retorted to the author: "Your head being whirligigged
by imaginary importance, you got your eye upon public money, and you
were immediately the self-constituted treasurer. It was certainly very shal-
low and impolitic to give the public money so early away, without convincing them [you] had some merit than mere noise as a claim upon it."

Such a storm of controversy can only whet the public interest all the
more. If the first edition could be sold out in a matter of weeks, a duplic-
ity of second editions may only double the speed with which this remarkable book is selling.[46]

Observations and Predictions

Although *Common Sense* is still to reach England, many of its conclusions are already there in a book now on sale in London.

Observations on the Nature of Civil Liberty, published this week by
Thomas Cadell, is the work of a Welsh-born minister named Dr. Richard
Price, who has already acquired a reputation, and no small measure of
controversy, with his writings on politics and economy.

To Dr. Price, a moralist by virtue of his religious training, the war with
the American colonies is wrong; but it is not so much on moral grounds as
on a practical basis that he opposes it; it is not so much a matter of what
the war is doing to the colonies as what it is doing to the mother country.
Says Price: "An important revolution in the affairs of this kingdom seems
to be approaching. If ruin is not to be our lot, all that has been lately done
must be undone, and new measures adopted."

Much the same is expressed in this: "In America we see a number of rising states in the vigour of youth, inspired by the noblest of all passions, the passion for being free, and animated by piety. Here we see an old state, great indeed, but inflated and irreligious, enervated by luxury, encumbered with debts, and hanging by a thread."

Just as Price has not yet seen a copy of *Common Sense*, neither has Paine, an ocean away, seen *Observations on the Nature of Civil Liberty*. And yet there are some remarkable similarities:

Paine: "Freedom has been haunted round the globe. Asia and Africa have long expelled her. Europe regards her like a stranger, and England has given her warning to depart. O! receive the fugitive, and prepare in time an asylum for mankind."

Price: "With respect to the Colonists, it would be folly to pretend they are faultless. They were running fast into our vices. But this quarrel gives them a salutary check: And it may be permitted on purpose to favour them, and in them the rest of mankind; by making way for the establishment, in an extensive country possessed of every advantage, a plan of government, and a growing power that shall astonish the world, and under which every subject of human enquiry shall be open to free discussion, and the friends of liberty, in every quarter of the globe, find a safe retreat from civil and spiritual tyranny."

What Dr. Price predicts may well be heeded. His public reputation as an economist rests in large part on his theories for calculating life expectancy—theories put to daily use by a number of insurance and benefit societies in England.[47]

This book sold extraordinarily well in Britain, and in America when a reprint was issued by John Dunlap in Philadelphia [See Week of July 22nd]. So great did Price's reputation become that, in 1778, the Continental Congress invited him to move to America and become a financial adviser to the government; Price declined. But he did eventually visit the United States, and in 1783, along with George Washington, received an honorary doctor of law degree from Yale College.

SUPPLEMENTARY NOTES

January

The Continental Congress

The Second Continental Congress convened May 10, 1775, and had been meeting regularly, Monday through Saturday (normally at 10 a.m., preceded by committee business, and sometimes at 9 a.m.) in the State House—now Independence Hall—in Philadelphia. John Hancock, of Massachusetts, had been president since May 19, 1775.

The size of Congress fluctuated. At the First Continental Congress (September, 1774) there appear to have been fifty-three members, this being the number signing the Articles of Association. But Georgia was not yet represented. The Declaration of Independence was signed by fifty-six members of the Second Continental Congress, including Georgia's three delegates. Shortly after this, however, on the expiration of the term of its members, Virginia sent a dele-

gation of five instead of seven. Connecticut then sent five members instead of four. In fact, fluctuations in the size of the delegations made no difference in voting since all votes were cast by states instead of by individual members; no matter how many were in attendance, there were never more than thirteen votes cast.

It should be observed that Congress at this time was without any constitutional foundation; it was able to be effective because its actions were accepted by a majority of the citizens of America simply through good faith and necessity. As British historian Sir George Otto Trevelyan noted more than a century later: "Possessed of no constitutional authority to legislate or govern, they passed, after searching debate and minute revision, resolutions which had the moral force of laws and the practical effect of administrative decrees."

Provincial Congresses and Conventions

These represent a transition from royal government to Independence; they began in October, 1774, in Massachusetts (when Governor Thomas Gage countermanded the convening of the Assembly, and it met anyway as a provincial congress) and ended in 1776 (at various times, when permanent governments were established under state constitutions). Although the provincial congresses were thus extralegal in their origins, they came to assume the essential functions of government, and generally supplied the aegis for establishing constitutional government. The terms "congress" and "convention" are basically interchangeable.

Lord North and the British Ministry

Frederick North, 2nd Earl of Guilford and 8th Baron North, is generally referred to as Prime Minister, but he was not so called at the time. He was, first and foremost, First Lord of the Treasury, which position, from the time of Elizabeth I on, was normally the most powerful among the ministers. The title of prime minister did not come into common usage until the nineteenth century, and the office itself was not given formal recognition until 1905. The term first minister was, however, occasionally used in Lord North's day [Characters. London: J. Bew, 1777. p. 140], and is used in this book. Lord North was also Chancellor of the Exchequer.

The government over which Lord North presided, beginning in January, 1770, was called either the Ministry or Administration. It was notable in British political history for being the first of one party—all Tories.

The second most prominent member of the North Ministry was Lord George Germaine, Secretary of State for the Colonies, a post to which he was appointed in November, 1775. It had been established in 1768 under the Ministry of the Duke of Grafton.

FEBRUARY

STILL *Flora* in her mother's womb doth hide
Herself, as yet unable to abide
Old *Boreas's* blasts; and therefore in the earth
Lies still entomb'd, till SPRING shall give her birth.

The Virginia Almanack
February, 1776

THE WEEK OF FEBRUARY 5TH

The War

New Commander

The acknowledgment was traditional. Richard, Lord Howe, vice admiral of the Royal navy, dutifully bowed and kissed the King's hand. The reason: Lord Howe's appointment as commander-in-chief of all British naval forces in North America. The occasion: a reception on Monday at St. James's Palace, London.

The swarthy and taciturn Howe, who first went to sea at the age of fourteen, is known as an able and effective officer. It was his ship that fired the opening shots of the last war, attacking and capturing the French warship *Alcide* in the Gulf of St. Lawrence, Canada, in 1755. Four years later Howe was in the vanguard of the assault on the French fleet off Quiberon Bay.

When Lord Howe reaches America he will be reunited with his brother, General William Howe, who is commander-in-chief of the British army at Boston.[1]

53

Command Performance

Act one, scene one, of "The Blockade of Boston," a farce. Enter "General Washington," tall and commanding, but clothed uncouthly, carrying a long, rusty sword. At his side is an orderly, a sergeant in country dress, carrying a gun perhaps seven or eight feet long, also rusty.

Enter some British sergeants crying out, "The Yankees are attacking our works on Bunker's Hill!"

Entrance One is in the script of a farce the British troops have been staging to while away the long hours of siege. Entrance Two is not.

To first-timers in the audience one night this week, the sergeants' alarm seemed a clever twist. To General William Howe, who had sat through the show before, it was obviously not. "Officers, to your alarm posts," he cried, thus bringing down the curtain for his soldier-actors, who now had more important roles to play.

For the audience, there was confusion and dismay. Ladies shrieked, then fainted.

Actors dropped their rusty weapons, sought real ones. "General Washington" headed for his post, prepared for an American advance.[2]

The cause of the alarm was an incidental attack by a small Continental force on British quarters near Bunker Hill, north of Boston. Eight houses were burned.

Army-Navy

One of Philadelphia's best known naval suppliers, Moulder the Sailmaker, has a job to do for the army. Washington's army in Cambridge, short on tents and shorter still on the material with which to make them, sent an appeal to Moulder to round up as many old sails as he can find and turn them into one thousand tents, each capable of sheltering five or six men. The request left no doubt as to the urgency: "Must have immediately."[3]

Congress

Military Funds

During a week of largely routine business, Congress approved additional appropriations for the Continental Army and for raising additional battalions. For the army at Cambridge, Congress authorized 250,000 dollars and directed Colonel Bull and two assistants to convey the funds. Congress also approved 12,000 dollars in assistance to New York for raising four additional battalions and 10,000 dollars to Pennsylvania for an unspecified number of battalions.[4]

The Cost of Being a Delegate

Very little is free these days, and that includes serving in Congress. But just what does it cost the United Colonies to maintain their delegates in Philadelphia while Congress is in session?

Here is an example. Virginia's Richard Henry Lee was in Philadelphia for 93 days from last September until January of this year. His statement of account with the Colony, filed on his return, shows a claim for 23 *l* for transportation, computed on the basis of 12 pence per mile for the 460-mile journey (there and back). A total bill of 209*l* 5*s* was submitted to cover his stay in Philadelphia, figured on the basis of a Half Johannes, or 2*l* 5*s* per day for each of the 93 days. Expenses for carriages totaled 12*l* 3*s*.

Thus for that period of service in Congress, Lee submitted to the Colony a total of 244*l* 8*s* in expenses. Subtracting the 200 *l* in cash and "by Mr. Treasurer's exchange" that he started out with last September, he has a balance of 44*l* 8*s* due from the Colony.[5]

The Colonies

Parading to the Polls

Tuesday was election day in New York, and a number of citizens—intent on reminding others that the time had come to select the city's representatives in the Provincial General Assembly—gathered early in the morning at the coffeehouse. Taking up a flag emblazoned with the motto, "In Union There's Strength," they set out parading through the streets, and as they went, attracted many others including the High Sheriff. All together they marched to the polls and helped elect Philip Livingston, John Alsop, John Jay and Alexander McDougall as the city's representatives.[6]

Opposite Direction

On November 7th of last year, Virginia's royal governor, John Murray, 4th Earl of Dunmore, declared martial law in Virginia. He did so not in Williamsburg at his royal palace, but off Norfolk on the flagship *William*, aboard which he had taken refuge last June when the Colony of Virginia appeared at patience' end with his loyalist arrogance.

Lord Dunmore remains afloat, and more unlikely than ever to set foot again in his elegant mansion. If the climate was hostile last June, it is incendiary now. Yet Dunmore, Governor of Virginia since 1771, was not unpopular at first—even following as he did one of the Colony's most esteemed and genuinely liked governors of all, Lord Botetourt. But whatever amity there was at the start went sour. When Dunmore dissolved the House of Burgesses in 1773, and again in 1774, the gulf between the people of Virginia and the one-time Scottish peer in Parliament became unpassable.

Dunmore took the clearly intimidating step of declaring martial law. He did something else carefully calculated to cause havoc in Virginia: he emancipated all slaves who would desert their masters and sign on with British forces. Not that many have left. But on a recent day, two of Dunmore's own slaves were observed passing through Fredericksburg—quite the opposite direction of enlisting in the British army, and quite the opposite direction of their own master.[7]

Foreign News

Three Treaties

For Britain's Minister Plenipotentiary Sir William Faucitt, the past month has been a busy one; for his Majesty's government, a potentially important one.

On February 5th, Faucitt and Privy Counsellor Frederic de Malsbourg, his counterpart in Hesse-Cassel, Germany, completed a treaty that will furnish the British army with additional soldiers in America. It was the third such treaty completed by Faucitt in the past month.

On January 9th, the Duke of Brunswick and Lunenburg agreed to furnish 3,964 infantrymen and 336 cavalrymen. For these, King George will pay thirty crowns per foot soldier in levy money that will prepare them for battle in America, plus 64,500 crowns per year for as long as they are needed.

Less than a week later, a far more important agreement was worked out between Faucitt and Baron Martin Erneste de Schlieffen, minister of state for the Landgrave of Hesse-Cassel. By this treaty, the Landgrave will provide 12,000 men comprising four battalions of grenadiers, fifteen battalions of infantry, and two companies of chasseurs, all fully equipped including tents. As for fighting ability, they are to be "none but the best fit for service."

The agreement provides that at least three battalions of grenadiers, six battalions of infantry and one company of the lightly equipped and fast moving chasseurs are to be ready to pass review by his Majesty on February 14th, and proceed to port of embarkation the next day. The rest must be ready to leave by March 14th.

All the Hesse-Cassel troops will fight as a unit, unless separated by reasons of war. The men will be paid at the same rate as British soldiers. For this ready-made army, Britain will pay 450,000 crowns per year, plus thirty crowns per foot soldier in levy money.

The treaty signed February 5th with the Hereditary Prince of Hesse-

Cassel provides for 668 infantry at an annual cost of 25,050 crowns plus the usual levy money.

The Brunswick pact, meanwhile, provides a few extras: a band numbering eleven drummers, one trumpet, four oboes, two French horns and two fifes, as well as a number of surgeons, carpenters, servants and laborers.[8]

Her Majesty's Favorite

In Russia, it is a woman—her Imperial Majesty Catherine II—who is all-powerful. Though clearly second to her, the most powerful of men is General Grigory Aleksandrovich Potemkin, 37, of whom there has been long surmised a role in the deposing of the late tsar (and her Majesty's late husband) Peter III, after a brief rule in 1762.

Others—Count Aleksey Orlov is most prominent—may have had as much, or more, to do with Tsar Peter's demise. But it is General Potemkin who has remained her Majesty's favorite. This week in St. Petersburg, Catherine II showed her affection by naming Potemkin Lieutenant of the Noble Guards and by making him a present of the government of Novgorod—its 16,000 peasants and all.

As Lieutenant of the Noble Guards, Potemkin succeeds none other than Count Orlov himself, who left the post, says the *London Chronicle*, as if to counter suspicion to the contrary, "by voluntary resignation."[9]

Press

Plain Dealing

Moored securely between America's two largest cities, and with no such center of population of its own, the colony of New Jersey looks east to New York or west to Philadelphia for whatever benefits a large city may provide.

Nowhere is this more evident than in the press: New Jersey has none. Residents of the northern and eastern sections of the colony read, and place their advertising in, New York newspapers; those in southern and western areas, in Philadelphia papers.

Although New Jersey has no newspaper of its own, its Cumberland County citizens are known to catch up on the latest local happenings by visiting Matthew Potter's tavern in Bridgeton and reading a modern version of the forerunner of many a newspaper: the news letter. Always handwritten, never more than a few pages in length, news letters flourished in the coffeehouses and taverns of Europe, beginning in the time of Elizabeth, and at the outset contained primarily news of shipping and trading. Later versions offered news of a wider sort.

Following the same tradition is Bridgeton's *Plain Dealer*, which made

its first appearance at the Potter tavern last Christmas day. Since then it
has been produced once or twice a week, the work of a small and informal association of interested citizens, and chiefly their secretary, Ebenezer Elmer, also a student of medicine. The several copies produced by
hand remain at the tavern, even after the next edition, for all who would
like peruse the *Plain Dealer*'s views.

Subjects of articles vary. One, signed "A Country Bachelor," considered the custom of bundling and denied it was widespread. ("I am a
bachelor of near thirty years of age. I know from experience that there
are many young ladies in this place who were never guilty of any such
thing and would even spurn at the mention of it. I can say, none ever
practised it in my house, either of my own girls or others, although I
have had a great many.")

More often articles are about the major political events of the day,
always from the eyes of a patriot. In a recent issue the *Plain Dealer*
sought to simplify the basic issues dividing Britain and the colonies by
drawing an analogy close to home. It did so by asking readers to suppose
New Jersey were a colony of Pennsylvania. Suppose, said the *Plain Dealer,* "at length, the Assembly of Pennsylvania taking it into their heads
that New Jersey was peopled by the subjects of Pennsylvania and belonged to the Governor of that province; that therefore they had a right
to make laws binding upon us. Every one would readily see the absurdity
of such a claim, and look upon himself bound in duty to oppose (even
by force if necessary) the execution of such laws. This is exactly similar
to our present dispute. The right of the Parliament of Great Britain to
make laws binding upon us in all cases whatsoever is founded on no
better principles; it is equally absurd and unconstitutional, and will be
attended with the most pernicious consequences, if not timely prevented
by a vigorous and manly opposition."

Besides analogy, the *Plain Dealer* also likes satire, and in another recent issue claimed the use of a "majic spyglass" to gather the news for
its readers.

"With the assistance of this miraculous glass," related the writer from
his table down at Potter's, "I can at any time day or night see clearly
through the brick walls of our Court House and observe all the proceedings of a certain venerable set of gentlemen, who now and then meet
there to smoke politics, chop logic, chaw tobacco, eat roast beef, drink
Madeira, snarl, hiccup, and transact many other great and mighty affairs
of state with the most profound secrecy. With the same glass I can distinctly read the journals of that right reverend and right honorable Privy
Council though kept close under lock and key; and look into all public
houses, societies and clubs in the place; by which means, I find I shall be
able to furnish myself with a very large stock of materials for carrying on
my trade; for happening the other day to use my glass pretty freely, I
got such a surfeit of absurdity and nonsense that I was obliged to take
a dose of Dr. Sangrado's Cure-all Physic."[10]

Theater

Forecast: Mostly Cloudy

London's 1776 theater season is in full sway, and like most theater seasons to most critics, not entirely pleasing to everyone.

London's *St. James's Chronicle* took upon itself a brief review of the major productions in what it called a "Theatrical Barometer." Were it reporting on the weather instead of the stage, Londoners would do well to keep their umbrellas handy.

The Drury-Lane repertory looks this way:

Little Gypsey—"muggy, with very light airs."

The Sultan—"sultry, heavy, dark and dull."

The Silent Woman—"dark, variable, gloomy, unfavorable for the season."

Blackamoor Whitewashed—"Thunder, many showers, hot, foggy, stormy, black and dull."

And at Covent-Garden:

The Man's the Master—"Fine, light and fair."

The Weather-cock—"Tempestuous, blown away."

Duenna—"Fair and pleasant."

The *Chronicle's* critic added an aside about Drury-Lane's managing partner, and otherwise noted actor and dramatist, David Garrick, lately taken up with the hobby of amateur astronomy. His production of *Blackamoor Whitewashed* at Drury-Lane had the worst weather forecast of all.

Said the critic: "Mr. Garrick is now very vigilant with his telescope, to discover whether the new black spot in the moon is his vanished Blackamoor."[11]

Fashion

Capital Structures

Ladies' wigs have gotten so high it is a wonder Madame doesn't topple over. Said London's *St. James's Chronicle* of the custom: "It is believed that unless the ladies think proper to reduce the size of their head dresses, that they must be obliged to enlarge the roofs of their carriages to prevent any mischief being done to their capital structures. It is a certain fact that a lady going lately to pay a visit in her coach was obliged to lean so far forward on the opposite seat that the people who passed by imagined she was seized with some violent disorder. However, she undeceived them by jumping out of her carriage with great agility, though she was obliged to thrust her head a yard or two before the rest of her body."[12]

THE WEEK OF FEBRUARY 12TH

The War

Confusion in New York

New Yorkers have long heard bitter tales of the British occupation of Boston. Last week they had a scare of the same. Into New York Harbor unexpectedly sailed General Sir Henry Clinton in the frigate Mercury, followed by two transports full of soldiers.

Anchoring, they stirred fear and confusion. By Sunday of this week, some New Yorkers, fearing the worst, loaded possessions on carts and left for the country.

The sudden threat of a far-off war suddenly at their own doorsteps brought out the best and worst in people. Some of New York's more affluent citizens were seen giving a helping hand to fellow citizens less fortunate. Others, sensing the opportunity, were observed setting exhorbitant rates for the use of carts.

By Monday, however, it was clear the alarm was a false one. Back out of the harbor sailed the Mercury and the transports—probably for the southern colonies—letting New Yorkers take a deep breath for the first time in nearly a week.[13]

Congress

False Alarm

Congress this week reacted with considerable speed in meeting a potential military threat to New York, and just as quickly reversed its action when the danger appeared to be over.

The source of the alarm in Congress Monday was a letter dispatched three days earlier by General Charles Lee, the Continental Army's second-in-command, now in New York. Lee told Congress a transport of British troops had arrived, and more could probably be expected, making American reinforcement necessary. Such assistance Congress directed in the form of New Jersey minutemen equal to one battalion, and Pennsylvania troops in four battalions, requesting the Committees of Safety of the two colonies to make them available under the command of Lee in New York. By Friday, however, the threat of any further concentration of British forces in New York appeared unlikely, and Congress rescinded its request to Pennsylvania.

Another consequence of the suddenly improved conditions in New York was Congress' reassignment of General Lee to bolster the badly sagging American operations in Canada. General Schuyler, as soon as his health permits, will take command in New York.

The question of Canada remains very much on the minds of the colonies' representatives in Philadelphia. In what could be a step of potential long-range importance, Congress appointed a committee of three to prepare to make the arduous journey to the provinces to the north. No specific mission has been cited except "to pursue such instructions as shall be given them by Congress." All expenses of the trip will be underwritten by Congress.

The three Canada-bound: Dr. Benjamin Franklin of Pennsylvania and Samuel Chase of Maryland, as members of Congress; and Charles Carroll of Carrollton (Maryland) a non-member whose Catholicism and knowledge of French are expected to be assets in dealing with the Canadians. Presumed objectives of the mission are to provide Congress with a firsthand view of the situation in Canada, and to interest Canadians in support of the American cause, up to and including union of the Canadian provinces with the thirteen colonies. Specific instructions for Franklin's committee will be drawn up by another committee, this one including John Adams of Massachusetts, George Wythe of Virginia and Roger Sherman of Connecticut.

Another major act of Congress this week was authorization for an emission of four million dollars in bills of credit, the first such issue since three million dollars of paper currency was approved last November 29th. The Committee for Superintending the Treasury (James Duane of New York, Thomas Nelson, Jr. of Virginia, Elbridge Gerry of Massachusetts, Richard Smith of New Jersey and Thomas Willing of Pennsylvania) will recommend details. As an adjunct to its financial responsibilities, the same committee is also directed to obtain from the Conventions and Assemblies of the colonies an account of the number of inhabitants of each, thus bringing up to date the census taken by Congress in September, 1774.

In other action this week, Congress approved additional appropriations of 35,000 dollars to New York, 30,000 to New Jersey and 20,000 to Virginia for raising additional battalions. Following the recommendation of the Virginia Convention, Patrick Henry was commissioned colonel-in-charge of Virginia forces.[14]

Charles Carroll became a member of Congress on July 4, 1776. Patrick Henry subsequently declined the commission. The census taken by Congress in September, 1774, showed the population of the colonies (excluding Georgia) at 3,026,678. That was likely on the high side.

Foreign News

A Bad Winter

In Chatham, England, one day last week, the temperature at eight o'clock in the morning had plummeted to an astonishing three and a half degrees below zero—setting a new record there by seven and a half degrees. And while temperatures in Chatham, and Kent generally, have been a bit lower than other regions—as they always are—all England this season has been shivering as hardly ever before, fighting the effects of cold and snow to a greater extent this year than in memory.

In York last month, during one sixteen-day period, there was snow or sleet on fourteen of those days; temperatures never rose above 34. In Bristol, no ships were able to dock for three weeks straight because of the ice. In Baldock, snow was reported to be deeper than at any time in at least two decades. Canterbury harbor was frozen over for the first time since the hard winter of 1739–40.

In London, on January 28th, the temperature dropped to a frigid eight and a half degrees; ice covered the Thames. Two days later, when the Epsom coachman arrived in London, he was numb from the effects of the seventeen-mile journey, soon complained of a fever, then lapsed into delirium, and died at eleven o'clock at night. Near Bath, Farmer Thomas went out one morning, found sixty of his sheep had smothered to death in the snow. Farmer Coomer lost an ox and twenty sheep the same way.

But here and there, some good has been found of this bone-chilling winter of 1776. A housewife in Ashford, Kent, had the longest night's sleep of her life, from Friday evening when she went to bed until Monday morning when concerned neighbors came for her. The snow had drifted up against the window of her first-floor bedroom, shutting out the light; thinking it was still night, she stayed in bed. And at Gillingham Reach, north of Chatham, townsmen found the River Medway—frozen over—a handy place for playing cricket.[15]

The accuracy of these temperature reports may be open to some question, but such extremes of cold are well within the range of possibility.

Medicine

Field Duty First

Dr. John Morgan, of Philadelphia, the Continental Army's new director-general of hospitals, is now on the job in Cambridge, his arrival noticeable by a change in priorities. Morgan's first major order: reduce the number of surgeon's mates in the central hospital to a minimum, and concentrate on filling vacancies in the field. Thus for many a surgeon's mate, life will be harder and medical services presumably more efficient.[16]

Science

Observing Air

Hardly content with some remarkable discoveries already made is

England's clergyman-scientist, Joseph Priestly, who continues his explo-ration of the everyday world.

His most recent contribution: a report to the Royal Society (of which he became a member at thirty-three) on his experiments into the phlo-gistic nature of blood. His latest curiosity: metals. "You may smile," he told a friend recently from his laboratory at the home of his patron, Lord Shelburne, at Bowood, near Calne, "when I tell you I do not absolute-ly despair of the transmutation of metals."

Priestly won entrance to the society with his "History of the Present State of Electricity," written mainly at the behest of America's Dr. Ben-jamin Franklin. But it is his obsession with air that dominates Priestley's work.

Living at one time next to a brewery in Leeds, he began by experi-menting with mephitic air collected from the fermentation vats. He found such air—the same given off in breathing—was soluble in water, and he proposed that the sparkling water which resulted might be a cure for scurvy. For his discovery of this so-called "soda water," he received the Royal Society's Copley Medal.

By 1772 he had completed enough experimentation to issue his *Ob-servations on Different Kinds of Air,* there recording the isolation of nitric air and marine acid air.

Perhaps his most notable discovery came two years ago. Heating red calx of mercury, he found an air given off which is many times more pure than ordinary air. In it, a candle burns with a far more vigorous flame. Recognizing the potential importance of this "dephlogisticated air," as he named it, he dispatched a description to Antoine Lavoisier in Paris. Lavoisier repeated the experiment, determined the air's elemental nature, and, observing its acid-forming properties, turned to the Greek word "oxys," meaning acid, in re-naming it "oxygen."

"Mephitic air" was carbon dioxide; "nitric air," nitrous oxide; "marine acid air," hydro-chloric acid; "red calx of mercury," mercuric oxide; "phlogisticated air," basically nitrogen; and "phlogiston," the supposed ingredient of combustion. Priestly, 43 at the time, went on to isolate and describe ammonia, carbon monoxide, nitrogen peroxide, silicon fluoride and sulphur dioxide, among other gases; made numerous other scientific contributions; and wrote many works on politics and theology. He moved to America in 1794, seeking greater freedom, and died in Northumberland, Pennsylvania in 1804. [17]

Books

Decline of an Empire

As a schoolboy in Kingston-on-Thames, Edward Gibbon learned Latin alternately by the book and by the birch rod. Whichever was more pro-ductive is no longer recalled. The eventual product of lessons well learned is *The History of the Decline and Fall of the Roman Empire,* the first volume of which was published this week in London by W. Strahan and T. Cadell. It sells for one guinea in boards.

Conceived on a trip to Rome and compiled in part through the pains-taking translation of Latin manuscript, *Decline and Fall* will surely affirm for its author—also a member of Parliament—Goldsmith's heirship as the leading classicist of the Royal Academy.

In its ultimate form of six or eight volumes, Gibbon's work will trace Rome's decline through the course of three major periods. The first (covered in part by Volume 1) begins with the age of Trajan and the Antonines, when the Roman monarchy, having attained its full strength and maturity, began its decline; the period extends to the subversion of the western empire by the barbarians of Germany and Scythia, the rude ancestors of the nations of modern Europe. This "extraordinary revolution," which subjected Rome to the power of a Gothic conqueror, was completed about the beginning of the sixth century.

The second period begins with the reign of Justinian, who through his laws as well as his victories, restored a temporary splendor to the eastern empire. This period encompasses the invasion of Italy by the Lombards; the conquest of the Asiatic and African provinces by the Arabs; the revolt against the feeble princes of Constantinople; and the rise of Charlemagne who, in the year 800, established the second, or German Empire, of the west.

Longest of all is the third period, spanning seven and a half centuries. It begins with the revival of the western empire and continues through the capture of Constantinople by the Turks. Encompassed are the extinction of "a degenerate race of princes" who continued to assume the titles of Caesar and Augustus after their dominions were contracted to the limits of a single city; the history of the Crusades, as far as they contributed to the ruin of the Greek Empire; the state of the city of Rome during the darkness and confusion of the Middle Ages. During this period, says Gibbon, the language as well as the manners of the ancient Romans had long since been forgotten.

Gibbon predicts the first period alone will take two volumes, so that the entire history will run to six, or perhaps eight. And not until the whole is complete will he list all the sources for his work. He does say, however, that he has consulted the lives of the emperors from Hadrian to the sons of Carus as compiled during the reigns of Diocletian and Constantine by such authors as Aelius Spartianus, Julius Capitolinus, Aelius Lampridius, Vulcatius Gallicanus, Trebellius Pollio and Flavius Vopiscus, whose manuscripts, he allowed, offer "much perplexity"—even for so distinguished a scholar.[18]

Gibbon's monumental work met with considerable public acceptance. Said the Annual Register *for 1776: "We do not remember any work published in our time which has met with a more general approbation than Mr. Gibbon's* History of the Decline and Fall of the Roman Empire. *We are happy in adding our suffrage to the public voice, which has so justly declared in its favor."*

The War

Mystery Fleet

The small British fleet that gave New York a shudder little more than a week ago is now under the wary eyes of the residents of southern Virginia, for whom the terror of the destruction of Norfolk is still fresh.

The *Mercury* and accompanying transports are now anchored in Hampton Roads. Aboard are General Sir Henry Clinton; his second-in-command, Lord Percy; and a force said to total about 600 men in four regiments of grenadiers and light infantry.

Clinton's mission continues to be a mystery. If his intention is to strike, he will need ample reinforcement. Meanwhile, he shows no signs of preparing to land.[19]

Defensive Devices

Sometimes called crow-feet, other times caltrops, they are scattered on the ground near defensive positions to impede attack. The devices, reportedly employed by the British at their fortifications at Roxbury, near Boston, are iron balls imbedded with four sharp points one inch in length. Whichever way they land when tossed around a defensive perimeter, at least one sharp prong is pointed up to pierce the feet of men or horses.[20]

"Frightful" Weapon

The story may not be new, and may not be true, but it is once again making the rounds at General Washington's camp in Cambridge. It's about some British redcoats who were put to rout by what seemed to be a new weapon, shortly after General Thomas Gage arrived in Boston as royal governor in 1774.

The redcoats were walking on Beacon Hill when the night air was penetrated by the ominous, whizzing sound of bullets. Whichever way the troops darted, the sound darted also; the soldiers took flight. "Frightful," one said of the attack, even though, in truth, no one was injured.

American soldiers, wise to the wilds of Beacon Hill at night, think the episode amusing, and would have less trouble telling the sound of a whizzing bullet from the buzzing of Beacon Hill's bugs and beetles.[21]

Congress

Background note appears on Page 78.

More Money

As it was instructed to do one week ago, the Committee for Superintending the Treasury this week reported back to Congress its recommendations on a four million dollar issue of bills of credit. Congress concurring, the printing of dollar bills will follow this schedule:

Number of bills	Denomination	Total value
600,000	⅙ dollar	100,000 dollars
600,000	⅓ dollar	200,000
600,000	½ dollar	300,000
600,000	⅔ dollar	400,000
130,436	1 dollar	130,436
130,437	2 dollars	260,874
130,436	3 dollars	391,308
130,435	4 dollars	521,740
65,217	5 dollars	326,085
65,217	6 dollars	391,302
65,217	7 dollars	456,519
65,217	8 dollars	521,736
3,182,612		4,000,000 dollars

Copper engravings prepared by Paul Revere of Boston for last year's issues of paper currency will be used for denominations of one to eight dollars. Smaller denominations—now being issued for the first time—will require new plates. Each bill will bear the inscription: "This bill entitles bearer to receive (no.) Spanish milled dollars, or the value thereof in gold or silver, according to resolution of Congress passed at Philadelphia, February 17, 1776." Three agents were appointed to inspect the printing at a salary of two dollars a day.

This emission brings to a total of ten million dollars the paper currency that has been issued since Congress began emitting bills of credit for the "defence of America" on June 22nd, 1775—five days after the Battle of Bunker's Hill

Recognizing that this issue of currency as well as other business has placed disproportionate demands upon them, Congress decided to give the members of the Committee for Superintending the Treasury a permanent staff. It authorized the committee to acquire suitable office space and to hire two people to keep up the accounts on a daily basis.

In other action this week, after suspending Monday's session to attend a memorial oration for the late General Richard Montgomery, Congress:

—Welcomed Carter Braxton as a delegate from Virginia, succeeding the late Peyton Randolph, the first president of Congress, who died last October at the age of 54;

—And received the credentials of New Jersey delegates William Livingston, John De Hart, Richard Smith, John Cooper and Jonathan Dickinson Sergeant, who were elected by the Provincial Convention February 14th. Cooper and Sergeant are new delegates.[22]

Parliament

Background note appears on Page 77.

The Long Debate

The lobby outside and hallways leading to the House of Commons began filling early, and by afternoon were so crowded with Londoners seeking seats in the gallery that Speaker Sir Fletcher Norton ordered the door locked.

What London citizens had come to watch—and now could not—was what promised to be one of the most important sessions of Parliament of the year. That unbending leader of Whig opposition, that notorious foe of King and North whom many regard as the greatest debater in Parliament—Charles James Fox would propose an enquiry into the conduct of the war with America.

The House as usual proceeded first with routine matters. It was half after three in the afternoon when Fox rose, and the great debate began. It being common knowledge that his subject would be an enquiry, he began by outlining with consummate care what such an enquiry would *not* encompass: it would not be directed to ascertain the rights of Great Britain or the subordinate claims of America; it would not seek to explain the constitutional connection between taxation and representation; nor what is rebellion and what is resistance; nor whether all America should be punished and proscribed for the "intemperate zeal or disobedience of a Boston mob."

It would, said Fox, be simply this question: If the ministers planned with wisdom the course of action in America, then a miscarriage of such a plan should rightly be laid to the military and naval commanders; if, on the other hand, these commanders acquitted themselves according to instructions, then the responsibility must fall upon the ignorance of those who planned such action.

Wherefore moved Fox: "That it be referred to a committee to enquire into the cause of the ill success of his Majesty's arms in North America, as also into the causes of the defection of the people of the Province of Canada."

No few members of Parliament saw fit to join the debate.

Thomas Townshend supported the resolution, attacking the North Ministry severely in doing so. If they oppose it, said he, "it would fairly prove that in smothering the enquiry they intend to cover themselves from public disgrace."

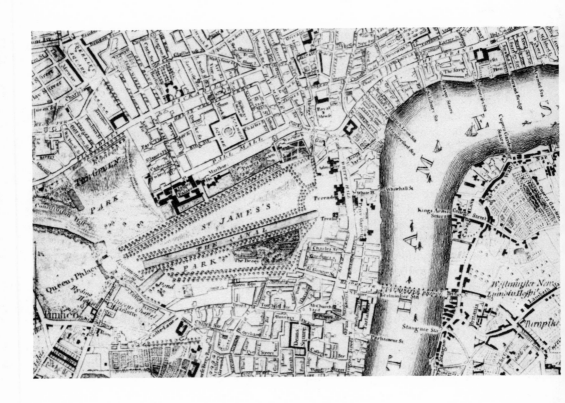

LONDON (John Rocque, London, 1746). Except for a few details (Piccadilly Circus wasn't there yet, for example) this part of London looked then substantially as it does now. Westminster Palace (lower center, just below Westminster Bridge) was, however, the older one, antedating the present Westminster Palace, or Houses of Parliament, built (except for ancient Westminster Hall) in the nineteenth century. Here met Parliament, as it does today. Across the way is the Abbey Church of St. Peter, otherwise known as Westminster Abbey. Just above St. James's Park is St. James's Palace, then the principal residence of the monarch. To the left of the park is the Queen's Palace, and so used by George III's Queen Charlotte; it was also known as Buckingham House, and after reconstruction by John Nash in the following century, it would become Buckingham Palace. Along Whitehall were then, as now, the various buildings of state: the Treasury, the old (on this map) Horse Guards Parade, and the Admiralty, and across from the Parade, Banqueting House and Whitehall Palace (long since gone).

Stuart Collection—Rare Book Division—
New York Public Library—Astor, Lenox
and Tilden Foundations

General John Burgoyne defended British operations in America as expected, delivering what one observer called "an indiscriminate eulogium on the commander-in-chief, officers and troops." But the general speaks with a low and indistinct voice. It was difficult to hear him, and many, though they sensed the nature of his comments, missed the effectiveness of his remarks.

If Burgoyne may have swayed a few votes against the resolution by virtue of his firsthand knowledge of military operations in America, there was another to counter them—one who had also served in the colonies.

Colonel Isaac Barré was at the side of General Wolfe when he fell at Quebec, and was himself wounded in the same fusillade. The bullet that rent his cheek left him permanently disfigured, causing a severe glare to his eye—a strangely distorted countenance with which he now offered his remarks to Parliament. As for British troops in America, he would not defend them. They misbehaved, he said, at Bunker's Hill and it was as simple as that. As for the position of the North Administration, he reminded his colleagues he had been telling them, for the past two years, that British policy toward the colonies was leading to dire trouble. America will never submit to be taxed, he pleaded, not even if "half Germany were to be transported beyond the Atlantic in order to effect it. "

The hours of debate went by . . . a speaker for, a speaker against; defense of the North Ministry, then bitter opposition to it. On into the evening.

Burgoyne spoke again . . . no louder, and a trifle less emphatic about the performance of his Majesty's troops. Now he allowed that they did give way a bit at Bunker's Hill, but only because their flank had been cut off by the fires in Charlestown. Then they rallied and advanced. "No men on earth ever behaved with more spirit, firmness and perseverance," he argued, reminding his colleagues he was there, a witness to the whole affair.

Lord Howe—not yet departed for his naval command in America—added his weight to Administration's cause, albeit conceding, for argument's sake, that British troops last year did not perform in accordance with their usual standards. What happened, he explained, can be attributed to the fact that the British were not "acquainted with the latest designs of the Provincials." Those designs are now fully known.

Still the debate continued . . . past midnight, and into the early morning hours.

Finally at half after one in the morning, Lord North himself entered the fray. He had no objection to an enquiry into the conduct of the war, provided there be a limitation of the enquiry to acts of his Administration. He would not be answerable for measures taken before he became first minister; he would stand ready for "the most rigid enquiry and examination" of his own record. At the same time, he asked his fellow members of Commons to remember that he did not seek his office. He remains ready and willing to resign if someone more capable—more fond of power—wishes to succeed him.

Then addressing himself to one particularly disturbing criticism— made far earlier in the day, or yesterday, as time would more accurately demand it be said—Lord North observed, with no little indignation, that his Administration had been accused of wickedness, ignorance and ne- glect. The last two, he said, remain to be proved; the first could only have been a mistake.

It was a quarter to three in the morning when the debate ended, worn down to a conclusion by its own length, and 344 weary members of the House of Commons prepared to be counted. By a vote of 240 to 104, they put a stop to Charles James Fox's enquiry into the conduct of the war in America before it started.[23]

Thomas Townshend should be distinguished from his cousin Charles, Chancellor of the Exchequer from 1766 until his death the following year; Charles was author of the hated "Townshend Acts" for taxation of the colonies.

Press

Worse Verse

Said Williamsburg's *Virginia Gazette* in a public notice to one of its anonymous contributors: "Antonio is desired to call for his verses, and to send no more of the same."[24]

Customs

Necessity and Invention

What may eventually make unnecessary the necessary house is still a novelty here and there in England and France, and then only for the very rich. And even at that, its shortcomings make it little improvement over what mankind has been using for time immemorial.

The so-called "water closet"—a mechanical privy constructed right in- side the house—is not altogether new; in rudimentary form it has been around a few years. Constructed sometimes of lead, sometimes of mar- ble, and taking up the space of a small closet, it consists of a pan or basin connected through a drain to a sewer and is designed so as to be emptied by the flow of water from an adjacent cistern.

Beyond cost, which is very high indeed compared to the customary necessary house, the device has some shortcomings: its mechanical de- sign is not altogether infallible and it has not yet been constructed so as to keep the closet always free of stink.

But improvement may be on the way. That such a contrivance is reaching the stage of refinement is evident from a fact of no small sig- nificance: last year, for the first time in its history, the British Patent Office issued a grant for such a device. It did so to Alexander Cumming, a mechanic better known as a watchmaker with a thriving business in London.

Cumming's device has an overhead cistern which supplies water to the pan by way of a sliding valve operated by a handle. Beneath the pan is a stink trap intended keep out odors from the sewer. When the water closet is used, the handle is pulled, operating the valve, or "slider," which simultaneously admits a flow of water from the cistern and empties the pan through the stink trap into a drain and thence into the sewer.

Such devices are obviously costly, and that limits their use to a very few who can afford such luxury. Beyond cost, usefulness is limited to locations with access both to piped-in water and a suitable system of drains and sewers.

Limitations aside, an improved version of the water closet is now being manufactured, and Londoners are even finding them advertised. One such "Patent Water Closet, of an entirely new construction," is being sold by William Allen of 129 New Bond Street, London. He claims it does not consume "a tenth of the water requisite for those of common construction." Moreover, he says, it is "perfectly sweet and easier managed."

But reading an advertisement is one thing. Advises the seller: "As words cannot give a just idea of their superiority, Mr. Allen has one fitted up for the inspection of such nobility and gentry as may chuse to see it, which he flatters himself will be more satisfactory to them than the most ample description."[25]

THE WEEK OF FEBRUARY 26TH

The War

Out to Sea

General Sir Henry Clinton and his mystery fleet, which anchored in Hampton Roads for no clear purpose more than a week ago, left the mystery unsolved when, on Monday, they went back out to sea.[26]

Alternatives

In weighing alternatives he has for regaining possession of Boston, General Washington knows one may be the very destruction of the city itself—no matter how reluctant he may be to resort to that extreme. Such an eventuality was seen by Congress last December 22nd when it gave

Washington that alternative if other means failed to dislodge the British.

Perhaps no single individual would suffer as much loss in the destruction of Boston as the President of Congress himself. John Hancock is one of the largest property owners in the city, and his home one of the most elegant. Though he would be severely affected, he wrote Washington giving his personal support to that ultimate measure if it would help the cause.[27]

Rout of the Highlanders

The hills of North Carolina may not be the Highlands of Scotland, but they do abound with McDonalds and McLeods and many another old clan name.

Many of them are refugees of the Second Jacobite Rebellion, settling there after the defeat of Culloden Moor in 1746. At Culloden, as the supporters of Charles Edward, the Young Pretender, they fought against the Crown, and lost. In North Carolina over the intervening years they have grown to be staunch supporters of the Crown—in fact, the Colony's most dependable loyalists. Their leader is a brave veteran of Culloden, who, notwithstanding his age—he is 80—has vast influence over his fellow Highlanders.

Such influence was not lost upon Governor Josiah Martin who, like Virginia's Governor Dunmore, has been in refuge aboard a British ship for some months, the former making his floating headquarters off Cape Fear. Martin commissioned old Donald McDonald a brigadier general of the colony of North Carolina, gave him a bagful of blank commissions and broad discretionary powers, and sent him roaming the countryside to compel all eligible subjects to join his army and put down the patriots. Governor Martin has maintained for some time that a show of force by loyalist Americans and by British troops is all that is needed to bring the southern colonies into line. Within the first few weeks of February, McDonald assembled a force of perhaps 1,500 men—mostly fellow Scots, but such other of North Carolina's men as he could also persuade, or compel, to his cause.

Such a blossoming of loyalist forces might ordinarily have been cut in the bud, but North Carolina's strongest regiment, under Colonel Robert Howe, has been at Norfolk, Virginia, since last December. Colonel James Moore, however, did manage to assemble a force of about 1,100 regulars and militiamen, and on February 15th set out for the Scots' encampment at Cross Creek, camping about twelve miles south. Upon hearing of this, McDonald began moving to meet Moore, and dispatched a warning for him to avert imminent bloodshed by joining with the loyalist Highlanders. Moore turned that offer down, warning McDonald he would be in for the same treatment he himself proposed for the patriots. About the same time, McDonald began receiving reports of additional minutemen gathering to reinforce Moore.

Apparently hoping now to avoid a battle until the expected arrival of British forces under General Sir Henry Clinton and Lord William Campbell, McDonald broke camp and headed for the coast and the presumed arrival of the British.

On the 26th, as he approached Moore's Creek, a small tributary of the Cape Fear River, McDonald and his Highlanders ran right into the camp of Colonels Richard Caswell and Alexander Lillington and the combined militia of four counties—all out looking for the Scots. Moore, meanwhile, was coming up on the rear of McDonald's force.

The inevitable battle came at dawn the next day, announced by the bleating of bagpipes; it was utter disaster for the Highlanders. Among their casualties were Captains McLeod and Campbell, first and second in command under McDonald. The old general himself was ill, and stayed in his tent through the few minutes of fighting.

The clearcut patriot victory at Moore's Creek leaves North Carolina's Tories without a military leader, without a military force, and without much hope for the future except in following the lead of their royal governor: leaving the colony.[28]

Congress

Change in Orders

Still weighing alternatives and shifting strategies, Congress this week did an about-face and canceled its order sending General Lee to Canada. It directed him to hold fast until further notice. That was on Wednesday. On Friday, it decided what the further notice would be. Instead of heading due north, Lee is to head due south and take command of the newly organized Southern Department (Virginia, North Carolina, South Carolina and Georgia) of the Continental Army.

At the same time, Congress raised six officers to the rank of brigadier general. Among them: Colonel Robert Howe, who commanded the ill-fated American forces at Norfolk at the beginning of the year. Howe will serve under Lee, but his command will remain in Virginia.

Congress on Thursday received the credentials of Josiah Bartlett, John Langdon and William Whipple, once again forming the New Hampshire delegation. They were re-elected by that state's House of Representatives January 23rd.[29]

First American Nobleman?

Can it be that the Continental Congress of the United Colonies—certainly not the world's foremost believer in orders of nobility—would, of all things, bestow a peerage because the world's foremost believer, the British House of Peers, would not?

In fact, Congress did not. But what it did do might well have had patriots raising their eyebrows and a certain American military figure allowing himself a wry smile.

Colonel of the 1st New Jersey Regiment since last November, William Alexander was born in New York fifty years ago, and though descended from a line of earls—from whence comes the "Lord Stirling" by which he is affectionately known—never managed to win the right to the title of "Earl of Stirling." And not for lack of trying. While in Britain twenty years ago, he pleaded his case before a jury in Edinburgh—how a court poet and forebear of his had been a favorite of James I, and was thus favored with a peerage and grants of land in America; how the peerage had continued down to the fifth Earl of Stirling, and then ended with his death in 1739; how he, William Alexander, by virtue of direct succession, should now be sixth Earl of Stirling.

The court was unconvinced by Alexander's argument. Undaunted, Alexander went all the way to the Committee on Privileges of the House of Peers, and another rebuff.

That ended the matter. Alexander may have smiled last week, however, when Congress, in its resolution promoting him to brigadier general, addressed him not by his given name of "William Alexander" nor even his affectionate pseudonym of "Lord Stirling"; but—at long last—as "Right Honorable William, Earl of Stirling."

Congress doubtless intended it as nothing but a compliment to a highly esteemed officer, and won't likely offer any privileges to go with the title.[30]

Foreign News

Uncertain Plan

Lord George Germaine, British Secretary of State for the Colonies, is reportedly proposing to his colleagues in the Ministry this plan for ending war in the colonies: Use the army to march along the coast and utterly destroy every city, town and village on the sea and on major rivers. This, he believes, would entirely cut off the naval potential of the Americans and prove the most effective way of putting an end to the war. Several other members of the Ministry are thought to be in agreement with Germaine. But Lord North is reported to be opposed, making such a strategy unlikely.[31]

Religion

Brothers' Keepers

That Church of England clergy in North America may not be faring well has become a very real concern to their brethren in England.

At the behest of a number of bishops, Britons are being asked to contribute to a relief fund for those of the American clergy remaining loyal to the Crown and thereby thought to be facing hardship until return to England or transfer to Canada. Thus far the fund has reached more than 775 l. Largest individual donations: 30l each from the Archbishops of Canterbury and York.[32]

Theater

Curtain for the Playhouse

Citizens of Milan have long taken pride in the Ducal Playhouse as one of Europe's finest theaters; this week they watched it disappear in a curtain of flame. The fire, of unknown origin, struck the day after it was used for a masked ball. Three persons died, a number of others were injured. The loss was estimated at the equivalent of 100,000 crowns.[33]

Press

Now There are Three (or Four)

In its forty-year history, the *Virginia Gazette* has had a steady succession of publishers, but never more than one publisher or partnership at a time. Lately there have been many of both. They have included:

—A newspaper published in Williamsburg by John Dixon and William Hunter entitled the *Virginia Gazette*;

—A newspaper published in Williamsburg by Alexander Purdie called the *Virginia Gazette*;

—A newspaper published in Williamsburg by John Pinkney bearing the title, *Virginia Gazette*;

—A newspaper published by the royal governor, Lord Dunmore, aboard his ship somewhere off Norfolk, called the *Virginia Gazette*.

—And until September, there was a newspaper published in Norfolk by John H. Holt and Company, also the *Virginia Gazette*.

Such a preponderance of reading material hasn't always been the case in Virginia. The colony's first recorded printer was John Buckner, of Gloucester County, who a century ago saw fit—presumably as a public service—to print copies of the laws of the Assembly. That was until a copy found its way into the hands of the governor, Lord Culpeper, and his Council. For failure to have a license for his work (something which he probably wouldn't have been granted) Printer Buckner was placed under 100 l bond not to print anything further "until his Majesty's pleasure should be known." When his Majesty's pleasure was known, it was decidedly negative: There would be no further use of the printing press without a special license. And licenses were few, far between, and stringently supervised.

It was not until forty years ago that a free press was finally established in Virginia with the founding of the *Virginia Gazette* by William Parks. A native of England, Parks first settled in Annapolis and established the *Maryland Gazette* in 1727. He moved to Williamsburg in 1736, and published the *Virginia Gazette* until his death in 1750. Then began a succession of owners that seems destined never to end. First came William Hunter (the elder) who died in 1761. Then came Joseph Royle. He died in 1766. Then came Alexander Purdie in March of 1766, and then a joint partnership of Purdie and John Dixon in June of that year. Then, last year, Purdie decided to drop out and begin his own newspaper. So Dixon took on a new partner, William Hunter, son of the second publisher.

Meanwhile, there is Pinkney's *Gazette*. It came about, in effect, as successor to still another *Gazette* that was published until 1773 by William Rind, and after he died, by his widow, Clementina, until her death a year later. Pinkney revived the newspaper, as the heading states, "for the benefit of Clementina Rind's children." No issues of this newspaper, however, have been published since February 3rd, and it is now understood that Pinkney has ceased publication.

Lord Dunmore's *Virginia Gazette*, which is intended primarily for circulation among his troops, first appeared last November. It was the successor to—and the reason for the demise of—the Holt *Virginia Gazette* published in Norfolk. Holt's presses were confiscated and hauled away by Dunmore's troops September 30th, and are now used for printing the loyalist version.

So many newspapers of the same name may sound like a guarantee of confusion, but readers can always tell them apart by observing the slogan in the heading of each. If it says "Always for liberty and the public good," they will be sure of having Purdie's; if it says "The freshest advices, foreign and domestick," they know they are reading Dixon and Hunter's. If a recent edition proclaimed "Open to all parties, but influenced by none," it was one of Pinkney's. On the other hand, if the heading is nothing but *Virginia Gazette*—and the news is all about the British—it's a sure bet to be Dunmore's.[34]

SUPPLEMENTARY NOTES

February

The British Parliament
   Parliament—this was the Second Session of the 14th Parliament—met at the old Westminster Palace, the House of Commons in St. Stephen's Chapel (as it had since 1547 and would for more than another half century) and the House of Lords in the adjoining White Hall, which in earlier days was the Court of Requests. This Westminster Palace, except for Westminster Hall,

was destroyed by fire in 1834 and replaced by the present Houses of Parliament. St. Stephen's Chapel was small by modern standards as a legislative chamber (86 by 38 feet), but it was never expected that the entire membership of the House of Commons would be there at one time; and it had the advantage, during debate, of allowing the speaker to be heard without straining his voice.

Daily sessions at this period nominally began at nine in the morning; but as a practical matter, it was usually three or four in the afternoon when major business got under way, and then often continued well into the evening.

The House of Commons had 558 members—489 from England, 45 from Scotland and 24 from Wales. The Tories had a sizable majority. The Speaker, since 1770, was Sir Fletcher Norton.

Continental Currency

In making the dollar the standard currency, the Continental Congress established the basic monetary system that exists today. But some other basic unit of currency might easily have been chosen; there was a plethora of coinage in common use in the colonies at that time.

Up until June 22, 1775, when Congress first authorized an emission of two million dollars in bills of credit in various denominations of Spanish dollars, the British pound sterling was necessarily the official currency. But even before 1775, the dollar (Spanish) was probably the more common in ordinary trade. The choice of the dollar instead of the pound sterling as the basis of the American monetary system had the dual advantage of perpetuating a popular unit of currency with which every one was familiar, and (once independence was declared and reconciliation forever abandoned) of removing from the American scene another vestige of the mother country.

Although the only backing for Continental currency at the outset was the good faith of the individual colonies, Congress recognized the need to provide for redemption; with the first emission in June, 1775, it directed that the issue be sunk by the colonies through "laying and levying taxes," in four equal amounts to be determined on the basis of population, beginning November 30, 1779, and continuing annually through 1782. But with the continuation of the war and further emissions in ever greater amounts—a total of 200 million dollars by 1780—that schedule was never kept.

It should be noted that the dollar (Continental) was not yet divided into cents. Transactions of small value continued to take place with shillings and pence. Nor was the dollar sign yet in use; as was the custom then, so is it done throughout this book; the word dollar *is spelled out after the amount.*

Meanwhile, the colonies were also issuing their own coin and emitting their own bills of credit, the latter—as was true of Continental dollars—without any concurrent backing whatever. The proliferation of paper of the colonies only served to weaken Continental paper, to the common detriment of the cause of independence. Of all the colonial currency, that of Pennsylvania (still in pounds) was the most stable.

As the war years went on, Continental bills depreciated drastically in value. At the close of 1776, it would have required about 105 dollar bills to purchase what 100 dollars in coin would obtain; by 1781, that same 100 dollar purchase would have required 7,400 Continental bills. Thus the origin of the saying, "Not worth a Continental." It was in part the chaotic currency situation during the war that led, after the peace in 1783, to moves for a strong central government with exclusive control over the monetary system of the United States.

Records of the Continental Congress show the following forms of currency in circulation in the United Colonies early in 1776, and these equivalent values in dollars of the United Colonies: Crown (French), 1⅑ dollars; Dollar (Spanish), 1; Guinea (French), 4⅝; Half-Johannes (Portuguese), 8; Pistole (French), 3½; Pistole (Spanish), 3⅔; Pound Sterling (British, as of December 23, 1775), 2⅔; Pound Sterling (August 19, 1776), 3⅓; Moidore (Portuguese), 6.

MARCH

NOW comes the time the birds begin to sing
Harmonious, to welcome in the spring;
And *Phoebus,* hastening to the *northern* wane,
Doth cause each vegetive to spring again.

The Virginia Almanack
March, 1776

THE WEEK OF MARCH 4TH

The War

Providence at Dorchester Heights

It was March the 5th—the anniversary of the Boston Massacre of 1770—but that significance of a late winter day paled before a greater significance this year. Six years ago it had been colonials who stared in disbelief as British troops fired at a mob on King Street in Boston. This time it was the turn of the British to stare in disbelief—at the crests of Dorchester Heights. There, to the south of Boston, across the bay, on high ground that the day before lay bare as it had all these months of siege, were extensive fortifications and a goodly number of cannon aimed not only at the British in Boston but at the fleet under Admiral Molyneux Shuldham in the harbor.

The fortification of Dorchester Heights may well be the turning point in the siege, and surely a military accomplishment that borders on the

BOSTON AND ENVIRONS (William Faden, London, 1777). This is how the Boston area looked at the time of the siege, all essential territory being included in this detail of a map published in London October 1, 1777. Most significant of the environs are Charlestown, to the north; Cambridge, to the northwest; and Dorchester and Roxbury, to the south. Boston, not marked, is the fist-shaped mass of land crisscrossed by streets just right of center. Boston then looked remarkably different than it does today—and for that matter, somewhat different than it had a century and a half earlier when the city was founded. Bostonians were continually enlarging the city by filling it in around the water line. Beacon Hill (just north of the common), now little more than high ground, really was a hill once, but lost a good deal of altitude in the nineteenth century as land was taken for fill, especially for what is shown here as Mill Pond. The present North Station is located about at the words "Mill Dam." Meanwhile even more significant expansion went on to the west and south. The Boston Public Garden (1839) is located just to the west of Boston Common, which was at city's edge in the eighteenth century; many of the city's present-day skyscrapers are still further west of this point. It is impossible to comprehend the events of the siege of 1775–76 using a modern map of the city.

Map Division—New York Public Library— Astor, Lenox and Tilden Foundations incredible. It may also at last explain why, in recent days, there has been so much cannon fire in other areas of the perimeter around Boston. While the steady roar of the cannon consumed the attention of the British, something else was going on. Sometime early Monday evening, General John Thomas and perhaps 2,000 men, marching in remarkable silence, reached Dorchester Heights and set about to do in one night's time what might have taken less resourceful and less determined men weeks to do: turn two barren promontories into armed embankments, notwithstanding the fact that the earth is frozen.

A disbelieving British army beheld the new fortifications on Tuesday morning, the 5th, and answered with a cannonade from its forts in Boston and from ships in the harbor. General Howe began massing his troops for attack on the now strategic Dorchester Heights.

Thus began a day of anxious waiting on both sides for that which would culminate these ten long months of siege. General Washington was there among his men. He had them filling barrels with earth and stone to set outside the breastworks. The British would have a steep hill to climb, and at the right moment he would order the barrels rolled down into the midst of the attacking force, breaking legs and scattering the ranks. Howe meanwhile had ordered perhaps 2,500 men to take to barges and rendezvous at Castle William in the harbor, there to stand ready for an attack on Dorchester Heights that night under the command of Earl Percy.

Thus by afternoon were the preliminaries completed; the field was ready for battle. These were preparations for war at its worst: "Preparations," said one in the American ranks, "for blood and slaughter." And then he added, as if in prayer, "Gracious God! if it be determined in thy providence that thousands of our fellow creatures shall this day be slain, let thy wrath be appeased and in mercy grant that victory be on the side of our suffering, bleeding country!"

Providence may well have intervened, but it was on the side of neither. What had been a gentle breeze off the harbor grew into a furious gale. By night the rains came—torrents of water that indiscriminately made landing boats swamped, muddy terrain impassable, hills unclimbable, gunpowder waterlogged, and powerfully armed men powerless against the greater force of nature.

Howe abandoned his plans; Washington returned to his camp. There was no battle.[1]

Hell, Hull or Halifax?

By Friday, the 8th, the real significance of the fortification of Dorchester Heights seemed apparent. There was a report of a message from General Howe to General Washington, relayed by Boston's Selectmen. That message: the British are ready to evacuate.

Plagued throughout the long winter with steadily dwindling supplies, a shortage of food and fuel, smallpox, and declining morale, the British are already in what is at best a stalemate, and potentially in what is at worst an unbelievable defeat. A decision to evacuate—if true—will therefore strike almost no one as a surprise.

If General Howe does leave Boston, where will it be for? A British soldier may have offered a hint. Complaining of the tribulations of the siege, he moaned: "Neither Hell, Hull nor Halifax can afford worse shelter than Boston." Of the three, the last is the most likely destination, though the first may not seem altogether inappropriate. Not to be ruled out, either, is New York, think a few observers.[2]

Although such a message from Howe to Washington was publicly reported at the time, Washington considered it "an unauthenticated paper" drawn up by the Boston Selectmen and in no way binding on Howe. He refused to take official notice of it.

Congress

Indian Recruitment

Congress has prohibited the direct recruitment of individual Indians as soldiers in the armies of the United Colonies. The regulation does not preclude the possibility that Indians may some day fight side by side with Americans. What it does do is to place the power of Indian enlistment in the tribal councils—and avoid the possibility of incurring the wrath, and retaliation, of Indian nations over the willing-or-otherwise induction of their braves into Colonial armies.

Henceforth, before Indians may join American ranks, two requirements must be satisfied: 1) the tribes to which they belong must, in national council, consent thereto; and 2) Congress must also approve.

In other action this week, Congress appointed a new commander in Canada, weighed the disposition of a case of contempt of Congress, and took further action on various monetary matters.

Hoping to bolster the campaign to the north, Congress promoted Brigadier General John Thomas to major general, and assigned him to take command of all American forces in Canada. Thomas is currently assigned to Washington's command in Cambridge.

The case of contempt involved one Isaac Melchior, who, the Saturday night before, is said to have treated President John Hancock with "great rudeness." Furthermore, said the charge against him, he "made use of several disrespectful and contemptuous expressions toward him and Congress." Congress ordered Melchior to appear at eleven Friday morning. When he did so, it was with contrition. He assured the House he did not remember behaving with disrespect—owing to the "circumstances he happened to be under"—and in any event begged the pardon of Congress and its president for his indecent behavior. The case was dismissed. The "circumstances" were not further explained.

Recognizing that the first of the recently authorized four million dollars in Continental bills are now coming off the presses, Congress appointed a committee of sixty (all non-members) to do the signing. To avoid risk of fire, robbery or negligence, press inspectors were ordered not to deliver more than two parcels of 200 sheets each to a group of signers at any one time.

In other action, Congress requested the Philadelphia Committee of Inspection to collect all the gold and silver coin possible—in exchange for Continental bills—so that coin will be available for use of the American military forces in Canada, where Continental bills are not readily accepted.[3]

No Place

The idea a military officer require a private citizen to give an oath of allegiance has no place in the American scheme of things. So said Congress this week. It directed that "no oath by way of test be imposed upon, exacted or required of any of the inhabitants of these colonies by any military officer."[4]

The Colonies

In Time for Spring Planting

Among them are staples of American gardens, but there are also some exotic varieties that, when grown, tempt one's taste. They're an assortment of seeds imported from Italy, and on sale by merchants in the colonies.

Among them: Roman small broccoli, cauliflower from Malta, Dutch lettuce, Lasagnino cabbage, green cucumbers, Naples watermelon, cantaloupe melon, early pumpkins, Italian loaf lettuce, early Charlton peas, endive, Turkey snap beans, asparagus, spinach, round and long radishes, cress, and red beets.[5]

Parliament

Hessian Treaties: Approved

Both houses of Parliament have now given their approval to the treaties negotiated in January for supplying German troops to fight in the colonies. But they did so in different ways: the House of Commons by an act appropriating 522,368 *l* for the purpose, and the House of Lords through defeat of a motion opposing the treaties.

In Commons March 4th the vote was 120–48 in favor of the appropriation, which will cover payments to the Duke of Brunswick, the Landgrave of Hesse-Cassel and the Hereditary Prince of Hesse-Cassel through December of this year.

Objections to the treaties were largely on technical grounds. Example: would Britain have to continue payments at the same rate if a substantial number of troops is killed and therefore no longer of service?

Colonel Isaac Barré asked if clothing for the troops (by the treaties, a British responsibility) is to be bought in England or in Germany. Barré said it appeared "this sale of human blood would turn out as advantageous to the woolen manufactures of Brunswick and Hesse in the clothing branch as it was already become lucrative to their respective sovereigns." The matter was resolved through a supplementary resolution requiring that the clothing be purchased in Great Britain.

The House of Lords two days later disregarded technicalities and devoted its debate to the substance of the treaties. It began with a motion by the Duke of Richmond asking that his Majesty stop the march of the Hessians, suspend hostilities in America, and lay a foundation for a speedy and permanent reconciliation.

As for the treaties, said Richmond, they acknowledge "to all Europe that these kingdoms [Great Britain] are unable, either from want of men or from disinclination to this service, to furnish a competent number of natural-born subjects." Furthermore, the treaties, through mutual assistance provisions, "will get us involved in every quarrel on the continent in which his Serene Highness [Landgrave of Hesse-Cassel] happens to be involved." Richmond's alternative: "Reconciliation of this unnatural war would be more agreeable to sound policy."

Support of the treaties and the policy of the North Ministry was acclaimed by Viscount Townshend: "The die is cast, and the only point which now remains to be determined is in what manner the war can be most effectually prosecuted and speedily finished, in order to procure that unconditional submission which has been so well stated by the noble Earl with the white staff [Talbot]. I know of no method so probable to insure success to our operations as that now adopted."

The vote: Contents, 32 (including three proxies) and Non-contents, 100 (including 21 proxies), thus defeating the Duke of Richmond's resolution and, in effect, approving the treaties.[6]

This Townshend was George, 4th Viscount Townshend and older brother of the author of the "Townshend Acts."

Foreign News

Reluctant Regiments

Among British and German troops bound for active duty in America, there is said to be growing resistance as embarkation day, March 18th, nears. Much the same situation is told in these three reports:

—From London: that both British and Irish troops are readying to embark only with "infinite reluctance" and that "strong guards are obliged to be kept on the transports to keep them from deserting wholesale";

—From Prussia: That there is great discontent among Brunswick and Hessian troops, and that two regiments have mutinied and killed the major general who tried to restore order through an appeal to reason;

—From Hesse: That soldiers are nearly mutinous, but recognize that the Landgrave is an absolute monarch and will have to be obeyed.[7]

They Were

Said the man named Reilly, "Innocent." Said another named Minerd, "Innocent."

The scene in a Dublin prison was not unlike many another before it: two men charged with robbery, tried, found guilty, sentenced to be hanged, still claiming innocence.

Now their final day had arrived. Still protesting, they were given the last sacraments, and taken away to be pinioned—the last step before execution. Then said a man named Lupton, "Wait." And another named Coleman, "Wait." Already in the jail for street robbery, Lupton and Coleman had nothing to lose, and admitted they were the guilty ones.

The Lord Lieutenant of Ireland suspended the last step for the men named Reilly and Minerd, and set them free.[8]

Books

Of Wealth and Nations

"The French economical writers," concedes the London-published *Annual Register*, "undoubtedly have their merit. Within this century they have opened the way to a rational theory on the subjects of agriculture, manufactures and commerce. But no one work has appeared amongst them, nor perhaps could there be collected from the whole together, anything to be compared to the present performance—for sagacity and penetration of mind, extent of views, accurate distinction, just and natural connexion and dependence of parts."

The "present performance" is a new work, published in London March 9th in two volumes by W. Strahan and T. Cadell, and entitled *An Inquiry into the Nature and Causes of the Wealth of Nations.* The author: Adam Smith, formerly professor of moral philosophy at the University of Glasgow, whose first major work, *The Theory of Moral Sentiments,* began to acquire recognition for the author seventeen years ago.

What sets *The Wealth of Nations* apart from other speculative treatises on economy—whether the author be philosopher or politician—is the totality of its approach. Rare even has been the attempt to consider the economic basis of the rise and fall of nations in so great a diversity of causes; and probably never has there been one that does it as convincingly.

The Wealth of Nations, to cite the opinion of the *Register,* "is a compleat analysis of society, beginning with the first rudiments of the simplest manual labor, and rising by an easy and natural gradation to the highest attainments of mental powers. In which course not only arts and commerce, but finance, justice, public police, the economy of armies, and the system of education are considered, and argued upon, often profoundly, always plausibly and clearly; many of the speculations are new, and time will be required before a certain judgment can be passed on their truth and solidity. The style of the author may be sometimes thought diffuse, but it must be remembered that the work is didactic, and the author means to teach, and teach things that are by no means obvious."

Smith's work—ten years in the writing—represents perhaps the most decisive break yet with the mercantilism of the past centuries (and its supremacy of the state, its rigid controls, its emphasis on exports over imports, colonial exploitation, and the idea that money alone is wealth), even though Smith would not dispense with government controls entirely. And while he is more akin than not to the physiocrats of France (whom he got to know while visiting there ten years ago) he differs significantly and materially from them in arguing that land alone is not the basis of wealth. For Smith, the wealth of a nation is that which it accrues through the production of goods of all sorts having a market (rather than merely utility) value. The extent of such production, and thus of wealth, depends on the amount of work invested, and clearly, says Smith, this will be greater in a state of economic liberty than it will be under government control. Production will be further increased where the labor is divided, each worker specializing in some facet of the production; and it will be perpetuated through a capitalist class that has reason to believe investment in its nation's business and industry is as much a matter of self-interest as of national interest.

In short, for Smith the *natural liberty* of man is manifested as significantly in his economic life as for a Locke it is in his political life—if indeed the two can be separated at all.[9]

THE WEEK OF MARCH 11TH

The War

Gone the Chariot Wheels

For several days it had been suspected by General Washington and his officers all around Boston that the British were making ready to leave. General Howe's troops in the city on Friday were seen parading toward the docks, and not returning to their quarters. And then, likewise, civilians—those Tories who had been promised protection by the British and now would rather leave their homes forever than risk the wrath of returning patriots. To American observers it appeared every bit to be the expected evacuation of Boston by the British.

On Sunday the 17th there was no longer a shadow of doubt. At nine in the morning, the last large British garrison, at Bunker's Hill, began an orderly march to waiting vessels, and as the day wore on, ship after ship departed the harbor, so loaded with troops and supplies that those Tories escaping had to leave most of their possessions behind. It was no doubt a particularly bitter moment for the people who had cast their lot with the British and were repeatedly assured that reinforcements were coming to break the siege and enable the King's troops to ravage the countryside and the American army. More than one Tory elected the course of suicide rather than face the choice of evacuation. In all, the British exodus meant the departure of about 11,000 troops and officers and perhaps a thousand civilians.

The Continental Army wasted no time in entering the just-vacated city, only slightly hindered by a scattering of crow's feet left for them by the British. There were outbursts of joy, tender embraces and shouts of mutual congratulation by those patriots-at-heart who had endured ten months of siege somehow confident this day would come. But the joy of the arriving Continentals lessened as they looked about them at what was once a beautiful Boston.

Churches and public buildings had been shamefully defaced; fine homes ransacked or destroyed; shade trees cut down. Gone was the North Church—used for fuel. So was the steeple of the West Church. Faneuil Hall had become a theater; and the Brattle Street and Hollis Street churches, barracks. And that large elm, called the Liberty Tree, under which the Sons of Liberty gathered for meetings during the summer of 1765, from whose limbs once hung in effigy enforcers of the Stamp Act— gone altogether, into fourteen cords of wood. On the other hand, the elegant home of Continental Congress President John Hancock, still listed as an outlaw by the British government, is in good order.

For the Americans now in Boston, it may have been disconsoling to view the wretched desolation of the object of their months of siege; but whatever its condition, Boston was once again in Continental hands.

For the departing British, it would be a relief to be free the rigors of siege, now to prepare for some new objective better the odds and more worth the trouble. Yet there would have to be some sense of ignominy among the commanders. Not long ago in England a general boasted about how he could take a mere five regiments and march victoriously from one end of America to the other. Here was a considerably larger force that never got west of Concord.

On the afternoon of the day Boston changed hands officers and men could ponder the significance as they listened to a sermon by the Rev. Mr. Leonard. Reflecting on the events of that historic day, the pastor quoted from the Book of Exodus—about the children of Israel being saved from the Egyptians, about God intervening to make impotent the Pharaoh's forces. He read from Exodus 14:24–25:

"And it came to pass, that in the morning-watch the Lord looked unto the host of the Egyptians, through the pillar of fire and of the cloud, and troubled the host of the Egyptians, and took off their chariot-wheels, that they drave them heavily: so that the Egyptians said, Let us flee from the face of Israel; for the Lord fighteth for them, against the Egyptians."[10]

Congress

Day of Prayer

The objective, said Congress clearly enough, is to impress upon people a "solemn sense of God's superintending providence, and their duty devoutly to rely in all their lawful enterprises on his aid and direction."

Toward that purpose, Congress has set aside Friday, May 17th, as a day of fasting and prayer throughout the Colonies. Christians of all denominations are asked to assemble for public worship, abstain from all labors. In so doing, says the resolution, "we may with united hearts confess and bewail our manifold sins and transgressions, and by a fierce repentence and amendment of life appease his righteous displeasure, and through the merits and mediation of Jesus Christ, obtain his pardon and forgiveness."

Earlier last week, Congress asked the colonies of Connecticut, New York and New Jersey to hold their militia in readiness in case they are needed for the defense of the city of New York—thus anticipating the possibility of attack there after the British leave Boston. The pay of militiamen called up is to be the same as Continental troops.[11]

Parliament

The Sword Now Drawn

"It will be the means of sheathing the sword now drawn, perhaps never again to be returned to the scabbard till a deluge of blood is spilt, and either Great Britain or America, or both, are brought into such a state as may inevitably produce their separate or total destruction."

So saying, the Duke of Grafton addressed his fellow members of the House of Lords Thursday in support of his motion for one last meaningful attempt at conciliation with the colonies. On such a proposal he was assured of extensive debate, and he got it. All in all it was a session that may well rank as one of the most significant in Parliament in the present crisis.

A follower of former First Minister William Pitt, and for a time leader of that Ministry after Pitt's withdrawal because of ill health, the 41-year-old Grafton argued long—and many would say eloquently—in behalf of a motion he knew would have rough-going. He could be long and eloquent, he said, because of "a thorough conviction on my part, that it, or some measure of a similar nature, is the only possible means now left of averting the destruction which seems suspended over the heads of the people of this devoted unhappy country."

Grafton's motion: A request to the Crown for a royal proclamation declaring that, if the colonies will submit a petition setting forth what they consider to be their just rights and real grievances, his Majesty will consent to at least a temporary suspension of arms and will assure the colonies that their petition will be received, considered and answered by Parliament.

The first to answer was the Earl of Dartmouth, an amiable man who rarely speaks during debates. He had plenty to say this time, and it was squarely in favor of proceeding with measures of force. "I was anxious to treat them [the Americans] with tenderness," explained Dartmouth, "to give them every reasonable indulgence, and even to give way to their prejudices, so far as it could be done with safety. What has been the consequence? They have treated those marks of favour as so many indications of national imbecility."

And then, one who has sided with the colonies throughout the past struggle spoke, and as expected, he was squarely in favor of the Grafton motion. Said the Duke of Manchester: "That we have no reason to rest in a state of security, I am well convinced. I have good reason to believe that France and Spain are meditating some blow against us. . . . In short, my lords, uniting all the causes, circumstances and probable events which first created, or may be consequent of the present dispute, I am heartily for agreeing with the motion made by the noble Duke."

And so the debate continued . . . the Earl of Sandwich, opposed; the Duke of Richmond, for; Lord Lyttelton, against; the Earl of Shelburne, in favor. Some argued against it on grounds it would only give America time to prepare more effective resistance. The Bishop of Petersborough spoke for it, suggesting that among other virtues it "will at least have this good effect, it will let us all into the real ground of the quarrel."

At last, late into the night, the Duke of Grafton took the floor again for his summation: "I once more conjure your lordships to reflect that the honour of Parliament, the prosperity and dearest interests of both countries, the lives of thousands of British subjects, are at stake; that the present is probably the only moment you will ever have to snatch them from the ruin which will otherwise inevitably await them; and that the consequences of neglecting this opportunity will be the source of endless mourning and lamentation to ages yet unborn."

Even as he said that, he undoubtedly knew that the prevailing senti-

ment for a harder line against the colonies would not change. And it did
not. The House of Lords voted 91 to 31 against Grafton's motion.

A contemporary evaluation of March 14th in the House of Lords was contained in the
Annual Register, written in part by Edmund Burke and then in its 17th year: "This day will,
perhaps, hereafter be considered as one of the most important in the English history. It
deeply fixed a new colour upon our publick affairs. It was decisive, on this side of the
Atlantick, with respect to America; and may possibly hereafter be compared with, and
considered as preliminary to, that on which, unhappily, in a few months after, the inde-
pendence of that continent was declared on the other. . . . No alternative now seemed to
be left between absolute conquest and unconditional submission." [12]

Foreign News

Another Destination

Algiers, the sanctuary of the Barbary pirates, has already been the target of one Spanish military expedition seeking a solution to piracy through
force instead of the often more common method of paying tribute. Now
it appears a second such expedition is being canceled by the Spanish government.

Noted a recent report from Madrid: "Our court seems to have quite
given up the proposed attempt of a second expedition against Algiers. All
the preparations for that expedition have now another destination, and are
said to be intended to watch over our settlements in America, as war between England and its colonies renders it necessary for all powers who have
settlements in those parts to put them in so secure a situation that they
may be in no danger of suffering from the abovementioned disputes." [13]

Music

"Sonorous and Awfully Majestic"

In London's Covent Garden this week there was a performance of the
recently published oratorio *Messiah* that proved its composer, the late
George Frideric Handel, beyond any question England's favorite.

Wednesday's rendition, marking the mid-point in Lent and thus the most
popular time for religious oratorios, was typical. An assemblage of nearly
eighty performers filled the stage, the members of the orchestra grouped
concentrically in back of the chorus and soloists. In the center was the or-
gan; on top of it, a portrait of Handel surrounded by a glory of rays such
as are placed around the heads of saints of the Roman Church—"our musical saint's performance," said one observer, "being as much read and
studied here as their manuals of devotion are by their admirers."

To the same observer, who listened to the performance from the first row, lower gallery, it was all in all an awesome occasion. Said he: "The music was noble, grand, full, sonorous and awfully majestic." When the performers got to the Hallelujah Chorus, everyone rose, as they have been doing since King George II set the example at the first London performance, thirty-three years ago in this same Covent Garden. And to the same listener: that "added a solemnity which swelled and filled my soul with an—I know not what; that it exalted it beyond itself, bringing to my raised imagination a full view of that sacred assembly of blessed spirits which surround the throne of God."[14]

Books

Independence is Slavery

Since its publication in early January, *Common Sense* has become the most successful publication ever to leave the presses of the colonies. The anonymously authored pamphlet, which unabashedly avows the cause of independence, has found a host of sympathetic readers, but no few opponents as well.

Whereas *Common Sense* equates independence with freedom, *Plain Truth* would have Americans believe "independence is slavery."

An outright Tory response to *Common Sense, Plain Truth* has now appeared from the same publisher, R. Bell, of Philadelphia, under the anonymous authorship of "Candidus." But it is not expected to become as popular. Its higher cost of three shillings is, says the publisher, a necessary result of the small number printed in the first, and so far only, edition.[15]

"Candidus" is believed to be either James Chalmers, a Scottish-born American then serving (or soon to serve) as a lieutenant colonel in a Loyalist regiment in Maryland, or the Rev. William Smith, Tory provost of the College of Philadelphia.

THE WEEK OF MARCH 18TH

The War

To the Point

The *Boston Gazette* reacted to the departure of the British in no surprising way. In its edition the day after evacuation, the *Gazette* called the events of March 17th "retreat of butchering, murdering and plundering banditti." With the British gone, the *Gazette,* published at nearby Watertown since last year, may soon return to town.[16]

Highland Gathering

In the weeks since the rout of old Donald McDonald's Tory High-landers at Moore's Creek Bridge, North Carolina, parties of patriots have been roaming the Colony in search of Highlanders still armed and at large. So far they have apprehended and disarmed (and subsequently released) more than 850 Loyalist soldiers and taken in (and kept) 250 guns and shotbags, 150 swords, 1,500 rifles in excellent condition, and 13 wagons and horses.[17]

Congress

Canadian Relations

Their departure date approaching, Congress at last has specific in-structions for the members of its diplomatic mission to Canada. To Dr. Benjamin Franklin, Samuel Chase and Charles Carroll, appointed Feb-ruary 15th, Congress gave these directions, along with a request to depart "with all convenient dispatch:"

—Explain to the Canadians that arms of the United Colonies have been carried into their province for the purpose of frustrating the designs of the British against our common liberties; that we will help our Cana-dian brethren pursue their own freedom and happiness in whatever way sound policy and their love of liberty shall dictate to them;

—But also, get them to see the necessity of coming under the protec-tion of the United Colonies;

—Inform them that if we are reduced to servile submission to Great Britain, they will share our fate;

—Explain our government to them; assure them it is our earnest de-sire to adopt them into union with us as a sister colony (with whatever form of government they want) as long as the terms of union are con-sistent with those on which the other colonies united.[18]

The Colonies

Change of Heart

On February 10th, Colonel Christopher Gadsden, having left the Con-tinental Congress to take the military command of South Carolina, ap-peared before the Provincial Congress in Charleston. Tucked under his arm was a copy of *Common Sense,* perhaps the first copy to reach that Colony.

Boldly, Gadsden told the South Carolina delegates the book did in-deed make sense to him, and he was himself in favor of the absolute independence of America. Not so the Provincial Congress. His remarks,

said one member, came "like an explosion of thunder on its members."
It was obvious the representatives of South Carolina abhorred the idea.

That was little more than a month ago. On the 23rd, having learned
of that December act of Parliament authorizing seizure of American ships,
the same Provincial Congress of South Carolina reversed its instruction
to its delegates in the Continental Congress, advising them they are now
free to agree with whatever steps Congress as a whole should judge to
be necessary with regard to independence.[19]

Dunmore's Black Regiment

Some are runaways otherwise bound for jail; others are former slaves
who took advantage of last November's proclamation freeing Virginia
Negroes who would join the forces of the Colony's royal governor. They
are the members of the Royal Regiment of Black Fusileers.

The regiment is stationed with the fleet of Virginia's Governor Dunmore in Hampton Roads. But it is a regiment in name, and not in number; there are only about eighty men so far. And it is not a regiment in
the full military sense. The Negro recruit, whatever his dreams of battlefield glory may have been, soon finds his lot in life is hardly improved
by Lord Dunmore's offer. The recruit's principal function is the drudgery;
for him, the life of a scullion is far more probable than that of a fusileer.
But army life is not totally lacking. When his chores are done, the Negro
soldier is given a full round of military exercises.

One concession the regiment does have. Instead of using the traditional fife and drum, Black Fusileers have permission to use the sprightly
African *barasoo* in playing their regimental tune, "The Blackbird March."[20]

Parliament

Pickles and Principles

To an uninformed observer in the House of Commons, it could only
have seemed a fallen *British* commander was the subject of such ardent
adulation. It was not, nor were fallen heroes the basis of debate.

The subject Monday night in Parliament was a Committee of Supply
report on expenses of the army in America—such mundane stuff as many
a legislative session is made of. But attention turned to the recently received report of the death of General Richard Montgomery, killed while
leading the unsuccessful American attack on Quebec last December 31st.

Once a rising young officer in the British Army, Montgomery resigned
his commission in 1772, moved to America, and took up farming. He was
subsequently coaxed into service in the American cause, and was second-
in-command in the American invasion of Canada last year. Still remembered in Britain, and by many affectionately, he was now being held up
by the Whigs as the model of an efficient military commander—the sort,

they argued, who could not be claimed by the British army penned up at Boston for the better part of a year.

The Whigs' oratorical phalanx—principally Edmund Burke, Charles James Fox and Colonel Isaac Barré—took turns extolling Montgomery. Even General Burgoyne, after first carefully denouncing the American cause, paid homage.

At last Lord North could bear it no longer, and rose to censure such "unqualified liberality of praise." He would not join in lamenting the general's death. Perhaps, he allowed, Montgomery was "brave, able, humane, generous"; but if so, he was still "a brave, able, humane, generous rebel." And in any event, the General brought to North's mind a verse from Cato: "Curse his virtues, they've undone his country."

With that, Fox rose for a second time and argued that the term "rebel" is no certain mark of disgrace. All the great asserters of liberty, the saviors of their countries, the benefactors of mankind, in all ages, have been called rebels, said he. And then, to bring the lesson home, Fox reminded his fellow members of Commons that the constitution that enabled them to be sitting right there in that House that night was likewise owed to a rebellion—the Glorious Revolution of 1688–89 that brought about the Bill of Rights and ended the divine right of Kings.

There ended the digression, as George Foster Tuffnal sought to get back to the business as hand—the matter of unexplained army expenditures. What, he wanted to know, was the reason for an extravagant outlay of several thousand pounds for pickles and vinegar for 6,000 men at Boston for three months. If they had lived on pickles and vinegar and nothing else the whole time, it could not have come to half the money.[21]

Foreign News

Disfavor in Vienna

Great Britain's recent treaties with Brunswick and Hesse-Cassel for the supply of troops for duty in America have been generally acclaimed in London, but they are looked upon with disfavor in Vienna. There, the Imperial Ministry is reported to be unhappy with the development. It is all too easy to recall that, some years ago, the Diet of the [Holy Roman] Empire, assembled in Ratisbon, adopted a formal resolution opposing any such use of the inhabitants of Germany. The Imperial Ministry appears to feel that such a policy should continue.[22]

Defining Debt

Britan's national debt, a phenomenon of modern times, is now about 140 million l, and the subject of increasing public concern.

To show just how much that amount is, a London paper recently published this short catechism, using for calculating purposes a debt of 130 million l:

Q. If a man could count at the rate of 100 shillings per minute, for twelve hours a day, how long would it take him to count out the national debt?

A. 98 years, 316 days, 14 hours and 40 minutes.

Q. How much would the national debt weigh (assuming 62 shillings to a troy pound)?

A. 41,935,484 troy pounds.

Q. How many carts (at a ton each) would it take to carry this amount?

A. 20,968 carts.

Q. If all those shillings making up the national debt were laid in a straight line (assuming a shilling is one inch in width), how far would the line extend?

A. Once around the world, and then around again for 16,035 miles.

Q. Suppose the interest on the national debt is three and a half percent per annum. How much is the interest?

A. 4,550,000 l.

Q. How doth the government raise this interest?

A. By taxing those who lent the principal in the first place.[23]

Mission Completed

Last year the King of Spain sent three ships halfway around the world to the western coast of North America. Their mission: spread the Gospel and explore those reaches of the Spanish Empire as far north as feasible.

The three ships—the *Santiago* under Don Bruno d'Aceta, the *Señora* under Don Juan Francisco de la Bordega, and the *San Carlo* under Don Juan d'Ayala—are back, and in Madrid the Spanish Court issued a brief report on the geographic side of their mission.

Concentrating their visit between 37 and 58 degrees north latitude, they inspected the harbor of San Francisco, explored various gulfs and bays along the coast northward, and visited a bit with the people, finding the natives of a mild and sociable disposition.

Such a report coincides with that provided by Don Juan Perez who, also sailing in the *Santiago*, visited the same area as far north as 55 degrees in 1774 and found "a civilized people, well-looking, and accustomed to wear clothes."[24]

Religion

Boston's Churches

Old South Church in Boston for more than a century has been consecrated to Christian service, and many a noted cleric has mounted its pulpit to preach the ways of righteousness and truth. More recently dragoons of General John Burgoyne's regiment used it—or what was left of it—as a riding school.

During the recent siege, the interior was completely destroyed by the British. The pulpit and pews were removed and the floor covered with earth to permit training and exercising of horses. One pew, carved of wood and adorned with silk, was ordered removed by an officer, used as a fence for a hogsty.

The North Church, meanwhile, suffered perhaps a kinder fate. Spared such profanement, it was merely demolished and used as fuel.[25]

This "North Church," made of wood, should not be confused with the "Old North Church" of Paul Revere fame, which was made of brick and is still standing.

Press

"Without Foundation"

A letter published in recent days by a number of London newspapers—including the *Public Advertiser, London Packet, Lloyd's Evening Post* and *London Journal*—hardly sounded like the Earl of Chatham (William Pitt) who, as the King's first minister a decade ago, was a champion of reconciliation with the colonies. Chatham, ill and unable to attend Parliament, was said to have taken this new position on the present state of affairs:

"Whilst America retained her allegiance, I was the friend of America; whilst there was room for honorable accommodation, I was happy to propose the terms. That era is past; it is now too late to negotiate. You cannot treat with rebels whilst arms are in their hands. . . . The deluded colonists running wildly after the shadow of liberty have lost the substance [of it]."

Whomever may have thought that strange coming from Chatham was right, says another London newspaper. Countered the *St. James's Chronicle*: "We have authority to assure the public that the exract [cited] . . . is totally without foundation, and in every respect a gross and scandalous imposition on the world."[26]

Books

Distinguished Critic

To Edward Gibbon, whose *History of the Decline and Fall of the Roman Empire* was published a month ago, this week went a glowing review of the work from a man whose judgment Gibbon could not fail to appreciate.

Said the distinguished critic, in a letter from Edinburgh: "Whether I consider the dignity of your style, the depth of your matter, or the extensiveness of your learning, I must regard the work as equally the object of esteem; and I own that if I had not previously had the happiness of your personal acquaintance, such a performance from an Englishman in our age would have given me some surprise. . . . I must inform you that we are all very anxious to hear that you have fully collected the materials for your second volume, and that you are even considerably advanced in the composition of it"

Then, less happily, added Philospher and Historian David Hume, increasingly enfeebled by illness: "I speak this more in the name of my friends than in my own, as I cannot expect to live so long as to see the publication of it."[27]

THE WEEK OF MARCH 25TH

The War

Threat to South?

Military reports reaching Philadelphia are convincing Congress, more and more, that a major British strike in the south can be expected sometime this spring. This week, concluding that the present strength of Continental troops in Virginia and South Carolina is insufficient, Congress directed the raising of three additional battalions in Virginia and two in South Carolina. Congress will bear the cost.[28]

The Cow and the Hare

To a London observer quoted in Philadelphia's *Pennsylvania Gazette*, it is astonishing that Great Britain is sending cavalry to America. Said he: "Only let us for a moment conceive a dragoon, with his bags, his bucket, his boots, his belts, his havre-sack, his cloak, his cantine, his broad sword and his carbine, galloping around a tree to catch a rifleman or an Indian. It is a cow catching a hare. The idea is laughable if the consequences were not serious."[29]

Congress

A Death in Congress

Member of the Continental Congress, and before that in his own colony a member of the General Assembly, Chief Judge of the Supreme Court and finally Governor, Samuel Ward was one of Rhode Island's most prominent citizens until that scourge of rich and poor, famous and unknown—smallpox—ended his life at the age of fifty-two.

Death came in Philadelphia, where Mr. Ward had been in residence during the present session of Congress. On Wednesday, he was buried there.

As befitted his position, the funeral was attended by members of Congress, wearing crepe armbands, and by members of the General Assembly of Pennsylvania and the mayor and other high ranking officials of the City of Philadelphia. The cortege set out at four in the afternoon for the Presbyterian Church on Arch Street, where the Rev. Samuel Stillman preached a sermon entitled, "Death, the last enemy, destroyed by Christ." Interment followed at the grounds of the Baptist Church.[30]

The Colonies

"Indispensably Necessary"

South Carolina this week became the second colony to adopt its own constitution and thus establish a government independent from that given to it as a colony by the Crown. Like New Hampshire, which adopted its own constitution in January, South Carolina declared its action "indispensably necessary" but intended only to last "until an accommodation of the unhappy differences between Great Britain and America can be obtained."

The new constitution was adopted March 26th as the culminating act of a Provincial Congress elected last year and convened in Charleston November 1st. Through adoption of the charter, the Congress has reestablished itself as a General Assembly which will remain in office until an election for new two-year terms is held in October.

Under the new form of government, the General Assembly has the power to elect a thirteen-member Legislative Council, and these two legislative bodies combined the duty to elect the President and vice President of the Colony. All money bills must originate in the Assembly.

The preamble cites in general the treatment of the colonies by Parliament, including taxation without colonial representatives in the British lawmaking body, as reasons for a new government. It adds another, specific to South Carolina: the late governor, Lord William Campbell, dissolved the old General Assembly last September 15th without providing for the calling of another within six months, as required by existing law; and furthermore, that he "used his utmost efforts to destroy the lives, liberties, and properties of the good people here, whom, by the duty of his station, he was bound to protect, [and] withdrew himself from the Colony."

Following adoption of the constitution, the new General Assembly convened at five o'clock and elected the Legislative Council. The two bodies then chose John Rutledge, formerly a member of the Continental Congress, as president and commander-in-chief, and Henry Laurens as vice president.[31]

Foreign News

Generals All

Henceforth, announced his Majesty in London, Major General William Howe, the commander-in-chief for North America, and Major General Guy Carleton, commander of British troops in Canada, will hold the rank of full general while in America. Similarly, Major Generals Henry Clinton, John Burgoyne, Earl Percy and Charles Earl of Cornwallis will have the rank of lieutenant general, thus following the custom of according to senior British officers the privileges and pay of the next higher rank while serving in a theater of war. At home, their permanent rank will obtain.[32]

Try Again

A royal proclamation has raised the bounty for men enlisting in the British Navy. It will now be 3l for those with some skill, 2l for ordinary seamen. Men must be able-bodied, at least eighteen years, but under fifty.

The last increase in enlistment bounties came only in January. The new proclamation shows the trouble his Majesty is having finding a sufficient number of seamen for the war with the colonies.[33]

Law

Retribution—Two Views

Suppose the American colonies lose this war? Suppose the British troops are victorious, and the King and Parliament regain the political domination of America? What, in defeat, would be the consequence for Washington, as leader of the military, and Hancock, as leader of the civil government? For Franklin, or the Adamses, or other prominent American leaders?

They themselves are doubtless too engrossed in their cause to give it thought, and too far along to care about their own safety. But two British viewpoints have appeared in recent weeks—one by a militant royal governor, the other by a former jurist who is now a member of the House of Lords. Their views are as different as the two men.

A recent issue of his own *Virginia Gazette,* published for his troops aboard ship by Virginia's governor-in-exile, Lord Dunmore, touched on the matter of retribution in an article exhorting British troops to redouble efforts against the colonies: "Let them [the American people] feel what it is to provoke and insult a great and powerful people, who have so lately astonished the world with their achievements. When they return to their duty and sue for pardon, let the conditions be: Lay down your arms; deliver up your leaders to just punishment; retire quietly to your homes, and submit to the [loyalist] legislature of your present state." In view of the fate of Colonel Ethan Allen, a British prisoner since last year, "delivering up leaders" could only be construed to mean having Washington and Hancock and the other leaders bound in irons, transported to England for trial, and then imprisoned or hanged.

But such a hard view is not universally shared. In a recent debate in the House of Lords, a former jurist who has long championed the rights of the colonies, including the right to be taxed only with representation in Parliament, took a wholly different position. Said Lord Camden:

"Great stress is laid upon the Americans seizing the castles, forts, munitions, &c., of his Majesty; and it is said this is rebellion. If this is true at all, the case can only apply to Canada. If, however, we are to examine the law, which in affairs of this nature can be our only guide, I question the truth of this assertion. Previous to Edward VI [1547–53] it was not punishable as treason; during the reign of that prince a law was enacted, which made retaining the King's castles, fortresses, &c., against his consent, high treason. In the succeeding reign [Queen Mary, 1553–1558] that, with all other laws passed since the 25th of Edward III [1352] were repealed; and I know of none since enacted for the purpose; and, for my part, I cannot see, if the offence was merely confined to that, how a person could be legally punished."

Such a liberal opinion is not the first for Lord Camden. His judicial career is perhaps best remembered for his decision, thirteen years ago as chief justice of the Court of Common Pleas, granting a writ of *habeas corpus* to the fiery John Wilkes, member of Parliament, who was arrested for libel of the King and his ministers. Camden, in that case, determined that the warrant was vague. Six days later, Camden again acted in Wilkes's favor, ordering him freed from the Tower of London on the grounds privilege of Parliament.[34]

On December 26, 1776, London's St. James's Chronicle *reported: "Administration are determined that the rebel leaders in America shall be put to death there in a manner that shall strike terror into the whole continent."*

Science

No New Continent

British Captain James Cook's voyage around the world in the good ship *Resolution* between 1772 and 1775 added measurably to man's knowledge of the southern hemisphere by a close inspection of it. But what it may have contributed most of all was the recognition of what was not there for the inspecting.

Geographers have long speculated on the existence of a new continent between the equator and 50 degrees south latitude. Crossing and recrossing that vast region, Captain Cook appears to have established, beyond any reasonable doubt, that there is none; our present list of continents will have no additions.

The *Journal of the Resolution's Voyage,* published in Dublin, treats of the scientific nature of the journey in a plentiful way; but it is also a delightful account of the countries visited (each seemingly more exotic than the last) and the people (often a lot like those back home). In fact, Captain Cook seems to take more pleasure in recording impressions of people and places than in reporting scientific data.

There was, for example, the time Cook and his officers talked several native chieftains into a drinking contest—a matter that involved no little persuading. "But some of them having at length been over-persuaded," Cook comments dryly, "and having been made very drunk, were the next day so very sick that they never afterwards would touch any of the liquors offered them."[35]

Books

African Poetess

Kidnapped in Africa at the age of eight and shipped off to America for sale as a slave, she had naught but a life of drudgery to expect. But life has proved far kinder to her than could have been foreseen on her arrival in Boston in 1761.

The young Negro slave named Phillis found as her master a kindly and prosperous tailor named John Wheatley. Showing signs of basic intelligence that would have been the pride even of many a white child, she was encouraged by the Wheatleys to learn not only English but history, religion, poetry, Greek mythology. Without any formal education, but with the continual and understanding help of her masters, she proceeded at such a pace that within two years she had not only developed a facile command of the English language but was translating Ovid —to the astonishment and delight of some of the most learned men of Boston.

Then, still barely into her teens, she began writing poetry of her own: "To the University of Cambridge in New England"; "To the King's most Excellent Majesty" (1768); "On the Death of Rev. Dr. Sewell" (1769). *An Elegiac Poem on the Death of the Celebrated Divine . . . George Whitefield* was published in 1770. Three years later there followed the first bound volume of her works, *Poems on Various Subjects, Religious and Moral.* In the same year, she was taken to England by Wheatley's son, Nathaniel, and became immediately popular for her personal charm as well as her writing.

Phillis Wheatley, now twenty-three, subsequently returned to the colonies and, working in Providence, devoted herself to a poem in honor of General Washington. She sent the poem to the commander-in-chief, and in a letter that accompanied it, explained her adulation: "Your being appointed by the Grand Continental Congress to be Generalissimo of the armies of North America, together with your fame and virtues, excite sensations not easy to suppress."

Replied the commander-in-chief: "The style and manner exhibit a striking proof of your poetical talents. In honor of which, and as a tribute justly due to you, I would have published the poem had I not been apprehensive that, while I only meant to give the world this new instance of your genius, I might have incurred the imputation of vanity. This, and nothing else, determined me not to give it place in the public prints."

The poem has found its way into print, none the less, in the *Virginia Gazette.* An excerpt:

> Proceed, great chief, with virtue on thy side.
> Thy every action let the goddess guide.
> A crown, a mansion, a throne that shine,
> With gold unfading, WASHINGTON! be thine.[36]

PART II

APRIL

WITH kindly moisture now the plants abound,
The grass securely springs above the ground;
Mountains and valleys, which of late were seen
Cover'd with snow, look cheerful now, and green.

The Virginia Almanack
April, 1776

THE WEEK OF APRIL 1ST

The War

Army to New York

Convinced the departure of the British Army from Boston is only an interlude until the next encounter, and convinced that encounter will come in New York no matter what the intervening itinerary of his Majesty's forces, General Washington ordered most of the Continental Army there. Five regiments and some artillery, under General Heath, left shortly after the British evacuation. The remainder—except for five regiments still defending Boston—left a week later. On the 4th Washington himself also departed for New York.[1]

Mercenaries or Emigrants?

What will happen to all the German soldiers, now on their way to America, when hostilities end? Will all then return to their homeland?

A report from London suggests not: that although there is a clause in the Hessian treaty providing that no soldier shall be suffered to settle in America without the consent of his commanding officer, "it is generally believed that very few will ever return; it is most probable that those who don't get their brains knocked out will insist upon staying among their own who have emigrated there."[2]

What the Siege Was Like

For British troops in Boston, the long months of siege made life more and more unendurable; evacuation became the only answer.

In a letter to his wife in Kent, a British captain told of the horror of it: "During the bombardment of the town many were killed, even in their beds, whither they went not more for rest from fatigue than to allay the gnawing appetite of hunger. Many of the sick and wounded found a remedy in death."

Toward the end, said the captain, food was nearly unattainable. What there was, cost dearly, and had little quality. Butter was selling for 3s 6d a pound, and wasn't "fit to grease wheels."[3]

Congress

Open to the World

Last December's act of Parliament cutting off all British trade with the colonies, authorizing seizure of American ships, and ending the protection of the Crown, is now common knowledge throughout the colonies. And it is bitter knowledge.

The news, which arrived in the last few weeks, has provoked many an irate comment from many an American. This week, Congress took official notice by opening American ports to the non-British world. Overturned is the resolution of Congress of last November 1st, which temporarily prohibited export of American produce and livestock other than from one colony to another. Preserved is the older prohibition—from the Articles of Association of October, 1774—banning the importation or consumption of goods from Britain, Ireland and dominions.

In opening the ports of the thirteen United Colonies to world commerce—whether other nations respond or not—Congress has done something of no small significance. It has declared, in a very real way, commercial independence—even though many in Congress yet may wince at that description. But that is the significance of what Britain did in December and what Congress has done now: to end, at least until otherwise changed by act of Parliament or resolution of Congress, and with a sense of finality which was not the intention of the Articles of Association of 1774, the era of American economic dependence on the mother country.

In its resolutions on trade this week Congress also reaffirmed its 1774 prohibition on the importation of slaves, a step that followed similar action in Virginia in 1768 and by other colonies since. Many believe there are already enough slaves, and that continued importation of Negroes from Africa is inherently wrong to begin with. Others are fearful that the slaves may be encouraged by the British to rebel against their masters—something which Virginia's royal governor has already attempted, without much apparent success. Whatever their reasons, the delegates were specific enough: "Resolved, That no slaves be imported into any of the thirteen United Colonies."[4]

The Colonies

Dr. Washington

"... *propter eximias virtutes, tam civiles quam militares* ... *summo honore dignum, GEORGIUM WASHINGTON, Doctorem* ..."

"... because of his outstanding virtues, civil as well as military ... worthy of the highest honor, GEORGE WASHINGTON, Doctor ..."

When the Continental Army came into being last June, it was still essentially a New England army. Would it not have been appropriate, then, to name a New Englander as commander-in-chief?

Many thought so, and yet it was one of New England's most prominent citizens, John Adams, who proposed that the high honor go to a man from Virginia—a man whose skill as a military leader would be sorely needed, and whose southern roots would help make the army a truly Continental one.

Whoever may have questioned the choice of General George Washington then, likely does no longer; his Excellency has been adopted by New England as if born in Wakefield, Massachusetts, instead of Wakefield in Virginia. So great has been his esteem since the British evacuation of Boston that the Massachusetts General Court—the Council on March 28th and the House of Representatives next day—paid him a heart-felt tribute by official resolution. Said they, in part: "(You) have exceeded our most sanguine expectations, and demand the warmest returns of gratitude. . . . May you still go on approved by heaven, revered by all good men, and dreaded by those tyrants who claim their fellow men as their property."

That followed by a few days the homage of the Continental Congress. For "his wise and spirited conduct in the siege and acquisition of Boston," Congress directed that a gold medal be struck in his honor.

Now still another tribute has come the way of General Washington: an honorary Doctor of Laws degree from Harvard College. The degree (quoted in part above) was approved and signed by the President and

Fellows of Harvard on April 3rd for presentation on the 4th. But the General had already left to rejoin the Continental Army in New York; it was awarded *in absentia*.[5]

They Drink to It

In Cambridge, in the best social circles, the toast that is now the favorite goes: "May the Independent principles of Common Sense be confirmed throughout the United Colonies."[6]

Parliament

Cost of War

In the opinion of Lord North, there is no way to tell the cost of the war in America during 1776 until the expense is fully incurred—and even then, in some instances, it may be long afterward until all the costs are entered in the ledgers of the Exchequer.

In the opinion of members of the Opposition, such an argument is evasive; in fact, they say, the cost is going to be so great the Administration has good reason for wanting to hide behind a veil of budgetary vagueness.

Thus did Opposition Member David Hartley try a ploy to force the issue: he moved a series of resolutions certifying or estimating military costs for the year; specifically: Supplies already voted upon in this session, 6,157,000 *l*; additional for the Navy for the year 1776, 2,500,000 *l*; extraordinaries for the land forces for one year from March 9th, 1776, 2,500,000 *l*; additional for the Office of Ordnance for the year, 300,000 *l*; Exchequer Bills outstanding, 1,250,000 *l*; Navy Debt outstanding last December 31st, 2,698,000 *l*; and payment of Navy, Victualling and Transport Bills outstanding last February 29th, 2,308,000 *l* (or at least the portion of this in public credit that is carrying four percent interest).

Only guesswork, argued North. There is no way to divine the expense of the campaign. The resolutions should be defeated because there is no way to comply with them. And indeed the resolutions were summarily defeated, without even the contrary vote of Hartley.

But the Member of Parliament for Hull never expected passage of the resolutions, and so he was not dissatisfied. In fact, he told the House, he was in part pleased with the whole matter . . . "for the noble Lord [North] has confessed the expense to be true by not contradicting it. The nation may therefore take it for granted that the expense of the American War for the year 1776 will be ten millions, which was more than was expended on an average the first four years of the late war when we had almost every great power in Europe leagued, and either directly or indirectly acting against us."[7]

Great Britain

Relief Fund

A committee of public-spirited citizens that organized March 18th at a London tavern has already raised 17,554*l* in a public subscription for relief of British soldiers serving in the colonies. The fund will provide for the soldiers such necessities as worsted caps, flannel waistcoats, mittens, stockings and shoes, as well as assistance to the widows and children of troops killed during the war. Many individual donations to the fund are no more than five shillings, others as high as ten pounds.[8]

Education

Hearing with the Eye

The deaf, hearing not, also do not speak, for they do not know what speech is. Nor, ordinarily, do they ever learn. Unless some special means is used to teach them, they are relegated to a life that is little more than human form detached from the world around them.

A few, for whom this might otherwise be their lot in life, have found such a handicap can be conquered: that they can learn to speak, and thence to read, and to write and to carry out their lives in a useful and productive way. Though it may not be the only one, perhaps the most remarkably successful school for the deaf is the Edinburgh academy of Thomas Braidwood. Here the deaf find they can "hear with the eye," as Dr. Samuel Johnson remarked after a visit three years ago.

Once a teacher of mathematics to ordinary students, Braidwood some years ago accepted the challenge of trying to teach writing to a boy who had been deaf from birth. The outcome was so satisfactory that Braidwood has now devoted his academy to such students, having about a dozen or so enrolled at all times. His only instrument—outside of patience and understanding—is a small silver-plated pipe, flat at the one end, with which to hold a student's tongue in the proper position for forming different sounds. A sure test of his success was provided when Dr. Johnson, during his visit, wrote out on a scrap of paper one of his famed *"sesquipedalia verba"*—foot-and-a-half-long words—and took great delight to hear the student pronounce it to his satisfaction. Still another recent visitor told of meeting "an angelic young creature, of the age of thirteen [who] honoured me with her new-acquired conversation [and] soon satisfied me that she was an apt scholar."

That same visitor came away awed with the accomplishments of the academy, as he so described: "I left Mr. Braidwood and his pupils with the satisfaction which must result from a reflection on the utility of his art and the merit of his labours: Who, after receiving under his care a being that seemed to be merely endowed with a human form, could produce the *divina particula aurae* latent—and but for his skill condemned to be ever latent in it—and who could restore a child to its glad parents with a capacity of exerting its rational powers by expressive sounds of duty, love and affection."[9]

THE WEEK OF APRIL 8TH

The War

British Strategy

Bit by bit, Britain's military strategy against the colonies has become clear. No longer any secrets are the following elements of that strategy, reported by a correspondent in London:

Commodore Sir Peter Parker sailed in February from Cork, Ireland, with Lord Cornwallis and about 3,000 men. Destination: Cape Fear, North Carolina, where General Clinton recently arrived from Boston. When Clinton and Cornwallis join, their objective is expected to be an invasion of South Carolina—or, as an alternative, Virginia by way of the James River. Commodore Parker's fleet would provide the naval cover for such an invasion.

General Burgoyne, meanwhile, recently sailed for Quebec from Portsmouth, England, with an army of about 4,000 men—including 3,000 Brunswickers as well as the 29th Regiment and a contingent of Marines. It is expected about 4,000 more troops will follow. If all goes well, Burgoyne during the summer will invade the colonies by way of Lake Champlain and Lake George, using 1,300 flat-bottomed boats.

By far the largest concentration of British troops in America, however, will be brought together on Staten Island. Totaling more than 20,000 men, this grand army under the command of General Howe will include his Boston occupation forces augmented by Hessian soldiers and a few regiments from England and Ireland. Howe's mission will be to subdue New York, and then march through New Jersey and take Philadelphia.

Throughout the course of land operations, seventy to eighty ships of war will be cruising the coast. Many, however, are woefully undermanned; some men-of-war have no more than a quarter of the proper crew; transports have hardly enough men to navigate them at all and will be prey for American privateers.

All in all, this is how the correspondent in London appraises these developments: "The designs of the British Cabinet are to make the greatest effort possible this year to reduce America to an unconditional submission, being thoroughly sensible that it is not in the power of this country to carry on the war another year, if the present armament should prove unsuccessful. Therefore all wise men think that the Americans will keep on the defensive, entrench themselves at every pass and never come to a general decisive engagement but when sure of victory."[10]

Congress

Message for Coquataginta

Still intent on assuring good relations with the Indians to the west, Congress this week summoned to Philadelphia—with all expenses paid—that good friend of the colonies and chief sachem of the Delawares, Captain White Eyes, better known among his own people as Coquataginta.

To White Eyes, Congress gave a message for the Delawares: "Brothers: We desire you will make it known among all the Indian nations westward, that we are determined to cultivate peace and friendship with them, and that we will endeavour, by making the best possible regulations in our power, to prevent any of our people wronging them in any manner, or taking their lands; and that we will strive to put the trade between us on such a footing as will secure the peace, and promote the interest of all parties; and we expect that all the wise men, of every Indian nation, will use their influence for the same purpose."

That declared, Congress sought to demonstrate its good intentions by directing the commissioners for Indian Affairs in the Middle Department to employ a minister of the Gospel to reside among the Delawares and instruct them in the Christian religion; a schoolmaster to teach their youth reading, writing and arithmetick; and a blacksmith to work among them. To White Eyes, who has befriended the patriot cause in many ways—not the least, keeping in check that other Delaware chief, Captain Pipe, who likes the British—Congress showed its esteem in its concluding comments: "As you are now about to depart, we present you with some money to buy clothes and necessaries, and pay your expenses, and we wish you a good journey, and bid you farewell." With those good wishes went the gift of two horses, complete with saddles and bridles, and the sum of 300 dollars.[11]

The Colonies

First for Independence

Resolved, That the delegates of this Colony in the Continental Congress be empowered to concur with the delegates of the other Colonies in declaring Independency. . . .

So saying, its Provincial Congress this week made North Carolina the first Colony to empower its delegates in Philadelphia to vote in favor of declaring the United Colonies independent states, when and if such a motion comes before the Continental Congress.

Thus will talk of independence undoubtedly redouble among the colonies as word spreads of what could well be a history-making resolution dated April 12th, 1776, in Halifax, North Carolina.[12]

Important Visitor

New Yorkers in recent weeks have greeted virtually the entire Continental Army; Saturday they welcomed still another soldier: his Excellency, General George Washingon, who arrived from Cambridge with Adjutant General Horatio Gates and a number of aides-de-camp. New York will be headquarters of the Continental Army for an indefinite time.[13]

Foreign News

A View from London

To a London observer it appears, "America now has no alternative but to submit to Turkish slavery, or declare itself independent of Great Britain, in which case many of the European powers would be glad to afford her all the assistance in their power."

He added: "It is supposed the Americans must be successful if they have either spirit or sagacity. . . . The Administration is depending on assistance from traitors in North Carolina and Scotchmen in Maryland, Virginia and the Carolinas."

The above comments, written in London on April 9, were first published in Philadelphia on July 3.[14]

Education

"Nor Prudent"

Financial support of colleges is not a proper function of the government. Congress has decided in turning down assistance to Dartmouth College in Hanover, New Hampshire. "Although the prosperity of [the college] is a desirable object," said Congress, "it is neither seasonable nor prudent to contribute towards its relief or support out of the publick treasury."

Opened six years ago, Dartmouth was intended primarily for the teaching of Indians, as well as the white missionaries to go among them, but has found the Indians often indifferent to their studies and whites more inclined toward other kinds of subjects.[15]

Theater

Wrong Cue

In productions of the *Irish Widow* at London's Drury Lane Theater, Madame Greville is used to looking into the barrel of a pistol, safe in the knowledge it is only a theatrical device.

Not so one night this week at dusk, when she was confronted by two highwaymen, whose pistols looked very real indeed. She begged they be put away, having never seen a weapon but on the stage.

One of the would-be robbers, recognizing her and perhaps having admired her on stage, was now chagrined at their choice of victim, declared he would rather give her ten guineas than take one. They settled instead on half a crown for her driver, then vanished.[16]

Press

"More Fatal Despotism"

As far as *New York Packet* Publisher Samuel Loudon was concerned, it was only a matter of allowing ample discussion of a question of the greatest importance . . . and ironically, a point of view with which he did not personally agree. For such liberality of purpose, Publisher Loudon found himself censored by a mob acting in the name of freedom.

It all began some weeks ago when Loudon was approached by an unidentified man who submitted to him a manuscript rebutting the pamphlet *Common Sense*. It was supposedly by a gentleman some distance away, which explained the reason for a third party. Would Loudon publish it, the man asked?

Loudon explained it would take some deliberation—since he had to be certain the manuscript was written with decency and did not express, or even imply, any disapprobation of the proceedings of the Continental Congress . . . or, as Loudon himself put it, "the glorious cause in defence of which Americans are spending blood and treasure."

Finally convinced the manuscript was a reasonably written argument, he agreed to publish it, and therefore thought nothing of advertising the impending sale of the pamphlet.

Public reaction to it came as a shock. New York's Committee of Mechanics asked him to appear before its members, and he did. There, Chairman Christopher Duyckink interrogated the publisher. "Who was the author?" he asked; "who gave you the manuscript?" To the first, replied Loudon, he did not know. To the second: "I got the manuscript from a man in this city, whose name, in my opinion, you have no right to demand."

Displeased with that answer, the Mechanics' Committee threatened to burn the printed pamphlets. Loudon argued that they should at least read the document first, and offered to make copies available. Furthermore, Loudon suggested the Mechanics' complaint be put before the city's Committee of Safety, by whose decision he would abide. Instead, the Committee of Mechanics sent six men to Loudon's office. They collected all the copies of the rebuttal to *Common Sense* and locked them away, keeping the key.

The following evening Loudon was summoned to appear before the Committee of Safety. Without even getting into the merits of the case, the Committee simply advised Publisher Loudon not to proceed further with publication, lest his personal safety be endangered. Loudon agreed to comply with the recommendation.

He returned home. Shortly after ten o'clock, Mechanics' Chairman Duyckink and a number of his cohorts arrived at Loudon's home to inform him they were about to burn all the copies of the controversial document. And they did—all 1,500 copies of what they had apparently not yet even read.

But the last word was Publisher Loudon's, and it appeared on the first page of the *New York Packet* this week:

"As the question concerning American Independence hath not, to the best of my knowledge, been decided by the Continental Congress, nor by any legal subordinate convention, there can be no criminality in publishing the arguments for and against it; and as it is a question of the greatest importance, it should not be decided before these arguments are fully discussed. . . .

"It is at any rate self-evident that if any set of unauthorized men shall be permitted to assume the power of legislating for their fellow citizens and punishing them as they please, our legal Conventions and Committees, with all the precious liberties for which we are contending, will be in effect annihilated, and we will be in a more miserable slavery than would arise from the most successful execution of all the tyrannic acts of Parliament.

"The freedom of the press is now insulted and infringed by some zealous advocates of liberty. A few more nocturnal assaults upon printers may totally destroy it, and America in consequence may fall a sacrifice to a more fatal despotism than that with which we are threatened."[17]

The controversial document may have been a copy of the pamphlet Plain Truth, *already published in Philadelphia. [See Week of March 11th.]*

Books

"One Hundred and Twenty Thousand"

Common Sense—in various editions and reprints from the presses of a number of printers throughout the United Colonies—has now been on the market for three months. If an estimate published this week is correct, it may well be the fastest selling book in history.

That estimate: one hundred and twenty thousand copies. It appears in the *Pennsylvania Journal* of April 10th in a letter by the anonymous (and hardly disguised patriot) "Forrester" to the anonymous (and equally undisguised Tory) "Cato."

The pseudonymous Cato has been complaining about *Common Sense* —about its message in general, about its author and publishers in more specific terms, as when he challenged: "[They] have but little cause to triumph in its success. Of this, they seem sensible: and, like true quacks are constantly pestering us with additional doses til the stomachs of their patients begin wholly to revolt."

To that, "Forrester" this week retorted: "It is Cato's hard fate to be always detected: for perhaps there never was a pamphlet, since the use of letters were known, about which so little pains were taken [to publicize], and of which so great a number went off in so short a time; I am certain that I am within compass when I say one hundred and twenty thousand."

"Cato" was the Rev. William Smith, Scottish-born Tory and then provost of the College of Philadelphia; the "Forrester" was Thomas Paine himself—British-born writer and editor, sometime corset maker, many-time failure, one-time Collector of his Majesty's Excises in England, other-time teacher, grocer, tobacconist. His authorship of Common Sense *Paine did not publicly admit until February, 1779; but public speculation had long since left little doubt about it. Meanwhile, sales set a record. Paine's own estimate of 120,000 copies the first three months (which represents the equivalent of a book today selling an astounding 10 million copies in its first three months) is entirely credible; indeed some estimates have placed the sale at 500,000 in the first few months, though that is probably high. Such record sales did not make a rich author, however. Paine let it be known that publishers were welcome to print and reprint it as often as they wished, without the formality of a contract. And that they did.18*

THE WEEK OF APRIL 15TH

Congress

Governor's Arrest Asked

Congress reacted decisively this week to reports that Governor Robert Eden of Maryland has been carrying on highly dangerous correspondence with the British Ministry. It asked that Eden be arrested and his papers brought to Philadelphia for examination.

Congress issued its "earnest request" to the Maryland Council of Safety to make the arrest after receiving reports that letters from British Secretary of State Lord George Germaine to Governor Eden had been intercepted by American agents. The contents of the letters have not yet been made public.[19]

The Colonies

The Brethren Slain

It was one year to the day from that fateful first moment of open warfare between armed American militia and the British regulars—a year in which bitterness, hostility and bloodshed have only increased.

Now were the loved ones, and the friends, and those who knew them not at all except by reputation, gathered at Lexington, Massachusetts, to commemorate the sacrifice of those eleven patriots who fell dead at that place. Now were the people of Lexington and its neighboring villages come to that fateful green to listen as the Rev. Jonas Clark, pastor of the Church at Lexington, spoke of one day's significance:

"From this remarkable day will an important era begin for both America and Britain. And from the 19th of April, 1775, we may venture to predict, will be dated in future history the liberty or slavery of the American world, according as a sovereign God shall see fit to smile or frown upon the interesting cause in which we are engaged.

"Yonder field can witness the innocent blood of the brethren slain. And from thence does their blood cry unto God for vengeance from the ground."

Pastor Clark used an Old Testament text, Joel 3:19–21, invoking a God of swift and sure justice: "Egypt shall be a desolation, and Edom shall be a desolate wilderness, for the violence against the children of Judah, because they have shed innocent blood in their land."

And then he paraphrased: "Great Britain shall be a desolation and England a desolate wilderness for the violence against the children of America." And he prayed: "May that God, who is a God of righteousness and salvation, still appear for us, go forth with our armies, tread down our enemies, and cleanse and revenge our innocent blood."

Were any in the assemblage lacking comprehension of his remarks, they could have no doubt by referring to the title of his 8,000-word sermon: "The fate of blood-thirsty oppressors, and God's care of his distressed people."[20]

Reasons for Independence

Why should America declare independence, as more and more people are saying? According to the *Pennsylvania Evening Post*, there are a lot of good reasons, and it listed seven of them this week as advantages which might well accrue from "a Declaration of the Independence of the American Colonies." Among them:

"France will immediately attack Britain in the most defenceless parts of her empire, and thus draw off her fleets and armies from our coasts."

"All the powers of Europe will conceive such ideas of our union, love of freedom, and military resources that they will not be tempted to accept of a share in us upon the condition of conquering us."

"The criminal correspondence with the enemies of this country will be prevented, or punished [as] high treason."[21]

Rooh of All Evil

Residents of Connecticut and surrounding colonies are being advised to watch out for counterfeit Connecticut forty-shilling bills being circulated in considerable quantity.

The bills, patterned on those of the emission of May 10, 1775, are considered good imitations on the whole. But there are a few tell-tale signs. For one thing, the ornamental border around the face of the counterfeit is much more distinctly engraved than on the genuine bill. For another, the name of a signer, Jesse Root, is misspelled *Jesse Rooh*.[22]

Tuesday of this week was an election day in New York, eligible voters choosing twenty-one of their number to represent the city and county of New York in the Provincial Congress. Among them was one with a name to become well known in American politics: Roosevelt. This one was Isaac.

Foreign News

Facetious Feast

April 19th, writes a correspondent from London, was being observed there as "St. Yankey's Day" in honor of what he calls the "tutelary saint of North America." It was properly and "honorably observed by all true and loyal friends of government." In America—with awe and solemnity —it was the first anniversary of the battles of Lexington and Concord.[23]

City in Ashes

Fire, that perennial peril, has once again wreaked wholesale destruction, leveling an entire community to ashes. This time it was the Croatian capital of Warasdin.

The first flames appeared in the suburbs, spread quickly from house to house; then, borne by a strong wind, they carried their peril to the city itself. In five hours Warasdin—a city large and opulent for that part of the world—was seven-eighths destroyed. The cause is believed to have been a man's shaking the tobacco out of his pipe without first extinguishing the ashes.[24]

Medicine

Inoculation: Official Approval

Smallpox kills at least one in every fourteen people throughout the world. Since its first appearance early in civilization it has marked its course through history with terror, death and devastation. Whole villages and towns have been laid waste.

It strikes with equal severity rich and poor, old and young, the famous and the unknown. Just last month a member of Congress, Samuel Ward of Rhode Island, succumbed to smallpox in Philadelphia. And to this day—more than forty years after it happened—another member of Congress, Benjamin Franklin, often recalls with a sigh the memory of his dear son, Franky, who died of smallpox at four years of age.

What can be done to control this killer has long been a concern of physicians, and over the years, some strides have been made. Perhaps the chief advance in treatment came a century ago when that "British Hippocrates," Thomas Sydenham, introduced the procedure—now so widely accepted today—of cooling the patient during the peak of the infection.

If method of treatment has been improved, what about prevention? Here there remains controversy. Physicians have known about and used inoculation since ancient times, but they are divided about the wisdom of its use. In effect, inoculation induces a case of smallpox in the subject— but a case far milder and far less dangerous than that which is otherwise contracted. The first major use of smallpox inoculation in the colonies was during the Boston epidemic of 1721. It has been used to varying degrees since then, but to the present has remained a scourge or a blessing, depending on which physician is asked.

Now from one of the most eminent physicians in America has come outspoken endorsement of inoculation. The physician: none other than Dr. John Morgan, director-general of hospitals and physician-in-chief of the Continental Army. Morgan is calling for widespread use of inoculation in the colonies as a precautionary measure, even though there is no epidemic at the present time.

His argument: "Smallpox by inoculation is always much lighter than the natural; it is a far less dangerous disorder, and is generally benign whenever the subject is well chosen. So great [have been] the improvements in practice, preparation of subject, and treatment that it is rare for a patient to be confined one day by it."

Dr. Morgan is optimistic that inoculation will eventually prevail. Though some still try to discredit it, said he, inoculation "should triumph at length over all opposition and over the fears and prejudices of weak minded persons."[25]

Law

Committees of Safety

Since the first one was established in Massachusetts little more than a year ago—and particularly since the Continental Congress last June recommended they be established everywhere—committees of safety have become a way of life in the United Colonies.

They were a natural outgrowth of the committees of correspondence which first sprang up four years ago to relay information from community to community and colony to colony and promote the patriot cause. But the committees of safety go further, often possessing judicial authority bestowed upon them by provincial conventions and congresses to safeguard patriot interests and root out Tories, as well as the power to raise troops and arms.

In recent weeks, committees of safety in Virginia demonstrated the diversity of dealing with Tory resistence. Three examples:

—In Goochland County, the Rev. William Douglas was summoned on complaints he had spoken disrespectfully of the American people. The committee of safety examined him and several witnesses, decided there was no truth to the complaints, and directed that he be acquitted with honor.

—In Acomack County, Curtis Kellum was summoned on charges that he interfered with the recruiting of troops, that he was generally inimical to the American cause, and that he was heard to exclaim, "Damn the Bostonians, what are they but a pack of G-d damn'd rebels?" At the hearing Kellum appeared penitent; on condition of a public apology, the committee recommended he be received back in the favor of his countrymen.

—In Culpeper County, the Rev. James Herdman was ordered to appear on a complaint he was a "person inimical to American liberty." The committee of safety found him guilty, expelled him from the county, and directed that the citizenry should have nothing further to do with him.

As constitutional government developed among the states this year and the next, the committees of safety were largely superseded by new state governments. 26

Theater

Tables Turned

London's *St. James's Chronicle* recently carried this letter from a reader to its theatrical critic: "On the morning after the representation of *The Orphan* at Drury-Lane Theater, I left town and am but just returned. Your papers ever since that date lay in a heap in my dressing room, and looking them over at my breakfast, I have just arrived at that of the 26th of March, where you give a critique upon the performance of the above-mentioned night. Pray, sir, were you present?"[27]

THE WEEK OF APRIL 22ND

Congress

Maintaining the Army

The army in Canada continues to be a major concern to Congress, and the colonies' delegates in Philadelphia acted again this week with the issuance of additional supplies and promises of more to come. They also directed General Washington to offer his opinion as to whether additional troops are necessary in Canada, and if so, whether they can be spared from the army at New York.

As immediate assistance, Congress ordered that 10,000 pair of shoes, 10,000 pair of stockings and 2,000 barrels of pork, at a total cost not to exceed 45,000 dollars, be sent with dispatch to General Schuyler for the army in Canada. Congress also asked that the general be advised that ten additional battalions and 4,000 barrels of pork are on the way. In turn, Schuyler was asked to advise Congress of how much gunpowder he has received since January 1st, and to "give the earliest possible notice" of what further supplies he may need.[28]

The Colonies

Disillusioned Tories

After they elected to remain during the siege, Boston's Tories were continually reassured by General Howe that British reinforcements would make not only Massachusetts but every other colony a loyalist stronghold once again.

As the long winter passed, and food and fuel ran almost out, Howe's oft-repeated promises took on a hollow ring. At last, disillusioned, Boston's Tories were confronted with a dismal choice: evacuate with the British, leaving behind homes and possessions, or stay and face the vengeance of the returning patriots.

Now it is clear that those who cast their lot with the departing British had only more disillusionment in store. This week, at Marblehead, hardly a month since the evacuation, a small boatload of Tory refugees returned. At Halifax, Howe had given the men still another bitter decision: Enlist in the British army as common soldiers and be provided for, or starve. For this small band, thus rewarded for their loyalty to the Crown, the decision was to return to Massachusetts—and plead the mercy of the patriots.[29]

Parliament

The British Budget

To the surprise of likely no one, the budget Lord North presented to Parliament this week for the year 1776 shows a substantial increase over last year. Outlays for the army and navy are generally double, and although there are some reductions in other areas, the overall budget will be nearly double that of 1775.

Despite such a sharp increase—to be financed in part through a higher land tax—the budget will be nowhere near what it was in 1762, at the height of the last war.

Lord North presented to Commons a statement of supplies [appropriations] totaling 9,097,577l 17s 10⅞d and ways and means totaling 9,154,230.4.4¾. How much of an increase that represents may be inferred from the respective totals for last year: 5,556,453.2.10 and 6,559,246.9.0. By comparison, supplies in 1762 (when Britain was embroiled in war on three continents) reached 18,299,153.18.11½, and ways and means 18,655,750.2.8½.

The largest increases are for the army, up by 1,865,280.13.6⅛ to a new outlay of 3,462,282.3.3⅞, and the navy, up 1,552,996.3.8 to a new total of 3,227,055.19.6. Likewise does the expenditure for ordnance show an increase of the same proportion, advancing by 212,020.3.7 to a total of 472,827.10.5. The increase alone for the army is more than the entire amount voted this time last year for army purposes.

Lord North has proposed meeting some of the increase for military purposes through a reduction in outlays for other services, and the total for miscellaneous services in the budget shows a marked decrease of 112,489.14.11 to a 1776 total of only 54,070.4.10. To do this, many programs included in last year's budget have been cut completely. Notable examples are African forts (13,000.0.0 last year), charts of North America (3,711.15.0), charts of Great Britain and Ireland (2,145.0.0), subsidization of the British Museum (3,000.0.0) and the expenses of preventing distempers among horned cattle (1,684.15.0).

Meanwhile a substantial increase in ways and means has been provided by increasing the land tax from 3s to 4s on the pound. The higher rate, voted by Parliament November 13th of last year (amid complaints from the Opposition it will amount to "a perpetual mortgage"), sets no new precedent, however; it was in effect prior to 1772. The change is expected to provide an additional 500,000*l* and bring to a total of 2,000,000*l* that portion of ways and means raised this way—making the land tax the largest single source of revenue. The malt tax, by comparison, is expected to yield 750,000*l*. Further revenue increases are anticipated through the issuance of 1,500,000*l* in exchequer bills instead of the 1,250,000*l* previously planned, and through 2,000,000*l* in new revenue, which Lord North proposes to accomplish through the sale of three percent annuities (1,400,000*l*) and a lottery (600,000*l*).

Although the budget was adopted, Lord North at the time warned that an additional appropriation might be needed. On May 2nd he requested, and got, an additional credit of 1,000,000 l. Over and above the budget, there was also the Civil List, an annual sum provided for the personal use of the Crown and totaling 800,000 l at this time. It should be noted that there was nothing comparable to a budget in the United Colonies in 1776.[30]

And How to Pay for It

The far higher cost of the budget presented to Parliament by Lord North this week will be felt by every subject of Great Britain. In addition to the increase in the land tax, approved by Parliament late last year, these new duties are to be instituted:

—On four-wheel carriages, an additional tax of 20*s* each (expected to yield 17,000*l* annually);

—On stagecoaches, a tax of 5*l* each (2,000*l*);

—On deeds and all other written instruments, a 1*s* stamp in addition to the shilling stamp that has been required since 1736 (30,000*l*);

—On newspapers, an additional halfpence stamp (18,000*l*);

—On each pack of playing cards an additional tax of 6*d* and on dice 2*s* 6*d* (6,000*l*).

These measures, estimated to bring in additional revenue of 72,000*l* per year, will do no more than pay interest on the new public debt which will be incurred to meet the most substantial part of the increase for 1776.

Even though the national debt is already "considerable," Lord North is confident Great Britain can bear the cost of the new budget. The nation's commerce is immense and its resources are great, he told the House of Commons; "the tradesmen, mechanics and labourers in this country live in a manner unknown to any country whatever. . . . the means of procuring the necessaries, nay, even the comforts of life, are easier attainable in this country than in any other under the sun." But in determining the new duties, he said, the emphasis was on comforts and not essentials; except where necessity compels otherwise, taxes should always be laid as much as possible on luxuries and the elegant conveniences of life.

Though some may disagree, he hastened to add that the new tax on newspapers is no contradiction to that dictum; newspapers, in general, are a very fit object of taxation, he declared; many persons think they do more harm than good.[31]

It should be noted that the land tax of 4 s on the pound (20 percent) was on the annual rentable value of a property, and not on its total assessed valuation.

Foreign News

BORN: April 25th, in London, to her Majesty Queen Charlotte and his Majesty King George III, a daughter, their eleventh child. Her Majesty was taken with labor pains at six in the morning, and had notice sent immediately to the Archbishop of Canterbury, the secretaries of state, and several of the nobility, all of whom are customarily in waiting at a royal lying-in. She did not keep them waiting long, giving birth at seven.[32]

France: New Ministry?

"A change in the Ministry of France is constantly talked of," reports a correspondent in Paris, and such a change would mean the end of A. R. J. Turgot, comptroller general of finances since August, 1774, and, as such, France's chief minister.

That Turgot's Ministry, in many ways the most promising in recent years, has been meeting considerable opposition in the government has become clear in recent months; and even a report from Paris late in January—"Secrecy is not less observed in everything that concerns the operations of M. Turgot, the Comptroller General of the Finances," as reported the *London Packet*—revealed more than it hid.

Liberal and reform-minded, strongly influenced by, though not limited to, the Physiocratic ideal of a free agricultural economy, convinced of the need of fundamental tax reform, and fresh from a successful tenure as intendant of Limoges, where his idea of meaningful reform showed the art of the possible, Turgot wasted little time after his appointment in setting forth a new economic policy for France. One of his first major acts was to permit free trade in grain throughout the country (except in Paris, where even he agreed the time was not yet right). How well it should have worked was not to be seen; the harvest of 1774 was the worst in many years, and prices immediately soared despite an increase in grain imports to offset the difference. By spring of last year, the shortages and high prices resulted in riots that reached all the way to the door of Versailles. Though order was swiftly restored, Turgot's economic reforms were off to a bad start.

Early this year—while simultaneously pursuing economy through a reduction in the French budget—he renewed his mission of reform with a series of six edicts. Four of them (reorganizing or suppressing useless offices and minor dues and impositions), caused little enough notice; the others (one suppressing most of the *jurandes,* or commercial guilds of Paris, and one substituting a moderate land tax for the *corvées* that have left road maintenance to peasant labor) have apparently met with rigorous opposition, particularly in the Paris *Parlement.*

The abolition of the *corvées* won Turgot many friends among the common people, who will benefit the most; and it assured him of many new enemies among the privileged classes, whose position is thereby weakened and whose taxes are raised. And in France, today, there is no question who holds the power.

Turgot's waning influence shows also that he has lost favor with two who earlier appeared to support him: his Majesty, King Louis XVI, and the Comte de Maurepas, that aging statesman (he is seventy-five) who knows well what it is to lose favor, having himself been dismissed in 1749 from a prominent position in the government of Louis XV, only to become the principal adviser to the present King on his accession to the throne two years ago.[33]

Won't Run Short

In York, England, this week, Mr. Thomas, of the Yorkshire Militia, standing six feet two inches tall, took as his wife Hannah Tonnich, of Clearham, height of three feet two inches. What the bride lacks in height she is said to make up in fortune, estimated at 5,000*l.*[34]

Law

Toward a Smooth Transition

If the colonies should break away from England, as is being argued more and more often, what will happen to the vast body of English law now in force in the American colonies? The probable answer is for the colonies, in their own constitutions, to declare continuance of the common law of England, and whatever statute law has been practiced here, until changed by statute or unless obviously in conflict with the provisions of that colony's constitution.

That being the case, there will be a need for all possible reference material to insure a smooth transition from English to American law.

One such volume recently left the press of publisher Hugh Gaine in New York. Entitled *A Collection of English Precedents Relating to the Office of Justice of the Peace,* it reprints from English sources the duties of a justice, cites precedents applying to the administration of his office, and prescribes the proper form of warrants and summonses for such offenses as robbery, burglary and other felonies, keeping a bawdy house, bigamy, forced entry, unlawful gaming, rioting, selling goods on the sabbath, and harboring runaway servants.[35]

Books

Thoughts on Government

Whatever form of government the individual American colonies might adopt—or the United Colonies as an independent nation—it is increasingly apparent that that form of government will not be parliamentary. The Parliament may be a venerable institution in England, but will never become so in America.

Such is the contention of a book gaining more and more attention throughout the colonies. Published in both Philadelphia and Boston under the title *Thoughts on Government Applicable to the Present State of the American Colonies,* it is ostensibly an anonymous document; even so, the authorship shows. It is presumably the work of John Adams, who apparently feels his reputation as a radical might reduce its readership.

Some excerpts:

On the nature of the times: "You and I, dear friend, have been sent into life at a time when the greatest lawgivers of antiquity would have wished to have lived. How few of the human race have ever enjoyed [such] an opportunity."

On federal powers: "If the colonies should assume governments separately, they should be left entirely to their own choice of the forms, and if a Continental Constitution should be formed, it should be a Congress, containing a fair and adequate representation of the colonies, and its authority should sacredly be confined to these cases, viz., war, trade, disputes between colony and colony, the post office, and the unappropriated lands of the Crown."

On public education: "Laws for the liberal education of youth, especially of the lower class of people, are so extremely wise and useful that to a humane and generous mind, no expense for this purpose would be thought extravagant."

On annual elections: "These great men [in office] in this respect should be once a year . . .

> *'Like bubbles on the sea of matter borne,*
> *They rise, they break, and to the sea return.'*

"This will teach them the great political virtues of humility, patience and moderation, without which every man in power becomes a ravenous beast of prey."

On form of government: "There is no good government but what is Republican. That the only valuable part of the British constitution is so: because the very definition of a Republic is 'an Empire of Laws, and not of men.' "

Whatever way government does develop in America, one thing is certain: it is not as simple a matter as it appeared to Alexander Pope when he wrote:

> "For forms of government let fools contest;
> Whate'er is best administer'd is best."

Such an oversimplification, says Adams, is fallacious. "Pope flattered tyrants too much when he said [that]. . . . But poets read history to collect flowers, not fruits—they attend to fanciful images, not the effects of social institutions."[36]

THE WEEK OF APRIL 29TH

Congress

"Except for Tea"

Following the course it adopted last month in regard to trade, Congress this week made another major economic move by removing price restrictions on all goods and commodities except green tea. Henceforth, the prices of goods will be allowed to find their own level on the open market—and that level, in view of a general scarcity, is almost certainly to be a higher one.

The prohibition on price increases was one provision of the Articles of Association adopted by the First Continental Congress in October, 1774. The series of fourteen articles prohibited importation and consumption of all goods and commodities from Britain, Ireland and their possessions, as well as exportation of American goods to the same lands. Recognizing that the resulting scarcity of many goods would drive prices upward, Congress sought to establish controls at least temporarily. Thus stipulated Article Nine: "Such as are venders of goods or merchandize will not take advantage of the scarcity of goods that may be occasioned by this association, but will sell the same at rates we have been respectively accustomed to do, for the twelve months last past. And if any vender of goods or merchandize shall sell any goods on higher terms, or shall in any manner, or by any device whatsoever violate or depart from this agreement, no person ought, nor will any of us deal with any such person or his or her factor or agent at any time thereafter for any commodity."

In repealing that provision, Congress reaffirmed its position that price restrictions were to be only temporary, and intended primarily to apply to goods then in stock. Since that time supplies of many commodities have been depleted, and merchants have had little incentive to arrange—at higher cost to themselves—for importation from other nations knowing they cannot pass along the additional cost to the buyer. Congress therefore decided it was only reasonable that merchants should be encouraged by the prospect of a "gain adequate to the danger" which may be incurred in the importation and free trade now being opened from the United Colonies to the non-British world.[37]

The Colonies

DIED: Suddenly, this week, in Fairfield, Connecticut: Mrs. Lydia Henchman Hancock, widow of the late Thomas Hancock of Boston, uncle and foster father of John Hancock, President of the Continental Congress. It was his marriage in 1730 to Lydia Henchman, daughter of Boston's most prominent bookseller, that turned unschooled Thomas Hancock's middling business career sharply upward. Trading in such diverse commodities as foodstuffs, building materials, tea, paper, whale oil, codfish, rum and molasses, he built so thriving a business that at the time of his death in 1764 he was likely the wealthiest man in Boston. Thomas, childless, virtually adopted young John Hancock when the latter's father died, saw to his education at Boston Latin School and Harvard College, later made him a partner in the business.[38]

The Eden Letters

Congress last month sought the arrest of Maryland Governor Robert Eden after reports of the interception of correspondence between Eden and the British Secretary of State for the Colonies. Now two of the letters in question—both from the Secretary, Lord George Germaine, and both dated Whitehall, December 23rd last—have been made public.

One letter, accompanying a copy of the late Restraining Act, discusses a proposal—now common knowledge—for a commission to discuss the restoration of peace with the colonies. The other is a letter complimenting the governor on his conduct after the outbreak of hostilities; thanking him for his "confidential communication of the characters of individuals, especially of such as come over to England"; and supplying information on "an armament consisting of seven regiments with a fleet of frigates and small ships now [December 23rd] in readiness to proceed to the Southern colonies in order to attempt a restoration of legal governments in that part of America." The military and naval force—which the letter said would proceed first to North Carolina, and then either to South Carolina or Virginia—is obviously the one which has been observed along the southern coast in recent weeks.[39]

Foreign News

Still Counting

A public subscription for troops in America, and for widows and children of those soldiers who have been killed, now totals more than 28,000 *l* in Great Britain. A similar subscription for the relief of British clergy in the colonies is reported to have reached more than 4,600 *l*.[40]

Aid Forbidden

No aid will America receive, at least officially, from the Austrian Netherlands. Under an ordinance published this week in Brussels, her Imperial Majesty, Maria Theresa, has decreed that the provinces under Austrian dominion in the Low Countries are forbidden to supply any military assistance to the British colonies in America.

The ordinance establishes fines of up to 1,000 florins for any person found guilty of sending arms or military supplies to America, either directly or indirectly. As a safeguard, effective for one year, any shipment of arms or military supplies from the Austrian Netherlands to any country whatsoever will be permitted by special license only.

The Austrian Netherlands comprised what is basically today Belgium.[41]

Science

North Pole: Still Possible?

"Nec sit terris ultima Thule . . ."
"Among lands Thule will no longer be farthest . . ."

SENECA – *Medea*

In antiquity, Thule was an island supposed to be the northernmost land on earth. This quotation from Seneca was a prophecy that, in a new age, the ocean will loosen its hold (vincula laxet) *and all land will lie open to man.*

Will man ever reach the North Pole? His other explorations of this globe of ours have by now revealed most of those mysteries about which man of old could only wonder. But the barriers that separate the pole from exploration remain as impenetrable as ever.

Many people—and indeed, many seafarers—doubt that reaching the pole is even possible; a few think it will someday be done; most only wonder why man should want to go up there at all. In fact, there is a good reason for trying: to establish a new and shorter trade route to the Orient. The present route around the Cape of Good Hope, since a sea route to India was first charted by Vasco da Gama in 1498, has had its drawbacks: violent storms, more or less throughout the year; a scarcity of good provisions, particularly drinking water; and a high incidence of

THE NORTH POLE (John Gibson, London, 1775). This map of "The Icy Great North Sea" appeared in [David Henry, ed.] An Historical Account of All the Voyages Around the World (London: F. Newberry, 1775) and provides as good a reference as any contemporary map for the accompanying story on exploration of a polar route from Europe to the Orient. The "Course from Japan to Portugal" shown on the map is purely hypothetical. The various "passages" ("1st Passage," "2nd Passage," and so on) are apparently purported voyages into the polar region rather than passages as such. The first commercial passage was not until 1969, the $50 million Manhattan project, using a ship of such technological sophistication as to have been beyond imagination then; and the Manhattan was confined to a course that ventured no further north than what is shown in this map as the southern coast of an erroneously elongated Greenland. That entire region was still a mystery to cartographers who were drawing most of the rest of the world with remarkable accuracy. The "Presqu Isle" (bottom center) on this map is a rough attempt at an outline of Alaska at a time when many maps did not show it at all.

Rare Book Division—New York Public Library
—Astor, Lenox and Tilden Foundations

disease. For British navigators, there is an added incentive to polar exploration. The British Parliament recently renewed an offer of a reward for discovery of a northwest passage to the Pacific.

Exploration to the north began the same time the route to the south became established: John Cabot in 1497, Martin Frobisher in 1576, John Davis between 1585 and 1587, Henry Hudson in 1610, among the many. William Baffin in 1614 penetrated the unknown as far as 81 degrees north latitude, and thought he saw land as far as 82 degrees.

In more recent years there have been any number of captains who have dared the northern ice—sometimes for no other reason than that it was breeding season for whales and there was ample time for such a diversion. One such voyage was that of Captain McCallan and the *Campbelltown* in 1751. Whaling in the Greenland fishery, faced with the hiatus of breeding season, he sailed north as far as 83½ degrees (his reckoning) without running into any appreciable amount of ice. But his mate complained that the compass was no longer steady, so McCallan turned back. If he did reach 83½ degrees, it is one of the northernmost voyages on record. But both McCallan and his mate are now dead, and their journal is lost; there is no way to verify their story.

Exploration of the polar region has been by no means limited to the British. The Dutch, for the most part, have concentrated on a northeast passage around Russia; a Dutch ship in 1670 is reported to have reached about 80 degrees north latitude exploring north of Siberia. The French have also been interested; among others, there was Samuel de Champlain, for whom curiosity about a northwest passage led to the exploration of Canada. And by no means insignificant have been the polar voyages of Russian navigators.

The major problem for northbound mariners, of course, is ice—sometimes in huge floating chunks that look menacing to even the largest ships; at other times in what looks like a solid mass extending all the way to the pole itself. But such an endless mass we now realize may be no more than a number of smaller banks that have jammed together; the mass will often break up in a few days' time, as two recent accounts show. In June, 1754, Captain James Wilson's *Sea Nymph* encountered extensive ice between 74 and 81 degrees; he could only conclude it extended to the pole, and he went no further. Yet Captain Guy and the *Unicorn*, the same month and year, sailed as far as 83 degrees—or nearly as far as northernmost Greenland—without encountering any significant amount of ice at all. Indeed, there may not even be ice at the North Pole. The sagacious Dr. Robert Hooke, whose legacy to mankind at his death seventy-three years ago included the microscope, the quadrant, and the Gregorian telescope, postulated that if ice is formed from fresh water, and fresh water comes from rivers and streams, and there is no land, and hence no rivers and streams at the North Pole, then there is no ice either.

It may well be after many years, if ever at all, that man will know what the pole is like. But as there have been ventures past, so will there be in the future. The noted British lawyer and naturalist, Daines Barrington, has begun a campaign to excite the interest of British seafarers, arguing that new paths to commerce and the possible cultivation of northern islands are all good reasons for sailing north. In a proposal to the Royal Society Barrington has sought to stir national pride as well. "A project," he said, "which has dwelt in the mouths and memories of some, in the judgment and approbation of a few, from the time of Henry VIII should be revived, and at length for the benefits of his subjects, carried in effect under the auspices of George the Third."[42]

The obstacles were even more formidable than 18th century navigators imagined. It was not until 1969 that the first northwest passage was made commercially—the Manhattan *voyage, at a cost of $50 million. In 1958, the U.S. atomic submarine* Nautilus *sailed under the polar icecap. In 1909, Admiral Robert Peary was the first to be recognized to reach the North Pole.*

Music

Incomparable

What can compare with the martial band, the drum and fife, the bugle horn and the shrill trumpet? Nothing, to the ears of a physician with Washington's army, who, one day between medical rounds, wrote in his diary some comments nearly as musical as the subject itself.

Observed Dr. James Thacher, about military bands: "They set the warhorse in motion, thrill through every fibre of the human frame, still the groans of the dying soldier, and stimulate the living to the noblest deeds of glory.

"The full roll of the drum which salutes the commander-in-chief, the animating beat which calls to arms for the battle, the reveille which breaks our slumbers at dawn of the day with 'come, strike your tents and march away,' and the evening tattoo which commands to retirement and repose; these form incomparably the most enchanting music that has ever vibrated on my ear."[43]

MAY

THIS is the merriest month in all the year;
Now all the groves new liveries do wear,
Each tree a fine green perriwig puts on,
And all's enliven'd by the returning SUN!

The Virginia Almanack
May, 1776

THE WEEK OF MAY 6TH

The War

Bound for Boston

A sea captain newly arrived in Newburyport, Massachusetts, reports a chance meeting in the mid-Atlantic with a brig out of Plymouth, England. The captain of the brig told of having parted company a few days earlier with a convoy of sixty British ships bound for Boston. Aboard: 12,000 Hessian soldiers.

Meanwhile, in Boston, nearly every able-bodied man has volunteered to work two days a week, for six weeks, building fortifications for the general defense of the city—just in case the British troops who evacuated the city in March should return. Work began last week on the fortification of Noddle's Island, to the northeast of the city. Since that time, Bostonians have been joined by volunteers from several neighboring towns.[1]

134

Financing the War

Despite Great Britain's recent proposal for a peace conference, it is clear that Congress is not optimistic about a settlement favorable to the colonies; this week it set about to raise ten million dollars to finance the war through the rest of 1776. Acting upon a recommendation of a special committee, Congress resolved to raise half of the amount through an emission of five million dollars in bills of credit. How to raise the remaining five million dollars is still a question.

In other action this week, Congress resolved to inform General Washington that whenever Britain's peace commissioners—Lord Howe and General Howe—seek a meeting, he is to follow the prevailing custom in such cases and direct them to apply for the necessary passports and safe-conduct papers. When these are formally requested, Congress will advise General Washington as to the proper measures for receiving the commissioners.

Congress this week also requested the Pennsylvania Council of Safety to investigate the jailer in Philadelphia from whose custody Moses Kirkland escaped, and to remove him from his post if he is proven culpable. Kirkland, a South Carolina army captain who deserted with his company of Rangers to the British last August, was imprisoned by order of Congress.[2]

New Delegate

In Providence, Rhode Island, this week, the General Assembly elected William Ellery one of the Colony's two delegates to the Continental Congress. Ellery succeeds the late Samuel Ward, who died of smallpox in March while attending Congress in Philadelphia.[3]

Parliament

Official Secrecy

What really happened when the British evacuated Boston in March? The British public has had little information outside of brief official announcements, and even members of Parliament have complained that the fullest account to which they have had access, and to which the rest of the country has had equal access, is an article in the *London Gazette* on Saturday, May 4th. Monday, the 6th, member of Parliament Colonel Isaac Barré took the floor of the House of Commons to complain of such official secrecy and, waving the *Gazette* in his hand, put his complaint into a motion: That the latest dispatches from General Howe and Vice Admiral Shuldham be made accessible to Parliament.

Supporters of the Administration argued that secrecy is necessary . . . that "otherwise our plans would shortly come to the knowledge of our enemies." Barré's resolution was easily defeated, 171–54.[4]

An "Everlasting Farewell"

After one of the less extensive debates on colonial issues of the year, the House of Commons on Friday—by an overwhelming margin—said no to any liberalization of its policies on the taxation of its American colonies.

At issue was a motion by John Sawbridge, the Lord Mayor of London, that would have permitted the colonies to raise taxes through their own representatives, as is the case in Ireland. The resolution was moved at the behest of the London Common Council, and was first proposed at its meeting on April 29th.

Rising to second the motion, London Alderman Richard Oliver argued that it " . . . might convince the people of that country that we did not mean to make slaves of them, but hold them as peaceful, useful and obedient subjects." Temple Luttrell, while agreeing with the motion, cautioned that he would have American interests and happiness better accommodated than by giving them a constitution on the model of the Irish —"a people so wretched, so oppressed [as] scarcely to be found in any part of the world."

Adding another voice for reconciliation—though now seemingly resigned to the contrary—was David Hartley: "We have now got nearly to the end of the session. All our propositions for reconciliation have failed. The Ministry are determined upon the trial of force. . . . The die is now cast for conquest or independence. We have bid an everlasting farewell to America. Whatever may be the event of the war, this at least is certain— reconciliation never comes by the sword."

Thereupon, the House of Commons voted—115 to 33—against any change in policy on taxation of the American colonies.[5]

Foreign News

British Policy: In Favor

While not all of the British citizenry agrees with the government's policies toward America, those policies are nevertheless the majority view in Parliament, and thus, it may be argued, throughout the kingdom. An example is this letter published by London's *Gazetteer and New Daily Advertiser*:

"From the conclusion of the peace [of Utrecht in 1713] till Mr. Grenville's administration, the Americans enjoyed a continual and uninterrupted repose, while Great Britain labored under an accumulated debt of forty millions contracted wholly on their account; nay, I might say the whole expense of the last war; for had we not been the dupes of America, a war would not have been thought of."[6]

Grenville's Administration was 1763–65; the "last war" was the Seven Years War/French and Indian War.

Turgot Dismissed

When he became comptroller general of finances of France in August, 1774, A. R. J. Turgot wasted little time establishing a reputation as a reformer. And little more time was needed to make clear the extent of opposition to such reforming, particularly among the privileged classes.

This week, as has been predicted for some months, Turgot was dismissed by his Christian Majesty, King Louis XVI. His post is likely to go to J. E. B. Clugny, whose idea of reform is more apt to be undoing whatever Turgot did.[7]

Clugny suspended free trade in grain, brought back the jurandes, *and reinstated the* corvées.

Medicine

The Enemy Within

The musket ball, the cannon shot and the bayonet are the most obvious killers of troops in the field. Not so far behind is another peril that attacks not from without, but from within: disease. The success of an army therefore depends not only on how well it can defend itself from the first, but from the second as well.

Likely to be of help to military surgeons in the field is a comprehensive manual published this week in Philadelphia. It is a new translation of a book by one of Europe's most prominent physicians, Baron Gerard Van Swieten, and bears the title, *Diseases Incident to Armies with Method of Cure.*

Van Swieten, who is director-general of the Vienna Medical School and physician to the crown of Austria-Hungary, has concentrated on those infirmities most likely to strike soldiers. Many of them are also the most frequent disablers of the civilian population as well. Among them are:

Coughs: Abstain from wine, salt, acid foods. Have only rice and barley broth, new milk, or the yolk of an egg. If the cough is severe, take a pill containing eight grains of cynogloss [hound's tongue].

Sore Throat: Can be dangerous, and sometimes fatal, especially when respiration is impeded. A large bleeding is called for. Apply hot mustard-seed poultice to the neck.

Pleurisy: Known by sharp pain in chest, accompanied by fever. In severe cases, the patient can scarcely draw a breath. Bleeding is the first and chief remedy—twelve ounces of blood or more. Repeat if pain is violent enough to restrict breathing. Every half-hour administer the following preparation: one and one-half drams of pure nitre, two drams of crab claws, two ounces of syrup of wild poppies and ten ounces of barley water. As illness recedes, drink plentifully.

Fever: If recurring and accompanied by dizziness, bitter taste in mouth and flatulant eruptions, give emetic of fifteen grains of tartar or one-half dram of ipecacuanha four hours before sweating fit is expected. When patient vomits, make him drink warm water plentifully until he vomits again. Repeat drinking and vomiting at intervals until the water that is taken remains in the belly one hour. If fever is accompanied by pains in back or wind in the bowels, or if belly is swelled and hard, patient must be purged with forty grains of carnachini or a draught made of six drams of senna, two drams of water scurvy grass, one dram of agaric and one-half ounce of tamarinds boiled with one-half ounce of syrup of rhubarb.

Dysentery: Most common in summer and early autumn, it is caused by: 1) bile grown acrid by heat and fatigue of war, especially when the soldier, overheated in battle, exposes himself to cold air or sleeps in wet clothes; 2) stagnant or marsh water used for drinking purposes; 3) meat or fish that is beginning to taint. For treatment, give emetic of forty grains of ipecacuanha followed by warm water to cause vomiting, and continue giving water to repeat the vomiting. At night, if necessary, administer one grain of crude opium in a pill. The well and the sick should not use the same boghouse. If necessary, dig trenches to serve the necessities of the sick soldiers, making sure to cover trenches several times daily with earth.

Among other maladies covered in the Van Swieten manual: scurvy, gangrene, venereal disease, worms, cholera, dropsy, jaundice, phrenzy, perineumony and rheumatism.

So far, the discussion has been cure. What about prevention? Van Swieten suggests these to military commanders:

1) Remember that the soldier has been lifted and torn from family, and can easily become melancholy. Make sure he has adequate amusement and diversion.

2) Make sure his diet includes ample garden stuff, fresh greens and ripe fruit.

3) Good water is essential.

4) Soldier should be well clothed and covered, including shoes of thick, strong leather, well waxed at the seams.

5) Pitch camp on dry ground. If there is dampness, soldiers should change their straw more often. Officers would benefit by spreading waxed cloth under their beds.

6) Don't stay too long in one camp. The unwholesome effluvia of so many bodies always occasions sickness, especially in hot and moist air.

Commanders of a ragged, ill-equipped American army in the field may find it easier to use the section on treatment than the one on precaution.[8]

With Equal Certainty

Pain, suffering and death know not the rich from the poor, the ranked from the unranked. In recent weeks death has come:

—May 7th, in Munich, to Maria Josephena Anna Augusta, daughter of the late [Holy Roman] Emperor Charles VII, of an apoplectic fit with which she was stricken the day before;

—April 26th, in St. Petersburg, to Grand Duchess Petrowna Alexiewna, 21, of Russia (nee Princess Wilhelmina of Hesse-Darmstadt) of complications of childbirth, four days after the stillbirth of a prince. She was the wife of three years of his Imperial Highness, the Grand Duke Paul, 22, son of her Imperial Majesty, Catherine II.[9]

Press

Rhyme and Reason

No mild sentiment was it that unfolded on the pages of the *Pennsylvania Packet* this week. Some excerpts, from an exhortation to *Packet* readers:

> Americans! awake, awake!
> Your Liberty, your all's at stake:
> Behold your foes, huge angry swarms,
> Proclaim loud war, to arms, to arms!
>
> Rude Britain's haughty, angry frown
> Freedom's strong wall would batter down:
> But the foundation stands secure,
> God laid it, and it must endure.
>
> Let the inglorious coward quake,
> And up, the yoke of slav'ry take:
> Liberty's sons shall gain the prize,
> And unto fame immortal rise.[10]

THE WEEK OF MAY 13TH

The War

"Don't Give Up the Vessel"

One of a growing number of American privateers who have effectively harassed British shipping and taken a few notable prizes is Marblehead's

Captain James Mugford, who plied his trade with the best of them. But privateering is as hazardous as it is glorious; this week Captain Mugford paid the ultimate price of a daring life.

In seizing the 300-ton armed British ship *Hope,* which had left England with a convoy April 4th, Mugford had claimed the kind of prize that demanded retaliation. For the British it was not only the indignity of losing a ship, but the practical consequences of parting with its cargo of 1,000 carbines and a substantial amount of other military equipment. Two days after the capture of the *Hope* the British had their opportunity for revenge. Spotting Mugford's schooner *Franklin* off Pudding Gut Point, outside Boston harbor, they moved in with thirteen vessels, among them oared barges that offered greater mobility.

Vastly outnumbered—Mugford had twenty-one men, the attacking party at least two hundred—the doughty American captain prepared for the worst, and let the British within close range before firing cannon loaded with musket shot. But superior British numbers prevailed, and although the American captain sent two enemy barges to the bottom, Mugford was at last closed in, now faced with no alternative but the hand-to-hand combat of firearms and spears—a battle with which he could not possibly cope. Mugford was one of the first hit, felled by a musket ball that left no doubt of its mortality. In a matter of minutes, he was dead. Before the end, the captain called over his lieutenant. "I am a dead man," he told him, "but don't give up the vessel. You will be able to beat them. If not, cut the cable and run her on shore."

It was the latter alternative. And as the lieutenant ran the boat on shore, the British vessels made off, their mission completed.[11]

Captain James Mugford is generally credited with being the first to tell his men not to give up the ship (followed by Captain James Lawrence and Commodore Oliver Hazard Perry in 1813). But that's as far as the modern quotation is concerned. One is hard put not to think some ancient sea captain also gave the same command.

Objective: Unconditional Submission

Critics in Britain of the war with America have condemned not only the morality of it, but the cost as well. The latter is conceded even by the Administration; but for them it is the what-to-do that differs. Given the premise that the war is too costly, the answer is not to quit it but to prosecute it more vigorously.

That in essence is what Lord George Germaine, Secretary of State for the Colonies, has declared. The expense, he said, is such that Britain cannot carry on another campaign of the scale it has over the past year. The cost has already exceeded twelve million pounds, and that coupled with a loss of two million in trade with America, is becoming more than even British resources can bear. The effect is evident in commerce: British stocks have declined three percent since Christmas. The solution, according to Germaine, is a more determined effort to reduce America to unconditional submission—this year.[12]

More Hessians

Military sources in London say another embarkation of Hessians is scheduled for the near future. That will bring to more than 60,000 the number of men, on land and sea, in the King's service in North America.[13]

Congress

"Adopt Such Government . . ."

In one of its most significant decisions ever, Congress this week advised the colonies to begin forming their own governments and in so doing suppress every kind of authority still representative of the Crown. Thus said Congress, in effect: it is the authority of the people of the colonies that is the basis of government, not that of King and Parliament.

Congress had already made such a recommendation in a specific case —New Hampshire, which adopted its own constitution and government in January. Since that time South Carolina has done likewise, and delegates of the Colony of Virginia have been gathered in Williamsburg since May 6th to consider doing the same. Now with Congress extending its stamp of approval to all colonies, others almost certainly will follow.

Congress first acted May 10th, in a resolution (not then publicized) calling for the formation of new colonial governments. On Wednesday, May 15th, the delegates also agreed upon a preamble setting forth the justification of its precedent-setting action, and adopted that along with an agreement to publicize the action widely among the people of America. That resolution:

"Whereas his Britannic majesty in conjunction with the lords and commons of Great Britain has by late act of Parliament excluded the inhabitants of these United Colonies from the protection of his crown . . . and whereas no answer whatever to the humble petitions of the colonies for redress of grievances and reconciliation with Great Britain has been or is likely to be given, but the whole force of that kingdom aided by foreign mercenaries is to be exerted for the destruction of the good people of these colonies. . . .

"And whereas it is necessary that the exercise of every kind of authority under the said crown should be totally suppressed, and all the powers of government exerted under the authority of the people of the colonies for the preservation of internal peace, virtue and good order, as well as for the defense of their lives, liberties and properties. . . .

"Resolved, it be recommended to the respective assemblies and conventions of the United Colonies where no government sufficient to the exigencies of their affairs hath been hitherto established, to adopt such government as shall in the opinion of the representatives of the people

best conduce to the happiness and safety of their constituents in particular and America in general."

There is one significant difference, perhaps, between the kind of government to be instituted under this resolution and those governments
established in New Hampshire and South Carolina: those two charters
expressed a hope that reconciliation might make it possible to return to
royal government; this resolution of Congress says nothing about new
governments being temporary in nature.[14]

Portugal saw this as, in fact, a declaration of independence [Week of July 1].

"Stop A Tory"

For finding lost watches and purses, public-spirited citizens are usually offered rewards of no more than a few dollars; for apprehending runaway slaves and other lawbreakers as well as horses, the rewards are
sometimes five to twenty dollars; rare indeed are rewards higher than
that in value.

It may be a measure of distinction to him that Moses Kirkland, who
escaped from jail in Philadelphia after being confined there by order of
Congress for deserting to the British, is now the subject of a reward of
two hundred dollars. An advertisement entitled "Stop a Tory," appearing
in many newspapers, describes Kirkland as a stout, corpulent man of fifty
to sixty years of age, swarthy of complexion, wearing his own gray hair
tied up in back.[15]

The Colonies

Prelude to Independence?

Gathered in Williamsburg and meeting daily as they have been since
May 6th are the elected delegates of sixty-five counties, cities, towns,
boroughs and the one college (William and Mary) of the Colony of Virginia. This convention, the first in the colony since January, faces no
shortage of issues and no small task. Warned Convention President Edmund Pendleton on opening day—as if any didn't know—it is "a time
truly critical."

Paramount in importance will be establishing a new government for
the colony. Virginia has been without any effective government for two
years since the nearly complete suspension of the old by royal order.
One consequence has been the lack of any machinery of justice: criminals have been confined but not tried.

While the matter of a constitution has not been settled, the convention has already set the depth and the seriousness of its deliberations. No
matter what else it may or may not do, in two separate resolutions
Wednesday the Virginia delegates assured the convention a place in history by:

—Voting unanimously to instruct Virginia's delegates in the Continental Congress to propose that independence be declared;

—Setting as a goal of the convention the adoption of a Declaration of Rights and a new form of government.

While independence has been talked about more and more since the beginning of the year, and indeed some delegates in the Continental Congress already have instructions on the matter from home, the most momentous political question of the day has not yet reached the fateful formality of debate on the floor of Congress. Now it will.

In a simply but forcefully worded resolution to delegates George Wythe, Thomas Jefferson, Benjamin Harrison, Richard Henry Lee, Francis Lightfoot Lee and Carter Braxton, the Convention gave these instructions, to be delivered by returning delegate Thomas Nelson, Jr.: ". . . Propose to that respectable body to declare the United Colonies free and independent states, absolved from all allegiance to, or dependence upon, the crown or Parliament of Great Britain; and . . . give the assent of this colony to such declaration and to whatever measures may be thought proper and necessary by the Congress for forming foreign alliances, and to a confederation of the colonies, at such times and in such manner as to them shall seem best; provided that the power of forming governments for and the regulation of the internal concerns of each colony be left to the respective colonial legislatures."

The convention, meanwhile, entrusted to a committee of twenty-seven members the task of proposing for the colony itself a Declaration of Rights and a plan of government. The objectives: "to maintain peace and order in this colony and secure substantial and equal liberty to the people."

In its resolution to the Continental Congress, the Virginia Convention took note of the tribulations of all the colonies as well as its own, the latter most notably the abolition of constituted government: "The King's representative in this colony [Lord Dunmore] hath not only withheld all the powers of government from operating for our safety, but having retired on board an armed ship, is carrying on a piratical and savage war against us. . . . In this state of extreme danger, we have no alternative left but an abject submission to the will of those overbearing tyrants, or a total separation from the crown and government of Great Britain, uniting and exerting the strength of all America for defence, and forming alliances with foreign powers for commerce and aid in war."

Then, appealing to the "searcher of hearts" for divine assurance of the wisdom of their action, Virginia's delegates unanimously approved their resolution, and thus set the stage for a debate of the profoundest nature by the delegates of all the colonies three hundred miles away in Philadelphia.[16]

Colonies to States

For perhaps the first time, the United Colonies have been called the

United States—a distinction as sweeping in its meaning as Virginia's proposal that Congress declare independence from Great Britain. It happened as part of a celebration among the citizenry of Williamsburg following the first public reading of the Virginia Convention's resolution for independence at the Capitol on Duke of Gloucester Street. The Union Flag of thirteen red and white stripes flying overhead, these salutes were offered, each one given a roar of approval by Virginia artillery:

—"To the American independent states";

—"To the Grand Congress of the *United States,* and their respective legislatures";

—"To General Washington and victory to the American arms."

At night, festal lights were hung throughout the town, and there were everywhere demonstrations of joy . . . "everyone seeming pleased," said Alexander Purdie's *Virginia Gazette,* "that the domination of Great Britain was now at an end, so wickedly and tyrannically exercised for these twelve or thirteen years past, notwithstanding our repeated prayers and remonstrances for redress."[17]

Foreign News

Alarm at the British Ministry

The specter of American independence haunts the British government as does nothing else among the affairs of man. Here is how a correspondent in London sees it:

"Should America this spring declare independence, it is most certain that France, and many other powers of Europe, will give her immediate assistance. . . . The Ministry are fully sensible of this; therefore, by cajoling and making friends in some of the southern colonies, they hope to create divisions, and prevent such a decided step being taken this year; and by the operations of the present campaign, they expect to be so successful as to make it too hazardous for foreign powers to interfere.

"Indeed the Ministry are more alarmed at the apprehension of America declaring herself independent than anything else, because they have been already given to understand, by most of the powers in Europe, particularly by France and Prussia, that in such a case they shall think themselves entirely at liberty to act as best suits themselves. But the truth is the king is so determined on unconditional subjugation of America—the present court phrase—that it is certain he will risk the utter ruin of the whole empire, rather than not succeed in what he has set his heart so much upon."[18]

Family Day

For England's newest princess—Mary, born April 25th—Sunday, the 19th was christening day. For her mother, Queen Charlotte—that pale, thin, genteel noblewoman from Mecklenburg-Strelitz, to whom his Majesty has been devoted husband nearly fifteen years now—it was a birthday, her thirty-second. The christening was performed by the Archbishop of Canterbury in the Great Council Chamber of St. James's Palace. Afterward, both events were celebrated by a host of lords and ladies, members of Parliament and foreign ministers all gathered to help the royal family mark this special day.

With eleven children in fifteen years of marriage, the union of George and Charlotte has been a fruitful one. It was one year after his Majesty ascended to the throne that they entered into the marriage arranged on their behalf by intermediaries who thought the young German princess would be just right for the new British King, whose forebears were also German. George and Charlotte met for the first time on September 8th, 1761 (in the morning), a date they readily remember since it also happens to be their wedding day (in the evening). She prepared for life in her new country by playing English folk songs on a harpsichord aboard ship going to England.[19]

May 19th was Queen Charlotte's natural birthday. She also had an "official birthday" which was celebrated publicly on January 18th. The King, meanwhile, marked both his official birthday and natural birthday on the same date, June 4th.

The Rivers of Russia

The region of Smolensk in west central Russia lies at the near-juncture of three major rivers (West Dvina, Dniepr and Volga) flowing to three seas (Baltic, Black and Caspian) which would make it a crossroads of waterbound trade if the three rivers joined and were navigable throughout. That, in fact, is what Russia now proposes to do in a far-reaching project outlined recently in St. Petersburg by her Imperial Majesty, Catherine II. The plan: construct canals where necessary to join the rivers, and provide a navigable passage.

Smolensk, a once prosperous center of land trade centuries ago, being at the heart of the new river route through Russia, would regain at least some of its former importance. That once great status, according to the report from St. Petersburg, can be judged from "the stupendous ruins . . . no doubt inhabited by a number of nations who were powerful, polished and industrious."[20]

Art

The "Masterly" West

For Pennsylvania-born painter Benjamin West, who left his homeland sixteen years ago to study in Italy, England is now home. Accepted and respected there, it is no wonder his paintings currently on exhibition at

London's Royal Academy have won such praise as "excellently expressed" and "masterly."

The current exhibition was reviewed in the *London Chronicle*. Its critic offered these observations about these paintings:

Devout Men Taking the Body of St. Stephen: Mr. West still maintains that high character as a history painter, which he originally obtained and has all along supported. It were to be wished, however, that he had taken more of his pieces in the present collection from profane [that is, secular] and fewer from sacred history; not that the latter does not furnish as good subjects for history painting as the former, but because the subjects borrowed from the sacred are much more hackneyed. . . . And the reason is evident: when the great painters, Michaelangelo, Raphael, &c lived, profane learning was just beginning to revive, and was not disposed through the general body of the people. These painters therefore confined themselves almost entirely to sacred subjects and they have given us such admirable pieces in that way as to leave nothing to their successors but the hope of equalling, and by no means that of excelling them. This work is possessed of much merit. The figures are numerous, but the countenance of each is distinguished by a different passion. The skin of St. Stephen seems to be too smooth. Perhaps it would be better if he had some contusions, and bore some marks of those stones with which he was murdered.

Daniel Interpreting to Belshazzar the Writing on the Wall: The surprise and consternation of Belshazzar and his courtiers, and the solemn air and firm conviction of Daniel and his attendants, are excellently expressed.

Isaac's Servant Tying the Bracelet on Rebecca's Arm: This, though a simple scene and extremely well known, is rendered somewhat new and sufficiently interesting by the masterly manner in which it is executed.

Rinaldo and Armida: Armida is a perfect Venus; Rinaldo, the true picture of a man enamoured.

Although West is one of the most important painters in England today, that stature does not spare him from those slights an artist of lesser renown might more likely meet. The painting of St. Stephen, which portrays life-size figures on a gigantic canvas measuring seven by sixteen feet, was painted for the altar of the Church of St. Stephen Walbrook in London. When a fee of only 600 guineas arrived, West grumbled that they might just as well take the painting as a gift.[21]

Press

Nobody Does Anything About It

To Britain's thirteen enemies in rebellion in America may be added a fourteenth: the weather. At least that is the opinion of one British newspaper, which thinks the Ministry ought to do something about it.

The weather was the formidable foe that made a scatter of the fleet of British Commodore Sir Peter Parker as he sailed recently for America.

Of it all, wryly reported Canterbury's *Kentish Gazette*: "A correspondent who observed with astonishment the attack which Opposition made upon Administration [in Parliament], in consequence of the storm which separated Sir Peter Parker's fleet, wonders that our patriots do not impeach Lord North for suffering the weather to prove so fatally unfavorable to the armaments of this Kingdom. As his Lordship has the command of the elements, he should certainly direct them to combat on the side of Great Britain, and his negligently suffering them to follow the directions of the Deity should as certainly expose him to a charge of secretly assisting the rebels of America."[22]

Comment apparently based on debate in the House of Lords May 10th on the wisdom of sending Parker off in risky weather. Parker left from Ireland in February; it was early May when he got most of his fleet gathered together off Cape Fear, North Carolina. A few ships were lost; more significant is the fact that the weather delayed Parker's arrival in America.

THE WEEK OF MAY 20TH

The War

Retreat in Canada

After its ill-fated assault on Quebec last December 31st—the battle in which the popular General Richard Montgomery of New York was killed—the Amercan force that devolved to the command of then-Colonel Benedict Arnold withdrew a short way from the city and set up camp; if it could not take the capital of Quebec, it would then lay siege until such time as reinforcements from the colonies made feasible a new assault.

In the city itself, General Guy Carleton, commander-in-chief of British forces in Canada, needed do little but have his troops maintain vigilance and await a spring thaw that would bring new troops and supplies down the now ice-locked St. Lawrence River. He found little difficulty in defending the town against a few attempts by Arnold's forces to burn British ships in the harbor and sprinkle the city with occasional artillery fire.

For the rest of the season the rigors of the Canadian winter proved a greater adversary to each than either army to the other. In the American camp food and military supplies grew continually more scarce; in the city fuel ran so short that houses in the suburbs were used for firewood.

By the beginning of this month the ice on the St. Lawrence was breaking up, and the Americans—perhaps 1,000 fit for duty and now under the command of Major General John Thomas—knew there would be little time left to attack Quebec before British reinforcements arrived. There was less than they thought. The first sight of British ships sent the Americans into disarray. Learning of the confusion, General Carleton on the 6th took his first offensive action in the long months of siege: with an estimated 1,200 men he waged a surprise attack on the American position, and turned disarray into full-scale retreat. The Americans, now outnumbered, completely disheartened, and lacking even an entrenchment for defense, fled west up the St. Lawrence leaving behind provisions, equipment, artillery and about 200 sick soldiers. Even so, half of these, stricken with smallpox, hobbled along with the main body.

On the 9th of this month, the shattered remnants of General Thomas's army had encamped at Point-de-Chambeau, about 45 miles up the river. From that camp has come this report, the most recent to reach the colonies: The retreat was considered the only recourse left; smallpox was so prevalent that, considering the number stricken and the number scattered about to prevent the further spread, there were only 200 healthy men left at headquarters; there were neither entrenchments nor breastworks because there were no tools with which to construct them; there were only enough provisions left for another six days.[23]

Congress

Varied Business

In six days of varied business, Congress this week, among other things:

—Implemented its earlier decision to emit five million dollars in bills of credit by approving a report of the treasury committee providing for 138,889 bills each in denominations of one to eight dollars, these bills to be printed from the plates used in the last emission;

—Directed General Washington to send to Ticonderoga as many light cannon as will be sufficient to arm the vessels now at Lake Champlain;

—Voted to advise the commanding officer in Canada that Congress is absolutely convinced of the strategic need for that country, and will continue to afford every support to its military forces there.

Congress also approved a policy for the treatment of prisoners of war. In general, the rules are these: Prisoners are to be treated with humanity. Soldiers are to receive the same rations as troops in the service of the United Colonies; officers are to supply themselves, being permitted to draw bills for payment of subsistence and clothes, and where they cannot, they are to receive an allotment of two dollars a week, which must be repaid before release from imprisonment. There is to be leeway in determining where an officer is quartered, but it cannot be in a seaport town or on a public post road. Such officers as surrender prisoners of war will be put on parole and given freedom to travel within six miles of their residence, unless

Congress directs otherwise. Prisoners are to be allowed to practice their trades to support themselves and their families.[24]

Despite good intentions, treatment of prisoners often bordered on the barbaric on both sides as the war went on.

The Colonies

To the Last Farthing

The citizens of Malden, Massachusetts, have already made up their minds about American independence. By unanimous vote in town meeting, they decided to tell the Colony's delegates in Congress: "We have unbounded confidence in the wisdom and uprightness of the Continental Congress. With pleasure we recollect that this affair is under their direction, and we now instruct you Sir, to give them the strongest assurance that if they should declare America to be a free and independent republic, your constituents will support and defend the measure to the last drop of their blood and the last farthing of their treasure."[25]

Parliament

The Whigs: Gaining Votes

Official secrecy on the part of the Administration of Great Britain continues to be a major issue for the Opposition in Parliament, and has now given the Whigs their most substantial vote on any major colonial matter in months.

The extensive debate developed over a motion by General H. S. Conway for a full disclosure to Parliament of the instructions to Lord Viscount Howe and General Howe, recently appointed as his Majesty's commissioners for a discussion of peace terms with the colonies. Since both reconciliation and governmental secrecy have been popular issues for the Whigs, such a motion was bound to bring forth all the oratorical fire of the Opposition, and it did.

Leading off in support of his own motion, Conway lamented that the Administration has all along played with Parliament, withholding information or deluging it with news as fitted Administration's purpose. "When a war was determined on," he argued, "the conduct of the Administration changed with their views; they first provoked the [American] people to resist Government, and only produced to Parliament such part of the state of affairs in that country as promised to inflame and irritate Great Britain. As soon as Great Britain had determined to assert her rights, the Administration again resumed their wonted taciturnity, and from the very instant that America was declared in a state of rebellion, the present Parliament has been kept in the most profound ignorance of everything passing on the other side of the Atlantick."

Before he was through, General Conway had a profound warning for the Administration: "If you have no traces of justice left in your minds; if you feel not for your own honour, for God's sake pay some little attention to your own individual interests, and for the safety of the nation. Do you think, however credulous you may be, that France and Spain will lie by, silent and inactive, with their hands across? . . . Spain is daily arming. France has a new Minister, who is fond of war, who is a man of enterprise and ability, and is well known not to be well disposed towards this country."

Lord North took the floor to argue that it is only normal, in matters of negotiation, to give instructions, to let the treaty go on, to wait for the issue of it, and then to form a judgment. If the treaty should miscarry, he said, if no fruits should be produced from it, then it would be time enough to inquire into the tenor of the instructions, to see whether they were such as ought to have been given, and such as, from their professed objectives, were likely to succeed. Defending the choice of the Howes as peace commissioners, North maintained: "In some situations, the business of a general is as much to negotiate as to fight. The knowledge of his own strength, as well as that of the enemy, leads him to many important secrets, which frequently serve as the basis of future accommodation."

The Opposition resumed:

Edmund Burke arguing that the House had a right to know what powers were delegated to the commissioners, that it was indeed a Parliamentary affair;

Charles James Fox, doubting the commissioners had been so much empowered to entreat or sound out as to carry fire, sword and devastation— as in the "wanton cruelties" exercised in the burning of Norfolk;

Colonel Isaac Barré, wondering aloud if the Administration, in selecting the Howes, could have "picked two men more unqualified for the effectuating of so abstruse, difficult and arduous a business," and predicting that North America is "forever lost."

As expected, Conway's motion went down to defeat. But with a vote of 171–85, the Whigs showed more strength than they have in months.[26]

Favorite Wish or Fateful Will

As the concluding business of the present session, Parliament on Thursday heard King George pledge "the full exertion of the great force entrusted me" to restore order in the American colonies no matter what the cost.

Said his Majesty: "I will still entertain a hope that my rebellious subjects may be awakened to a sense of their duty, that they will justify me in bringing about the favorite wish of my heart, the restoration of harmony and the establishment of order and happiness in every part of my dominions. But if a due submission should not be obtained from such motives, and such a disposition on their part, I trust I shall be able, under the blessings of Providence, to effectuate it by a full exertion of the great force with which you have entrusted me. . . . I am convinced you will not think any price too high for the preservation of such objects."

Thereupon, Parliament adjourned until August 1st.[27]

Technically speaking, this was a prorogation—the termination of a session of Parliament at the order of the King. It put to an end all current business and killed all bills which had not become law, but did not change the membership. Lesser breaks—as at Christmas and Easter—were recesses called at the discretion of Parliament itself. At the other extreme was dissolution, which under the Septennial Act of 1715 had to come at least every seven years, and brought about election of a new Parliament.

Counterfeit Scheme

Unofficial reports from London say the North Ministry may try to encourage the counterfeiting of Continental currency, knowing that to flood the colonies with such money would play havoc with their economy.[28]

Foreign News

DIED: In Paris, May 23rd: Julie de Lespinasse, forty-four, who from humble roots blossomed into one of the distinguished *salonnières* of Paris, particularly in literary and intellectual circles. Born in Lyon, both illegitimate and poor, her companionship to the blind Marquise du Deffand eventually led to Paris society, where her own charm, wit and intelligence proved all that was needed to establish her own salon and acquire the friendship of such distinguished Frenchmen as Turgot and d'Alembert.[29]

Law

A Trying Profession

In London, an attorney's clerk who charged prisoners in Old Bailey two guineas each for a promise to get their trials put off, found himself on trial in Old Bailey for tampering with justice, and was made a prisoner himself in Newgate Prison.[30]

Science

Visitors in Dublin

In France it is known as a *becasse des bois;* in Germany, as a *Waldschnepfe;* in Holland, as a *houtsnip;* and in Ireland as a rarity.

The woodcock is otherwise the same throughout Western Europe: a game bird slightly more than twelve inches in length, with feet as short as his bill is long. His coloring provides virtually perfect camouflage among fallen leaves. During flight the male makes a peculiar, soft, croaking *"orrrt-orrrt"* but also a high, sneezing *"tsiwick."* His habitat, true to his name, is the woods, particularly where wet and overgrown.

Distinctly untypical a habitat is Phoenix Park in Dublin where, one recent day, a young man happened upon a nest sheltering two young woodcocks. He took them home, tried to nurse them along. But they died within two days. Recognizing the rarity of the species in Ireland, he had them stuffed for others to see.[31]

Books

Mr. Author?

The *London Evening Post* of May 21st, printing extracts of the American pamphlet *Common Sense,* thinks it knows the author of the anonymous document: "Mr. Adams."[32]

THE WEEK OF MAY 27TH

The War

Objective Clear

A British fleet of perhaps forty or fifty sail of ships is at anchor north of Sullivan's Island, outside Charleston harbor in South Carolina. There appears no doubt it is the fleet of Commodore Sir Peter Parker, which for nearly a month has been reported preparing for invasion of either Virginia or South Carolina. Now the objective is clear.[33]

The "forty or fifty sail" included mostly troop transports.

Congress

Like Tea

Even before it voted April 30th to remove rules on prices, Congress had found an exception, and retained a restriction on the price of green tea. Now it has made another exception: salt.

Advised that "avaricious, ill designing men" have been taking undue advantage of the removal of restrictions, Congress acted this week by recommending to local authorities that the price of salt again be regulated, provided however that in setting a price, some consideration be given to the risk and cost of importation so that merchants receive a fair return on their investments.

Among many routine matters, Congress took time to consider the welfare of prisoners, and agreed to let three at the Philadelphia jail—John Connolly, John Smith and Allan Cameron—have permission, because of ill health, to walk two hours per day in the prison yard in the company of at least two guards.[34]

The Colonies

Some Burning, Some Glowing

The spirit of independence has burned in Massachusetts to the north and Virginia to the south, and glowed at best in the colonies between. The difference in intensity shows in the adopted resolutions of assemblies in the north (Boston) and between (Maryland) in recent weeks.

Meeting at Annapolis, the Maryland Convention on May 21st unanimously adopted resolutions arguing:

—That people of the province have the sole and exclusive right of regulating its internal government and police;

—That they have the power to draw the forces of the province into action against armed force carrying out the "unconstitutional and oppressive acts of Parliament";

—That they will continue with cheerfulness in the common cause, and if it appears necessary, will enter into further compact with other colonies;

—That they are firmly persuaded "re-union with Great Britain, on constitutional principles, would most effectually secure rights and liberties."

Nine days later, a meeting of the freeholders and inhabitants of Boston, called for the choosing of representatives to the General Assembly of Massachusetts, produced these conclusions:

"We have seen the humble petitions of these colonies to the King of Great Britain repeatedly rejected with disdain. For the prayer of peace, he has tendered the sword; for liberty, chains; and for safety, death.

"A reconciliation with them [Britain] appears to us as dangerous as it is absurd. . . . We therefore think it absolutely impracticable for the colonies to be ever again subject to, or dependent upon Great Britain, without endangering the very existence of the state. Placing, however, unbounded confidence in the supreme councils of the Congress, we are determined to wait, most patiently to wait, till their wisdom shall dictate the necessity of making a declaration of independence."

The Boston citizens' specific instructions to their provincial representatives: Use your endeavors that the delegates in Congress be advised that if it is necessary to declare independence, the "inhabitants of this colony, with their lives and the remnants of their fortunes, will most cheerfully support them in the measure."[35]

Foreign News

Turgot: A British View

The dismissal of A. R. J. Turgot as France's comptroller general of finances May 12th is viewed as likely to have an impact well beyond the status of economic reform in France.

Such reform under his successor, J. E. B. Clugny, is almost certain to be set back; the fact that his Majesty, King Louis XVI, dismissed Turgot after once seeming to espouse his cause, attests to that. But a far wider effect may be felt in international relations. The removal of Turgot makes French intervention in the American war a great deal more likely. It means the French government, which for two years has been concentrating largely on internal reform, will now be paying more attention to what role it will play in world events.

This, at least, is the assessment in England. Said a correspondent in London this week: "The change in the French ministry has alarmed Administration exceedingly. The comptroller general of the finances, Turgot, was a warm friend to peace and domestic improvements . . . but the new arrangement is of a very different complexion." Affirming that view is a report that the British Board of Admiralty met this week and ordered twelve additional men-of-war to be put into commission. Said another correspondent in the British capital: "Those that are now to take the lead [in France] have not the same pacific sentiments as their predecessors."

The London Chronicle, meanwhile, commented on still another aspect of change in ministry: "The removal of Mr. de Turgot from the post of comptroller general, and the appointment of Mr. Clugny in his stead, occasions the greater surprise because the integrity and capacity of the former are generally allowed. The affair furnishes us with a fresh instance of the instability of royal favour."[36]

Medicine

Feeling Better

Like many another American, Mrs. George Washington is putting up with the discomforts of smallpox inoculation. She is in Philadelphia, where she has now passed her thirteenth day since inoculation, and appears to be reacting very favorably, with only mild symptoms and few pustules. She feels well enough to write a letter to her sister, but was persuaded to wait a few days longer.

Her husband arrived in town the afternoon of the 23rd to meet with Congress, but will likely return to his headquarters in New York in a few days. He is already immune, having suffered smallpox while visiting in Barbadoes with his brother Lawrence in 1751. It was a severe case which has left his face slightly pocked to this day.[37]

Press

Newest Newspaper

Boston, the home of America's first newspaper, is also the home of its newest. The first was *Publick Occurrences,* which appeared September 25, 1690. Intended as a monthly publication, it lasted one issue before being suppressed by the authorities. A far longer life is the hope of publisher John Gill, whose *Continental Journal and Weekly Advertiser* is Boston's newest paper. The first issue was Thursday, May 30th.

Meanwhile, the city's oldest surviving paper, the *Boston Gazette,* is still being published in nearby Watertown, where publisher Benjamin Edes— once Gill's partner—fled during the occupation of the city. At that time there was also the *Massachusetts Gazette and Boston News-Letter,* established in 1704 by John Campbell as the *News-Letter.* No editions, however, have appeared since February.[38]

Books

Rise of the Rabble

If the Colonials are "cowardly poltroons . . . psalm-singing provincials . . . a flock of wild geese," and the British army is a host of "valiant sons of Mars . . . self-sufficient heroes," then what happened at Concord bridge, or that first attack on Bunker's Hill?

If the Americans are cowards, and "the sound of the drum, the piercing squall of the fife, the sight of regular troops . . . were to frighten them into submission," then what happened at Boston?

The answer, says one Janus, is the "contempt which the Ministry and their friends had of the American spirit . . . the Ministry were dreaming about the affairs of state."

What makes the anonymous Janus's commentary interesting, beyond its vehemence, is that it is part of a book, *Rise and Progress of the Contest in America,* published in London. Not surprisingly, the publisher has chosen to remain as anonymous as the author.

Unlike his namesake, Janus doesn't see two ways in the present struggle. As far as he is concerned, the war in America is not the result of the rebelliousness of the colonies but the ridiculousness of the British government in its colonial policies. Says he: "the Americans were, unhappily for this country, considered as a rabble who would soon disperse at the appearance of the King's regular troops. The first lord of the admiralty spoke freely of driving them with a few hundred soldiers all thro' their country." But in the Americans, "we find an enthusiastic zeal for liberty; a spirit ready to brave danger and death. . . . It appears the mother country has been the cause of the present calamities."

Nevertheless, Janus doubts there will be a move toward independence. Argues he: "The insinuations that the Americans aim at independence are stories invented and circulated to increase our animosities; but there is nothing more untrue. It is impossible for the colonists to be happier than under the protection of Great Britain, and they will understand their own interests."[39]

JUNE

Hail, genial Goddess, blooming Spring!
Thy blest return, O let me sing,
  And aid my languid Lays:
Let me not sink in Sloth supine,
While all Creation at thy Shrine,
  Its annual Tribute pays.

Burlington Almanack
June, 1776

THE WEEK OF JUNE 3RD

The War

Forewarning

The Colony of South Carolina, which adopted a constitution and a new government March 26th, now has the choice of dissolving the Provincial Congress thus established or "answer the contrary at utmost peril."

So have the citizens of South Carolina been warned by Major General Henry Clinton, commander of his Majesty's forces in the southern Provinces of America, who, with Major General Lord Cornwallis, commands a force of perhaps 3,000 troops at the portals of Charleston.

Clinton's ultimatum was delivered to a representative of the American commander, Colonel William Moultrie, and leaves no doubt—were there any—about the reason for the British fleet anchored outside of Charleston harbor or the troops of General Clinton, transported here by that

157

same fleet, and now encamped on Long Island, adjacent to nearby Sullivan's Island.

In his message Clinton declared it his "duty inseparable from the principle of humanity first of all to forewarn the deluded people of the miseries ever attendant upon civil war," before proceeding with his military mission. He promised pardon to all who will lay down their arms and "return to their duty to our common Sovereign"—and the "utmost peril" to all who will not.

The reaction of South Carolina, if the past is any guide, may well be only more zealous preparation for battle.[1]

Congress

Independence: Debate Assured

"Resolved, That these United Colones are, and of right ought to be, free and independent States, that they are absolved from all allegiance to the British Crown, and that all political connection between them and the State of Great Britain is, and ought to be, totally dissolved.

"That it is expedient forthwith to take the most effectual measures for forming foreign Alliances.

"That a plan of confederation be prepared and transmitted to the respective Colonies for their consideration and approbation."

So, as the Convention of the colony directed on May 15th, Virginia on Friday, the 7th, placed independence on the agenda of the Continental Congress. With those three resolutions—for dissolving all political union with Great Britain, for making foreign alliances, and for devising a plan of government for an independent United Colonies—it has handed Congress the most difficult assignment in its history. Independence has been thought about, talked about, written about, debated about throughout the land; now will it be taken up in the one place that counts.[2]

The resolution for independence was moved by Richard Henry Lee and seconded by John Adams. Their names were specifically not publicized by Congress—as was the case with all the signers subsequently—to protect them as much as possible from retaliation by the British.

The Debate Begins

Congress spent most of Saturday in committee of the whole debating the question of independence, as usual in complete secrecy. This much is known:

"The Congress . . . resolved itself into a committee of the whole, and after some time the president resumed the chair, and Mr. Harrison reported that the committee have taken into consideration the matter to them referred, but not having come to any resolution thereon, directed him to move for leave to sit again on Monday."

In resolving itself into committee of the whole, with Virginia's Benjamin Harrison as chairman, Congress is following a procedure it frequently adopts on matters of major importance. Committee of the whole permits more flexible and informal debate, of which no official record is kept at all.[3]

Other Matters

Virginia's resolution for independence dominated the work of Congress this week. In other action, the colonies' representatives:

—Directed that 13,800 militia be employed to reinforce the Continental Army at New York, of these, 2,000 coming from Massachusetts, 5,500 from Connecticut, 3,000 from New York and 3,300 from New Jersey;

—Ordered that a flying camp be established in the middle colonies, to be made up of 6,000 men from Pennsylvania, 3,400 from Maryland and 600 from Delaware, with Continental pay to commence the date of their marching from home, and with additional payment for traveling expenses to consist of one penny per mile in lieu of rations plus one day's pay for every twenty miles between home and general rendezvous;

—Appointed John Whitecomb and Hugh Mercer as brigadier generals, Joseph Reed as adjutant general, and Stephen Moylan as quartermaster general of the Continental Army.[4]

A "flying camp" was defined in a military dictionary published in 1776 as "a body of lighthorse or foot who are always in motion, either to cover an army or garrison, and to keep the enemy in continual alarm."

The Colonies

The Cost of Patriotism

In the farm country around Fairfield, Connecticut, William Prindle has long had a reputation for being: 1) a Tory; and 2) a little insane. Last week, were there any doubt, he proved both.

Prindle had hired a new laborer, and soon found to his utter distress that the man was not only patriotically inclined, but talking at every opportunity about American rights and freedom. His aversion growing to the point of desperation, Tory Prindle watched for an opportunity to put an end to such talk, found the right moment when the laborer was fast asleep, took an ax, and severed the man's head from his body. Then around the countryside he went, boasting to his neighbors about how he had cut off the head of a "damned Whig" and wished he could sever theirs as well.

Before he had the chance, authorities had Prindle locked securely in Fairfield jail.[5]

Sea Spoils

Lord North—but not Britain's first minister—is the most recent, and unusual, prize of American privateers.

He was among the booty of two Philadephia privateers, Captain McElroy, commanding the *Congress,* and Captain Allen of the *Chance,* who recently captured three ships bound from Jamaica for London laden with rum, sugar, molasses and other commodities as well as 22,400 dollars.

Also aboard: two fine sea turtles intended as a present for Lord North —one of them bearing his Lordship's name nicely inscribed in his shell. He was forwarded instead to Continental Congress President John Hancock.[6]

Foreign News

Thirty-Eight

The front of London's Opera House was ablaze with festal lights and afull with the King's Arms and symbolic figures of "Liberty" and "Plenty"; from the apartments over the Great Piazza, a band played; in the Haymarket, thirty-eight cannon—one for each year—boomed a salute; fireworks streaked into the sky turning night to day; and all the while, Londoners downed strong beer handed out among the crowds.

A visitor might have wondered what the celebration was all about; Londoners knew. It was June 4th, the King's birthday.

For George III, now thirty-eight, the occasion was marked with a daylong series of social functions, culminating in a grand ball in the evening. Queen Charlotte, however, waited until the ball to put in her first appearance; it was thought more active participation might be too much for her so soon after the birth of their youngest child, the Princess Mary, a little more than a month ago.

In honor of the King's birthday, Poet Laureate William Whitehead composed an ode that finds Britain—and thus his Majesty—strong and wise among the tribulations of the times. A sample:

> Can Britain fail?—The thought were vain!
> The powerful empress of the main
> But strives to smooth th' unruly flood,
> And dreads a conquest stain'd with blood.[7]

Weapon of the Future?

The flintlock musket with its attached bayonet is the mainstay of the British army and the other armies of the world. It is a relatively rugged weapon, simple enough to use that almost any soldier who can carry it can be taught to load and fire it. The user need not be expert since the maximum effective range is not very great to begin with. On the other hand it is slow to reload and unpredictable in wet weather.

The principal weapon of the future may well prove to be the rifle, which has already found use among some American troops, particularly those who used it before the war for hunting. Unlike the musket, the bore of the barrel is "rifled," or grooved in a spiral fashion, to give the bullet a spinning motion and hence greater accuracy. Although the concept is centuries old, the rifle as a military weapon is new. One reason: the barrel is too long to permit the attachment of a bayonet.

The British army is now known to be considering the use of such a weapon, prodded on by a captain who has developed a working model said to possess many advantages over the muskets now in use. Besides the greater accuracy produced by its rifling, it is also breech-loading, which makes it easier and faster to re-fire. It is also said to be less affected by dampness.

To demonstrate his model at Woolwich Arsenal before some of the top men in the British army (among them, Lord Amherst, officiating commander in chief of the forces; Viscount Townshend, master-general of the ordnance; and Major General Thomas Desaguliers, commandant of the Royal Artillery) Captain Patrick Ferguson could not have picked a worse day—or a better one. There was a heavy constant rain, and a high wind. Despite those disadvantages, or rather to prove his weapon's superiority in spite of them, the captain from Scotland did four experiments:

—He fired at a target 200 yards away at the rate of four shots each for four or five minutes;

—He fired at the target six times in one minute,

—He fired four times per minute while advancing forward at a rate of four miles in the hour;

—He reportedly poured water into the pan and barrel of the gun when loaded, so as to wet the powder, and then, in less than half a minute, fired it as well as ever without first extracting the ball.

Whether the British army is ready to try Captain Ferguson's rifle is still to be decided. But what is a matter of record is the captain's skill. In the course of the four experiments, firing at least thirty times, he only missed the target thrice.[8]

For his design, Ferguson received British Patent No. 1139 on December 2, 1776.

Common Protection

British officers destined for America are reported under orders to wear the same uniforms as common soldiers, and to dress their hair in the same manner. The reason: so they will not be as easily distinguished by American riflemen, who are said to aim first at officers.[9]

New Titles

According to court sources in London, at least two well-known names are on the list of those who will be created or raised in the peerage by his Majesty in coming months: Sir Fletcher Norton, speaker of the House of Commons, who will be titled Baron Fletcher; and Lord Howe, the British naval commander in America, who will become Viscount Howe and Earl of Nottingham.[10]

Press

New Motto

Reflecting a growing spirit of independence and a recognition of the tumult that must accompany it, Printer Alexander Purdie's *Virginia Gazette* has a new motto at the top of the first page: "High Heaven to Gracious Ends Directs the Storm."[11]

Books

"True Happiness"

Readers of the *London Chronicle* of Thursday, June 6th, could hardly miss a synopsis of the American Tory document, *Plain Truth;* it covered all of the first page and most of the second. Nor could readers fail to appreciate its value to the *Chronicle,* which introduced it by observing: "The author of it, in answer to the writer of *Common Sense,* undertakes to shew the scheme of independence is ruinous, delusive and impracticable . . . that perfect liberty and true happiness can only be obtained by reconciliation with the parent country."

Not to be partial, the *Chronicle* also ran extracts from *Common Sense* a week earlier. Displayed much less conspicuously, on the third page, that story could have been missed.[12]

THE WEEK OF JUNE 10TH

The War

"Huzza for Washington"

> "Great WASHINGTON prepares the way,
> Nor can he doubt to win the day."

From the *Pennsylvania Packet*
May 13, 1776

In the year since he was appointed commander in chief of the Continental army (June 15, 1775), a tall, imposing man from Virginia has become the unquestioned hero of America and his name the certain symbol of its cause.

No other name so summons confidence as his to the patriot who sings of the British army:

Urg'd on by North and vengeance, these valiant champions came,
Loud bellowing TEA and TREASON! and George [III] was all on flame!
Yet sacrilegious as it seems, we REBELS still live on—
And laught at all your empty puffs, and so does WASHINGTON!

No other name so lends pride as his to a soldier who observed late last year: "I have been much gratified this day with a view of General Washington. His excellency was on horseback, in company with several military gentlemen. It was not difficult to distinguish him from all others; his personal appearance is truly noble and majestic, being tall and well proportioned. His dress is a blue coat with buff-colored facings, a rich epaulette on each shoulder, buff under dress, and an elegant small sword; a black cockade in his hat."

No other name so catches the spirit of the times—except, perhaps, that also of his wife. In Cambridge, Massachusetts, in January, an infant girl was baptized Mary Dandridge, in honor of the maiden name of Mrs. Washington. For her christening the child was dressed in blue and buff; in her hair was a sprig of evergreen—"emblematick," said her father, "of his excellency's glory and affection of people."

No surprise is it, then, that Americans sing this new song to the tune of "The British Grenadiers":

Vain Britons, boast no longer with proud indignity
By land your conquering legions, your matchless strength at sea!
Since WE your braver sons, incens'd, our swords have girded on,
Huzza, huzza, huzza, huzza for WAR and WASHINGTON![13]

Congress

The Debate is Postponed

Congress on Monday resumed debate on independence—again in committee of the whole, again in secret—and then postponed any further discussion by the whole of Congress until July, apparently to allow time for delegates to receive further instructions from home. This much is known of the day's events:

"After some time spent thereon, the president resumed the chair, and Mr. Harrison reported that the committee have had under consideration the matters referred to them, and have come to a resolution thereon: That the consideration of the first resolution be postponed to Monday, the first day of July next; and in the meanwhile, that no time be lost, in case Congress agree thereto, that a committee be appointed to prepare a declaration to the effect of the first resolution, which is in these words, 'That these United Colonies are, and of right ought to be, free and independent states; that they are absolved from all allegiance to the British crown; and that all political connection between them and the state of Great Britain is and ought to be totally dissolved.' "[14]

The Committee

As it resolved to do Monday, Congress on Tuesday named five of its members a committee to draw up a written declaration so that "no time be lost" should it later proclaim the independence of the United Colonies. The five, in the order appointed:

—Thomas Jefferson, thirty-three, of Virginia, one of the youngest members of Congress (though there are seven his junior) and a delegate since June of last year. A lawyer, tall and personable in manner, he is nevertheless a reluctant public speaker, rarely debates in Congress. Throughout his career in the Virginia House of Burgesses and now in Congress, he has shown the written and not the spoken word as his way of swaying minds. Few would deny that he is adept.

—John Adams, forty, one of Massachusetts' original delegates to the First Continental Congress and a guiding spirit still. He is a lawyer who has leaned more to public life than private practice. Learned and forthright. even if sometimes short-tempered, he is surely one of the most prominent members of Congress and one of its most effective and eloquent champions of independence.

—Dr. Benjamin Franklin, seventy, of Pennsylvania. Printer, postmaster, politician, philosopher, experimenter, inventor, diplomatic agent, and America's best known public citizen. Though he once saw the British Empire as a "big family" watched over by a "good mother," he has, like many another American, changed his mind. Ten years ago, as Pennsylvania's diplomatic agent in Britain, he told the House of Commons, in effect, America ought to be its own family even while it keeps the same mother. Today he would say it should be its own mother as well.

—Roger Sherman, fifty-five, of Connecticut. A cobbler and then a lawyer, he turned merchant at forty, sold books so successfully to students at Yale (while turning some of the profits into contributions toward a new chapel) that the college named him treasurer. He has been a judge of the Connecticut Superior Court as well since 1766. A member of Congress from the start, he is sometimes thought of as an "old Puritan" and a clumsy debater. But he is among the most independence-minded of all.

—Robert R. Livingston, twenty-nine, of New York. Nephew of his own colony's Philip Livingston and of New Jersey's William Livingston and brother-in-law of the late General Richard Montgomery, he has been a delegate since last year. Though less ardent a proponent of independence than the others—he would wait a while—he is sufficiently recognized as a patriot that the British Crown last year refused to renew his two-year-old appointment as Recorder of the City of New York. His appointment is likely meant to encourage New York to authorize its delegates to vote for independence. As of now, they cannot.

As of this date, there appear to have been seven delegates younger than Jefferson. Besides Robert R. Livingston, they were Elbridge Gerry (Massachusetts), thirty-one; Thomas Heyward, Jr. (South Carolina) twenty-nine; Thomas Lynch, Jr. (South Carolina), twenty-six; Edward Rutledge (South Carolina), twenty-six; Jonathan Dickinson Sergeant (New Jersey), thirty; and Thomas Stone (Maryland), thirty-three, though exact date of birth is uncertain. Sergeant resigned on June 22nd. Livingston, with other New York delegates, abstained from voting for independence July 2nd, and left Congress before the signing of the engrossed copy August 2nd. [15]

What Kind of Government?

Even though a vote on independence will not come until sometime in July, and even though there are still several delegations under instructions to oppose it, Congress has nevertheless begun exploring two major questions that must confront the government of an independent nation:

—In the first place, just what kind of a government should it be?

—And secondly, what will be that government's role in the world of nations?

To the first, Congress assigned a committee made up of one member from each colony. Its responsibility: "Prepare and digest the form of confederation to be entered into between these colonies." Its members: Josiah Bartlett, New Hampshire; Samuel Adams, Massachusetts; Stephen Hopkins, Rhode Island; Roger Sherman, Connecticut; Robert R. Livingston, New York; John Dickinson, Pennsylvania; Thomas McKean, Delaware; Thomas Stone, Maryland; Thomas Nelson, Jr., Virginia; Joseph Hewes, North Carolina; Edward Rutledge, South Carolina, and Button Gwinnett, Georgia. There is none from New Jersey. Two of its five delegates resigned earlier in the month, one is on military duty, and another has taken no active part in the proceedings. A new delegation is expected.

The second committee—Dickinson, Benjamin Franklin, John Adams, Benjamin Harrison and Robert Morris—must prepare a plan of treaties to be proposed to foreign powers in the event that independence is declared.

In this same eventful week, Congress also established a Board of War and Ordnance to supervise the war effort, and named as members John Adams, Harrison, Sherman, Rutledge and James Wilson. Under the committee will be a War Office, headed by a secretary, which will keep all records relating to the land forces of the United Colonies, including a register of all officers, records of the disposition of troops, and accounts of all artillery, arms, ammunition and stores of war supplies. The War Office will also supervise the raising, fitting out and dispatching of all land forces, and have care and direction of prisoners of war.[16]

Faithful Servant

A month late—understandable, perhaps, in view of the nature of recent business—the second Continental Congress this week took note of its first anniversary by paying tribute to one who has been an essential part of every matter of business, although he has never moved a resolution and never cast a vote.

To Charles Thomson, secretary of Congress, and by virtue of that position, secretary of the United Colonies, Congress awarded 1,200 dollars in consideration of his faithful services throughout the year that ended May the 10th.

Thomson might well have come to move a resolution or cast a vote as a member of the Pennsylvania delegation had he been less controversial in his views in the days that preceded the convening of the First Continental Congress in 1774. In his outlook, he was akin to John Adams, of whom, in fact, he was and is a close friend. But where that kind of spirit might have assured his election in Massachusetts, it did not in Pennsylvania. Once the First Continental Congress assembled in 1774, however, Thomson's acceptance among the more radical delegates—such as both John and Sam Adams—and his friendship with the more moderate Pennsylvania delegation, made him the uniquely acceptable choice for all. He was elected as secretary of the First Continental Congress, served for its duration, and was duly elected to the same position in the Second Congress that convened May 10, 1775. By now he is sufficiently a fixture of the governmental process that he seems likely to continue as long as he wishes—serving, in many ways, a more important role than he might have as a delegate.[17]

President "Great Tree"

Although of no small import in its own right, Congress's policy toward the Indians provided a moment of diversion from the weighty consequence of matters that dominated the colonies' delegates this week.

As it did with the Delawares a month before, Congress entertained representatives of the Six Iroquois Nations to assure them of the peaceful intentions of the United Colonies. Specifically, said Congress: "We hope the friendship that is between you and us will be firm, and continue as long as the sun shall shine, and the waters run . . ."

Congress then presented the Indian delegates with a number of gifts. In return, Iroquois Chief Onondago announced that President John Hancock will become an honorary chieftain, and henceforth be known among the Six Nations as Karanduaân, or "Great Tree."[18]

The Colonies

The Inherent Rights of Man

". . . it devolves to the people, who have a right to resume their original liberty, and by the establishment of a new legislative (such as they shall think fit) provide for their own safety and security, which is the end for which they are in society."

John Locke
Two Treatises on Government, 1690

If all men are equal, it is a fact not universally conceded by governments throughout history. If all men are entitled to acquire property, to have free exercise of their religious beliefs, to have free suffrage, to have a free press—it is not the case that they have always been accorded those rights.

The rights of man have been more often the province of theorists, such as John Locke nearly a century ago, or a few years before him, Thomas Hobbes, whose *Leviathan* (1651) addressed itself this way: "The *right of nature,* which writers commonly call *jus naturale,* is the liberty each man hath, to use his own power, as he will himself, for the preservation of his own nature."

Nor are the rights of man only a question for modern times. In the ancient world Cicero, in *De Officiis,* (45–44 B.C.) said much the same: *"Jus enim semper est quaesitium aequabile; neque enim aliter esset jus."* (What people have always sought is equality of rights before the law. For rights that were not open to all alike would be no rights.)

From time to time, the charters of government have caught up with such theory, and established new and broader standards of individual freedom and liberty. The Magna Charta in 1215 sought to resolve the relative powers of the king and the barons, but also set forth certain rights of the people. Among them:

> *Nullus liber homo capiatur vel imprisonetur, aut disseisiatur, aut utlagetur, aut exuletur, aut aliquo modo destruatur, nec super eum ibimus, nec super eum mittemus, nisi per legale judicium parium suorum vel per legem terrae.*

> No freemen shall be taken or imprisoned or disseised or exiled or in any way destroyed, nor will we go upon him nor send upon him, except by the lawful judgment of his peers or by the law of the land.

And it interpreted the concept of equality in terms even the least literate could understand:

> *Una mensura vini sit per totum regnum nostrum, et una mensura cervisie. . .*

> Let there be one measure of wine throughout our whole realm, and one measure of ale . . .

In more recent times, the "Act declaring the Rights and Liberties of the Subject and Setleing the Succession of the Crowne," more commonly known as the English Bill of Rights, in 1689 concluded the Glorious Revolution, ended the divine right of kings, established the pre-eminence of Parliament, and asserted additional rights of the common man: the right of subjects to petition the king; the right of subjects (provided their being Protestant) to bear arms; the right of free elections to Parliament; and the prohibition of "cruell and unusuall punishments."

Nowhere, however, have man's notions of freedom been more sweepingly translated into political principles than in a document debated over the last few weeks and approved June 12th by the representatives of the Colony of Virginia gathered in Convention in Williamsburg. A Declaration of Rights, it is intended not as an idle assortment of governmental virtues, but as the very "basis and foundation of government"—the latter being the next major question facing the Convention.

Among the declaration's tenets, and thus the principles of a new government in Virginia:

—"That all men are by nature equally free and independent and have certain inherent rights . . . namely, the enjoyment of life and liberty, with the means of acquiring and possessing property, and pursuing and obtaining happiness and safety."

—"That government is, or ought to be instituted for the common benefit, protection, and security of the people . . . and that when any government shall be found inadequate or contrary to these purposes, a majority of the community hath an indubitable, unalienable and indefeasible right to reform, alter or abolish it."

—"That elections of members to serve as representatives of the people in assembly ought to be free, and that all men having sufficient evidence of permanent common interest with, and attachment to the community, have the right of suffrage."

—"That in all capital or criminal prosecutions a man hath a right to demand the cause and nature of his accusation, to be confronted with the accusers and witnesses, to call for evidence in his favour, and to a speedy trial by an impartial jury of his vicinage, without whose unanimous consent he cannot be found guilty; nor can he be compelled to give evidence against himself."

—"That excessive bail ought not to be required, nor excessive fines imposed, nor cruel and unusual punishments inflicted."

—"That the freedom of the press is one of the great bulwarks of liberty."

—That "the military should be under strict subordination to, and governed by, the civil power."

—That "all men are equally entitled to the free exercise of religion, according to the dictates of conscience; and that it is the mutual duty of all to practise Christian forbearance, love, and charity towards each other."

Thus distilling the wisdom and consolidating the virtues of both the theory and practice of government from ancient times to the present, the Virginia Declaration of Rights must rank as one of the most significant political documents of them all—and a model others will likely follow.[19]

The Influence of Locke

Clearly influential in the writing of the Virginia Declaration of Rights, and perhaps more so than those of any other, are the writings of the English philosopher, John Locke, whose *Second Treatise on Government* must be regarded a source of inspiration to George Mason and the others who wrote the Virginia declaration. A reprint of that treatise was published three years ago in Boston by Edes and Gill under the title, *An Essay Concerning the True and Original Extent and End of Civil Government*. Precursing even the language of that adopted in Williamsburg, Locke's *Essay* asserted, "Men being, as has been said, by nature all free, equal and independent, no one can be put out of this estate and subjected to the political power of another without his own consent."

From the same document are other concepts which will undoubtedly have a measure of significance in the same convention's deliberations on a new form of government for Virginia. Said Locke:

On separate legislative and executive functions: "The legislative power is that which has a right to direct how the force of the commonwealth shall be employed for preserving the community and the members of it . . . . But because the laws that are at once and in a short time made have a constant and lasting force, and need a perpetual execution or an attendance thereunto, therefore it is necessary there should be a power always in being which should see to the execution of the laws that are made and remain in force."

And further: ". . . because it may be too great a temptation to human frailty, apt to grasp at power, for the same persons who have the power of making laws to have also in their hands the power to execute them, whereby they may exempt themselves from obedience to the laws they make, and suit the law, both in its making and execution, to their own private advantage."

One other of Locke's works, *A Letter Concerning Toleration*, has also been published in America. A copy of the third edition was printed in Boston by Rogers and Fowle in 1743 and a copy of the fourth edition in Wilmington in 1764.[20]

Boston Port: An Anniversary

June 14th, 1774, was the last day that trading vessels, other than British ships serving the garrison, were allowed to enter or leave the port of Boston. It was the day the Boston Port Act went into effect, Parliament thus punishing the people of Boston for turning the harbor into a pot of tea one winter night six months before.

June 14th this year Boston was once again an open port, the siege ended and British forces long departed. His Majesty's ships were allowed to enter only at the peril of becoming the prizes of American privateers.

The closing of the port two years ago, observed a correspondent in

Boston, was "through the cruelty of an act of Parliament"; the reopening of the harbor was "through the blessing of God upon the operations of a much injured and oppressed people."[21]

Georgia: All Above One

In weighing the great issues of the day, Georgia's delegates in the Continental Congress are under instructions to consider the good of all the colonies above the interests of Georgia.

Said that colony's Congress to its delegates in Philadelphia: "[We] . . . recommend it to you always to keep in view the general utility, remembering that the great and righteous cause in which we are engaged is not provincial, but continental."[22]

Voting on Independence

In Philadelphia, to the 2,000 militiamen of the 1st, 2nd, 4th and 5th Battalions of Associators of the city and its suburbs, was proposed the question of independence for the colonies. The answer was not unanimous. Four officers and twenty-three privates in the 1st Battalion, and two privates in the 2nd were opposed. The other 1,971-odd men declared themselves in favor.[23]

Advice to Women

With summer and the increased likelihood of thunderstorms approaching, *Pennsylvania Magazine* took occasion to warn women that some of their fashionable modes of dress can be hazardous. The magazine's advice: Don't wear wires in caps or pins in the hair, thus risking death by lightning.[24]

Foreign News

The Demurring Sister

Though it was the site of the first European settlement in North America, the colony of East Florida—a British possession since it was ceded by Spain in 1763—has remained for the most part a quiet wilderness unmarked by those signs of growth that characterize the colonies to the north. It has likewise spurned the hot passion of rebellion in favor of the warm lassitude of the southern sun.

That may not always be so. A correspondent in London thinks a cool and cloudy day may yet admit the spread of rebellion from the north, and that the "infant colony" of East Florida may yet follow "the example of her elder sisters."[25]

Theater

Into the Wings

> "And when this transient world's gay scenes are o'er;
> When life's dark curtain falls to rise no more,
> May your good actions, like your acting shine,
> And plaudits gain, immortal and divine."
> *The London Chronicle*
> June 15, 1776

When he made his first appearance on stage—at Goodman's Fields, London, more than thirty years ago—British theater was in a state of decline. Performances were no match for the earlier days of Booth and Wilkes and Cibber. Passion and feeling had given way to ranting and vociferation. Shakespeare, once revived, was again lapsing into obscurity.

When he made his final appearance on stage—at Drury-Lane on Monday night as Don Felix in *The Wonder*—British theater was strong, healthy, diversified, again replete with Shakespeare worthy of admiration. In large part, the story of the revival of the British stage is also the story of David Garrick, now beginning his retirement at the age of fifty-nine.

It was perhaps more through his mastery of Shakespeare than through any other accomplishment that Garrick the actor first gained recognition. "He was," said an acquaintance, "like a hawk who flies directly at his prey, seizing the most finished and difficult parts of our great bard and making them his own." Hamlet, Macbeth, Richard and Lear—these roles in particular, but others as well—Garrick seized and polished to a new luster, and made popular again. Outside Goodman's Fields, where before the customers of any sort were sometimes scarce, the coaches of the nobility now lined up and passers-by knew why. At his start, there were never more than six or eight Shakespearean productions a season in the repertory of the entire British theater; in recent seasons, Garrick's company alone has been producing on the average eighteen or twenty. Thus, more than any other actor, has Garrick returned Shakespeare to his place of eminence.

As a manager he had the trying job of reconciling jealousies, controlling tempers, and directing competitiveness toward the constructive end of excellence in performance. He never pleased all, as indeed no one could, but he approached these demands with the same sort of understanding that he devoted to his acting roles. Like Molière a century ago, his managerial role was that of the affectionate father: he raised salaries because he felt a better standard of living was due and owing the profession; he established a perpetual fund so that aged and infirm actors would never have to face the poverty so many have known in the past. Indeed, said one, the tears of his actors on his leaving the stage will be the truest compliment of all.

If as manager he was thus dedicated to the players, he was equally committed to those who wrote the plays he produced. Once he espoused a new work, he would never forsake it, even risking the displeasure of the public to do justice to the author. As playwright himself, and as that only, Garrick would also have commanded attention.

Actor, manager, author—David Garrick has dominated British theater so completely that another of his stature is not even in the wings. Said one who knows him well, quoting David Garrick's own favorite author:

> ". . . take him for all in all.
> I shall not look upon his like again."[26]

Press

Biggest Story?

"The important day is come, or near at hand, that America is to assume a form of government for herself."

So said the *New York Journal* last week in a story that could well be a sound prediction. If so, the *Journal* believes it will be not only the biggest story it has ever covered, but the most important told by any newspaper anywhere in the world in centuries.

Said the *Journal*: "The affair now in view is the most important that ever was before America. . . . it is the most important that has been transacted in any nation for some centuries past. If our [new] civil government is well constructed, and well managed, America bids fair to be the most glorious state that has ever been on earth."[27]

Books

Popular Pamphlet

As a condemnation of his country's policies toward America, Richard Price's *Observations on the Nature of Civil Liberty* was immediately popular in England, where it was published early this year. So great was the demand that it was in its fifth edition by the middle of March. On the 14th of that month, the anti-Administration government of the City of London showed its opinion of *Observations,* on the one hand, and of the national Administration on the other, by according Dr. Price its highest honor, the Freedom of the City.

Since then, thousands of copies more have been sold in England, and many have reached the United Colonies. Now there is also an American edition. It was published in Boston by T. & J. Fleet, and went on sale June 13th.[28]

THE WEEK OF JUNE 17TH

The War

Alert in New York

Warned by Congress to prepare for the worst, the city of New York is girding for the possibility of invasion by the British.

The alert came in the form of a letter from President of Congress John Hancock to the convention of the colony, requesting that the militia be called forth. Said Hancock: "Congress this day received advice, and are fully convinced, that it is the design of General Howe to make an attack upon the city of New York as soon as possible. . . . The important day is at hand that will decide not only the fate of the city of New York but of the whole province.

"On such an occasion there is no necessity to use arguments with Americans; their feelings, I well know, will prompt them to do their duty, and the sacredness of the cause will urge them to the field."

With the arrival of two battalions from Pennsylvania and militia from New Jersey and Connecticut, American troops in and around New York are expected to total about 25,000.[29]

Agonizing Delay

"Their decisions are most afflictingly slow," wrote General Artemas Ward in Boston to General Washington in New York, "when everything calls for the utmost ardour and despatch."

Ward was reporting on the progress of the Massachusetts Assembly in raising additional soldiers for the relief of troops in Canada and New York. He explained that the Assembly, meeting in Watertown, is an unusually large body, and that half its members are new this year.

"My soul," said Ward, "at times is ready to die within me at the delays; at others, my blood to press out of the pores of my body."[30]

Congress

A Warning on Justice

Congress this week reminded local government and citizen alike throughout the colonies that the exigencies of war and tumult should not be considered grounds for groups of citizens taking the law into their own hands.

Instructed Congress: "No man in these colonies charged with being a tory, or unfriendly to the cause of American liberty, [should] be injured in his person or property, or in any manner whatever disturbed, unless the proceeding against him be founded on an order of this Congress or the assembly, convention, council or committee of safety of the colony, or the committee of inspection and observation of the district where he resides; provided however that this resolution shall not prevent the apprehending any person found in the commission of some act destructive of American liberty, or justly suspected of a design to commit such act and intending to escape."

In such a case, the accused must still be brought before the proper authority for examination and trial.

Congress this week also acted to improve the clothing situation of Continental army soldiers by asking each colony to be responsible for procuring, or having manufacturered by contract, one set of clothes for each soldier who enlisted in that colony. Each set is to contain a waistcoat and breeches, which may be made of deer leather if the price is reasonable: one blanket, a felt hat, two shirts, two pair of hose, and two pair of shoes.

The colonies, while paying directly for such clothing, may later apply to Congress for reimbursement. Ultimately, however, it is each soldier himself who will bear the cost—through a deduction from pay when the clothing reaches him in the field.

In other action, Congress resolved to hold no further regular sessions on Saturday—instead to use that day for committee business.[31]

The Colonies

Poor William

In his thirteen years as Governor of New Jersey, Pennsylvania-born William Franklin has never wavered in his allegiance to the crown that appointed him. During the same period, the prevailing mood of the people of New Jersey has shifted markedly.

For New Jersey's Provincial Congress and for its leading Tory, a breech thus became inevitable. It was hastened when Franklin, on May 30th, called for a convening of the colony's General Assembly, a constituent part of royal government now effectively supplanted by the popularly elected Provincial Congress. The Congress, meeting in Burlington. answered Franklin's call on June 14th with a resolution that it "ought not to be obeyed," and the next day determined to end the breech in government once and for all by deposing the governor.

In part reacting to its suspicion that Franklin's chief public duty of late has been supplying intelligence to Great Britain, and in part to its desire to establish a new government in the colony, the Congress on June 15th found that Franklin's call for a convening of the Assembly was in direct violation of a resolve of the Continental Congress on May 15th [advising the colonies to begin forming their own governments], and therefore, by a vote of 42 to 10, declared Franklin "an enemy of the liberties of this country," and ordered him arrested and held for a hearing.

Friday, playing his loyalist role to the hilt, Franklin appeared before the Provincial Congress, but with characteristic stubbornness refused to answer the charge; he argued only that the Congress, having usurped the King's government in the Province, was therefore an illegal body with no authority to take action against him—or, for that matter, any action whatsoever.

The Provincial Congress saw it differently. It now declared Franklin a "virulent" enemy, and ordered him held for the Continental Congress to dispose of as it sees fit.

Thus comes the end of the public career of one of America's most enigmatic men. A once idle youth who came to apply himself industriously in government, first as a comptroller of the post office and then as clerk of the Pennsylvania Provincial Assembly, he might have joined the ranks of the patriots but for a visit to England with his father in 1762 that led—without his father's knowledge—to appointment as a royal governor.

Those who saw his selection as a hopeful sign thirteen years ago, however, could not long overlook Franklin's show of loyalty to the crown and could only abandon hope that the native-born son of a famous American would make any more conciliatory a royal governor than the rest. Surely not the least disappointed has been Franklin's father, Benjamin.[32]

New Delegation

Its old regarded as at best lukewarm to independence, New Jersey has sent a new delegation to the Continental Congress. The new members —Richard Stockton, John Witherspoon, Francis Hopkinson, John Hart and Abraham Clark—are not only independence-minded themselves, but have instructions to vote for a declaration establishing the colonies as free and independent states.[33]

"To Toasting!"

General George Washington, his staff officers, and the commanding officers of regiments stationed in or near the City of New York this week were guests of the New York Provincial Assembly at—said an observer— an "elegant entertainment."

The evening included no fewer than thirty-one toasts, starting with, "To the Congress," and ending with, "To civil and religious liberty to all mankind." In between participants also: saluted "the friends to the rights of mankind in every part of the earth"; opined that "the crown of tyrants be the crown of thorns"; and exhorted "the generous sons of St. Patrick [to] expel all the venomous reptiles of Britain."[34]

Foreign News

Prussian Influence

According to a report from Hamburg, Great Britain has renewed a request to Russia for the loan of 15,000 Cossacks for service in America. Such an agreement has been frustrated in the past through the influence of King Frederick II of Prussia, who is known to consider many policies of the British Administration toward its colonies to be "highly impolitic."

In the view of this same correspondent in Hamburg, Prussia is not alone in taking such a position. He reports: "Foreign powers hesitate to lend aid to Great Britain to subdue America, as their interest absolutely consists in the latter's independency, and particularly in the abolishment of the Navigation Act, which as long as it remains in force, all the foreign nations are obliged to purchase all the productions of America from the English, after paying enormous duties and commissions to England."[35]

Music

Upward Modulation

Now in its thirty-ninth year, the London-based Fund for the Support of Decayed Musicians and their Families is a form of mutual assistance society dedicated to seeing that aged and destitute musicians, or their survivors, will not face the penury so many of their profession have in times past.

Among its benefits: subsistence payments to infirm musicians, in amounts determined by the governors of the fund; care for children of musicians, if they are otherwise destitute; a weekly allowance of up to seven shillings for widows (to cease upon remarriage) ; and up to five shillings toward the funeral expenses of a member (if he died without leaving provision for same).

In part the fund operates through charitable donations. The largest such contribution, 1,000 *l*, was provided through the will of the late George Frideric Handel, who died in 1759. But by far the largest source of operating revenue has been the annual payments of subscribers. When the fund was established in April, 1738, these payments were fixed at ten shillings per year. This week, taking note of the steadily increasing cost of living, the Board of Governors voted to raise the cost of subscription in the fund to 20 shillings per year.[36]

THE WEEK OF JUNE 24TH

The War

The Plot Against Washington

An apparent Tory attempt to infiltrate the personal guard of General Washington, and then murder him and other staff officers, blow up magazines and block entrances to the city, was uncovered and broken up last weekend by the Headquarters of the Continental Army in New York.

Arrests were made throughout the weekend, including New York's mayor, two members of Washington's personal guard, and a noted gunsmith. At least thirty-four persons were imprisoned. There is also a report that the general's housekeeper is involved. Money to finance the scheme allegedly came from Loyalist Governor William Tryon.

It is understood that Mayor David Matthews was questioned Sunday, and that he asknowledged paying 140 *l* received from Governor Tryon to a gunsmith named Gilbert Forbes for guns to be used in the plot. Matthews remains under guard.

Among those arrested were six Tories captured Saturday on Long Island and now under confinement in the Jamaica jail. A seventh was killed by Continental soldiers during the capture.

While it appears the plot was broken up before any injury or damage was done, it is thought that as many as 500 persons may be involved in the scheme and that many thus remain at large.[37]

Court-Martial of a Plotter

By Tuesday, there emerged a key suspect in the plot on the life of General Washington: one from his own guard, a private sentinel named Thomas Hickey. The Army wasted no time, ordered Hickey before a court-martial the next day. He is the only one thus far brought to trial, though the others remain imprisoned.

The court, presided over by Colonel Samuel Parsons, heard four witnesses. William Green, a fellow member of Washington's guard, told of a political discussion three weeks ago with gunsmith Gilbert Forbes, in which the plot first came to his attention. Green said Forbes invited him to enlist in the King's service, and he did so only "with a view to cheat the Tories and detect their scheme." Green said he in turn was to enlist others, but in the case of Hickey, secretly swore him to fight for America. Then he proposed to Hickey to reveal the plot to the general, but said Hickey suggested waiting to uncover further details. That, said William Green, was the extent to which he was involved.

Gilbert Forbes then testified that he had received more than 100 *l* from Mayor Matthews, and had given Green eighteen dollars of this with which to pay those enlisted in the plot one dollar each and ten shillings a week in subsistence. He himself gave Hickey half a dollar. But, contradicting the earlier testimony, the gunsmith claimed it was Green who drew him into the scheme, and not the other way around.

Next was William Welch, who told of a conversation with Hickey in a grog shop. Hickey, he said, claimed that the colonies had no chance against the British, and that it was best for "us Old Countrymen to make our peace before they came, or they would kill us all." Welch said he "did not relish the project," spurned the offer of a dollar as encouragement, and parted Hickey's company.

An admitted Tory, Isaac Ketchum, was then the last to testify for the prosecution. He had met Hickey in jail a week before, where Hickey had been committed on suspicion of counterfeiting. Hickey told him of the plot, and that eight of the General's guard were involved, but mentioned only Green by name. The accused, said Ketchum, stated clearly that they were to turn against America when the King's troops arrived.

In his defense, Thomas Hickey offered no evidence, and only a simple statement: that he engaged in the scheme at first for the sake of cheating the Tories, and getting some money from them, and afterward consented to have his name sent on board a British man-of-war so that if the enemy won, and he were taken prisoner, he might be safe.

The court took little time to reach a unanimous verdict: guilty of the charge and of a breach of the Fifth and Thirtieth Articles of the Rules and Regulations of the Continental Forces. Thomas Hickey was sentenced to be hanged by the neck until dead.[38]

An Unhappy Fate

Just off Bowery Lane in New York, in a field between the encampments of Brigadier General Spencer and Lord Stirling, at eleven o'clock Friday morning, Thomas Hickey was hanged by the neck, his death throes watched under order by all available members of the Continental Army for whom, if need be, the execution might serve as a lesson. Were it not enough, Continental Army Headquarters later in the day issued a terse reminder: "The unhappy fate of Thomas Hickey, executed this day for mutiny, sedition, and treachery, the General hopes, will be a warning to every soldier in the Army to avoid those crimes and all others so disgraceful to the character of a soldier, and pernicious to his country, whose pay he receives and bread he eats. And in order to avoid those crimes, the most certain method is to keep out of the temptation of them, and particularly to avoid lewd women, who, by the dying confession of this poor criminal, first led him into practices which ended in an untimely and ignominious death."[39]

No other suspects in the plot were ever brought to trial.

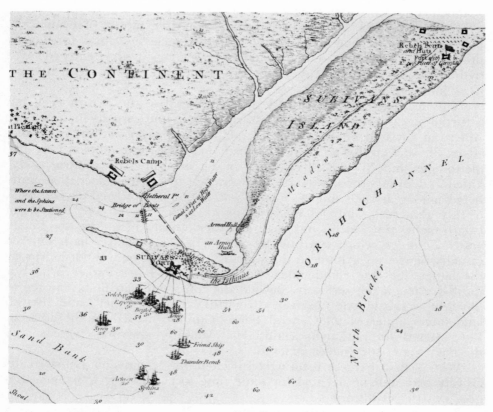

THE BATTLE OF SULLIVAN'S ISLAND *(William Faden, London, 1776).*
The essential action of the engagement of June 28th is contained in this map
published in London August 10, 1776. Not shown in this detail is Long Island,
which is to the northeast of the "Rebel Tents and Huts" shown in the upper
right. The city of Charleston is about four and a half miles across the harbor
to the west.

Map Division—New York Public Library—
Astor, Lenox and Tilden Foundations

Battle of Sullivan's Island

For most of the month of June it was clear the next clash of arms between America and Britain would come in the harbor of Charleston. And so it has—with an outcome neither side could have predicted with as much certainty as the inevitability of the battle.

For an untested American command, comprised mostly of troops who had never seen a shot fired in anger, it was a clear victory; for a well-prepared British force—even though its attack was apparently delayed by unfavorable wind and tide conditions—it was an equally clear, if somewhat inexplicable defeat.

The decisiveness is evident by the withdrawal of the British fleet, but a further measure of the contest is apparent in the casualty figures. The American garrison on Sullivan's Island, in Charleston harbor, commanded by South Carolina's Colonel William Moultrie, was protected by palmetto logs and by the effectiveness of its own fire; it counted twelve killed and twenty-three wounded. Meanwhile the British fleet, that numbered among it such mighty men-of-war as the *Bristol* and *Experiment*, of fifty guns each, and the *Solebay*, *Sphinx*, *Active*, *Syren* and *Acteon*, of twenty-eight guns each, and many smaller vessels including the bomb vessel *Thunder*, which can hurl mortar shells a mile and a half, suffered casualty figures far grimmer: an estimated 180 killed or wounded. Among the latter: the fleet commander, Commodore Sir Peter Parker, who was injured, though not seriously. Beyond the toll in human flesh, damage to the fleet was, said one observer, "frightful." On the other hand, British land forces under Major General Henry Clinton, massed on the adjacent Long Island for onslaught against the American garrison, were spared the navy's fate; they never attacked.

Why a British force seemingly sufficient for its mission failed so decisively may well be debated for some time to come; how it happened is now a matter of history.

At half after ten Friday morning, the 28th, the *Thunder* began a mortar barrage from a mile and a half away, and the *Bristol*, *Experiment*, *Active* and *Solebay* began moving in for the attack on Sullivan's Island. From their fort on the island, Moultrie's Second Regiment of Provincials, a detachment of artillery and some volunteers, answered the fire. For the next eight hours, virtually without interruption, there ensued, to use an observer's words, "one of the most heavy and incessant cannonades perhaps ever known." The sky darkened with a hail of lead and iron and billowing clouds of smoke.

For the British, things went badly from the start. Only an hour into the battle, the *Sphinx*, *Acteon* and *Syren* got entangled on a shoal. Two managed to get free; the *Acteon* remained aground, all the while devastated by American fire, and later was abandoned and burned. The American cannonade, meanwhile, was exacting a dreadful toll. The *Bristol*, Parker's flagship, was extensively damaged, and had the sea not been calm, probably would have sunk. The mizzenmast shot away and the mainmast badly damaged, sails and rigging plummeted to the deck. Every man stationed on the quarter-decks appeared to have been either killed or wounded as at least 70 cannon balls found their mark. The ship's commander, Captain John Morris, was reported to have lost an arm. Commodore Parker was said to be injured. Other ships suffered their share of damage, but particularly the *Experiment*. It was obvious the Americans were concentrating their fire on the fifty-gunners.

On the island garrison, British shelling was doing nowhere near the same sort of damage. The *Thunder* hurled more than fifty shells into the fort, but many landed in a moat filled with water, their fusees thus extinguished before they could explode. Others plowed into the sand, exploding harmlessly. The palmetto walls of the fort also dissipated much of the effectiveness of the British fire; cannon balls and bullets alike were merely absorbed in the spongy wood.

Somewhere in the course of the afternoon, the troops under Clinton and Major General Cornwallis were obviously to have stormed the American garrison from their staging ground on Long Island. They did not, perhaps unsure of the terrain, perhaps feeling the naval cover insufficient.

After seven at night, the fire slackened considerably. By eleven it was over, Commodore Sir Peter Parker's wrecked fleet and dispirited crews retiring into the darkness. A further assault on Charleston—at least for the present—is remote. It therefore remains for Commodore Parker to reclaim General Clinton's troops from Long Island, and then to depart entirely.[40]

A military dictionary published in 1776 described a bomb as a shell of cast iron filled with powder and detonated by means of a fuse which ignited from the flash in the chamber of the mortar from which it was fired. Bombs ranged in weight from 50 to 500 pounds.

Misnomer

Americans defending Sullivan's Island against attack by the British may have wondered about the choice of names when they found that one of the ships firing against them was called the *Friendship*.[41]

Fraternity

The Continental Army, Northern Department, has a new Deputy Paymaster. He is Ebenezer Hancock, of Boston, brother of the President of the Continental Congress.[42]

Congress

Imprisonment for Franklin

As it promised New Jersey it would do if the colony found its governor guilty of being an enemy of America, Congress this week ordered the confinement of William Franklin as a prisoner of the United Colonies.

The New Jersey Convention's finding was clear: Franklin is a "virulent enemy to this country, and a person that may prove dangerous [and should] be confined in such place and manners as the Continental Congress shall direct."

Thus for the Tory son of one of America's most distinguished citizens and patriots, the end of a public career more British than American in its interests will be in the custody of another governor—Jonathan Trumbull of Connecticut, whose disposition has been more American than British. By directive of Congress, Franklin will have some latitude in the form of confinement. He will be offered parole, with some degree of freedom, in exchange for his word to remain neutral throughout the hostilities. Should he not agree to that, he will be held as a prisoner of war in accordance with the recent regulations established by Congress.

In other action this week, Congress asked General Washington to compile a list of all officer vacancies in the Continental army, and to furnish the same to Congress along with his recommendations for filling them.[43]

Added Incentive

By resolution of Congress, a bounty of ten dollars is now being offered to every noncommissioned officer and soldier who agrees to enlist in the Continental army for a term of three years. Enlistments in the past have normally been for one year at a time.[44]

The Colonies

For Independence: Pennsylvania

Slowing down the move toward independence has been the simple reality that the largest delegation in the Continental Congress—Pennsylvania's nine representatives—has been bound by orders to vote against it since November 9th of last year.

That is now one reason less. Pennsylvania's Provincial Congress, meeting in Philadelphia, has changed its orders, and voted unanimously "its willingness to concur in a vote of the [Continental] Congress declaring the United Colonies free and independent states." Moreover, said the Provincial deputies with considerable conviction: it is a change of heart deemed to have "the approbation, consent and authority of our constituents."[45]

For Independence: Maryland

As Pennsylvania did earlier in the week, so has the Colony of Maryland also: withdrawn its refusal to vote for independence. Thus, the debate that is to begin July 1st more and more appears leading to a formal separation from Great Britain.

The resolution of the Convention of Maryland was a cancellation of the instructions of last December that prohibited Maryland's representatives voting in favor of independence. Henceforth, the delegation—if at least three of its members so agree—may concur with the other of the United Colonies in declaring themselves free and independent states. The middle colonies, heretofore glowing, are beginning to burn.[46]

Moderation for Moderation

Since correspondence of his with Lord George Germaine, British Secretary of State for the Colonies, was intercepted in early April and forwarded to Congress, Maryland's royal Governor Robert Eden has been a marked man. Congress, believing Eden to be wholly aiding the British cause and subverting the American, asked the Maryland Council of Safety to take the governor into custody and begin an investigation pending the next meeting of the Convention of Maryland, which would make a final disposition of the case.

The Council did act, but with considerably more moderation than an irate Congress had intended. Instead of keeping Eden in custody, the Council gave him parole upon only his promise to remain in the colony until the Convention could meet.

Such moderation would have been unlikely in many another colony, where royal governors themselves have been much less moderate to begin with. Governor since 1768—and that largely by virtue of having three years earlier married Caroline Calvert, sister of the Lord Proprietor of Maryland—Eden nevertheless has made a point of attempting to see both sides in the dispute between the colonies and the mother country, and perhaps more than any other royal governor has attempted to be a mediating force even though his ultimate allegiance is doubtless to England.

The Convention that assembled in Annapolis May 7th appears to have taken that spirit of moderation in mind when it rendered its verdict on May 23rd. Stopping short of what Congress likely intended, the Convention merely found that Eden's "longer continuance in the province, at so critical a period, might be prejudicial" and asked him to leave. To do so, Eden had to await the arrival of a British ship, and he did so with ever mounting apprehension that, in the meantime, the Convention might change its mind and mete out a harsher penalty.

At last, some weeks late, the frigate *Fowey* arrived, and this week Eden left for England.

Governor Eden once talked of his job as requiring him to "steer as long as should be possible, clear of those shoals which all here must, sooner or later, I fear, get shipwrecked upon." While at last he may not have been able to steer entirely clear, his helmsmanship of moderation was ultimately recognized. It is hard to conceive of Virginia or New Jersey or Massachusetts judging their last royal governors as benevolently as Maryland has judged Governor Eden.[47]

A Parting Word

Still every inch a Tory—although no longer the Tory governor of New Jersey—William Franklin delivered a parting word Thursday to the all-but-defunct Council and Assembly of the colony, which like Franklin himself, has been superseded by the popularly elected Provincial Congress.

Even as he conceded the Council and Assembly would not likely meet again, he sought to exhort their members—and indirectly, the people of the colony—in a proclamation issued at Perth Amboy, and what he exhorted was this: "Avoid, above all things, the traps of independency and republicanism now set for you, however temptingly they may be baited."

The outcome, said Franklin, will only be "an independent republican tyranny—the worst and most debasing of all possible tyrannies. . . . It will never suit a people who have tasted the sweets of British liberty under a British constitution. When the present high fever shall abate of its warmth, and the people are once more able coolly to survey and compare their past with their present situation, they will, as naturally as the sparks fly upwards, wreak their vengeance on the heads of those who, taking advantages of their delirium, had plunged them into such difficulties and distress."[48]

Still Another

Virginia this week became the third colony to adopt a constitution and establish a government independent from that set up by royal authority. As in New Hampshire and South Carolina, where constitutions were adopted earlier in the year, effective government had been suspended through absence of the royal governor.

Virginia's new government is similar to those of the other two colonies, except that both houses of the legislature—the House of Delegates (comprised of two representatives of each county) and the Senate (one representative from each of 24 districts)—will be elected by the people. In New Hampshire and South Carolina the members of the second house are elected by the first. Virginia's governor, meanwhile, will be elected by joint ballot of the House of Delegates and the Senate, as in the colonies earlier adopting constitutions.

Otherwise noteworthy are the use of the term "Senate" for the upper house, the first formal use by a legislature in modern times, and the term "Commonwealth," reminiscent of the writings of both John Locke and Thomas Hobbes as well as the government of England under Cromwell (1649–60).

The Constitution, like the Declaration of Rights adopted June 12th, is largely the work of George Mason.[49]

"Senate" was not the only use of historic terminology. Virginia's state house was called "The Capitol," the first such use of that term in America, and quite possibly the first time that term was applied to a building since Roman times.

Economy

"In these times of difficulty and distress, it is necessary to practice the utmost economy in the distribution of the public money."

So read the resolution of the delegates to the Convention of Virginia, meeting in Williamsburg. This week, backing principle with practice, they did something to economize: they reduced their own pay from forty-five to thirty shillings a day.[50]

Foreign News

Strike Averted

A threatened strike by London carpenters over a pay increase of two shillings a week has apparently been averted through the concerted resistance of their employers and magistrates' warnings of the full imposition of the law against conspiring to strike.

The threat of a strike developed out of a meeting of the carpenters and joiners of London, Westminster, Southwark and surrounding towns on June 17th at the Kings-Head Tavern. There the workers agreed upon a series of steps intended to bring about not only an increase in pay but, in the long run, greater power in their dealings with employers. Thus did the workers agree:

—To ask their masters for an advance in wages of two shillings per week "and upon his refusal, every man employed in his service to strike and quit his business on Saturday next, until he complies with all reasonable requests;"

—To accept no raise as an individual, unless the same raise is given to all others in the same employ;

—To contribute to a fund for the support of those out of employ;

—To refuse to work for any master who has not yet settled the matter of wages;

—To purchase, at five shillings, a card showing membership in the carpenters' committee, which card would then entitle him to work for any master with whom he could find employ;

—To compile a list of all carpenters continuing to work without a raise, and to strike each new employer to whom that worker thereafter goes.

That kind of action could not be taken lightly by employers, and was not. The Master Carpenters and Joiners of London met the following week, and jointly agreed not to comply with the wage demands of the journeymen. Furthermore, they would henceforth refuse to hire a new journeyman unless he presented a certificate of good behavior from his last employer.

A crisis was averted this week when London magistrates issued a public proclamation warning that the circulation of a handbill listing the workers' demands was "inciting conspiracy" and punishable under the law. To prevent the unwary from being drawn into such unlawful activity, the magistrates published an extract of an Act of Parliament dating back to the 2nd and 3rd years [1548–49] of Edward VI: "That if any artificers, workmen or labourers do conspire, covenant or promise together, or make any oaths that they shall not make or do their works but at a certain price or rate, or shall not enterprize or take upon them to finish that another hath begun, or shall do but a certain work in a day, or shall not work but at certain hours and times, that then every person so conspiring, covenanting, swearing or offending, being lawfully convicted thereof by witness, confession or otherwise, shall forfeit for first offense 10 *l* . . ." An alternative to a fine for the first offense is twenty days' imprisonment on bread and water; for the second offense, 20 *l* or the pillory; for third offense, 40 *l* or to sit on the pillory and lose one ear.

Should such penalties not be sufficient, the magistrates took a further precaution: they announced a reward of 5 *l* for anyone submitting the names of at least two of the workmen who took part in the meeting June 17th at the Kings-Head Tavern.[51]

Science

The Deft Dionaea

Botanists have long been aware of mimosa and certain other types of plants that can open and close their leaves. But one that can close its leaves around a prey, thus catching food, is a new one.

What may seem a product of the imagination does indeed exist, and is the object of no small amount of attention and curiosity both in America and Britain. Already given the technical name of *Dionaea muscipula*, such a plant is native to shady, wet areas in North and South Carolina, flowering in July and August. Its largest leaves are three inches in length, with a width of about one and a half inches across the lobes.

Some specimens were collected in the colonies more than ten years ago, and a dried sample was shipped to England in 1765 by Philadelphia Botanist John Bertram. But it was only this year that the first live *Dionaea* reached London for examination. John Ellis, a fellow of the Royal Societies of London and Uppsala, recently made public a report on *Dionaea* he sent to the eminent Carl Linnaeus in Sweden. Explained Ellis:

The leaf is formed like a "machine to catch food." Many minute red glands cover the inner surface, and may discharge a sweet liquor to attract the victim (a fly or other form of insect). The instant these tender parts of the leaf are touched by the feet of the victim, the two lobes rise up, grasp the insect and squeeze it to death as rows of spine lock together. The lobes will not again open until the meal is digested.

While *Dionaea* may have amazing power for a plant, it also has a shortcoming: It cannot tell an insect from something less suitable to its diet. A pin or piece of straw placed on its lobe will cause the same reaction.

The technical designation of this new plant as *Dionaea muscipula* follows the new system of nomenclature proposed twenty-three years ago by Linnaeus in his *Species Plantarum*. Laymen may find it easier to call it by the common name scientists themselves are already using: Venus's-flytrap.[52]

Education

Numeratio Harvardiae

Founded in 1636 and opened in 1638, Harvard College in Cambridge is America's oldest. (Next: William and Mary, 1693.) Therefore Harvard also has the distinction of having conferred degrees upon more young men than any other college (2,677).

In its first graduating class, in 1642, nine were so honored. A measure of Harvard's growth in the intervening years is evident in the comparable number for the current year: forty-three. That record is contained in the latest *Catalogus eorum qui in Collegio Harvardino,* published in Cambridge. Basically a record of the years 1642–1776, and showing the number of degrees given in each, it won't be very popular reading except among those with training in the classics. In proper academic tradition, it is entirely in Latin.

Thus, in looking at Harvard's cumulative record over the years, *Catalogus* observes that the *numerus integer* (overall number) of men who received degrees totals 2,677. Of this number, one must now deduct 1,319 as *vivis cesserunt stelligeri* (departed from the living and now bearing stars). Thus 1,358 *supersunt adhuc;* which is to say, 1,358 are still around to call Harvard *alma mater.*[53]

PART III

JULY

THE farmers now will work, and not delay;
For while the sun shines they must make their hay,
And all in earnest be; who mean to thrive
Must (like the bee) bring honey to the hive.

The Virginia Almanack
July, 1776

THE WEEK OF JULY 1ST

Congress

The First Day of July

Congress could not move further on independence, when it was formally proposed by the Virginia delegation June 7th: too many delegations lacked the necessary instructions from home, and it was a subject of far too great magnitude to proceed without the certainty of each colony's support. Congress postponed the debate until July 1st.

When the fateful day arrived, independence was duly the agenda. This much is what Congress reports of Monday, the 1st:

"Resolved, That this Congress will resolve itself into a committee of the whole to take into consideration the resolution respecting independency:

"That the declaration be referred to said committee.

"The Congress resolved itself into a committee of the whole. After

191

some time the president resumed the chair, and Mr. Harrison [chairman in committee of the whole] reported that the committee had come to a resolution which they desired him to report, and to move for leave to sit again.

"The resolution agreed to by the committee of the whole being read, the determination thereof was at the request of a colony postponed till tomorrow."

The Second Day of July

Years of dissent and months of debate have made more and more inevitable that one day when the supreme issue of the time could be postponed no further. That day has come. The issue is decided. Thirteen colonies—by resolution of their elected delegates—are colonial no longer. This day the Continental Congress declared the United Colonies free and independent states.

But, to another day, Congress left the adoption of a formal declaration setting forth for Great Britain and, more important, for the world, the justification of so profound an act.

This much does Congress report of Tuesday, the 2nd of July:

"Resolved, That these United Colonies are, and of right ought to be, Free and Independent States; that they are absolved from all allegiance to the British crown, and that all political connection between them and the state of Great Britain, is and ought to be totally dissolved.

"Agreeable to the order of the day, the Congress resolved itself into a committee of the whole; and after some time, the president resumed the chair, and Mr. Harrison reported that the committee have had under consideration the declaration to them referred, but not having had time to go through the same, desired him to move for leave to sit again:

"Resolved, That Congress will tomorrow again resolve itself into a committee of the whole, to take into their farther consideration the declaration respecting Independence."

The Third Day of July

As word of independence began spreading—it was announced late Tuesday by the *Pennsylvania Evening Post*, even as one Philadelphian was already telling another—Congress went back to work:

"Agreeable to the order of the day, the Congress resolved itself into a committee of the whole, to take into farther consideration the declaration, and after some time the president resumed the chair, and Mr. Harrison reported that the committee not having yet gone through it, desired leave to sit again.

"Resolved, That this Congress will tomorrow again resolve itself into a committee of the whole, to take into their farther consideration the declaration of independence."

The Fourth Day of July

"Agreeable to the order of the day, the Congress resolved itself, into a committee of the whole, to take into their farther consideration the declaration, and after some time the president resumed the chair, and Mr. Harrison reported that the committee have agreed to a declaration which they desired him to report.

"The declaration being read, was agreed to, as follows;

"A DECLARATION by the Representatives of the UNITED STATES of AMERICA in Congress assembled.

"WHEN, in the course of human events, it becomes necessary for one people to dissolve the political bands which have connected them with another, and to assume, among the powers of the Earth, the separate and equal station to which the laws of nature and of nature's God entitle them, a decent respect to the opinions of mankind requires that they should declare the causes which impel them to the separation.

"We hold these truths to be self-evident; that all men are created equal; that they are endowed, by their Creator, with certain unalienable rights; that among these are life, liberty, and the pursuit of happiness.— That to secure these rights, governments are instituted among men, deriving their just powers from the consent of the governed; that whenever any form of government becomes destructive of these ends, it is the right of the people to alter or to abolish it, and to institute new government, laying its foundation on such principles, and organizing its powers in such form, as to them shall seem most likely to effect their safety and happiness. Prudence, indeed, will dictate, that governments long established, should not be changed for light and transient causes; and accordingly all experience hath shewn, that mankind are more disposed to suffer, while evils are sufferable, than to right themselves by abolishing the forms to which they are accustomed. But when a long train of abuses and usurpations, pursuing invariably the same object, evinces a design to reduce them under absolute despotism, it is their right, it is their duty, to throw off such government, and to provide new guards for their future security. Such has been the patient sufferance of these colonies; and such is now the necessity which constrains them to alter their former systems of government. The history of the present king of Great-Britain is a history of repeated injuries and usurpations, all having in direct object the establishment of an absolute tyranny over these states. To prove this, let facts be submitted to a candid world.

"He has refused his assent to laws the most wholesome and necessary for the public good.

"He has forbidden his governors to pass laws of immediate and pressing importance, unless suspended in their operation till his assent should be obtained; and when so suspended, he has utterly neglected to attend to them.

"He has refused to pass other laws for the accommodation of large districts of people, unless those people would relinquish the right of representation in the legislature; a right inestimable to them, and formidable to tyrants only.

"He has called together legislative bodies at places unusual, uncomfortable, and distant from the depository of their public records, for the sole purpose of fatiguing them into compliance with his measures.

"He has dissolved representative houses repeatedly, for opposing, with manly firmness, his invasions on the rights of the people.

"He has refused for a long time, after such dissolutions, to cause others to be elected; whereby the legislative powers, incapable of annihilation, have returned to the people at large for their exercise; the state remaining, in the mean time, exposed to all the dangers of invasion from without, and convulsions within.

"He has endeavoured to prevent the population of these states; for that purpose obstructing the laws for naturalization of foreigners; refusing to pass others to encourage their migrations hither, and raising the conditions of new appropriations of lands.

"He has obstructed the administration of justice, by refusing his assent to laws for establishing judiciary powers.

"He has made judges dependent on his will alone, for the tenure of their offices, and the amount and payment of their salaries.

"He has erected a multitude of new offices, and sent hither swarms of officers to harass our people, and eat out their substance.

"He has kept among us, in times of peace, standing armies, without the consent of our legislatures.

"He has affected to render the military independent of, and superior to the civil power.

"He has combined with others to subject us to a jurisdiction foreign to our constitution, and unacknowledged by our laws; giving his assent to their acts of pretended legislation:

"For quartering large bodies of armed troops among us:

"For protecting them, by a mock trial, from punishment for any murders which they should commit on the inhabitants of these states:

"For cutting off our trade with all parts of the world:

"For imposing taxes on us without our consent:

"For depriving us, in many cases, of the benefits of trial by jury:

"For transporting us beyond seas to be tried for pretended offences:

"For abolishing the free system of English laws in a neighbouring province, establishing therein an arbitrary government, and enlarging its boundaries, so as to render it at once an example and fit instrument for introducing the same absolute rule into these colonies:

"For taking away our charters, abolishing our most valuable laws, and altering fundamentally the forms of our governments:

"For suspending our own legislatures, and declaring themselves invested with power to legislate for us in all cases whatsoever.

"He has abdicated government here, by declaring us out of his protection, and waging War against us.

"He has plundered our seas, ravaged our coasts, burnt our towns, and destroyed the lives of our people.

"He is, at this time, transporting large armies of foreign mercenaries to complete the works of death, desolation, and tyranny, already begun with circumstances of cruelty and perfidy, scarcely paralleled in the most barbarous ages, and totally unworthy the head of a civilized nation.

"He has constrained our fellow-citizens, taken captive on the high seas, to bear arms against their country, to become the executioners of their friends and brethren, or to fall themselves by their hands.

"He has excited domestic insurrections amongst us, and has endeavoured to bring on the inhabitants of our frontiers the merciless indian savages, whose known rule of warfare is an undistinguished destruction, of all ages, sexes, and conditions.

"In every stage of these oppressions we have petitioned for redress in the most humble terms: Our repeated petitions have been answered only by repeated injury. A prince, whose character is thus marked by every act which may define a tyrant, is unfit to be the ruler of a free people.

"Nor have we been wanting in attentions to our British brethren. We have warned them, from time to time, of attempts by their legislature to extend an unwarrantable jurisdiction over us. We have reminded them of the circumstances of our emigration and settlement here. We have appealed to their native justice and magnanimity, and we have conjured them by the ties of our common kindred to disavow these usurpations, which would inevitably interrupt our connexions and correspondence. They too have been deaf to the voice of justice and of consanguinity. We must, therefore, acquiesce in the necessity, which denounces our separation, and hold them, as we hold the rest of mankind, enemies in war, in peace friends.

"We, therefore, the representatives of the UNITED STATES OF AMERICA, in GENERAL CONGRESS assembled, appealing to the supreme judge of the world for the rectitude of our intentions, do, in the name, and by authority of the good people of these colonies, solemnly publish and declare, That these United Colonies are, and of right ought to be, FREE AND INDEPENDENT STATES; that they are absolved from all allegiance to the British crown, and that all political connexion between them and the state of Great-Britain, is, and ought to be, totally dissolved; and that as FREE AND INDEPENDENT STATES, they have full power to levy war, conclude peace, contract alliances, establish commerce. and to do all other acts and things which INDEPENDENT STATES may of right do. And for the support of this declaration, with

a firm reliance on the protection of DIVINE PROVIDENCE, we mutually
pledge to each other our lives, our fortunes, and our sacred honour."[1]

Signed by Order and in Behalf of the Congress,

Attest   JOHN HANCOCK, President.
CHARLES THOMSON, Secretary

*The events of the first four days of July, 1776, are set forth here to the extent they were
publicly reported that year. The text of the Declaration of Independence is exactly as
entered in the* Journals *of Congress; the signature line is as it appeared in published
versions (newspapers and broadsides).*

Among Other Things:

Dwarfed by the enormity of proclaiming the independence of America
and turning thirteen colonies into thirteen free and equal states, no other
business of Congress this week could seem of great importance.

And yet it was a week as packed with the routine, necessary stuff of
government as any other. In this momentous week, Congress also, among
other things:

—Directed that the postmaster general proceed immediately to have
expresses established between Philadelphia and New York;

—Instructed the Marine Committee to contract with shipwrights to
go to Lake Champlain at a salary, in advance, of thirty-four and two-
thirds dollars per month, plus a half pint of rum and one and a half rations
per day;

—Requested General Washington, if he thinks it advisable, to send
three regiments stationed in Massachusetts to Fort Ticonderoga, and take
an equal number of Massachusetts militia into Continental pay to make
up the difference;

—Named as members of the Indian affairs committee Thomas Jefferson, Philip Livingston and Samuel Huntington.[2]

Another Unalienable Right

A matter more serious Congress could not consider. Yet when it was
done—when the Declaration of Independence was formally adopted—
the profound nature of the act and all its potential consequence could
not be allowed to restrict man's additional unalienable right to see the
lighter side of things.

Thus it is said to have happened a short while after the signing that
Benjamin Harrison of Virginia met Elbridge Gerry of Massachusetts in
the corridor of the State House. Harrison, a very portly man, smiled as
he encountered Gerry. "When the hanging scene comes," said Harrison,
"I shall have the advantage over you on account of my size. All will be
over for me in a moment, but you," he told the very slender Gerry, "will
be kicking in the air for half an hour after I am gone."[3]

The World

Elsewhere . . .

"Sou servido Ordenar, que em nenhum dos Portos destes Reinos, e seus Dominios, se dê prática, ou entrada a Navio algum, que a elles chegar com carga, ou sem ella, vindo de qualquer dos Portos da sobredita América Septentrional Ingleza."

"I hereby order that, in none of the ports of these kingdoms or their dominions, shall entry be permitted to any vessel arriving at these ports, with or without cargo, from any of the ports of the aforesaid British North America."

His Most Faithful Majesty, José I
Lisbon, July 4, 1776

Elsewhere in the world on a day that will be remembered in history, there was this happening on the fourth day of July, 1776:

—In Lisbon, his Portuguese Majesty, an ally of Britain, issued a decree prohibiting all trade with America, and ordering all American ships to depart from Portuguese ports within eight days.

—In Oxford, England, former loyalist governor Thomas Hutchinson of Massachusetts, and his deputy, Peter Oliver, received honarary degrees from Oxford University at the annual commemoration of the university's founders and benefactors.

—At the same ceremony, the son of the Lord Bishop of Oxford and a fellow student of New College were both recipients of academic prizes awarded annually by Lord North who, besides being first minister, is chancellor of Oxford University, and something of a neighbor, making his permanent home at Wroxton Abbey outside nearby Banbury.

—In London, former Lord Mayor and now Alderman John Wilkes, also a member of Parliament, addressed the Gentlemen of the Livery on his loss of the election for City Chamberlain, lamenting a decline in public virtue in "this selfish and degenerate age," and upholding those citizens of bygone days who would have scorned to sacrifice public trust "at the altar of power"; he was interrupted with hisses and groans, but continued, only to be stopped again with a more violent outburst of derision; he finally bowed, and left the Common Hall.

—In Annapolis, the *Maryland Gazette* reported plans for electing a convention to form a new government; the convention is to meet in Annapolis August 12th and complete its work no later than December 1st.

—And in the shipbuilding center of Newburyport, Massachusetts, on the Merrimack River, Thursday, July the 4th, was the occasion of the launching of the second Continental frigate, a warship of thirty-six guns. It was named the *Hancock*, after the president of the Continental Con-

Laſt Wedneſday the Fowey failed from Annapolis with Governor Eden on board.

The following Captains, belonging to this port, were at the bay of Honduras the 24th of laſt February, viz. Spain, John Green, Taylor, Philips ; alſo Capt. Buchannan of Baltimore.

In CONGRESS, June 27, 1776.

Reſolved, That four companies of Germans be raiſed in Pennſylvania, and four companies in Maryland, for to compoſe the German battalion.

That it be recommended to the Committee of Safety of Pennſylvania immediately to appoint proper officers for, and direct the inliſtment of the four companies to be raiſed in that colony. By order of Congreſs,

JOHN HANCOCK, Preſident.

In COMMITTEE of SAFETY, July 1, 1776.

The Committee taking into conſideration the reſolution of Congreſs, and being of opinion that the public ſervice requires that it be carried into execution, without any delay, and the recruiting ſervice be entered on as ſoon as poſſible,

Reſolved, That this Board will on Friday the fifth inſtant appoint Captains, and on Friday the twelfth inſtant Lieutenants and Enfigns, for the four companies of Germans directed to be raiſed in this province by order of Congreſs, and that it is the opinion of this Board that, confiſtent with the reſolve of Congreſs, no perſons but ſuch as are Germans born, or the ſons of Congreſs, ſhould hold any office in ſaid companies.

All ſuch gentlemen, who fall under the above deſcriptions, and are deſirous to enter into the ſervice, are requeſted to ſend in their applications as early as may be.

Extract from the minutes,

WILLIAM GOVETT, Secretary.

☞ Threepence a pound given for clean LINEN RAGS by the printer.

TO be SOLD, the brigantine TWO FRIENDS. She is a prime ſailor, but three years old, and carries nine hundred and fifty or a thouſand barrels of flour.

The ſchooner MARY ANN. She is a prime ſailor, but four years old, and carries four hundred and fifty barrels of flour.

The ſchooner is loaded and ready to go, and will be ſold with her cargo, or alone. She has an inventory ſuitable and complete. The brig may be fitted for ſea with a very ſmall expence, and the ſchooner requires none. Both veſſels are very good, but any gentleman inclining to purchaſe may have them viewed by proper perſons. Inquire for Mr. JOHN PARRY, on board the brig, at Vine-ſtreet wharf.

Philadelphia, July 2, 1776.

RAN away laſt Sunday week from the ſubſcriber, baker, in Second-ſtreet, an Iriſh ſervant man named SIMON GIBNEY, thirty years of age or upwards. He had on, when he went away, a blue coat; ſpotted ſtuff jacket, a pair of Wilton drilling breeches, white ſhirt, half worn beaver hat, thread ſtockings, a pair of pumps half worn, and pinchbeck buckles. He is ſuppoſed to be in or about Philadelphia.

Whoever takes up ſaid ſervant, and ſecures him ſo that his maſter gets him again, ſhall have TWENTY FIVE SHILLINGS reward, and reaſonable charges.

LAWRENCE POWEL.

N. B. All perſons are forbid to harbour ſaid ſervant at their peril.

Choice INDIGO to be ſold by John Hart.

Philadelphia, July 2, 1776.

THIRTY SHILLINGS Reward.

RAN away laſt Saturday night, from his maſter, a certain WILLIAM WRIGHT, a bought apprentice lad, by trade a ſhoemaker, about eighteen years of age, pale complexion, ſhort brown hair, to which he generally ties a falſe tail, is knock kneed, and very ſlovenly in his dreſs. He took with him the tools of his trade, and ſome clothes, in a bag made of old ſail cloth, drawn together at the mouth like a purſe, with a calf ſkin thong. He is with his mother, who is ſuſpected of having inticed him to abſcond. Any perſon ſecuring him in jail, ſhall receive the above reward and all reaſonable charges, by applying to his maſter between Market and Cheſnut ſtreets, in Front-ſtreet.

ANDREW HUCK.

FOR the accommodation of paſſengers going up and down to the FORT, a STAGE BOAT, well provided for that purpoſe, which will ſet off from Joſeph Price's wharf, oppoſite the ſign of St. Patrick, Southwark, three times a week, viz.

Sundays, Wedneſdays and Fridays, between eight and nine o'clock. Each perſon paying one ſhilling and ſixpence for going and coming the ſame day, or not returning one ſhilling. *6 JAMES SLOAN and JOHN DONNAL.

THREE DOLLARS Reward.

RAN away the fifth inſtant, a Negro man named ISHMAEL, twenty-five years of age, above ſix feet high, ſtrong made, his colour between a Mulatto and a Black, rocks in his walk, or rather ſomewhat lame, occaſioned by his having his thigh bone broke when a boy. Had on when he went away a ſmall brimmed hat, a brown cloth jacket without ſleeves, let out in the back, new tow ſhirt and trouſers, old ſhoes. Whoever takes up and ſecures ſaid Negro in any jail, ſo as his maſter may have him again, ſhall have the above reward and reaſonable charges, paid by the ſubſcriber living in Second-ſtreet, oppoſite the Swede's church in the diſtrict of Southwark.

WILLIAM THOMAS.

N. B. All maſters of veſſels and others are forbid to carry, take, or harbour him at their peril.

A QUANTITY of white and brown BUCKRAM to be ſold by Mary Flanagan, the corner of Front and Spruce ſtreets.

A FEW hogſheads of old Jamaica SPIRITS, very good green TEA in quarter cheſts, Goa ARRACK, and two CANNON, four pounders, to be ſold by Dominick Joyce, at Capt. John Sibbald's in Second-ſtreet, oppoſite the New Market. Philad. June 11.

STRAYED from the ſubſcriber, living near John Jones's, inn-keeper in Carnarvan townſhip, Berks county, a BAY MARE, one quarter blooded, a natural trotter, ſhod all round, remarkably bad to ſhoe behind, and difficult to catch when out of hand, between thirteen and fourteen hands high, ſix years old this ſummer, a few white hairs mixed with brown on her forehead, by way of a ſtar, a little roundiſh brand on her nigh ſhoulder. Whoever takes up ſaid Mare and brings her home, or gives notice where ſhe is, ſo that the owner gets her again, ſhall have FIVE POUNDS reward and reaſonable charges. ROBERT SMITH.

PHILADELPHIA: Printed by BENJAMIN TOWNE, in Front-ſtreet, near the London Coffee-Houſe.

LATE-BREAKING NEWS Shown here is the back page (the number at the top is a cumulative one for the year) of the Pennsylvania Evening Post, *Philadelphia, Tuesday, July 2, 1776. At the left is the page as it appeared when Publisher Benjamin Towne began his press run—before he got the news. When he heard what had happened at the State House some blocks away, he stopped the press, dropped out what we would call a "house ad" for linen rags to be used in papermaking (first column, halfway down), inserted all he had time for of the biggest story in his career, and sped on its way the first public announcement that America had declared its independence. The page on the*

Laſt Wedneſday the Fowey failed from Annapolis with Governor Eden on board.

The following Captains, belonging to this port, were at the bay of Honduras the 24th of laſt February, viz. Spain, John Green, Taylor, Philips; alſo Capt. Buchannan of Baltimore.

In CONGRESS, June 27, 1776.

Reſolved, That four companies of Germans be raiſed in Penſylvania, and four companies in Maryland, for to compoſe the German battalion.

That it be recommended to the Committee of Safety of Pennſylvania immediately to appoint proper officers for, and direct the inliſtment of the four companies to be raiſed in that colony. By order of Congreſs,

JOHN HANCOCK, Preſident.

In COMMITTEE of SAFETY, July 1, 1776.

The Committee taking into conſideration the reſolution of Congreſs, and being of opinion that the public ſervice requires that it be carried into execution, without any delay, and the recruiting ſervice be entered on as ſoon as poſſible.

Reſolved, That this Board will on Friday the fifth inſtant appoint Captains, and on Friday the twelfth inſtant Lieutenants and Enſigns, for the four companies of Germans directed to be raiſed in this province by order of Congreſs, and that it is the opinion of this Board that, conſiſtent with the reſolve of Congreſs, no perſons but ſuch as are Germans born, or the ſons of Germans, ſhould hold any office in ſaid companies.

All ſuch gentlemen, who ſall under the above deſcriptions, and are deſirous to enter into the ſervice, are requeſted to ſend in their applications as early as may be.

Extract from the minutes,

WILLIAM GOVETT, Secretary.

This day the CONTINENTAL CONGRESS declared the UNITED COLONIES FREE and INDEPENDENT STATES.

TO be SOLD, the brigantine TWO FRIENDS. Sheis a prime ſailor, but three years old, and carries nine hundred and fifty or a thouſand barrels of flour.

The ſchooner MARY ANN. She is a prime ſailor, but four years old, and carries four hundred and fifty barrels of flour.

The ſchooner is loaded and ready to go, and will be ſold with her cargo, or alone. She has an inventory ſuitable and complete. The brig may be fitted for ſea with a very ſmall expence, and the ſchooner requires none. Both veſſels are very good, but any gentleman inclining to purchaſe may have them viewed by proper perſons. Inquire for Mr. JOHN PARRY, on board the brig, at Vine-ſtreet wharf.

Philadelphia, July 2, 1776.

RAN away laſt Sunday week from the ſubſcriber, baker, in Second-ſtreet, an Iriſh ſervant man named SIMON GIBNEY, thirty years of age or upwards. He had on, when he went away, a blue coat, ſpotted ſtuff jacket, a pair of Wilton drilling breeches, white ſhirt, half worn beaver hat, thread ſtockings, a pair of pumps half worn, and pinchbeck buckles. He is ſuppoſed to be in or about Philadelphia.

Whoever takes up ſaid ſervant, and ſecures him ſo that his maſter gets him again, ſhall have TWENTY FIVE SHILLINGS reward, and reaſonable charges.

LAWRENCE POWEL.

Choice INDIGO to be ſold by John Hart.

Philadelphia, July 2, 1776.

THIRTY SHILLINGS Reward.

RAN away laſt Saturday night, from his maſter, a certain WILLIAM WRIGHT, a bought apprentice lad, by trade a ſhoemaker, about eighteen years of age, pale complexion, ſhort brown hair, to which he generally ties a falſe tail, is knock kneed, and very ſlovenly in his dreſs. He took with him the tools of his trade, and ſome clothes, in a bag made of old ſail cloth, drawn together at the mouth like a purſe, with a calf ſkin thong. He is with his mother, who is ſuſpected of having inticed him to abſcond. Any perſon ſecuring him in jail, ſhall receive the above reward and all reaſonable charges, by applying to his maſter between Market and Cheſnut ſtreets, in Front-ſtreet.

ANDREW HUCK.

FOR the accommodation of paſſengers going up and down to the FORT, a STAGE BOAT, well provided for that purpoſe, which will ſet off from Joſeph Price's wharf, oppoſite the ſign of St. Patrick, Southwark, three times a week, viz.

Sundays, Wedneſdays and Fridays, between eight and nine o'clock. Each perſon paying one ſhilling and ſixpence for going and coming the ſame day, or not returning one ſhilling.   *6   JAMES SLOAN and JOHN DONNAL.

THREE DOLLARS Reward.

RAN away the fifth inſtant, a Negro man named ISHMAEL, twenty-five years of age, above ſix feet high, ſtrong made, his colour between a Mulatto and a Black, rocks in his walk, or rather ſomewhat lame, occaſioned by his having his thigh bone broke when a boy. Had on when he went away a ſmall brimmed hat, a brown cloth jacket without ſleeves, let out in the back, new tow ſhirt and trouſers, old ſhoes. Whoever takes up and ſecures ſaid Negro in any jail, ſo as his maſter may have him again, ſhall have the above reward and reaſonable charges, paid by the ſubſcriber living in Second ſtreet, oppoſite the Swede's church in the diſtrict of Southwark.

WILLIAM THOMAS.

N. B. All maſters of veſſels and others are forbid to carry, take, or harbour him at their peril.

A QUANTITY of white and brown BUCKRAM to be ſold by Mary Flanagan, the corner of Front and Spruce ſtreets.

A FEW hogſheads of old Jamaica SPIRITS, very good green TEA in quarter cheſts, Goa ARRACK, and two CANNON, four pounders, to be ſold by Dominick Joyce, at Capt. John Sibbald's in Second-ſtreet, oppoſite the New Market. Philad. June 11.

STRAYED from the ſubſcriber, living near John Jones's, inn-keeper in Carnarvan townſhip, Berks county, a BAY MARE, one quarter blooded, a natural trotter, ſhod all round, remarkably bad to ſhoe behind, and difficult to catch when out of hand, between thirteen and fourteen hands high, ſix years old this ſummer, a few white hairs mixed with brown on her forehead, by way of a ſtar, a little roundiſh brand on her nigh ſhoulder. Whoever takes up ſaid Mare and brings her home, or gives notice where ſhe is, ſo that the owner gets her again, ſhall have FIVE POUNDS reward and reaſonable charges.   ROBERT SMITH.

PHILADELPHIA: Printed by BENJAMIN TOWNE, in Front-ſtreet, near the London Coffee-Houſe.

---

right is as it appears in most of the existing copies of the newspaper. This was probably the first time in American journalism that a publisher literally stopped the press to report late-breaking news. And what more appropriate occasion? (Actual size of page is 9½ x 7¾ in.)

"Early Edition"—Rare Book Division—
New York Public Library
"Late Edition"—Library Company
of Philadelphia

gress, who was in Philadelphia helping to make news of another sort himself.

The decree of his Most Faithful Majesty José I barring American ships from Portugal clearly demonstrated that country's long standing alliance with Great Britain. It appears, however, to have been based upon a misunderstanding about America already declaring independence. Said King José's proclamation: "We have lately been informed that the British colonies of North America have, by an act of the Congress on the 5th of May last past [apparently the resolutions of May 10th and 15th calling for the formation of new colonial governments] not only declared themselves entirely free from all subjection to the crown of Great Britain, but were moreover actually employed in forming and enacting laws by their own private authority in opposition to the lawful rights of our brother, friend and ally, the King of Great Britain." That, said King José, is "so pernicious an example [as] ought to engage every Prince, even those it interests the least, not to abet, favour, or assist, by any means, directly or indirectly, such subjects united in such direct and open rebellion against their natural sovereigns."[4]

In some sources, the date of the edict of the King of Portugal is given as July 5th. The edict actually was promulgated on the 4th, but was announced on the 5th, and the latter date is thus often attached to it.

Press

Rags to Rights

When Congress voted in favor of independence, printer Benjamin Towne, over on Front Street in Philadelphia, had already completed part of the printing of the July 2nd edition of his thrice-weekly *Pennsylvania Evening Post*. He stopped his press when the news reached him, and made the only expedient change that time permitted: on the back page he dropped out an advertisement of his own for rags to be used in paper-making. What appeared in early copies as:

> ☞ Threepence a pound for clean
> LINEN RAGS by the printer.

in later copies that same day became:

> This day the CONTINENTAL CON-
> GRESS declared the UNITED COLONIES
> FREE and INDEPENDENT STATES.

Thus was American independence first announced to the world.[5]

Little Inkling

Almanac readers are apt to shake their heads in awe when a given day turns out as long before predicted, and only smile knowingly when the prognostication misses.

How well did America's almanacs do with that most noteworthy of days? Was there even a hint in this year's editions (written last year) that readers ought to expect an out-of-the-ordinary day on Thursday, the fourth day of July?

Forecast *Gaine's Universal Register*: "Cloudy, and it may rain." (In fact, it was fair and warm.)

Advised *George's Cambridge Almanack*, "good hay weather," after noting that Naumkeak, in Massachusetts, was first called by its new name of Salem on this date in 1629.

Said *Bickerstaff's New England Almanack*, "rain"; and the *New York Pocket Almanack*, "cloudy."

Predicted *Der Hoch Deutsch-Americanische Calendar* of Germantown, Pennsylvania: "Wind, Regen oder Donner" [Wind, rain or thunder].

Both *Saunders' Pocket Almanack* and *Poor Richard Improved* observed only that the day would be fourteen hours and forty-six minutes long.

Thus to the prognosticators who through whim or divination last year assigned the lot of each day this year, July the fourth loomed no larger than the fourth of any other month.

But readers of *Freebetter's New England Almanack* may have suspected something was in the wind when they turned to the prologue for July:

> "Hail! Happy day, while patriotic fire,
> Glows in the breast the noble mind t' inspire
> Flam'd by this spark *America* will shine,
> And lighten distant worlds with rays benign."[6]

The War

Arrival of the Locusts

Like "a swarm of locusts escaped from a bottomless pit," said one observer dismally. The swarm is a fleet of perhaps one hundred thirty British vessels that has arrived off New Jersey's Sandy Hook, leaving no further doubt that New York is the next military objective in the British strategy.

Aboard the fleet is General Howe's command, estimated at 8,000 men, which last saw duty in Boston. Both the army and the naval force have been stationed in Halifax since the evacuation of Boston in March, although it has long been evident the stay would be only temporary.

On Monday about 1,000 of the troops landed on the western end of nearby Long Island [Brooklyn], but returned to their ships later in the day.[7]

Royal Recognition

Britain's military success in Canada—in contrast to Lexington, Concord, Boston, and now Sullivan's Island—has not gone unnoticed at home. Announced this week by his Majesty for creation as a Knight of the Bath: Canada's commander-in-chief, General Guy Carleton.[8]

The States

Governor Patrick Henry

Without one since Lord Dunmore took refuge aboard ship last year, Virginia again has a governor—and no royal flunkey this one. By a vote of 60 to 45, Virginia delegates in convention this week in Williamsburg gave the honor to Patrick Henry. They also gave him an official residence, Dunmore's former palace, by rescinding an earlier resolution that would have converted the elegant mansion into a public hospital.

Replied Governor Henry in acknowledgment of his election: "I lament my want of talents; I feel my mind filled with anxiety and uneasiness to find myself so unequal to the duties. . . . The errors of my conduct shall be atoned for, so far as I am able, by unwearied endeavors . . ."[9]

Fourth Constitution

New Jersey this week became the fourth colony in America to adopt its own constitution and establish its own form of government, and in so doing, set what may be a precedent: it is the first to establish a truly bicameral legislature.

The constitution was adopted July 2nd by the Provincial Congress, meeting in Burlington, by a vote of 26 to 9. It establishes a legislature consisting of two houses: the Legislative Council, made up of one member from each of the thirteen counties; and the General Assembly, with three from each. What makes this legislature unique among the newly established governments of the colonies is that each house, unlike New Hampshire and South Carolina, will be elected directly by the people; and each house, unlike Virginia, will have the power to originate legislation. Following the custom of the British Parliament, however, only the lower house may originate or alter a money bill. As in the other colonies, the two houses jointly will elect the governor.[10]

Foreign News

Applauded and Condemned

> ". . . aucune résolution du Roi, depuis son avènement à la Couronne, n'a peut-être été plus applaudé ni plus condamnée, par les deux partis qui divisent publiquement le peuple."

The dismissal in May of Turgot, the comptroller general of finances, has not been soon forgotten. Reports a correspondent in Paris:

"The change which some time ago took place in the ministry here still engages the conversation of all ranks; and no determination of the king, since his accession to the throne, has perhaps been more applauded or condemned by the two orders of society into which this people are remarkably divided. The people of rank and the Parlement are of the former opinion; all the Bourgeois, and the lower class of people, are to a man of the latter, except such as have actually suffered by the late regulations [the six edicts of January].

"This originates from the various alterations which have been made in many departments of the State, materially affecting the personal interest of great numbers. Turgot, who has from his first entrance into office laboured to free the people from the great burthens by which they have been long oppressed, esteemed the suppression of the many unjust monopolies very necessary. . . . [These changes] claimed the attention of both Turgot and Malesherbes [secretary of state for the royal household, who resigned in April]. Their advice to have the body of poor *noblesse*, so heavy a charge upon the royal purse, reformed, was carried into execution. The same principle of economy occasioned the suppression of the Military School. Hence these two men raised up implacable enemies in the members which compose the Parlement, for curtailing their schemes of usury; in the nobles, because so many were thrown out of employment; and lastly, they were opposed violently by the Q[ueen], because her vanity had been severely wounded in the removal of so great a number of men of rank from being her attendants. Against so powerful a combination, it was impossible to make any effectual stand. The king was obliged to give up the only men in whom he placed any confidence, to the great regret of every disinterested man in the nation."[11]

Press

"Semper Eadem"

An additional halfpenny tax on British newspapers is now in effect.

It is the tax Lord North asked of Parliament in April, arguing that newspapers are a good source of taxes since some people think they do "more harm than good."

Printers, who would scarcely agree, are bitter about the additional duty. They must pay the tax, and then consider whether or not to pass it on to their customers. Since the margin of profit in publishing news is already paper-thin, many feel they are bound to suffer whichever way they turn: taking a loss by trying to absorb the tax themselves, or risking a decline in readership by raising the price.

London's *St. James's Chronicle,* which announced a price increase from two-and-a-half to three pence effective with its issue of July 6th, presented this account of the dilemma in newspaper publishing:

"Town and country printers complain heavily of the hardship and injustice of the additional halfpenny on newspapers. They already pay a penny [tax], which with the halfpenny allowed to the hawker, leaves but a penny for the expenses of the paper and print, and it is well known, even to the Ministry, that tho' the newspapers pay a penny a piece to the Revenue, they do not clear even a fraction of a farthing a piece to the proprietor, and yet the government are now adding an additional halfpenny, which will turn the balance on the other side, and make the paper a loss instead of a gain."

It is apparent, many feel, that the Ministry would have the newspapers simply pass along the cost—treating the public like a "beast of burthen," one said—so as to make a profit. But not all publishers like that approach. Lamented an Oxford printer: "If power is obstinate, we may be obliged to wish the public would bear part of our loss, but however happy we should be to put a few plums into our Sunday pudding, by our labours in defence of liberty, we do not wish even to eat bread and cheese at the expense of the freedom of the press."

He might have added a wry comment about the course of taxation by quoting the adage that appears on the newspaper stamp itself: *Semper Eadem*—"Always the same way."[12]

Religion

And Mercifully Spare Us

When he worshiped in New York's Trinity Church on recent Sundays, along with other ranking officers of the Continental Army, General George Washington may have winced when he heard the minister read, as part of the standard Church of England service, a prayer that God "give the

King victory over all his enemies"—the general currently being foremost among them.

The time-honored Book of Common Prayer is plentiful with references to the monarchy. In Morning and Evening Prayer, worshipers throughout the English world pray, "O Lord, save the king; and mercifully hear us when we call upon Thee." Likewise in the communion service, in the Prayer for the Church Militant, are they called upon to acknowledge royal authority. The fifteenth through eighteenth sentences of the Litany are devoted to supplication for the King's majesty and for the royal family.

Not only General Washington—who is symbolically more an enemy of the king than any other man on earth—but others of lesser renown have come to question the continuance of such prayers in American services. Late in May, the *New York Journal* published a letter from a reader, who signed himself only as "An Episcopalian." It happened he was in Trinity Church when Washington worshiped there on May 12th—when the traditional prayers for the royalty were offered. Personally offended, and believing many others including Washington to have been offended, he wrote the *Journal*:

"I not only could not join in the prayers abovementioned, but prayed in direct opposition to them—for the present conductors of our public affairs, that justice and wisdom might direct their counsels, and that heaven would bless and succeed their measures against our enemies, viz., the king and ministers of Great Britain, as dangerous and rancorous enemies as any nation ever had.

"The conduct of our Episcopal Clergy, in thus praying in our public devotions for the king, is a most daring and open insult upon the United Colonies of America, whom he has forced to be his enemies; and for the minister, as the mouth of the congregation, or (for us) as joining with them to pray that God would 'give the king victory over all his enemies' is directly praying against all the United Colonies of America, of which the congregation is a part; that their united efforts in defense of their rights and freedom may be defeated, and supposes them to pray against themselves! This is to the highest degree absurd and unnatural, and a most unpious prostitution of the ministerial office and the sacred privilege of prayer to the Almighty."

This week, the Convention of the new Commonwealth of Virginia did something about it there. It directed, among other things, that:

—the phrase "O Lord, save the king; and mercifully hear us when we call upon Thee," be omitted from Morning and Evening Prayer;

—the fifteenth through eighteenth sentences of the Litany be omitted;

—that all reference to the authority of the king be omitted from the Prayer for the Church Militant in the service of Holy Communion, and that supplication be offered instead, at the appropriate places, for the "Magistrates of this Commonwealth."[13]

THE WEEK OF JULY 8TH

Independence

Now It's Unanimous

When Congress voted to declare independence last week, it did so without the votes of New York's delegates. Still unauthorized by their Colony to support independence, they were excused from voting.

This week a copy of the Declaration of Independence reached the Convention of New York in White Plains. What the Convention had to say about it now makes independence truly unanimous: The "reasons assigned by the Continental Congress for declaring the United Colonies free and independent states are cogent and conclusive, and that while we lament the cruel necessity which has rendered that measure unavoidable, we approve the same, and will, at the risque of our lives and fortunes, join with the other colonies in supporting it."[14]

The War

Into the Breech

As commander of the British naval force that unsuccessfully stormed Sullivan's Island, near Charleston, South Carolina, last month, Commodore Sir Peter Parker not only lost a battle, but something else as well. The American shot that struck his flagship, wounding him slightly, also ripped off part of his breeches. That prompted an anonymous poet to say of Sir Peter's disaster:

> "If honor in the breech is lodged,
>   As Hudibras hath shown,
> It may from hence be fairly judged,
>   Sir Peter's honor's gone."[15]

Shame at the Cedars

Except for the capture of Fort St. John and Montreal in November of last year, and despite the heroic commitment of such men as those who lasted the arduous march overland to Quebec, the war in Canada has presented the American army with nearly every example of military failure: defeat, retreat, disorganization, desertion, despair.

But perhaps no one event in the entire northern campaign has so provoked anger and remorse at home as that which Congress this week heard described in detail, and to which it reacted with such terms as "shameful," "horrid" . . . "a gross and inhuman violation of the laws of nature and nations." It was the surrender of an outpost called The Cedars, and what made it so bitter was that it was an apparently unnecessary capitulation by an American officer that resulted in his troops becoming not only prisoners of war, but victims of torture.

The Cedars—about forty miles southwest of Montreal on the St. Lawrence—was a small fortification held in May by about 390 Continental soldiers. On the 15th, anticipating an attack by about 600 British Regulars, Canadians and Indians, the commander, Colonel Bedel, left the post to a subordinate, Major Butterfield, while he went to Montreal for reinforcements. The attack came on the 17th, and continued for two days. Then—although the garrison had sustained no injury from enemy fire and had weapons and supplies, and although reinforcements were on the way—Major Butterfield surrendered.

The terms of capitulation were supposed to have provided against it, but the Americans were immediately turned over to the hostile Indians. Many were stripped of possessions and clothes; several were killed at once and others from time to time; some were carried off by the Indians; one, first shot but still conscious, was roasted over a fire; several others, worn down with hunger and cruelty, were left naked to die of cold and famine.

Congress showed its outrage by finding the commanding officer of The Cedars chargeable of a "shameful surrender." Then it turned its wrath toward the British army, demanding indemnification for the murder and plunder of The Cedars. It also put Britain on notice that the United States will react in kind if necessary, declaring in a message to Generals Howe and Burgoyne:

"That, if the enemy shall commit any further violences by putting to death, torturing, or otherwise ill treating the prisoners retained by them, or any of the hostages put into their hands, recourse be had to retaliation as the sole means of stopping the progress of human butchery; and that, for that purpose, punishments of the same kind and degree be inflicted on an equal number of the captives from them in our possession, till they shall be taught to respect the violated rights of nations."

Both Colonel Bedel and Major Butterfield were subsequently tried before a court-martial, found guilty, and dismissed from the service.[16]

Congress

Confederation: Veil of Secrecy

Although all matters can be kept secret indefinitely under a resolution of May 11, 1775—closing its doors during business sessions—Congress has gone to an unprecedented degree of secrecy in its handling of the draft of the Articles of Confederation just received from committee.

The draft at first will go only to a printer. The printer is to make eighty—neither more nor fewer—copies and deposit them with Charles Thomson, secretary of Congress, who is to deliver a copy personally to each member. The printer, meanwhile, is to be under oath to divulge the contents to no one, either directly or indirectly, and to keep no copy of the document. Each member of Congress, in turn, is under orders not to show his copy to anyone, and not to take any steps by which it might be reprinted.

Thus, until Congress decides to make it public, a veil of secrecy will protect the proposal for perpetual union of the colonies as drafted by the committee appointed June 12th.

Other matters in a busy week not subjected to such restriction:

—A decision to exempt from military duty all postmasters while in office;

—Reappointment of the Rev. Jacob Duché of Philadelphia as chaplain to Congress, his attendance continuing to be desired every morning at 9 o'clock. The Rev. Mr. Duché has held the post since the opening of the First Continental Congress in October, 1774.[17]

Accounting but not Reporting

Back home from a trip that appears to have been as basically unproductive as it was arduous, Congress's three commissioners to Canada have thus far issued no public report of their mission.

This week Congress took its only official notice of their return by settling accounts for the expenses incurred. To Benjamin Franklin, Congress approved payment of 1,221 and 18/90 dollars, of which was the amount of 560 dollars to be charged to Brigadier General Arnold, 124 dollars that had been advanced to fellow commissioner Charles Carroll for expenses, 164 and 78/90 dollars that was paid for bedding and other necessaries for the commissioners (these items were then turned over to the commissary of stores in Albany), and 372 and 30/90 dollars that had been expended by Franklin and Commissioner John Carroll during the journey.[18]

> The curious procedure of counting in 90ths of dollars may be due to the fact that equivalent values of English currency were calculated in ninths: a shilling was valued at two-ninths of a dollar and a crown at one and one-ninth dollars.

The States

Celebrating Independence: Philadelphia

From a correspondent in Philadelphia Tuesday: "Yesterday at 12 o'clock, INDEPENDENCY was declared at the State House in this city, in the presence of many thousand spectators, who testified their approbation of it by repeated acclamations of joy."[19]

Celebrating Independence: New York

" . . . the fall of leaden majesty."

Over New York's Bowling Green since August, 1770, has reigned an imposing lead-and-gilt replica of George III astride his horse—the first such equestrian statue ever crafted of his Majesty. Now, as no longer he reigns over thirteen independent states, neither does his Majesty continue to rule over Bowling Green. The statue was tumbled down from its high pedestal, broken to pieces, in the celebrating of independence Tuesday.

The "ominous fall of leaden majesty," said the *New York Journal*, concluded the proclamation of independence to the Continental army stationed there. General Washington, as soon as he received a copy from Philadelphia, ordered the army assembled at 6 o'clock Tuesday so that the Declaration of Independence might be read at the head of each brigade. By general orders he expressed his hope that "this important event will serve as a fresh incentive to every officer and soldier to act with fidelity and courage . . ."

He need not have wondered about incentive. The reading of the declaration was greeted with loud huzzas. And soon afterwards the statue was, "by the Sons of Freedom, laid prostrate in the dirt, the just desert of an ungrateful tyrant." So said the *Journal*, which further reported that the lead of which the monument was made will be run into bullets to "assimilate with the brain of our infatuated adversaries." The *Journal's* story concluded with this comment on recent British policy: "*Quis* [sic] *Deus vult perdere, prius dementat.*" [Whomever God wants to bring to destruction, he first causes to become mad.]

There is still to be an official proclamation of independence for the civil population; that will come at 12 o'clock Thursday, July 18th, in front of City Hall, at the head of Broad Street . . . "when and where," the *New York Packet* advises, "it is hoped every true friend to the rights and liberties of this country will not fail to attend." The declaration will also be read the same day at nearby Westchester. Meanwhile, independence is also being observed at New York's city jail by giving debtors their freedom.[20]

Celebrating Independence: Princeton and Trenton

Last night, reported a correspondent in Princeton on Wednesday, Nassau Hall was grandly illuminated; "independency was proclaimed under a triple volley of musketry and universal acclamation of the United States." In Trenton, day before, the Declaration of Independence was read along with the state's new constitution.[21]

Farewell, Two Governors

When he left his palace in Williamsburg last year, fearing for his safety, Virginia's Royal Governor Dunmore took refuge aboard the ship *William* and made a small British fleet his dominion. But life at sea could not long please him, and he soon found a haven on Gwynn's Island, north along Chesapeake Bay some forty miles from Norfolk.

Dunmore back on Virginia soil, however, could not long please the new Commonwealth, and a confrontation was assured. It came Monday.

At Gwynn's Island, Dunmore had begun the likes of a permanent settlement with houses and fortifications. But the fortifications were largely against assault by sea. So an assault by land was carried out by troops under the command of Virginia Brigadier General Andrew Lewis, who touched a match to the first cannon shot, an 18-pounder that ripped through the hull of one of Dunmore's vessels, named in fact the *Dunmore*. The continued barrage did further damage to the ship and others anchored off the island, among other things making bits and pieces out of all of the royal governor's fine china and wounding his lordship slightly in the leg. While his ships were at least still operable, Dunmore decided his only alternative was evacuation, and he hastily put to sea, finally leaving Virginia soil for what is probably the last time.

Meanwhile, exiled Royal Governor William Franklin of New Jersey, ordered out of that state last month by its Provincial Congress, is now quartered in Wallingford, Connecticut, where he was taken under guard.

His arrival in Connecticut last week was an occasion for comment by Hartford's *Connecticut Courant,* which referred to Governor Franklin as a "noted Tory and Ministerial Tool . . . a mischievous and dangerous enemy" who had been "exceedingly busy in perplexing the cause of Liberty and in serving the designs of the British King and his minions."

"If his excellency escapes the vengeance of the people, due to the enormity of his crimes," said the *Courant,* "his redemption will flow not from his personal merit but from the high esteem and veneration which this country entertains for his honored father [Benjamin]."[22]

Medicine

Epidemic in Boston

In the face of a real smallpox epidemic around Boston—an estimated 10,000 are down with it—Massachusetts' legislature, the General Court, this week removed a standing prohibition on smallpox inoculation in the city. It will permit the procedure for four days, after which time inoculation in the city will again be forbidden under penalty of the law.

The position of the General Court is not a condemnation of inoculation. It is only an attempt to keep the practice under control, and to keep persons under inoculation separated from the healthy population. To do that, the General Court this week also approved legislation permitting inoculating hospitals to be set up in each county in the state.[23]

A hospital in Petersham, Massachusetts, operated by Ephraim Woolson, advertised smallpox inoculation as follows: Persons twelve years of age and up, nine dollars; children between seven and twelve, forty shillings; children under seven, one guinea. For these sums, patients would be inoculated, dieted, lodged and attended for twenty-one days. Longer confinements would be at the rate of seven shillings a week for adults and less in proportion to age for children.

Religion

The Pulpit Patriots

In the war with Great Britain, the army's chaplains have often played important roles—and not always through prayer and preaching. At Lexington, Concord and Bunker's Hill, clergymen took an active part in the fighting. And it was in the home of a clergyman, the Rev. Jonas Clark of Lexington, that Samuel Adams and John Hancock found asylum from British troops. In their more traditional role, few clergymen have been as spirited in their patriotism—and none has had a better flock to influence —as the Rev. Jacob Duché, who, as chaplain to the Continental Congress, has effectively preached the patriot cause.

The influence wielded by the clergy—and it has been clearly against the mother country—had not gone unnoticed by the British even before the outbreak of revolution. When in 1774 the Assembly of Massachusetts requested a general fast throughout the colony, the royal governor explained his refusal by saying, "The request was only an opportunity for sedition to flow from the pulpit."

Those clergymen who join the army as chaplains can often contribute significantly to the success of military operations by helping to maintain morale among the fighting men, by lifting downtrodden spirits, by reaffirming a sense of humanity to the dehumanizing experience of mortal conflict. To a good military commander, a cadre of chaplains is thus no more dispensable than guns and ammunition. So thought Colonel George Washington in the late war, when he sent back to the Governor of Virginia repeated requests for chaplains.

In this war, now as general and commanding officer, he is still making the same requests—with a little more success. Last December he wrote to Congress that "frequent applications have been made to me respecting the chaplains' pay, which is too small to encourage men of abilities. Some of them who have left their flocks are obliged to pay the pastor acting for them more than they receive." At that time, when his twenty-seven regiments at Cambridge had a total of nine chaplains, he was working his way around the problem by assigning chaplains to several regiments at a time, even while recognizing this would not be a permanent solution.

Now, he is beginning to get from Congress the support for which he has been looking. He announced this week from his headquarters in New York:

"The honorable Continental Congress having been pleased to allow a chaplain to each regiment, with the pay of thirty-three and a third dollars per month, the colonels or commanding officers of each regiment are directed to procure chaplains—accordingly persons of good character and exemplary lives—[and] to see that all inferior officers and soldiers pay them suitable respect, and attend carefully upon religious exercises. . . . The General hopes and trusts that every officer and man will endeavor so to live and act as becomes a Christian soldier, defending the dearest rights and liberties of his country."[24]

Athletics

Bruisers: In the Ring and Out

Boxing is not only a sport for two contenders; it is just as much a sport for hordes of onlookers who often wager huge sums of money on the outcome. For a recent bout at Chingford Hatch, near London, a sum estimated at more than 700 *l* was laid on two combatants whose admirers, in this case, were divided not only by their interest in boxing but by national pride as well.

The contenders: Englishman William Wood, a horsehair weaver by trade, and the Irish Bruiser, of unknown occupation. When they took the ring at two o'clock, they wasted little time getting down to business, and to the delight of spectators, business was the utmost fury between the two. But no more than three minutes into the fight, the Englishman landed a violent blow that sent the Irish Bruiser reeling, and gave every appearance of ending the fight. With that the Bruiser's compatriots—about 150 Irishmen in the crowd—pulled previously hidden sticks and bludgeons from under their coats and attacked the ring. Englishman Wood fled for safety.

Such an outcome was mild. Still well remembered is the fight in which the distinguished bruiser, James Parrot, was beaten so dreadfully he was given up for dead. That time the loser's partisans were not content to chase the winner; they stirred up a riot that left ten mortally wounded.[25]

This story is the only one in the book related to sports—bearing out, more or less, the proportion of sports to other news at that time. There was really nothing at all in American newspapers (and indeed there was very little in the way of sports to begin with, most people being too busy working to have time for such diversions). What few newspapers we have from Continental Europe present the same picture. In the British newspapers of 1776 there was this boxing story; there were on rare occasions brief mentions of a boat race or a cricket match; and there were frequent advertisements about horse races (though no follow-up stories about winners, one being obliged to be at the track to find that out).

"Cunning Evasions"

The *Scottish Gazette,* says a correspondent in London, is so prone to "falsehood" and "cunning evasions" that it is not to be trusted. Complains the correspondent: "If an engagement happens at sea, we hear nothing of the ships which are taken from us. If there are any taken from the enemy, though the bulk of an oyster boat, we are sure to have it added to the list on the *Gazette.* If Howe is forced from Boston with ten thousand men, who were to have conquered all America, the *Gazette* calls it 'a resolution to remove.' "[26]

THE WEEK OF JULY 15TH

The War

Peace: Proffered, Doubted

"So that the good people of the United States may be informed of what nature are the [British peace] commissioners," Congress has directed the publication of a declaration by Lord Howe to the royal governors on ways of restoring peace.

Essentially the declaration promises pardons to individuals who will return their allegiance to the crown. It was issued by Lord Howe—he and his brother, the General, are the king's peace commissioners—aboard his ship, *Eagle,* off the coast of Massachusetts June 20th.

Since the British peace proposal makes no attempt whatever to treat of the basic causes leading to the declaration of the colonies as free and independent states, and would restore tranquility only through submission to British policy, Congress—in ordering publication—apparently feels most Americans will be angered, and not persuaded, by its message. That message:

"Whereas the King is desirous to deliver all his subjects from the calamities of war and the other oppressions which they now undergo, and to restore said colonies to his protection and peace . . . I do, therefore, hereby declare that due consideration shall be had to the meritorious services of all persons who shall aid and assist in restoring the public tranquility in the said colonies, or in any part or parts thereof; that pardons shall be granted, dutiful representations received, and every suitable encouragement given, for promoting such measures as shall be conducive to the establishment of legal government and peace, in pursuance of his Majesty's most gracious purposes aforesaid."

At almost the same time Congress sent Howe's proposal to the news-papers, General Washington in New York was preparing for a preliminary meeting on the subject with the British Adjutant General, Colonel James Patterson. The meeting, held at Patterson's request, came on July 20th; it produced no discernible progress.

The first order of business was a British apology for the way in which General William Howe proposed such a meeting in the first place. His letter, addressed to "George Washington, Esquire," was refused by Washington on the grounds it was directed to a private citizen and not to an officer of the United States. Patterson apologized for the misunderstanding, claiming there was no intent to disrespect Washington's rank, and then gently reminded the General that he, last summer, once addressed a communication to "The Honorable William Howe, Esquire."

That settled, the meeting is said to have proceeded to the only substantive issue discussed: treatment of prisoners. Both sides exchanged assurances of fair treatment, and discussed procedures for exchange of prisoners. But on the question of Canada, where British mistreatment of captured Americans has been rampant, no accommodation appeared possible. Colonel Patterson explained that the operations of war to the north are out of Howe's jurisdiction.[27]

Congress

Notable Absence

Congress this week received the credentials of the newly elected Pennsylvania delegation, largest in Congress. For the most part they were old faces, but one was missing. No longer a delegate from Pennsylvania is John Dickinson, that outspoken doubter of independence, who after long and zealous debate, proved his convictions by voting against the Declaration. The Provincial Congress of Pennsylvania has now voted against him, refused to return him as a delegate. Those elected: Dr. Benjamin Franklin, Colonel George Ross, George Clymer, Robert Morris, Colonel James Wilson, John Morton, Dr. Benjamin Rush, Colonel James Smith and George Taylor. Each receives a salary of twenty shillings per diem.

Dickinson was later elected to the Continental Congress from Delaware.[28]

No Rest

For his acknowledged labors as the principal author of the Declaration of Independence, Virginia Delegate Thomas Jefferson appears to be getting not a respite but new responsibility. Of seven committees appointed in Congress since the Declaration was adopted, young Jefferson has been named to five—more than any other member. He now adds to his duties: a committee to investigate an alleged plot to free prisoners at the Philadelphia jail; the committee on Indian affairs; a committee to revise the journals of Congress and direct what parts shall be published; a committee to consider the propriety and means of augmenting the flying camp in the Middle Department; and a committee to examine the intercepted letters of royal governors Franklin (New Jersey), Penn (Pennsylvania), Eden (Maryland), Dunmore (Virginia), Martin (North Carolina) and Wright (Georgia).[29]

Nor Read Nor Talk

As the limited objectives for which it organized have more and more broadened in scope and begun to assume a character of permanency, so too has Congress broadened its facilities and acquired the necessities of permanency. An example of the former is the appointment of staff for the president and the committee on the treasury; an example of the latter is the adoption of permanent rules and orders, a matter settled this week. Among the new rules:

—No member shall read any printed paper in the House during the sitting thereof, without leave of Congress;

—No member shall speak more than twice in any one debate, without leave of the House;

—When the House is sitting, no member shall talk to another so as to interrupt any member who may be speaking in the debate;

—No member shall depart from the service of the House without permission or order from his constituents;

—Not until nine colonies are present in the House shall the Congress proceed to business;

—No person shall be appointed to any office of profit unless he shall have the consent of seven colonies, nor shall any ballot be counted, unless the person for whom the ballot shall be given be first named to the house before the balloting be gone into.[30]

Not Too Soon

The Declaration of Independence, according to Samuel Adams, has given "vigour to the spirits of the people," and had such a step been taken nine months ago, it would have resulted in Canada being a part of the union. "But what does it avail to find fault with what is past?" said Adams; "let us do better for the future."[31]

The States

Celebrating Independence: Boston

Independence was proclaimed here Thursday from the balcony of the State House as two regiments of Continental troops formed into thirteen divisions on King Street and crowds of people gathered around. Inside the State House were members of the Council and the House of Representatives, magistrates, ministers, selectmen, officers of the Continental Army, and many prominent citizens of Boston and surrounding towns.

At one o'clock, the sheriff of the County of Suffolk read the Declaration to a chorus of huzzas from the crowd. Then, at a signal, thirteen cannon were fired at nearby Fort Hill, their raucous ovation echoed in turn around the city by artillery at Dorchester Neck, Castle William, Nantasket and Point Alderton. Finally, an artillery regiment on King Street did likewise—thirteen times; and then the regiments in thirteen divisions, in succession, a series of thirteen salutes with their muskets. Said one who was there: it was the "greatest joy."[32]

Exempt Firemen

Members of fire engine companies in the city of New York will henceforth be exempt from military duty in either the city or county militia. City officials have advised fire captains to engage as many able citizens as possible to fill vacancies of such firemen as have already left for military service.[33]

Foreign Affairs

Worsening Relations

In Madrid, there is increasing speculation that a break in diplomatic relations, and even war, may be in the offing between Spain and Portugal. Giving credence to such speculation are reports of continued hostilities between the Portuguese and the Spanish in South America. Further evidence of a new cleavage in Europe came earlier this month when the Portuguese government—an ally of Britain—issued a prohibition of trade with America and ordered all American ships out of Portuguese ports within eight days.[34]

Medicine

Something in Common

The separate stations of nobility and common man are hardly anywhere more apparent than in Paris. Yet of late the young King Louis XVI, twenty-one, his younger brother, the Comte d'Artois, and other nobility are sharing something with many an ordinary Frenchman: the measles.

The disease, which has reached epidemic proportions, appears to be of the sort described by the great British physician, Thomas Sydenham, as having swept London in 1670. This form of measles usually runs its course in eight days, but requires the same cooling regimen as smallpox. French physicians have advised the public against using either a hot or invigorating regimen.[35]

Press

America in 1976?

What will England and America be like two hundred years hence? Will the present hostilities be a turning point in the life of each? Will one go on to greatness, and the other wither away, a declining culture whose day in the sun has turned to dusk?

An anonymous correspondent, writing last month in the respected London journal *Lottery Magazine* has some definite ideas. If his vision of the future is as clear as his sentiment on the colonial question, here is the way the two countries will be after two centuries:

America as a whole: Rich, flourishing, cultivated, with new cities, towns and villas; *Great Britain as a whole*: Barren, wasted, wild, with some few remains of its ancient splendor.

Philadelphia: An imperial city, rich in all the products of the earth, carrying on immense commerce with half the globe; *London*: A village supporting a few fishermen who make a wretched subsistence by catching plaice, flounder and other small fish.

Boston: A large mercantile city; *Bristol*: Just like London.

New York: Famous for its shipping; *Liverpool*: Just like Bristol.

Quebec: A fortress commanding the whole district of Canada and adjacent counties; *Dover*: In the possession of the Prussians, who overran France and took this place in the last century.

Reading, Massachusetts: Famous for its extensive woolen manufacture; *Norwich*: Three houses, in one of which they show the remains of a weaving machine.

New Jersey: A collegiate city, famous all over the world for the learning of its members; *Oxford and Cambridge*: About twenty houses each; in either place is a ballad-printer's.

In what is Philadelphia: A palace, a high court of justice, a cathedral, grand mews; *In what was London*: Buckingham-house turned to a dunghill, Westminster-hall turned to a Methodist meeting house, St. Paul's turned to a brothel, and the Guildhall a stable.

To a Londoner opposed to his country's policy on America, that's the way things will be going over the next two centuries. It will take a future generation, in that distant year of 1976, to pass judgment.[36]

Lottery Magazine *was so called because its one-shilling price included a stub with a number, such number—if it matched the first or last drawn tickets or either of the 20,000 1 tickets in the State Lottery—being worth 100 guineas to the reader, courtesy of the publisher. Gimmickry aside, the magazine was a good one.*

Amusements

Exercise in Ingenuity

Among the fashionable in England, a new amusement is rapidly gaining popularity. It is called charades.

A charade has something of the nature of a riddle, but follows a certain formula. The subject must be a word of two syllables, each of which alone constitutes a word (as for example, *sack-cloth, sea-son, Corn-wall*). It must be guessed from an enigmatical description which hints at first the two syllables separately, and then the whole subject word. Thus:

> To my *First* may I never be put!
> On my *Second* may I never be sordidly
> intent!
> My *Whole*, upon my modesty, I
> will never sell.

will, to an astute student of charades, reveal the word *bar-gain*.

The game, of course, has its detractors. Some call it "void of thought"; others say it is "nonsensical." "On the contrary," says *Westminster Magazine*, "it may be pronounced an exercise for the ingenuity, and where there is any to display, will be sure to display it. It serves to fill up, and agreeably too, an interval at breakfast, or a gap in conversation; and if not greatly instructive, is at least innocent and amusing. . . . The conceited pedant may wrinkle his front at their appearance, but the man of real learning knows the necessity of such relaxations."

Some other samples:

1.

> My *First* is called or bad or good,
> May pleasure or offend ye;
> My *Second*, in a thirsty mood,
> May very much befriend ye.
> My *Whole*, tho' stiled a "cruel word,"
> May yet appear a kind one;
> It often may with joy be heard,
> With tears may often blind one.

2.

> My *First* is equally friendly to
> the thief and the lover, the toper and
> the student. My *Second* is light's
> opposite; yet they are frequently seen
> hand in hand; and their union, if
> judicious, gives us much pleasure.
> My *Whole* is tempting to the touch,
> grateful to the sight, fatal to the
> taste.

3.

> My *First* has been called the seat
> of honour; it seems to resent some
> salutes and invite others. My *Second*
> it behoves us all to appear in. My
> *Whole* is frequently sought for by the
> baffled projector, the determined
> vermin-killer, and the desperate lover.

1. *Fare-well*   2. *Night-shade*   3. *Arse-nick*[37]

THE WEEK OF JULY 22ND

The War

"Determined and Cool"

The Americans, both officers and men, who defended Sullivan's Island in Charleston Harbor against British attack last month were for the most part raw troops, untested in battle. That they proved themselves that day is since obvious.

The commander-in-chief of the Southern Department of the Continental army, General Charles Lee, was there, and yet sufficiently removed from both the preparation for the battle and conduct of the defense to be able to profess an objective view of the battle. He has now offered his assessment to Congress, and it is one that ought to make the whole garrison proud.

Said Lee of Moultrie and his men: "I found them determined and cool to the last degree; their behaviour would, in fact, have done honour to the oldest troops. I therefore beg leave to recommend in the strongest terms to the Congress the commanding officer, Colonel Moultrie, and his whole garrison, as brave soldiers and excellent citizens."[38]

Inducement

The Continental army will seek to induce British officers and soldiers to defect by offering grants of land ranging from 200 to 10,000 acres beyond the Ohio River. The amount of acreage would depend on rank.

The offer, to be announced by Washington's headquarters in handbills written in both English and German and circulated among British troops, will seek defectors among those who might consider the war a direct violation of the British constitution—those who might quit the

King's service and settle in America "rather than imbue their hands in the blood of their best friends."

Meanwhile, intercepted letters indicate the British are planning a similar scheme, and will try to cajole Americans to lay down their arms in return for land at the conclusion of hostilities.[39]

Congress

"Some Progress"

On Monday, after he presided at a committee of the whole of Congress, Virginia's Benjamin Harrison reported "some progress." On Tuesday, he told of "farther progress." On Wednesday, he reported "not having finished." Thursday it was that we "desired leave to sit again." And on Friday, it was much the same, only this time from Pennsylvania's John Morton, substituting for Harrison.

The subject of Congress's most intensive deliberation since the Declaration of Independence was another matter of vast significance: the Articles of Confederation for the perpetual union of the colonies, reported out of committee on July 12th. Still confidential, the committee's draft appears likely of continued debate by Congress in committee of the whole for some time to come.[40]

The States

BAPTIZED: Last Sunday, in East Windsor, Connecticut: a child, Independence by name.[41]

Celebrating Independence: Williamsburg

The Declaration of Independence was proclaimed Thursday at the Capitol, the Courthouse and the Palace to the acclamations of the people and the firing of cannon and muskets. Several regiments of Continental troops paraded.[42]

Signs of the Times

Throughout its colonial days Boston, like other towns in America, displayed its British heritage in the signs that adorned its places of public accommodation: the Lion and Crown; the Pestle and Mortar and Crown; the Heart and Crown, and so on. Colonial no longer, Boston should be rid of anything that even looks like a crown, decided its citizens this week. Throughout the town they went, tearing down every last sign of old times, and turning such vestiges of colonialism into a giant bonfire on, of all places, King Street.[43]

Aptly Named

Operating out of Salem, Massachusetts, under the command of Captain John Fisk, carrying fourteen carriage guns and two swivels in its mission of menace to the ships of his Majesty's fleets, is a privateer called the *Tyrannicide*.[44]

"State" of Rhode Island

Rhode Island is now officially a "state" instead of a "colony" by act of the General Assembly. By concurrent legislation, the Assembly has also voted formal approval of the Declaration of Independence, and has made any show of loyalty to the crown a high offense: Specifies the latter act: ". . . if any person within this state shall, under pretence of preaching or in any other way and manner whatever, acknowledge or declare the said king to be our rightful lord and sovereign, or shall pray for success of his arms, or that he may vanquish or overcome all his enemies, shall be deemed guilty of a high misdemeanor." Such an offense will carry a fine of 100 *l*.[45]

Appropriate Symbol

Since late last year, American ships have been flying a flag, either striped or plain, depicting a coiled rattlesnake and the motto, "Don't Tread on Me."

The immediate symbolism is obvious: the rattlesnake is a potent beast when set upon. But there may be a deeper symbolism that makes the rattler particularly appropriate for America. For example, this appraisal:

"Ancients accounted a snake or serpent an emblem of wisdom, and in certain attitudes, [a symbol] of endless duration. The rattlesnake is properly representative of America, as this animal is found in no other part of the world. The eye of this creature excels in brightness, most of any other animal. She has no eyelids, and is therefore an emblem of vigilance. She never begins an attack, nor ever surrenders; she is therefore an emblem of magnanimity. She is frequently found with thirteen rattles, and they increase yearly."

What makes that account particularly interesting is that it was printed this week in London's *St. James's Chronicle*.[46]

It was originally printed in the Virginia Gazette *(Dixon & Hunter), May 11, 1776.*

Household Hints

Ink or wine spilled on linen or woolen cloth ought not to be a reason for discarding that article, according to the *South Carolina and Georgia Almanack*, which offers this advice: Take the juice of lemons and wet the spot with it divers times, letting dry between each application; then wash the soiled area with white soap and vinegar. The spot will go out.

Other suggestions offered by this year's *Almanack*:

For pimples on the face: Boil together in water a handful of the herbs patience and pimpernel; wash with this decoction every day.

To destroy moths, bugs and fleas: Take one gill of spirits of turpentine and two gills of spirits of wine—or in the same proportions, greater or smaller quantities—mingle them together well, then brush lightly over hangings, easy chairs, coverlids, bedspreads, &c, taking care to let the solution enter the joints of wood. This will effectually kill the insects mentioned and destroy their eggs, as well as prevent the approach of every other insect.[47]

Foreign Affairs

The Stubborn Dutch

The States General of Holland, in recognition of a standing agreement with Great Britain, have in the past maintained a prohibition on the export of gunpowder to the American colonies. Now the Dutch have refused to renew that prohibition, and have furthermore turned down British requests for military support. Thus have relations between the two countries become mired as in no recent year.

In part the ill feeling stems from an agreement, dating back to 1750, providing for four Scotch regiments to be stationed in the service of the Dutch states. The officers and men of these regiments have begun chafing at the duty, and would like to be transferred to America, or to go home. Britain, badly in need of troops, would like to have them back anyway. But the Dutch have thus far refused to back down on the agreement, and are insisting that the Highlanders stay. They have also declined to furnish Dutch soldiers for service to the British Crown.

Britain has retaliated for the Dutch stubborness by temporarily seizing several of the smaller nation's ships. The States of Holland have reacted by beginning to build up their own armed forces. Nevertheless, open hostilities are not considered likely.

Britain might not have expected otherwise had it paid heed to what Johan Theodor Vander Capellen, Deputy for the Dutch Province of Over-Yessel, said last December: "The very idea of employing our troops against America, in my opinion, is detestable in the highest degree. I take the Americans to be deserving of universal esteem: they are brave, they took up arms in defence of their rights, rights which they as men received from God himself, and not from the legislative power of Great Britain. . . . Their cause, I hope, will stir up all other nations and people whose liberty is hurt."[48]

DIED: Tuesday evening, in Pimlico, London, of unknown causes: the older of two elephants in the royal menagerie. His Majesty made a present of the carcass to the noted surgeon and anatomist Dr. John Hunter who, with the help of twenty of his students, set to work dissecting the beast Friday.[49]

Change of Cargo

Sailing down the Thames, said a correspondent in London recently, used to be a "rational amusement." One could thrill to the sight of an immense number of merchantmen unfurling their sails for every quarter of the globe. Now mostly to be seen are transports bound for America, "laden with instruments calculated to carry death to the bosoms, and desolation through the country of our unfortunate fellow subjects, friends and brothers."[50]

Science

Lunar Eclipse

Barring clouds or rain, America's astronomers will have their most exciting event of the year next Tuesday, July 30th: a three-hour, thirty-one-minute total eclipse of the moon.

The eclipse will begin at thirty-two minutes after five in the evening, with onset of total darkness coming fifty-nine minutes later. At eighteen after seven, the eclipse will be at its maximum. At three after nine, it will be all over.

This eclipse is the only one of five, solar or lunar, visible this year in the United States.[51]

Education

Of Bachelors and New Arts

"Leave nothing undone which ought to be done; do nothing which ought to be omitted . . . encounter troubles with magnanimity; enjoy prosperity with moderation."

Graduates have heard those exhortations before, and doubtless will at commencement exercises of the future. What distinguished the valedictory address of Timothy Dwight at Yale College this week was another exhortation peculiar to current times. Said young Dwight, twenty-four, to his fellow students receiving bachelor of arts degrees:

"All of these [the lessons learned here] are the arts of peace. But you may, especially at the present period, be called into the active scenes of a military life. Should this be your honorable lot, I can say nothing which ought more to influence you than that you fight for the property, the freedom, the life, the glory, the religion of the inhabitants of this mighty [American] empire; for the cause, for the honor of mankind and your Maker."

Except for that, Dwight's address contained no reference to the awesome events of the past months. He explained later that he drafted the address last summer and was prevented, by failing eyesight, from amending his remarks, as he would like to have done. In an oblique way, however, he sounded a note of confidence in his fellow graduates there and at Harvard, William and Mary, New York, Rhode Island, New Jersey, Queens, Philadelphia and other colleges, and other young men throughout the United States, and in the new nation they are being called upon to build. He concluded with a quotation from the prophet Isaiah: "Nations shall come to thy light, and kings to the brightness of thy rising."

Timothy Dwight (1752–1817) went on to be a chaplain in the Continental Army, and eventually served as President of Yale from 1795 to 1817, as did his grandson, Timothy Dwight, from 1886 to 1898. [52]

Early Commencement

Commencement exercises were held this week at Dartmouth College in Hanover, New Hampshire, five weeks earlier than usual because of "the situation of our public affairs." Despite the shorter term the trustees of the college were reported well satisfied with the qualifications of the ten students receiving bachelor of arts degrees and the six being honored as masters of arts.[53]

Trade and Commerce

Rural Economy

For one who has never tried it but is interested in starting a new business, how good is farming? The answer is it can be very rewarding for one willing to persevere a few probable difficulties at the outset.

So says *Rural Economy,* a guide to farm management originally published in London and now reprinted and sold by James Humphreys, Jr., in Philadelphia. An extract, offering some wise advice for the novice: "There is no doubt the gentleman farmer may turn farming to good account, and yet be cheated for some time by the people around him; he pays for experience; but he gets it, and that will, with good management, afterwards pay him again; but then large sums of money are requisite for this; and in the stocking of a farm, good allowances ought to be made for such unseen expenses."[54]

Press

Two Coppers to Three

Philadelphia's *Pennsylvania Evening Post,* which was founded a year and a half ago by Benjamin Towne, has announced its first price increase.

Beginning with its July 27th issue, the newspaper went from "two cop-
pers" an issue to three. Although no explanation for the increase was
given, it is assumed that a scarcity—and hence rising cost—of paper is
the primary reason. The *Post* is published Tuesday, Thursday and Saturday evenings. The *Pennsylvania Packet, Pennsylvania Gazette,* and *Pennsylvania Ledger,* meanwhile, remain the same at ten shillings per year,
or a little more than two pence a copy, once a week.

The Pennsylvania Evening Post *seven years later became America's first daily newspaper.*[55]

THE WEEK OF JULY 29TH

The War

Heroes and Non-Heroes

The popular hero of the American defense of Sullivan's Island in
Charleston Harbor is clearly the garrison's commander, Colonel William
Moultrie. In tribute to his gallant leadership, the garrison has been re-
named Fort Moultrie.

Meanwhile, still recovering from his dismal defeat at Sullivan's Island
the end of June, Sir Peter Parker and his shattered squadron finally departed Charleston Harbor this week. Passing Charleston bar, Parker's
ships were confronted by a floating American battery sent only to annoy
them, found the results more than simple harassment: captured was a brig
having on board an entire company of Royal Highlanders who are now
in American custody.[56]

Congress

A Final Formality

The entry in the journal of Congress Friday, August 2nd, gave little
hint of the sweeping significance behind it. It merely noted:

> "The Declaration of Independence being
> engrossed and compared at the table, was signed
> by the members."

Thus was a final formality accomplished. The document approved by
Congress the fourth of last month, and signed then only by President
John Hancock and Secretary Charles Thomson, was since engrossed on
parchment. Now, were any to doubt its universal acceptance, it has been

signed by each and every member of Congress—even those who were not yet members when the declaration was first approved—and it is thereby guaranteed to be the unanimous expression of thirteen separate but now more than ever united states.[57]

Failure in Canada: Why?

That the American campaign in Canada has been a disaster is generally admitted; why it has been, may be debated. This week Congress set forth what it believes are the three principal reasons. In concurring with the report of a committee that investigated the failures of the northern campaign, Congress concluded:

"That the short enlistments of the Continental troops in Canada have been one great cause of the miscarriages there, by rendering unstable the number of men engaged in military enterprises, by making them disorderly and disobedient to their officers, and by precipitating the commanding officers into measures which their prudence might have postponed could they have relied on a longer continuance of their troops in service;

"That the want of hard money has been one other great source of the miscarriages in Canada, rendering the supplies of necessaries difficult and precarious, the establishment of proper magazines absolutely impracticable, and the pay of the troops of little use to them;

"That a still greater and more fatal source of misfortunes has been the prevalence of the small-pox in that Army, a great proportion whereof has thereby been usually kept unfit for duty."[58]

"No Decision"

For five successive days this week, Congress resolved itself into a committee of the whole for more discussion of the Articles of Confederation, and for five successive days reported "progress" but no decision. The debate continues.[59]

Parliament

Postponement

When both houses of Parliament adjourned on May 23rd, they set August 1st as the date for opening the new session. Accordingly this week members of the House of Commons and the House of Lords returned to Westminster, but only to postpone the reopening still further—now at least until Thursday, September 5th.

Further prorogation would make Thursday, October 31st, the opening date.[60]

Major Mission (If True)

As the intended ambassador-extraordinary to Russia ten years ago, Britain's Hans Stanley was given the task of negotiating a defensive treaty with Prussia and Russia. But the plan in preliminary form was so poorly received by Prussia that Stanley never took the assignment, and has filled the intervening years primarily as Governor of the Isle of Wight and Cofferer of the Royal Household.

That proposed assignment and the record of Charles Jenkinson as an Undersecretary of State and more recently as a Lord of the Admiralty and a Lord of the Treasury may explain the conjecture in London that the two men have been given a joint mission which, if true, might have an incomparable bearing on the war in America. Reports a correspondent in London: "We have it from undoubted authority that Mr. Stanley and Mr. Jenkinson are gone to Paris with proposals to cede all Canada to the crown of France upon conditions of their taking an active part against the Americans."

Apparently only conjecture.[61]

Execution at Tyburn

Said London's *Lottery Magazine*: "May the premature deaths of these unhappy men be a warning to the young, the thoughtless, the extravagant! May they consider that 'Honesty is the best policy,' and that a shilling earned by labour and spent with prudence is of more value than any sum acquired by dishonorable practices."

That exhortation concluded a story on the execution at Tyburn, a common hanging place outside London. Seven young men accused of various crimes—James Standish, James Humphreys, John Mayo, Thomas Askew, Joseph Bissel, George Rowney and Archibald Girdwood—faced the gallows together; they did so in different ways.

As they were tied to the gibbet, caps over their eyes, Bissel and Askew clasped their hands together in apparent penitence and contrition. Rowney showed only unconcern. Girdwood, who earlier told a bystander to "go to hell" when asked how he felt, now laughed as the halter was placed around his neck. He would have none of the cap over his eyes, pushing it back up and looking around with astonishing indifference. That, however, would be his final act of defiance. As thousands of people watched, and groaned, the seven were "launched into eternity" while pigeons were set into flight to announce the fatal event.

Standish, Humphreys and Mayo had been convicted of footpad robberies; Askew and Bissel, for illegal coining; Rowney and Girdwood for sending a threatening letter. Rowney's younger brother, Thomas, was spared death because of his age.[62]

Religion

Minimum Ages

An edict by the Duke of Modena, Italy, has set minimum ages for girls who wish to take the veil. Henceforth, no parent or guardian may enter a daughter, niece or ward in a convent until the girl is at least ten years of age. The girl may not then wear the habit until she is twenty, nor make her vows until the year her novitiate is completed.[63]

Press

Reporting Independence

> " . . . the most important event that ever happened to the American colonies, an event which will doubtless be celebrated through a long succession of future ages, by anniversary commemorations, and be considered as a grand era in the history of the American states."
>
> New York Journal
> July 11, 1776

It has been one month since the *Pennsylvania Evening Post* of July 2nd first told the news: "This day the Continental Congress declared the United Colonies free and independent states." Within those weeks the extraordinary news has spread like a grass fire, up and down the land, reprinted from one newspaper to another.

Not all newspapers covered the story in the same way. The Tory *Pennsylvania Ledger* ignored the news entirely in its July 6th issue (when four other Philadelphia papers had already announced it) and devoted most of that edition to an account of debate in the House of Lords on March 5th. Finally on July 13th the *Ledger* presented the full text of the declaration—without comment on the second page. Likewise did the *New York Packet* (July 11th), the *Providence Gazette* (July 13th), and *Connecticut Courant* (July 15th) give conspicuous display to reports on Parliament as old as October 26, 1775, while presenting the text of the declaration as a seemingly secondary matter.

Other newspapers rushed to print an announcement as soon as the news was heard. Reported Alexander Purdie's *Virginia Gazette* on July 12th:

"The postmaster in Fredericksburg writes, of last Wednesday, that by a gentleman just arrived from Philadelphia, he had seen an Evening Post of the 2nd instant, which mentions that the Hon. the Continental Congress had that day declared the United Colonies free and independent states."

The *New England Chronicle* broke the news in Boston, telling its readers on July 11th:

"We are assured that on July the second the Congress voted INDE-PENDENCY, not one colony dissenting; but the delegates of New York remained neuter, for want of being instructed on the head."

Meanwhile, in New York on the 6th, John Anderson's *Constitutional Gazette* was the first to announce independence outside of Philadelphia. It was very late news for a paper nearly one hundred miles away, and the report was necessarily brief: "On Tuesday last, the Continental Congress declared the UNITED COLONIES FREE and INDEPENDENT STATES." On the following Wednesday the bi-weekly *Gazette* carried the entire text of the declaration.

In Philadelphia, Heinrich Miller's *Pennsylvanischer Staatsbote* on July 9th published for that area's German-speaking population the first text of the Declaration in a foreign language. In the *Staatsbote,* that document is *Eine Erklärung durch die Repräsentanten der Vereinigten Staaten von America, im General-Congress versammelt,* and it begins, *Wenn es im Lauf menschlicher Begebenheiten . . .*

In Newport, Rhode Island, printer Solomon Southwick rushed out a special edition, a *Newport Mercury EXTRAORDINARY,* to give readers the full text on the 18th. The news had arrived too late to permit more than a brief announcement in his regular edition on the 15th.

John Holt's *New York Journal,* on the 11th, predicted the Declaration of Independence "will doubtless be celebrated through a long succession of future ages" (see above) and to help get the celebration started it offered this suggestion:

" ☞ The Declaration of Independence of the United States of America is inserted in this paper in the present form [on a separate page, to be detached] to oblige a number of our customers who intend to separate it from the rest of the paper and fix it up in open view in their houses as a mark of their approbation of the Independent Spirit of their representatives."[64]

Better Late than Never

Absent from Charleston since May 31st, the *South Carolina and American General Gazette* now is back. Explained the publishers, R. Wells and son, in their issue of August 2nd: there were no issues the past two months because the printing presses were removed from town during the alarm.

The *Gazette* made a special effort to bring readers up to date, observ-

ing that "the transactions in this province during that period will probably make it a distinguished one in the American annals." Among the
distinguished events reported better late than never: the Declaration of
Independence and the American victory at nearby Sullivan's Island.[65]

Medicine

The Air in London

As London has grown to become a metropolis of some 800,000 in population, so has it acquired those problems of public health that go with a
great concentration of people. Though nothing on the order of the Great
Plague that swept the English capital 111 years ago (one year before the
Great Fire), matters of public health and sanitation today are causing
steadily increasing concern and a search for appropriate remedies.

Perhaps the most immediately detectable problem is the air: it is sometimes so loaded with impurities that many Londoners reckon it "most
dangerous to health and life." Often stinking and sulphurous, loaded with
human effluvia, vitiated and spoiled, the London atmosphere on a bad
day leaves no solution but a visit to the country for a precious mouthful
of fresh air.

London is chronically damp, and except for the middle of summer,
perennially chilly if not outright cold. That fact of nature is combatted
chiefly through coal fires, which represent the prime source of the bad
air. London's *Gentleman's Magazine* recently described the cycle this
way: Because of the "inflammable, mephitic, and other matters thrown
out, probably an acid is decomposed, and exhaled from the sulphur in
the coal; and thereby certain miasmata of a putrid tendency, may be
neutralized; but . . . there is reason to presume that the injury introduced
into the atmosphere overbalances the good effects arising from the acid
decomposition." Inhaling and exhaling that kind of chemical reaction all
day, it is no wonder many Londoners become valetudinarians and would
rather stay indoors. But that may not necessarily be a better place, warns
Gentleman's Magazine. Places of public assembly such as coffeehouses,
public markets, and other places of business and amusement are all
sources of infection through the transfer of human effluvia in the air. And
what is worse, all have been getting busier and more crowded as population has increased.

"The Royal Exchange," noted the magazine, "affords a striking instance. The exchange hours a few years ago seldom exceeded two o'clock,
and now three is considered the time of high 'change. The crowds of
people that usually remain at this place for upwards of an hour must certainly be pernicious, of which every one may be convinced who enters
upon full 'change immediately from the [relatively] fresher atmosphere
of the street."

Meanwhile, there are these other sources of putridity in the air, according to the magazine: playhouses, public exhibitions, kitchens under ground, night cellars, routs, masquerades and nocturnal revels of all kinds.

Whether it's breathing stinking, sulphurous air outside, or effluvia-laden air inside, the worst affected are always those who are ill to begin with. Lamented a recent observer: "Valetudinarians who have not the leisure to go into the country under a notion of purchasing a mouthful of fresh air, rush into an atmosphere loaded with human effluvia, which of all others, when become vitiated, is the most dangerous to health and life."[66]

Education

Rhetoric and Religion

Delaware Indians, in the formative era of their language, may have decided that a walk through the woods would more likely produce an encounter with a deer than with an evil spirit. Thus to the deer they gave the simple word, *actu;* to the spirit, *machtapequonitto.*

Still other words in their tongue range up to nine syllables, as for example *wilawelensitebewoagan,* which means "highmindedness." But for the expressions of everyday life, the Delaware vocabulary is rich in its simplicity. "To go" is merely *aan,* and "thou comest" is the equally simple *koom.* "The woods" are *tekene,* "summer" is *nipen* and "roasted corn" is *gachgamun.*

In the Delaware language, as in German or Latin, every syllable is pronounced—but not always as one would do it in English. *Ch,* for example, is always a hard sound as in the word *choir; w* before a consonant sounds like *uch; oa* after a *w* is a diphthong. The letters *f* and *r* are non-existent in the Delaware tongue, making it in theory a shade more difficult for a tribesman to learn English than the other way around, although an American confronting the Delaware language for the first time might disagree.

A substantial amount of what we know about the Delawares and their language is the result of the teaching and writing of a Moravian missionary named David Zeisberger, who has settled upon a life on the frontier after wandering from his native Moravia to Saxony, from Holland to England, and finally, by the time he was eighteen, from Georgia to the Moravian colony in Pennsylvania.

Zeisberger's first real contact with the red men was among the Iroquois, and for a while he lived with one of their chiefs, learning the language. Such knowledge as he gained soon made him valuable to both sides, and in 1745 he helped arrange a treaty between the British and the Six Nations of the Iroquois. The intervening years—and particularly the late war—have only doubled the measure of his reputation, and his effectiveness as mediator between white and red. But it is not this role, or arranging treaties of military significance, or extending the white man's knowledge of his Indian brothers that is his first concern. For Zeisberger, the real reason for being out there on the frontier is spreading Christianity.

These days the missionary work is among the Delawares along the Muskingum River and it is out there that he built what is probably the first church building and school house in the West. A school house needs books, however, and the lack of them in both Delaware and English was resolved by Zeisberger by the writing of one. Recently published in Philadelphia, *Essay of a Delaware-Indian and English Spelling Book* is one hundred thirteen pages of lexicon, simple rules and sample translations.

With typical missionary spirit, Zeisberger has seen to it that the translations serve as a double lesson of rhetoric and religion. Thus does the young Delaware tribesman translating *Katschi a pili Gopatamawosemiwon ni elinquechinak* not only improve his English, but he already knows the First Commandment as well.

Other samples (besides the other nine commandments) include selections from the Gospels (about when Jesus was twelve years old); from the Epistles ("Children, obey your parents," as Paul exhorts in Ephesians); and various prayers.

Not surprisingly, Missionary Zeisberger concludes the book by saying *Nihillalquenk gulapensohalgun woak knenatschiechquon,* which, as any one of his young Indian students might tell you, means "The Lord bless thee and keep thee."

When David Zeisberger died in 1808, at the age of eighty-seven, he had spent sixty-two years among the Indians and established settlements as far west as Michigan and as far north as Canada.[67]

AUGUST

NOW the industrious harvest-man must sweat,
Scorched all day, basted with his own heat,
Reaping the full ears, with their well-stor'd top,
Which pays his labours with a plenteous crop.

The Virginia Almanack
August, 1776

THE WEEK OF AUGUST 5TH

The War

Hessian Hesitation

The mass of British military and naval power around New York leaves not a shadow of doubt that attack will come. Why it has not so far can only be a matter of speculation. One theory advanced is that General Philipp Von Heister, who commands the Hessian troops attached to General Howe, is sticking to the terms of the treaty that brought the German soldiers into the war. That treaty provides that the Hessians would not go into combat except as a body, and so far, only about two-thirds are thought to have arrived in America. Reports a correspondent: "The old soldier [Heister] will not stir a step until he is joined by the last division."[1]

"Impracticable"

The British Admiralty this week released Sir Peter Parker's report on the British debacle—and American victory—of Sullivan's Island in South Carolina June 28th. The report clearly concedes a defeat.

At the time of Parker's naval bombardment, British troops under General Clinton were to land and take control of the American fortress. The plan, of course, failed. "I perceived that the troops had not got a good footing on the north end of Sullivan's Island," reported Parker. "I was perfectly satisfied that the landing was impracticable, and that the attempt would have been the destruction of many brave men without the least probability of success."

On Parker's flagship, the *Bristol,* there were forty killed and seventy-one wounded. The admiral duly reported his own injuries from shell fragments, and called them minimal.[2]

Practicable

The British Admiralty has also released a report from Vice Admiral Lord Shuldham that the British landing on Staten Island the beginning of July was accomplished without incident. Said Shuldham's report: "The inhabitants having immediately, on the troops' landing, surrendered and put themselves under the protection of his Majesty's arms . . . that the whole island has taken the oath of allegiance and fidelity to the king."[3]

Congress

Still No Decision

Congress this week continued debate in committee of the whole on the Articles of Confederation, and again reached no decision. In action, Congress:

—Scheduled a hearing on complaints against Commodore Esek Hopkins, Commander-in-Chief of the Continental Fleet, who is accused of disobeying orders;

—Determined that any enemy seaman captured by the American fleet can be enlisted into service, as an alternative to being held as a prisoner of war, but cannot receive pay;

—And appointed, as new major generals in the Continental army, William Heath, Joseph Spencer, John Sullivan and Nathanael Greene.[4]

The States

Celebrating Independence: Charleston

From a correspondent in Charleston, South Carolina, on Monday: "The Declaration of Independence was proclaimed here, amidst acclamations of a vast concourse of people."[5]

Celebrating Independence: Savannah

Savannah, Georgia, celebrated independence Saturday with a solemn funeral—the mock interment of his Majesty, George III—although towns-people earlier observed the occasion in more traditional fashion with the reading of the Declaration of Independence, followed by a volley of musket fire and a procession to the Liberty Pole.

In the evening was that solemn funeral procession, to the beat of muffled drums in front of the Courthouse; and there—before the largest public gathering in the history of the province—was this eulogy offered: "Forasmuch as George III of Great Britain hath most flagrantly violated his coronation oath and trampled upon the constitution of our country and the sacred rights of mankind, we therefore commit his political existence to the ground, corruption to corruption, tyranny to the grave, and oppression to eternal infamy; in sure and certain hope that he will never obtain a resurrection to rule again over these United States of America."[6]

A Mother's Farewell

"My children, I have a few words to say to you," the mother in Elizabeth Town, New Jersey, advised her four sons as she helped them gather their equipment and go forth to defend against a British attack sooner or later expected. "You are going out in a just cause, to fight for the rights and liberties of your country. You have my blessings and prayers that God will protect and assist you. But if you fall, his will be done. Let me beg of you, my children, that if you fall, it may be like men; and that your wounds may not be in your back parts."[7]

Foreign News

Near Death

At sixty-two, Europe's second oldest monarch—Frederick II of Prussia is sixty-four—King José I of Portugal is reported seriously ill in Lisbon. So poor in fact has his condition become that he is being kept alive only by having a nourishing syrup administered to him through the spout of a teapot. Although the nature of the illness has not been announced, it is known that many in the Court of Lisbon fear his death daily.

He lived until Feb. 24, 1777. [8]

Justice in Pest

In the town of Pest, on the Danube in Upper Hungary, a magistrate who should have known better gave a box on the ear to a townsman during the last carnival. That started a brawl in which eventually many people were involved, and several were killed. By order of the Court of Vienna the participants were tried, and the sentences are such that others may well think twice before entering into such a fray in the future. The magistrate was condemned to spend the rest of his days in the Fort of Spieglberg; a number of townsmen were ordered to a chain gang to clean the streets for three months; others, to be fined. But for seven the penalty will be the maximum: their heads cut off. [9]

Science

Known, and Still to Know

In earliest civilization, man's first concern was his own subsistence—food, clothing, shelter and the like. But as the ages passed, and these basic needs of life could be satisfied routinely, man began to look about him, wonder why things should be the way they are, and consider how he might influence his environment through his increasing knowledge of it. In the words of the late Oliver Goldsmith, "He feels the grateful vicissitudes of day and night, perceives the difference of seasons; he finds some things noxious to his health, and others grateful to his appetite; he would therefore eagerly desire to be informed how these things assumed such qualities."

Where, then, does Man stand today in his quest for the origin of these qualities? In an epic, two-volume *A Survey of Experimental Philosophy*, published posthumously in London in May, Goldsmith reviews the state of knowledge on a wide assortment of matters. Samples:

Electricity: It is a phenomenon, named from the Latin *electrum*, and is most easily defined by examples. Glass, resinous substances, wool, silk and hair, when rubbed, will attract particles of dust to their surfaces. Some substances, such as those cited, have their electrical properties more quickly excited than others, and are therefore called electric bodies. Those which take a long time, or show no signs at all, are called non-electric bodies. Among the latter are water, spirits, mercury, all metals and semi-metals, marble, limestone, all living animals, and all green plants and trees.

Experimentation has been done with a globe of moderately thick glass, one foot in diameter, that is rotated quickly upon a vertical shaft. Considerable friction is thus created, and the globe will attract particles of dust and so forth. If it is then touched by a non-electric body (a piece of metal, a stick, or by the hand) its attracting power immediately ceases. If, however, that which touches the globe has no contact with the earth, the attracting power is not released.

The air is often charged with vast quantities of electrical effluvia. An iron wire can imbibe this fluid from the clouds. At times of thunder, the air is particularly charged. In some countries, the damages sustained by thunder are frequent and terrible. Dr. Benjamin Franklin, in America, has invented a method of securing houses and protecting the inhabitants from its violence. The device consists of an iron rod erected on or near a house. The rod, touching the electrified cloud, imbibes the electrical fluid and carries it down to the earth, where it is dissipated without further mischief.

Hydraulics: There has long been considered an advantage to know the causes by which water spouts from vessels of different heights and distances. It can be reduced to a theorem: the velocity with which water spouts out at a hole in the bottom or side of any vessel whatsoever is in proportion to the square root of the height of the water in the vessel. In other words, if the water in one vessel is nine times higher than in another, it will spout three times as fast. Examples of hydraulic machines include the pump, the siphon, the fire engine and the intermitting fountain.

Effects of air on human body: Air is necessary for the support of all human life, but "why" is a question philosophers cannot easily resolve. Some say there is salt in the air and this is taken into the blood. The reason for this theory is the fact that blood in the arteries is scarlet in color, having been mixed with air in the lungs, while blood in the veins is darker. Scarlet is the color a salt would give to the blood. This is an interesting theory, but not convincing. There is no salt in the blood except part of the salt we eat. Others are of the opinion that air is necessary to drive blood through the body. By this theory, air presses down upon the large surface of blood in the lungs like the piston of a syringe. This is not true either. A child in his mother's womb has blood circulating through his whole body, and no air comes into his lungs whatsoever.

Fire: What is it? The answer has divided the greatest men from ancient to modern times. For Boerhaave, Hombers and Lemery it is a body actually existing, like air and water, and is found in all places and needing only to be collected into a narrow compass to become manifest. That view is opposed by no less than Bacon, Boyle and Newton. They deny fire is a body, and say it is that which arises from the attrition or rubbing of bodies one against another. Such bodies sometimes cast forth flame, which is nothing more than excessively small parts put violently into motion. Modern philosophers in general incline to the opinion of Boerhaave and concur with the ancients in affirming that fire is an element of a particular kind, inscrutable in nature.

While man has thus come a long way in learning "how these things assumed such qualities," he has also come to discover just how much there is still to learn. Says Goldsmith: "At present the real philosopher seems to rest satisfied that there is much in this science yet to be discovered, and that what he already knows bears no proportion to what remains unknown. He no longer therefore pretends to assign causes for all things, but waits till time, industry or accident shall bring new lights to guide the enquiry."

The word "philosophy" at this time included within its meaning what we today call science, and the two words are virtually interchangeable in this story. "Experimental" philosophy was that based on research and experiment as opposed to the earlier "scholastic" philosophy based merely on observation. Goldsmith pointed to Descartes, more than a century earlier, as perhaps the principal force in the transition from old to new.[10]

Press

Earlier Intelligence

Philadelphia's *Pennsylvania Packet,* always a Monday newspaper, is now being published Tuesday mornings. The reason, Publisher John Dunlap told readers: "communicate the earliest intelligence concerning the operations of the American arms in the northern and southern states." Since the posts from both New York and Virginia arrive in Philadelphia on Mondays, that intelligence will no longer have to lie over for a week before appearing in the *Packet.*[11]

Resurrection II

After the siege of Quebec halted publication last November 30th, *La Gazette de Quebec* spent a dormant winter and did not reappear until March 14th with its first accounts of the fighting there at the turn of the year. But one more issue, on the 21st, was all publisher William Brown could manage before continued hostilities in and around Quebec sent him back into hibernation.

Now *La Gazette* is back, proudly proclaiming in large type on the first page of the August 8th issue, *"La Resurrection No. II."* On the first page there is a reprint of an old proclamation (August, one year ago) of his Majesty for "suppressing rebellion and sedition," thus reminding readers that Quebec remains as loyal to the crown as its sister colonies to the south are otherwise.

On the third page, publisher Brown adds his own comment on the turn of events in Quebec: *"C'est avec le plus sensible plaisir que l'Imprimeur trouve que les tems [sic] sont assez heuresment [sic] changés selon ses souhaits . . . de lui offrir de nouveau ses services par le moien d'une* Gazette." In an adjoining column—as for all stories in *La Gazette de Quebec*—there is the same text in English: "It is with the most sensible pleasure the printer finds the times here so agreeably altered to his wishes . . . again to make them a tender of his service by way of the

Gazette." There is also a reminder, to French and English readers alike, that the price of *La Gazette* is still three Spanish dollars a year.[12]

THE WEEK OF AUGUST 12TH

The War

Grand Strategy: A Delay?

It has been apparent for some time that the concentration of British troops in Canada and New York is part of a coordinated strategy: General Burgoyne to push south from Canada, and General Howe to press north from the city of New York, and to meet, perhaps at Albany, cutting the northern states from the southern, breaking up the union, and ending the war.

Thus far, Britain has been dominant in Canada; Howe is massed and ready at New York, and even the most optimistic American concedes that a battle there imminent, even if victory for the United States, will be the bloodiest ever fought on these shores.

Now there is reason to believe that Britain's grand strategy—regardless of the outcome in New York—will have to be postponed. The latest reports from Canada indicate General Burgoyne has concluded that it is impracticable to cross the northern lakes and complete a march to Albany this season. Two reasons, in particular, are given:

—the British army does not have boats of sufficient size and will have to build them, which will take until next summer;

—opposing American forces are thought to be too great to contend with for now.

Thus Burgoyne's army appears to be preparing to spend the winter in Canada, probably around Montreal. General Carleton, commander in chief for Canada, has reportedly sent a request to London for more provisions.[13]

> Notwithstanding a delay in Burgoyne's march south, the British strategy was described this way in a report from London June 15th: "A footing once made from the back settlements [by way of Albany and the Hudson River] and a holdfast established, must be of infinite service, as all the most turbulent of the colonies will thereby be very soon under subjection: and that when once Philadelphia and New York provinces are in the King's hands, the rest of the colonies will be like the twigs in a broom, which when once the bandage that ties them together is cut, are very easily broken to pieces."

Evacuation in New York

A long feared British invasion of the city of New York now appears a certainty; women, children and infirm persons are leaving the city.

They were so ordered by General Washington himself, who said attack upon the city "by our cruel and inveterate enemy may be hourly expected." In the opinion of Washington and his staff, the continued presence of women, children and the infirm would not only be hazardous to such persons, but an impediment to military operations as well. Thus the request for evacuation.

"I do therefore recommend it," said Washington, "to all such persons, as they value their own safety and preservation, to remove with all expedition out of the said town at this critical period, trusting that with the blessing of heaven upon the American arms, they may soon return to it in perfect security; and I do enjoin and require all the officers and soldiers in the army under my command to forward and assist such persons in their compliance with this recommendation."

The best estimates place the British forces on Staten Island at about 22,000 men, making it substantially larger than the force which occupied Boston and the largest yet assembled for deployment against the colonies.

The force is believed to be comprised of these troops: General Howe's command from Halifax, and formerly at Boston: 8,000 men; the Scotch, who embarked from Glasgow for Boston, losing 850 men to American cruisers along the way and now totaling 2,350 men; the defeated troops of Cornwallis and Clinton, from South Carolina, 2,500 men; two divisions of Hessians, Waldeckers and English guards, which arrived on Monday, the 12th of August, 9,000 men.[14]

Congress

Civil Over Military

Tall, aggressive, strong-willed, and a seafarer most of his life, Esek Hopkins of Rhode Island has all of the qualities of a naval commander. And indeed, when those very qualities were called to the attention of the Continental Congress—not the least so by his brother, Stephen, a delegate from Rhode Island and member of the Marine Committee—Esek Hopkins was a likely choice to become the first Commander-in-Chief of the Continental Fleet, and was so confirmed last December.

Now, the same qualities may have run him aground before a Congress zealous in maintaining within the civil government a final say over the military. Tried before Congress for disobedience, Commodore Hopkins is still in command; but he has a mark of censure on his record that may well number his days as the highest ranking naval officer in America.

Ordered by Congress early in the year to have his fleet patrol the coasts of the southern states, Hopkins instead decided on an attack against a British supply depot in the Bahamas and, while successful there, paid dearly when a subsequent encounter with a British ship off Long Island caused extensive damage to his fleet. This defeat and decline of morale among his sailors resulted in his summons to appear personally before Congress.

After a hearing this week, Congress adjudged that Hopkins "did not pay due regard to the tenor of his instructions, whereby he was expressly directed to annoy the enemy's ships upon the coasts of the southern states, and that his reasons for not going . . . immediately to the Carolinas are by no means satisfactory." The result: "Said conduct of Commodore Hopkins deserves the censure of this house, and this house does accordingly censure him."

In other action this week, Congress:

—Approved a further emission of five million dollars in bills of credit, of which 76,923 dollars will be issued in each of the denominations of thirty, eight, seven, six, five, four, three and two dollars;

—Agreed to exempt tutors at the College of New Jersey from military service in the flying camp of the Middle Department.[15]

South America: Land of Dispute

By the Treaty of Tordesillas in 1494, Spain and Portugal agreed to a mutually convenient division of the non-Christian world for the purpose of colonization and spreading of the Gospel. Instead of the New World becoming the exclusive province of Spain, and Africa and India of Portugal, as decreed by Pope Alexander VI (a Spaniard) the year before, the two major powers agreed to divide the New World in such a way that Portugal was given claim to what is now the vast Viceroyalty of Brazil, while Spain took substantially the rest of that continent. What they did not do was establish a fixed boundary between the two.

In the wilds that form the interior, a line of demarcation has never been a great problem, and to the extent it created dissension, it was largely resolved through a treaty in 1750. It is along the settled portions of the coast between Portuguese Brazil and Spanish Buenos Aires to the south, that dispute and conflict have become a way of life. This disputed land, the Banda Oriental, remains the claim of both powers.

Last year General Juan José de Vertiz y Salcedo, the Spanish governor of Buenos Aires, reported to Madrid that the Portuguese were daily encroaching on the colony's rights. Spain complained to the Court of Lisbon, and received a reply that it was only "a quarrel among neighboring inhabitants." Seeking to keep the matter a colonial one, Spain advised General Vertiz the dispute should be settled on his side of the Atlantic. But matters worsened, and Vertiz again sent home a report, this time in more alarming terms. Spain again entered a formal complaint to Lisbon.

It was months later when Lisbon replied—again denying hostile intentions—but by then Spain had decided to take action: it had three regiments of soldiers on their way to Buenos Aires. It was ostensibly a defensive move; at the same time it would at least in part satisfy many Spanish

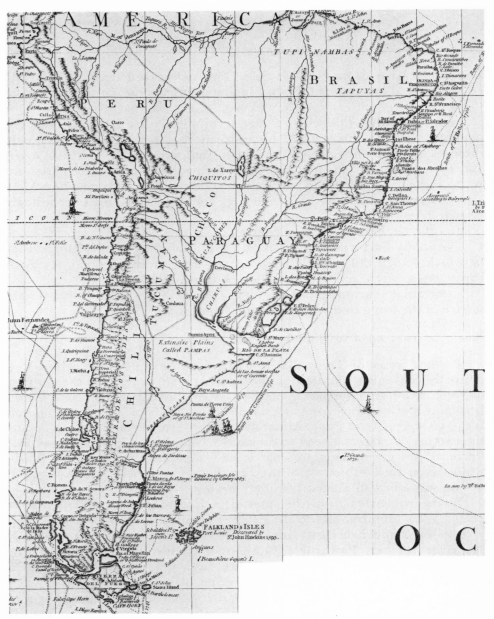

SOUTH AMERICA (Thomas Jefferys, London, 1775). Not surprisingly, this 1775 map shows no line of demarcation between Portuguese-speaking Brazil to the north and Spanish-speaking Paraguay, Tucuman, Charcas and Buenos Aires to the south. The absence of such a line had long been a source of conflict, and resulted in hostilities between Portugal and Spain in 1776. The center of the controversy was the Banda Oriental (now part of Uruguay) just north of the Rio de la Plata. A naval battle occurred on Lagoa dos Patos (a 125-mile-long tidal lagoon, the extent of which is not accurately shown here; the name appears on the eastern coast on a line with the "u" in "Tucuman"). Military engagements occurred at Rio Grande (on the coast, between Lagoa dos Patos and Lagoa Mirim, here spelled "Merum") and at Fort Santa Teresa (on the coast, just below the latter lake). The now-principal cities of Rio de Janeiro, São Paulo, Montevideo, Buenos Aires, Santiago (St. Jago), Valparaíso and Lima are all shown here.

nobles who were then and still are urging war against Portugal. Their argument is that Britain, being at war in America, will not come to the defense of its ally Portugal. Others in Spain are more cautious; they point out that the British minister in Madrid recently declared that Britain will not neglect its allies because of "the present civil war," and that Gibraltar and Minorca remain heavily fortified.

Encounter was no longer avoidable, and it came March 17th of this year. A Portuguese squadron of twelve ships, reportedly commanded by a British officer, attacked five Spanish vessels on Lagoa dos Patos. Although a violent wind blew up, scattering the Portuguese force and diminishing the attack, there were many Spaniards—some reports say in the hundreds—killed and wounded. During the engagement the British captain is said to have had two officers, also British, thrown overboard for cowardice, and then to have shot himself in the head. Spain filed a strong protest over the attack. Replied Lisbon: it must have happened prior to receiving orders to maintain peace.

Spain appears to have been suspicious of the reply, and eventually found its doubts well founded. A Portuguese force of thirty transports with nine regiments, commanded by British and German officers, attacked at Rio Grande in the Banda Oriental on April 2nd, then pressed on to take Fort Santa Teresa and finally Montevideo, where General Vertiz was defeated and four hundred of his men killed.

Spain has now demanded that the officers involved be put to death— that the alternative is a war in which it fully expects the participation of France. But it may not come to that. Britain and France have both now declared they believe Spain's demand for retribution is founded "in justice and equity." Diplomatic pressure may therefore avert a new war.

Meanwhile, Spain is moving in another way to strengthen its position in the disputed areas of the southern continent. Whereas Portugal's territory is consolidated into the one Viceroyalty of Brazil—and Spain's other major possessions of New Spain, New Granada and Peru, in the western and northern parts of the continent are also consolidated as viceroyalties—the Spanish lands in the south and the interior of the continent have never been more than separate provinces. Now Buenos Aires, Paraguay, Tucuman, Potosi, Santa Cruz de la Sierra, Charcas and the territories of the cities of Mendoza and San Juan del Pico will all become part of a new Viceroyalty of Rio de la Plata, answerable only to King Carlos III himself. Named by his Majesty to preside over the new nation: Lieutenant General Don Pedro de Cevallos, who was governor of the Province of Buenos Aires a decade ago.

Cevallos left for Rio de la Plata in November, 1776, with a substantial military force, but an agreement between Spain and Portugal the following year made the additional troops unnecessary. The Treaty of San Ildefonso, October 1, 1777, established a new line of demarcation. The Banda Oriental is now part of Uruguay.[16]

Customs

Latest Paris Fashions

From head (wigs higher than ever) to toe (glittering with diamonds) and in between (hoops smaller), this year's best dressed *femme parisienne* will owe apologies to no one when it comes to fashion.

Here is how she looks this year:

Madame is wearing her hair extremely high, the toupee slightly forward. When she wears a cap, it is huge, brightly ornamented with flowers, trailing ribands of all the brightest colors.

Her gown likewise is brightly trimmed with lace or Paris-net, of which there are no fewer than 150 kinds. The color *le plus chic* this year is *cheveux de la Reine* (the color of the Queen's hair). The cloak is out of fashion. In its place is used a coverlet of lace. Hoops are smaller.

Trimmings have become so specialized that each has its own distinctive name. A few samples: *les plaints indifférentes* (indifferent complaints); *l'insensible* (the insensible one); *le désir marqué* (marked desire). Others are dedicated: *à la préférence* (to one's favorite); *aux regrets* (to one's regrets); *aux doux sourires* (to sweet smiles).

But for the *pièce de résistance* of madame's fashion one must look down. Fashion in shoes is carried to such an extent that no woman of reputation can appear anywhere unless her feet look like jewelers' caskets. They are adorned with diamonds and other precious jewels so profusely that jewelry is rarely worn elsewhere on the body. There is thought to be nothing so beautiful as the foot of a woman of fashion.[17]

Children's Exercise

Of all the causes which conspire to make the life of man short and miserable, says Dr. W. Buchan's book, *Domestic Medicine,* hardly any has as much effect as the lack of proper exercise. And if exercise is important to adults, it is even more essential to growing children.

Thus observes the London-published *Domestic Medicine*:

—The habits of the young throughout the animal world show the propriety of giving exercise to children. Every young animal uses its organs of motion as early as possible.

—As the very young are not able to take exercise for themselves, it is the business of parents and nurses to assist them.

—The best method of exercise with infants is for them to be carried gently in the nurse's arms. This is much safer than swinging an infant around like a machine.

—When children begin to walk, adults should lead them about with their hands. The common method of swinging a child about with leading-strings fixed to its back can lead to undesirable consequences.

—When exercise (in adults as well as children) is neglected, none of the animal functions can be duly performed. Thus, the whole constitution will go to wreck.

Dr. Buchan, whose book is now in its fifth edition, is a fellow of the Royal College of Physicians in Edinburgh.[18]

Religion

"Let Tyrants Shake"

Hymns of the Christian church, by such eminent poets as Isaac Watts a half-century ago, recount the glories of heaven ("There is a land of pure delight, where saints immortal reign") or the essential beliefs of the church ("When I survey the wondrous cross, where the young Prince of Glory died"). John Milton, a century earlier, paraphrased portions of the Psalms: ("The Lord will come and not be slow, His footsteps cannot err; Before him righteousness shall go, His royal harbinger.").

It is a measure of both the nature and faith of many Americans that, in this time of war and revolution, their firm belief is that God will take the side of America against Great Britain. A hymn reflecting that sentiment will find many ready voices.

A collection of such hymns, written by the Rev. Elhanan Winchester, was recently published by M. K. Goddard in Baltimore. From its title alone the patriotic nature of the hymns is evident: *Thirteen Hymns, Suited to the Present Times, Dedicated to the Thirteen United Colonies.* Typical of the forthright spirit of all is Hymn V, entitled "America's Encouragement":

> Let tyrants shake their iron rod,
> And slav'ry clank her galling chains;
> We fear them not, we trust in God.
> Our God alone for ever reigns.

Winchester, a native of Massachusetts, is a Baptist minister who for the last two years has been preaching in South Carolina.[19]

THE WEEK OF AUGUST 19TH

The War

Omen of Violence?

Since their arrival on Staten Island early in July, the more than 20,000 British and Hessian troops of General Howe were presumed to be maintaining only a temporary camp, sooner or later to move on to their military objective of New York. On Tuesday that fateful move began. Out across The Narrows went ship after ship, throughout Tuesday and Wednesday, and into Thursday morning, pouring thousands of troops to a landing between New Utrecht and Gravesend on Long Island.

On Wednesday night, as if to announce the tumult ahead, the heavens unleashed a violent thunderstorm—a worse outpouring of fury than even the oldest man could remember. Lightning struck a field tent within the American camp in New York, killing a captain and two lieutenants. Four other soldiers on Long Island were killed. In Tappan, several houses and barns were burned to the ground.[20]

Congress

Still Secret

After weeks of debate, the committee of the whole of Congress has finally agreed on a final draft of the Articles of Confederation. But, as was the case when the first draft was reported from committee, so too will the second draft be clouded in secrecy. Copies will be printed only for distribution to members, and printer and as well as delegates are under oath to divulge the contents to no one.

The Articles of Confederation were not adopted until November 15, 1777, and did not go into effect until March 1, 1781.[21]

The States

Women to the Harvest

As harvest time approaches, so many men have left their farms for the fields of battle that there are scarcely enough around to bring in the crops. The job is being done wherever necessary by the women and by men too old to go off to war.

Said the *Pennsylvania Packet*: "Many ladies have declared they will take the farming business on themselves so long as the rights and liberties of their country require the presence of their sons, husbands and lovers in the fields." As for how they are managing, said the *Packet*: "A laudable job."[22]

Dunmore: New Refuge

Former Virginia Governor Lord Dunmore, driven from his palace at Williamsburg by the wrath of Virginia patriots and driven from a temporary haven on an offshore island by Virginia troops, has now joined General Howe's forces on Staten Island, along with the remnants of his "Aetheopian Regiment," according to reports received in Philadelphia.[23]

Foreign News

Ships and Soldiers

Both France and Spain continue to build their military resources as the war in America continues to intertwine with the affairs of Europe, reinforcing old alliances and antagonizing old enemies. From Paris and Madrid, allies, have come these reports in recent weeks:

—At the principal naval port of Brest, in Brittany, the French navy is fitting out eighteen new vessels, including twelve capital ships;

—At Toulon, another eighteen, including eight capital ships, are nearly ready;

—At Rochefort, six new vessels will soon join the French fleet;

—In Madrid, the Spanish government is reported to be raising 30,000 soldiers, of whom 14,000 will be incorporated into the regular army and the rest will become part of the militia;

—At Cadiz, the Spanish navy is reported ready to dispatch twenty-two new ships for deployment at Buenos Aires, along with a contingent of nearly 7,000 troops.[24]

DIED: In Edinburgh, August 25th: David Hume, sixty-five, philosopher, historian, economist, one-time British chargé d'affaires in Paris and later under-secretary of state. A follower of Locke and Berkeley, Hume at the outset of his literary career set about to introduce an experimental method of reasoning into moral subjects (in fact, the subtitle of his first published work in 1739) and from there to assert his argument that human knowledge is in all respects restricted to what can be experienced, that beyond that there is no truth that can be verified. His major works were *A Treatise of Human Nature* (1739), *Essays Moral and Political* (1741 and 1742), *Philosophical Essays Concerning Human Understanding* (1748), *Political Discourses* (1752), *Four Dissertations* (1757), and *History of England During the Reigns of James I and Charles I* (1754). Personally amiable and energetic, he was a friend to many of the other literary figures of the time, and, notwithstanding his own quest for recognition, a ready admirer of their works. By a will drawn up in January, he left the disposition of his literary works to his close friend and fellow author, Adam Smith. Said Canterbury's *Kentish Gazette* of Hume: ". . . he made so rapid and distinguished a progress (in the study of philosophy and belles lettres) as has placed him on an equality with the most celebrated names either in ancient or modern history." Shortly before Hume's death, the *Gazette* reported that Hume and Adam Smith recently urged a peaceful settlement with the United States and had "given the king their opinions that if a reconciliation does not speedily take place with America, the country is lost."[25]

Predicting Population

Last month, a writer in London's *Lottery Magazine* offered his personal prediction of what Great Britain and America will be like in 1976. Somewhat partial to the cause of the Americans, he found unbounded prosperity ahead for the New World, only steady decline for the old.

This month finds *Lottery* gazing ahead again—this time on the subject of the population of America. The report, says the editor, is a compilation of the thoughts of a number of different writers, all of whom are close enough in their reasoning to draw a consensus. It looks this way:

1792 —	4 million	1892 —	64 million
1817 —	8 million	1917 —	128 million
1842 —	16 million	1942 —	256 million
1867 —	32 million		

The report thus foresees a doubling of the population of America every twenty-five years, concluding that marriages are more general, come at an earlier age, and produce larger families in the New World than the old.

But, as time goes on, other factors will conspire to slow down the population rate so that the projection above should be lowered for the latter years. The article warns:

"There are several obstacles to their increasing in future periods at the rate they do at present. A large proportion of them will be fixed at so great a distance from the fresh land (the only cause of their quick increase) that the difficulty of getting at it will prove an obstruction to population.

"Great cities will be raised among them; vast luxury and debauchery will reign in these, the influence of which will extend to the extremities of the empire: and these causes, which certainly will operate, must render their increase slower in a distant period than it is at present."

Lottery Magazine was close to the mark in the early days of the nation, and not as far off as it looks in more recent years if its prediction for a gradual decline in population growth is also kept in mind. These are U.S. Census figures for the decennia closest to the dates in Lottery's table, with the 1776 predictions following in parentheses: 1790—3.9 million (4 million); 1820—9.6 million (8 million); 1840—17 million (16 million); 1870—40 million (32 million); 1890—63 million (64 million); 1920—106 million (128 million); and 1940—132 million (256 million). Population growth has indeed slowed markedly over the years. Between 1790 and 1800, growth was 35.1 percent; between 1960 and 1970 it was 13.1 percent. The 1970 population was 203 million.[26]

Law

Allegiance or Death

Congress in June established a test of citizenship by decreeing that every person living in one of the then United Colonies and deriving protection from the laws of same owes allegiance to those laws; and whoever does not, by waging war against the colony or by espousing loyalty to the king or by giving aid and comfort to the enemy, shall be considered guilty of treason.

Now Congress has gone a step further and declared that any person who has failed to give allegiance and who is found lurking as a spy near a military installation of the United States shall suffer the death penalty.[27]

Religion

A Public Blessing

Men who hold public office are used to having favors asked of them. Noteworthy it is when a group of constituents says it has nothing to ask.

That was in part the message that Virginia Baptists sent to recently elected Governor Patrick Henry after a meeting of their ministers and delegates August 12th at Louisa, Virginia. The message began by explaining what its purpose was not: "As a religious community, we have nothing to request of you," the message stated; and then it got to its purpose of merely offering the Baptists' congratulations: "Your constant attachment to the glorious cause of liberty and the rights of conscience leaves us no room to doubt. . . . May God Almighty continue you long, very long, a public blessing to this your native country . . . and crown you with immortal felicity in the world to come."

Replied Governor Henry: "I am happy to find a catholic spirit prevailing in our country, and that those religious distinctions which formerly produced some heats are now forgotten." As Governor Henry knows, it has not been long since Baptist ministers were fined, and even jailed, for conducting services without the permission of the General Court of Virginia.[28]

Press

Reporting Independence

"Het Generaal-Congres te Philadelphia . . . openlyk voor de onafhankelykheid van Groot-Britannien verklaard."

It was the *London Gazette* that broke the news to England: her colonies had declared their independence.

The *Gazette* of August 10th reprinted two dispatches from General Howe to Lord Germaine, dated July 7th and 8th at Staten Island, New York, and released at Whitehall the day of publication. Readers who made their way through lengthy detail about the military situation would come to this in the next to last paragraph: " . . . and I am informed that the Continental Congress have declared the United Colonies free and independent states." That was the extent of the news.

On the 13th the *St. James's Chronicle* provided a slightly more detailed report: "Advice is received that the Congress resolved upon independence the 4th of July; and, it is said, have declared war against Great Britain in form." The *London Chronicle* and the *Whitehall Evening Post*, the same day, reprinted the same dispatches that appeared in the *Gazette*. Other London papers followed.

Within the week the text of the declaration, all or in summary, was appearing—on the 16th in the *London Packet*, on the 17th in the *St. James's Chronicle*, the *London Chronicle*, the *Daily Advertiser* and the *Morning Post and Daily Advertiser*; and on August 21st, the *Kentish Gazette* in Canterbury.

For the most part, British newspapers have simply announced the news and reprinted the text of the American declaration without further comment. But London's *Morning Post and Daily Advertiser*, which on the 12th was the second to announce the news, thought it worthy of commentary. Said the *Post* in its issue of that date, adding more facts than seemed to have arrived: "Tho' the Congress have at last carried their favourite point, in voting by a small majority [sic] the United Colonies free and independent states, it will prove the most impolitic measure they could have devised; it has already driven most of the dispassionate members from their councils, and caused a general desertion through their camps; if their declaration of independency was founded on views of forming allies with some powerful European nation, the absurdity of the idea will soon be made manifest."

Although the news of independence is clearly of more significance in Britain than anywhere else, it was not the British press that had the news first. Five days before the *London Gazette* had the story, the Dutch could read it in The Hague's *'s Gravenhaagse Courant* (August 5th), which was followed next day by the *Rotterdamsche Courant* and Delft's *Hollandsche Historische Courant*. The latter reported the news this way:

"*Het Generaal-Congres te Philadelphia heeft eindelyk het lang betwiste gewigtige pund bepaald, en zig openlyk voor de onafhankelykheid van Groot-Britannien verklaard, en tevens beslooten om in elk van de 12 [sic] geconfedereerde colonien een byzonder gouvernement te vestigen, tot dat'er eene algemeene Wetgeeving geformeerd zal zyn.*"

"The General Congress at Philadelphia has finally decided the long disputed important fact, and it openly declared for independence from Great Britain, and also decided to establish a special government in each of the 12 [sic] confederated colonies, until there will be formed a general law."[29]

The Delft account, using the specific words verklaard *("declared") and* onafhankelykheid *("independence") make it entirely plausible that the Dutch did have the news first. On the other hand, it may have been a coincidence. A week earlier, London papers carried their first reports of the July 4th edict of the King of Portugal banning American ships and the May 15th resolution of the Convention of Virginia proposing independence. These* two strongly worded documents may have been the basis of the Dutch reports. The Gazette D'Utrecht, August 6, cites "Londres, le 30 Juillet," as the source of its account of a similar nature. The newspapers quoted above cite no sources.

Elsewhere in Europe, there were these reports of American independence: in GERMANY, the Altonaischer Mercurius [Hamburg] August 20 (" . . . der Congress die Colonien für völlig frey erkläret hat, den 4ten Julii geschehen";) in IRELAND, the Freeman's Journal Dublin, August 22 (full text; first report in Ireland); in FRANCE, the Mercure de France, Paris, never did quite come out and report independence but did allude to it in the October issue; in SPAIN, the Diario de Madrid, principal newspaper in this heavily censored nation, was not published in 1776–77.

Britain's Annual Register for 1776, published late in the year, summed up the Declaration of Independence in this one paragraph in its history of the year: "The fatal day [July 4th] at length arrived, which (however the final consequences may be) must be deeply regretted by every true friend to this empire, when thirteen English colonies in America declared themselves free and independent states, abjured all allegiance to the British crown, and renounced all political connection with this country. Such are the unhappy consequences of civil contention. Such the effects that may proceed from too great a jealousy of power on the one side, or an ill-timed doubt of obedience on the other. The declaration has been seen by everybody; it contains a long catalogue of grievances, with not fewer invectives; and is not more temperate in stile or composition, than it is in act."

Customs

Cook on Cookery

Among the gentry on South Sea islands, a primitive form of cookery has been refined and is said to rival the best Europe has to offer.

As reported by Captain James Cook, the British explorer lately returned from his second voyage around the world, ordinary tribesmen on the islands of the South Pacific must make do with broiled meat. The chiefs and other gentry meanwhile have servants do it this way: A hole is dug in the ground. At the bottom is placed a layer of wood, followed by a layer of stones, and so on until the hole is filled. Then a fire is kindled. When the stones are hot, the fire is put out, and a piece of meat (properly cleaned and seasoned) is placed on the stones in the bottom. This is covered with fresh green leaves, in turn covered with more of the hot stones, and the entire hole is then filled with the dirt dug out in the first place. The meat is left to cook three or four hours, then exhumed.

Plainly a method for those with servants to do the work, the results are supposedly fit for a king. Says Captain Cook: "So savoury as not to be exceeded by the best European cooking."[30]

Books

Shakespeare in French

". . . misérable."

To France's foremost playwright and poet, Shakespeare may have had some genius—for indeed, it was Voltaire himself who introduced the

Bard to France, and thus to the world, nearly a half century ago—but England's most famous playwright and poet was nonetheless a mere Englishman, whose tastelessness and barbarity will never allow him into such sublime company as a Racine or a Corneille . . . or a Voltaire.

What Voltaire has done already—to adopt some of the good moments of Shakespeare to the French language and French taste—as he did in several works, beginning with the preface to *Oedipe* in 1730—ought therefore to be enough. What reason is there to go further? And certainly, what good can come from taking all of Shakespeare and translating him word for word into French, particularly in view of all varieties of verse and blank verse, meter and rhyme?

Just such a translation is under way, and two volumes, including *Hamlet* and *Julius Caesar*, have already been published. They are the work of Pierre Le Tourneur, who has performed a similar task with the novels of Samuel Richardson (1758) and the somber blank verse poem, *Night Thoughts,* of Edward Young (1769).

What Voltaire is likely to think of Le Tourneur's Shakespeare may be easily guessed. As he wrote recently to a friend: "Pray, have you read the two miserable volumes, in which he would have us look upon Shakespeare as the only perfect model of tragedy? He calls him the god of the theater: he sacrifices all the French dramatists without exception to his idol, as they used to sacrifice hogs to Ceres. . . . Do you feel sufficient hatred against this impudent blockhead?" And then Voltaire adds perhaps his angriest comment:

> Ce qu'il y a d'affreux, c'est que le monstre a un parti en France; et pour comble de calamité, et d'horreur: c'est moi qui autrefois parlai le premier de ce Shakespear; c'est moi qui le premier montrai aux Français quelques perles que j'avais trouvées dans son énorme fumier.

> The worst of it all is that the monster has a following in France; and what is peculiarly unfortunate: 'twas I who first talked of this Shakespeare; 'twas I who first showed the French such pearls as I found on his enormous dunghill.

This week—by letter, since his age permits little travel—Voltaire took his complaint to the French Academy, where it was read at the public meeting on the Festival of St. Louis. It was in large part a discourse on the inherent beauty and harmony of great French drama, and what he would call the vulgarity and improbability of English drama. An example, said Voltaire, is from the first scene of "that monster called *Hamlet.*" Francisco, a soldier on sentry duty, is asked by an officer, Bernardo, if he has had a quiet guard, and he replies: *Not a mouse stirring.*

"Yes," M. Voltaire told the academy, "a soldier might make such an answer when actually upon guard; but not upon the stage, before the first persons of distinction, who express themselves nobly, and before whom everyone should express himself in like manner. . . . There is neither harmony nor anything interesting in the low expression of Shakespeare's soldier: *Not a mouse stirring.*

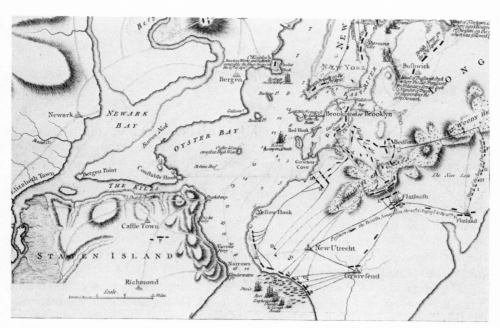

THE BATTLE OF LONG ISLAND (William Faden, London, 1776). Events related to the battle of August 27th are shown in this detail of a map published in London October 19, 1776. The land mass generally on the right is today all Brooklyn. Then—Brooklyn being only the little village so indicated—the countryside, and the battle, went by the name of Long Island.

Map Division—New York Public Library—
Astor, Lenox and Tilden Foundations

"Whether the soldier had seen or had not seen a mouse stirring is a matter of very little consequence to the tragedy of *Hamlet*. It is a mere St. Giles's phrase, a low proverb that can have no effect. There is always a reason why a beauty is a beauty, and a defect a defect."[31]

THE WEEK OF AUGUST 26TH

The War

The Battle of Long Island

Tuesday, August 27th, said one who was there, "proved a very distressing one on Long Island. Great numbers were killed on both sides, and I fear (though we cannot get certain accounts) that numbers of our people are taken." Another reported more bluntly: it was a night and a day of "bloody work."

What happened on the western tip of New York's Long Island was the utter rout of an American army; it was by far the blackest day of this war for the patriot cause. And for a British army which has had little with which to be pleased in more than a year of fighting, it was the first occasion outside of Canada for which a report to the Ministry in London will need no explanation.

The outcome of August 27th had been a specter to many Americans since the arrival of Lord Howe and General Howe at Staten Island early in July—and only the more so last week when an estimated 20,000 of General Howe's troops—nearly the entire command—crossed The Narrows and landed between New Utrecht and Gravesend on Long Island.

Throughout the weekend and into Monday, despite often heavy rain, there was scattered skirmishing between British scouting parties and American riflemen. But the main body of British troops under Sir Henry Clinton and Lord Cornwallis met no resistance marching its way toward the town of Flatbush. Beyond the town there is a thickly wooded ridge of high ground from The Narrows to Jamaica, and by Monday night advance parties of the American forces under the overall command of General Israel Putnam entrenched along the ridge and prepared for what was now inevitable. It came at four o'clock Tuesday morning.

What happened, from an American observer: "The British forces in three divisions, taking three different roads [through three passes in the ridge] and the advantage of the night, almost surrounded the whole of our out-parties. . . . The New York first battalion behaved with great bravery. Lord Stirling's brigade suffered the hottest of the enemy's fire; it consisted of Colonel Miles's two battalions, Colonel Atlee's, Colonel

Smallwood's and Colonel Hatch's regiments; they were all surrounded by the enemy, and had to fight their way through the blaze of their fire—they fought and fell like Romans! Lieutenant Colonel Barry, of the Pennsylvania Musquetry, was shot through the head as he was giving orders to, and animating his men. The major part of Colonel Atlee's and Colonel Piper's regiments are missing. Dr. Davis and his mate were both taken prisoners as they were dressing a wounded person in the wood. Colonel Miles is missing (a truly amiable character) and supposed to be slain. Generals Stirling and Sullivan are thought to be killed. General Parsons, with seven men, came in [this] morning, much fatigued, being for ten hours in the utmost danger of falling into the enemy's hands. . . . Our killed, wounded and missing are imagined to be above 1,000. . . . Our out-guards have retreated to the main body of the army within the lines. The British have two encampments about a mile from our lines, and by their maneuvers, 'tis plain, they mean to attack us by surprise and storm our entrenchments."

By noon Tuesday it was clear the American army, in its first full-dress, formal battle of this war, was not only outmanned but outfought as well. On the western flank General Lord Stirling was overwhelmed by the British General James Grant, though he held out for hours. Nearer the center of the American line, General John Sullivan faced the German regiments of General Philipp von Heister, and then, incredibly, to the rear, the main body of British troops which had maneuvered undetected around the flank to the east. Now largely disorganized, the Americans retreated to the village of Brooklyn on the East River, fatefully aware that a far larger British army is almost certain to press a new attack.[32]

Stirling and Sullivan were captured, not killed.

"A Doubtless Wise Measure"

By Thursday it was clear to the American command—despite a fog hanging over the East River—that Long Island was lost. To counterattack would have been to meet the British on their own ground; to remain would have meant a siege until surrender, with the British fleet ready to command the East River as the weather lifted. It was left to a council of officers and General Washington therefore to make the inevitable also official and—towards nightfall—to order a retreat silent and secret enough to be executed, hopefully, without detection. Almost incredibly, it was done.

The sick and wounded were moved first, and then the main body of 9,500 men with all military stores and almost all the cannon, crossing the river, turn by turn, in whatever small boats could be commandeered for the purpose. By six o'clock Friday morning, with the help of the fog, the evacuation to New York was completed . . . "with so much secrecy and silence that the enemy never so much as suspected it till we called off our sentries from the main lines after the break of day."

One who saw it credited the Commander-in-Chief for the remarkable efficiency of the whole operation: "There never was a man that behaved better upon the occasion than General Washington; he was on horseback the whole night, and never left the ferry stairs till he had seen the whole of his troops embarked."

Another reported: "It perhaps equalled almost any thing of the kind with which history gives us an acquaintance, and it was doubtless a wise measure, and much of the goodness of God is to be seen in it. The army are now much more collected and able to make a defence, whenever a grand attack shall be made. The troops in general are in good spirits, and I believe will do their best to defend the country."[33]

In The Debris

Britain's Brigadier General James Grant is well remembered by Americans for having once boasted in Parliament that he could take 5,000 men and march clear through America, restoring the entirety of the rebellious colonies to British domination.

In the debris of the Battle of Long Island this week, only a few miles into America, was found the tattered hat of a British officer, a bullet hole fringed with torn strands of gray hair through the middle of it. The hat bore the name of "James Grant."

It was later determined the hat belonged to a different "James Grant" who was killed in the battle. The general, also at Long Island, lived until 1806. [34]

Churches Closed

Although Tuesday had been long appointed in New York as a day of fasting and prayer to implore Divine assistance for the nation's new government, churches remained closed and public worship was canceled—so great was the alarm over the battle raging on Long Island.[35]

Soldier's Woes

The combined British naval and military assault on Sullivan's Island, South Carolina, June 28th ended in complete failure. In part it has been laid to a storm beforehand that reduced the strength of the fleet, in part to insufficient knowledge of the terrain. Now, a letter written before the battle by a British soldier suggests low morale may also have been a factor.

The letter, written by William Falconer to his brother in Montrose, Scotland, was found in July, forwarded to Philadelphia as intelligence, and then made public by direction of Congress. Wrote Falconer: "We have been encamped on this island for this month past, and have lived on nothing else but salt pork and pease. We sleep upon the sea shore with nothing to shelter us from the violent rains but our coats or miserable paltry blankets. There is nothing that grows on this island, it being a mere sand bank, and a few bushes which harbour millions of musketoes, a greater plague than there can be in hell itself."[36]

Congress

Pensions and Postal Service

Despite an agenda of mostly routine work, Congress this week took up two matters which may result in benefits to many Americans. It devised a system of disability pensions for war-injured members of the armed forces, and it worked out the details of an improved postal system.

Pensions will be granted to commissioned and noncommissioned officers in the Army and Navy, as well as to private soldiers, marines and seamen in both services who lose limbs during a military engagement or who are disabled to such an extent that they are incapable of maintaining a livelihood. Such pensions will consist of one-half of monthly pay, and will continue throughout life, or until the disability subsides. For naval personnel, there is one exception: should the disability be incurred during an engagement in which a prize is taken, the value of that man's share of the prize will be deducted from the pension.

In case of a partial disability that does not prevent earning a livelihood but does preclude further military service, a pension not to exceed one-half pay may be determined by the assembly or other representative body of the state in which such person resides. Such a person, however, if found capable of doing guard or garrison duty, will be required to join a Corps of Invalids for that purpose as a condition for receiving the pension.

Postal service improvements—in part dictated by the needs of war—will be sought through several steps:

1) The government will directly employ riders on the public post roads, each rider to be responsible for three trips a week, night or day, along a segment of twenty-five to thirty miles. He is to be prepared to leave immediately whenever the mail is received and travel without stopping until he reaches the next rider. The postmaster general is to institute use of way bills or some other system to insure efficiency, and to see that dilatory riders are discharged.

2) The states will be asked to consider freeing deputy postmasters from any other public responsibilities.

3) Three mail boats are to be established, operating on routes between the seat of Congress and the states of North Carolina, South Carolina and Georgia, which are not as easily served by overland mail. The boats will be armed, and will carry commercial freight to defray the cost of operation.[37]

Making Good

When Harriot Temple of Charlestown, Massachusetts, looked out around her farm one day last winter, she was dismayed to find soldiers of the Continental Army cutting down her trees for firewood. While no doubt sympathetic to the purpose, she was angry that permission had never been asked. Eventually her complaint found its way to the Continental Congress, and this week it ordered the Quartermaster General of the army to make compensation.[38]

The States

Military-Exempt Jobs

In an effort to encourage a continued flow of manufactured goods sufficient to meet the needs of the war effort, the Convention of New York, meeting at the village of Harlem north of the city, has acted to exempt from military service employees in a wide range of manufacturing jobs throughout the state.

To be excused from bearing arms while actually employed in these positions, provided they are properly registered with the commanding officers of their districts, are workers in the following job classifications:

At each manufactory: one founder, two keepers, one stock-jobber, one moulder, two fillers, one ore-burner, one ore-breaker, four miners and four master colliers at each furnace for melting iron ore into pigs and castings: at each forge for making bar iron: two men at each fire and two attendants to supply the same with coal; at each steel manufactory: two firemen and one coal carrier for every fire; at the anchor forge in the County of Orange: ten anchor makers, four carriers and one bellows man at each bellows; at each salt works under contract to the state: the master workman and six laborers; at each powder mill: the master workman, or overseer, together with three laborers for every twenty mortars; and at each paper mill: the master workman and two attendants.[39]

Need for Nurses

Hostilities in and around New York have added to demands on New York General Hospital to such an extent it has issued an appeal for nurses. Wanted for such service are all women (and men as well) who can be "recommended for their honesty." Also needed: dry herbs (for baths, fomentations, &c.) and linens.

The appeal for help was issued by Thomas Carnes, steward and quartermaster of the hospital, who said he hoped "many will attend to this matter, which is really of consequence, and cheerfully contribute to the relief of their sick and wounded brethren." Such volunteers, he added, will have to attach small importance to "pecuniary considerations."[40]

MARRIED: August 29th, in Williamsburg: Edmund Randolph, 23-year-old attorney general of the new Commonwealth of Virginia, whose father, uncle and grandfather were attorneys for the old colony; and Elizabeth (Betsey) Nicholas, whose father, Robert Carter Nicholas, is the treasurer of the new Commonwealth.[41]

Foreign News

Defense of Ireland

There is a report in Dublin—attributed to "undoubted authority"—that British military commanders in Ireland have been ordered to bring the country's defenses up to the highest state of readiness. The reason, it is said, is speculation that if war comes between Britain and Spain, the latter would attempt an invasion of Ireland as its first move.[42]

Marie Antoinette: Can It Be?

Suffering in recent days repeated fits of sweating, shivering and fever, France's young Queen Marie Antoinette, twenty, has become the subject of increasing concern. Each fit seems to be getting worse. One result has been the cancellation of several festive events, one of them scheduled for the king's name day, the feast of St. Louis, August 25th. The reason for her Majesty's indisposition has not been made known. But there are many in France who think it is a sign of pregnancy, and fervently hope so.[43]

It was not.

Without Peer

Among the recent monarchs of Great Britain, the distinction of creating the most new peerages belongs to the present king, George III, who, since ascending to the throne sixteen years ago, has granted peerages fifty-five times, roughly twice as many as any of his four predecessors. He is also ahead of the pace of the first three Stuart kings, who bestowed more titles, but over longer periods of time.

The record back to the beginning of the Stuart line in 1603: James I, sixty-two; Charles I, fifty-nine; Charles II, sixty-four; James II, eight; William and Mary, thirty; Anne, thirty; George I, twenty-nine; George II, thirty-eight, and George III (to date) fifty-five.[44]

Summer Is Agoing Out

London's Vauxhall Gardens is a traditional spot for summer merry-making, and the closing night of the season is traditionally the merriest of all. This week, an estimated 3,000 people turned out to drink good wine and much ale, dine on oysters, salmon, shrimps, and hot leg of beef, sing songs, enjoy noisy humor, have some more good wine and much ale, and in general bid one last salute to the succumbing summer. It was, said one, "drunkenness in perfection and riot in the abstract," and it all went on until five in the morning, when coffee was served. Not until six did the last of the weary merrymakers leave.

Said one reveler later—much later—the next day: "The whole scene of the night afforded an admirable proof that however absurd one man may behave, he will certainly find another to keep him countenance."[45]

Music

English Pitch

Just as English music differs in the color and subtlety of its composition from that of the other nations of Europe, so does it even differ in the playing: basic pitch in England is a shade lower.

To many a listener, the difference is moot; but to many musicians, their sense of pitch more highly trained, it is not only a noticeable distinction but another reason for some in France, Italy and Germany to argue the inferiority of English music.

The late Oliver Goldsmith, in his posthumously published *A Survey of Experimental Philosophy,* offered a defense on practical grounds. Said Goldsmith: "It has been objected by foreigners to modern English music that the concert pitch has been injudiciously altered. There is, say they, a certain stretch at which all strings give their finest tones; that, in general, is the pitch which the other nations of Europe have found by experience to be their concert tone.

"In the colder climates, this pitch, if it be altered at all, should be let down; for sounds strike brisker in cold air than in warm; in frost, for instance, than in the sultry heats of autumn. A humid air also braces the string, and only adds to the tension of strings already raised above their tonic pitch."

Standard pitch has been gradually rising over the centuries. Handel's tuning fork for Concert "A" had a frequency of 422.5 cycles per second. Today, 440 is generally standard.[46]

Medicine

Mad Wolf Bite: A Cure?

Among the most virulent afflictions known to man is that which follows the bite of a mad animal. It is an illness which severely constricts breathing and swallowing, and causes excessive salivation, in turn leading to exhaustion, and then paralysis, and then, almost always, death.

Now, from France, comes a report that a cure may at last have been found—at least in the case of the bite of a mad wolf. The government has directed the publishing of a report of the cure, developed by Monsieur

De Laponne, and tested, at the direction of the comptroller general, by the provincial physcian, Monsieur Blais, on inhabitants of the village of Maconnois. There, so far, the cure is said to have proven infallible.

Under the De Laponne method, the patient who has been bitten is first given a clyster, and then bled once or twice in the arm or foot. The wound must be washed in lukewarm water containing sea salt, and if large, cut deeply to remove pieces of foul flesh. Further bathing should then be done with lukewarm water, or if available, with sal ammoniac diluted in water.

Next comes treatment of the wound itself. It should be anointed around the edges with a mercurial unguent or with pomatum, a procedure to be repeated every twenty-four hours. Then the wound should be dressed with a suppurative ointment or with oil of basilicon—and this repeated twice each day. The body, meanwhile, should be kept open with daily clysters, and every fourth or fifth day, a gentle purge, along with an occasional vomit.

The following bolus [medicinal compound] should also be administered daily: Four ounces of camphire, two grains of musk and six grains of powdered nitre incorporated into a little honey. At night, if the patient is restless, a sleepy draught may be given but not repeated.

According to Monsieur De Laponne, this regimen should be continued for a least one month, and longer if the bite was a severe one.

Like so many supposed remedies of the time, this one also lacked any medical validity. No certain treatment of rabies existed until hydrophobia vaccination was developed by Louis Pasteur in the late nineteenth century.[47]

SEPTEMBER

THE winter's nights approaching are apace,
And *Sol* more near the south doth run his race.
The ripe fruit drops, the verdant herbs are done,
And winter soon will waste what summer won.

The Virginia Almanack
September, 1776

THE WEEK OF SEPTEMBER 2ND

The War

Uneasy Calm

Since the retreat of American forces from Long Island, the British have extended their position on the Sound-side of the island a considerable distance, thus making any attempt by the Americans to retake the island an even more remote possibility. On Thursday the British landed a large number of troops on Blackwell's Island, three miles from the city of New York, but pulled them back after encountering strong fire from American batteries. Otherwise, New York has been calm—but it is of a distinctly uneasy sort.[1]

Personal Effects

American soldiers who are prisoners of war on Long Island have been given a flag of truce by their British captors to send a request to the

American command for their personal effects. Their friends in the American ranks in New York are to deliver baggage trunks of the imprisoned men to the house next to General Putnam's headquarters for forwarding to Long Island. Any cash belonging to the captured men should be left at General Putnam's house.[2]

Congress

Jefferson Resigns

Though he is one of its youngest members and though he rarely debates, he has already attained a place of eminence as a member of Congress that few other delegates can claim. Yet for Thomas Jefferson, his contributions a matter of record, the important work now lies at home and not in Philadelphia. He has accordingly resigned from Congress.

His departure is not a complete surprise. Even before Virginia's delegates were re-elected to a new one-year term that began on August 11th, Jefferson had asked to be replaced—for "private causes," he told the Convention of Virginia. But it is also known he has been eager to return and lend a firm hand in the shaping of the new Commonwealth. Although he was prevailed upon to remain in Philadelphia a while longer, he has now resigned in time for the opening of the new Virginia House of Delegates in October.

The "private cause" was apparently the protracted illness of his wife.[3]

Peace Talks: Nearer

The possibility of finally entering into peace talks with the British was renewed this week by Congress as it appointed a committee of three to meet with Lord Howe on Staten Island. The meeting, which will be no more than exploratory, came about as the result of a message from Howe to Congress. While Congress rejected a substantial portion of Howe's proposal, it did conclude that enough was offered at least to pave the way for discussing how a formal peace conference might be brought about.

Despite this new development, many in Congress remain doubtful that either Lord Howe or his brother, General William Howe—while officially designated as peace commissioners of his Majesty—are empowered to make more than a superficial settlement. It is felt the fundamental issues of the war, as enumerated in July's Declaration of Independence, can be settled only by act of Parliament.

Lord Howe's informal message, relayed through General John Sullivan, offered a conference with members of Congress "as private citizens" to discuss peace terms. He said he and his brother had full power to compromise the dispute in America, and indeed that it was the arranging of these full powers in England that had delayed their return to America until after the signing of the Declaration of Independence. He urged that a settlement be reached before one side or the other struck so severe a blow that the other would be compelled to make a settlement.

In offering to meet with members of Congress "as private citizens," Howe apparently seeks to weaken the stature, and therefore the influence of Congress among the new American states. To Congress it was not so much apparent as obvious, and the nation's representatives in Philadelphia last week said no to that—even though Howe had left open the possibility of having the private citizens' peace agreement later ratified by Congress.

In its reply to Howe, also sent with General Sullivan, Congress did however propose an exploratory discussion, specifically: "to know whether he [Howe] has any authority to treat with persons authorized by Congress for that purpose on behalf of America, and what that authority is, and to hear such propositions as he shall think fit to make respecting the same." As its representatives for such informal, preliminary talks, Congress appointed Dr. Benjamin Franklin, John Adams and Edward Rutledge. If and when Howe replies, a date will be set. The meeting almost certainly will be held on Staten Island.

In other action this week, Congress agreed to an exchange of top-ranking prisoners of war. It will give up General Richard Prescott, who was captured in Canada last November, and Donald McDonald, the North Carolina Tory captured at the Battle of Moore's Creek Bridge in February and considered by the British to have the rank of a brigadier general. In turn the British will release two American generals captured August 27th during the battle of Long Island: Lord Stirling and John Sullivan. The latter was paroled from British custody to convey Lord Howe's message to Congress.[4]

Foreign News

Crime in London

Many in London complain that crime is more rampant than ever. As if to prove them right, a highwayman this week took on none other than the city's Lord Mayor himself. Near Turnham Green, a lone robber armed with a gun stopped Lord Mayor John Sawbridge, who was riding in a chaise and four with several city officials. Swearing to shoot the first man who offered resistance, the highwayman took an undisclosed amount of money, and fled.

Last March, Alderman and former Lord Mayor John Wilkes was the target of a pick-pocket on Fleet Street in London.[5]

Fire Prevention

It was September 2nd, 110 years to the day since the great fire of London, that incredible holocaust that, from a spark somewhere near London Bridge, swept across a city of a half-million people and turned 13,000 homes to ashes, laid to ruins old St. Paul's Cathedral, destroyed the Royal Exchange and the Custom House, and badly damaged Guildhall.

It was too long ago for the memory of any Londoner, and yet London still remembers. Aware it could happen again despite the most modern fire fighting equipment and the most sensible of precautions, the city is always ready to examine new methods of fire control and prevention.

So it was on this infamous anniversary that David Hartley—member of Parliament for Kingston upon Hull, scientist, friend and correspondent of America's Dr. Benjamin Franklin—chose to demonstrate his theories to the Lord Mayor and gentlemen of the Corporation of London. For that purpose—and for planned demonstrations to their Majesties and to members of Parliament—Hartley had acquired a house on the common in nearby Wimbledon. Workmen, following his instructions, had carried out his plan for lining sections of the interior, and particularly floors and ceilings, with very thin metal plates to resist flame. Such a method, seemingly cumbersome, is estimated to add no more than three percent to the cost of construction.

Hartley then sought to prove his fire prevention device by having piles of wood shavings set afire at various points around the house. According to one witness, the fires burned themselves out with no damage, leaving it looking "as if no fire had been in the house."

Futher demonstrations are now planned for their Majesties and for members of Parliament.[6]

Time Out

Londoners near St. Paul's Cathedral will have to find a new way to keep track of the time for a while. The cathedral's huge clock is undergoing repair, a job that will take about a month. The clock measures eighteen feet, ten inches across the dial, and is circuited by an hour hand as tall as a man (five feet, eight inches) and by a minute hand four feet longer. Each of its twelve numerals is two feet, two inches in height.[7]

Education

What They're Learning

Schoolbooks being read, marked and inwardly digested by the student of 1776 are the same titles that have enriched or entangled students for years—and in some cases, centuries—past. Among the books on sale this fall: the poet Horace, the satirist Juvenal, the biographer Suetonius, the Castellio Bible, Bailey's Latin and English Exercises, Ruddiman's Grammatical Exercises, Holmes's Latin Grammar, Dunlop's Greek Grammar,

Chambaud's French Grammar, Martial's Epigrams, and that old standby, Aesop's Fables.

Nor are subjects any but the traditional, though many a student might wish otherwise: reading, writing, English grammar, French, Latin, Greek, Euclid's elements, arithmetic, algebra and other branches of mathematics are all in store, along with such practical courses as merchants' accounts, navigation, surveying of land in theory and practice, mensuration of superficies and solids, altimetry or the taking of heights, and longimetry or the taking of distances.[8]

THE WEEK OF SEPTEMBER 9TH

The War

New York Is British

The strategic value of New York as headquarters for the British army has been clear to American and British commands alike: it is easily accessible by sea; it is centrally located; and it is in a region where Tory support is relatively strong. That the British would try to succeed the taking of Long Island with the greater prize of New York itself has been only a question of when. At the same time, the American command is known to have considered the continued possession of the city of New York impossible. Last week it began removing troops, military stores and artillery northward eight miles to Harlem; on Saturday night, the sick and wounded were taken to Newark, New Jersey.

Late Sunday morning, the 15th, General Howe answered the question of when. Under cover of a furious cannonade from ten ships of war in the East River, wave after wave of flat-bottomed boats full of British troops plied across the river from Long Island to Kip's Bay, a few miles north of the city. This force, under General Henry Clinton, estimated at about 4,000, and followed later by thousands more, easily outnumbered two small brigades of American militia holding the shore at makeshift entrenchments. The militia, raw, never before in battle, panicked and fled.

General Washington, it is reported, was at the American camp at Harlem, further to the north, when the attack was begun. Hearing the cannonade, he rode south in time to observe, astonished and mortified, the retreat of the militia. What happened next was told this way: "[Washington] made every effort to rally them, but without success; they were so panic-struck that even the shadow of an enemy seemed to increase their precipitate flight. His excellency, distressed and enraged, drew his sword and snapped his pistols, to check them; but they continued their flight without firing a gun; and the general, regardless of his own safety, was in so much hazard that one of his attendants seized the reins, and gave his horse a different direction."

Meanwhile, about 3,500 American troops under the command of General Israel Putnam were reported to have evacuated the city of New York itself, somehow managing to escape undetected up the western shore of the island on which New York is located, and have rejoined the main body of American troops at Harlem.

It took the British only a few hours to gain possession of New York. At sunset, American militia at Paulus Hook, New Jersey, looked across the Hudson and lamented the sight of a British flag flying over Fort George at the southern tip of the city.[9]

Putnam's escape from otherwise certain surrender, heroic in its own right in view of an arduous twelve-mile march, is also popularly credited to a Quaker housewife, Mrs. Robert Murray, who, when Howe and his aides stopped at her house asking refreshments. plied them with cake and wine for two hours and delayed their march.

Little Better Treatment

American sick and wounded evacuated to New Jersey from the city of New York may not be faring much better than had they been left behind to the British occupation. Reported one along with them from Paulus Hook: "Most of them could be got no further than this place and Hoboken. and as there is but one house at each of these places, many were obliged to lie in the open air till this morning, whose distress, when I walked out at daybreak, gave me a lively idea of the horror of war than anything I ever met with before."[10]

Peace: No Report Yet

Back in Philadelphia are Benjamin Franklin, John Adams and Edward Rutledge after a trip to Staten Island, New York, to represent Congress in a discussion of peace with Lord Howe. Details of the three-hour conference have not yet been made public. But it is suspected the delegates of the United States found that his lordship possesses no more power for bargaining a peace than was spelled out in the act of Parliament establishing a peace commission. The principal power authorized to Lord Howe and General Howe is the granting of pardons. That, Americans realize, will not get to the basic issues that have brought about the war in the first place.[11]

Congress

Major Matter, and Secret

An undisclosed report of the Board of War kept Congress in committee of the whole much of this week. While even the subject of the discussion has been kept secret, there can be little doubt it is a matter of major importance—particularly in view of the origin of the report. In the past Congress has chosen the recourse of going into committee of the whole, with its more flexible and informal rules of debate, whenever there has been some matter of urgency requiring day-after-day consideration. First it was debate on the Declaration of Independence; then it was a committee draft of Articles of Confederation. Now, what? In reported action this week, Congress resolved that all continental commissions and other legal instruments bear the title "United States" instead of "United Colonies," a largely technical step since the new name has come into general usage after being officially inaugurated in the Declaration of Independence.[12]

The Colonies

Delaware's Declaration of Rights

The State of Delaware, in adopting a "Declaration of Rights and Fundamental Rules," has become the second state to set forth as a basis for government the inherent rights which that government is constituted to protect.

Delaware delegates gathered in convention at New Castle since August 19th used the Virginia declaration as a model, even retaining some of the same phrasing. On the other hand, the Virginia declaration also borrowed from earlier documents, taking some of its language, for instance, word for word from the English Bill of Rights of 1689 ("cruel and unusual punishment").

The Delaware declaration, passed on September 11th, contains several new provisions, among them:

—"That retrospective laws punishing offenses committed before the existence of such laws are repressive and unjust, and ought not to be made."

—As a corollary to the provision on freedom of religion, the demurrer: ". . . unless under colour of religion any man disturb the peace, the happiness, or safety of society."

—A prohibition against quartering troops in private homes without consent during time of peace, and in time of war except as directed by the legislature.

The original draft of the Virginia declaration also had a prohibition of ex post facto law, but it was deleted by the Convention after a good deal of debate.[13]

Foreign News

Little Zeal

The war in America has placed upon the British shipbuilding industry the greatest demands in more than a decade. British workmen are responding—according to a report from Plymouth—with something less than zeal.

Said Canterbury's *Kentish Gazette,* in a report of the near-completion of the frigates *Apollo* and *Mermaid* in Plymouth: "The men somehow do not work with that spirit and alacrity which they did in the war with France and Spain; they go through their day's work now, but it seems like labour, whereas in the late war they appeared to play at their work, they were so brisk at it."[14]

Shortages of War

One certain way for many in Britain to be reminded of the war with America is the growing scarcity of snuff. Along with other imports from America, snuff is harder and harder to find, and when it is, the price is high. In Dublin, an ounce is up to two pence in price. The *London Packet* took note of the predicament recently when it observed: "Some cynical grey-bodies may endeavour as they please to sneer us out of conceit with that American herb; but it will, we fear, be found difficult to eradicate our old prejudices in its favour."

Still another effect of the trade stoppage has been felt by people in Ireland who are in the linen industry. Flax had come primarily from America, at favorable prices. Now it must be obtained, if it can be got, by way of Amsterdam and St. Eustasia at a much higher cost.[15]

Press

Non-Reporting Independence

According to a report from Boston, the royal governor of Nova Scotia received the text of the American Declaration of Independence at least four weeks ago, but has not permitted "the poor dupe of a printer to publish any more of it than barely the last clause ('We, therefore, the representatives. . . .')." Thus omitted are the grounds for such a declaration, and the reason is obvious, said the correspondent: the full declaration might win over many converts to the American cause and "inflame the minds of his Majesty's loyal and faithful subjects of the Province of Nova Scotia."[16]

THE WEEK OF SEPTEMBER 16TH

The War

Peace: No Nearer

In accepting a proposal from Lord Howe to explore terms of peace with Great Britain, Congress knew it faced two dilemmas:

1. It could not surrender its own integrity by permitting "private citizens" instead of representatives of Congress to negotiate peace terms, as Lord Howe demanded;

2. It could not, in any event, go into a peace conference expecting any fundamental issues to be open to settlement.

The meeting last Wednesday of Benjamin Franklin, John Adams and Edward Rutledge with Lord Howe on Staten Island has now been disclosed in detail by order of Congress, and it is obvious that peace is no nearer than before.

Lord Howe's proposal for a peace conference was held contingent on its being carried out by private citizens. Congress answered by saying that only representatives of Congress could negotiate. The three United States representatives, therefore charged with upholding the position of Congress while still attempting to make what they might of the meeting, trod their fine line this way, as they so reported to Congress this week: "We observed to his Lordship that, as our business was only to hear, he might consider us in what light he pleased, and communicate to us any propositions he might be authorized to make for the purpose mentioned; but that we could consider ourselves in no other character than that in which we were placed by order of Congress."

The second dilemma—the substance of negotiation if in fact the question of negotiators could be resolved—proved to be wholly outside the realm of settlement. It became clear, said the committee, that Howe could make "no explicit proposition of peace except one, namely, that the Colonies should return to their allegiance and obedience to the government of Great Britain." Beyond that, he had—as expected—no real authority to treat of the deeper issues. Said the committee to Lord Howe: he might "much sooner obtain fresh powers" than Congress would obtain agreement "from the several Colonies, to consent to a submission."

"We gave it as our opinion," Franklin, Adams and Rutledge reported to Congress, "that a return to the domination of Great Britain was not now to be expected. . . . His Lordship then saying that he was sorry to find no accommodation was likely to take place, put an end to the conference."[17]

"Misguided Americans"

The text of a declaration issued September 19th at New York by Richard Viscount Howe and General William Howe, his Majesty's commissioners for restoring peace to the colonies:

"Although the Congress, whom the misguided Americans suffer to direct their opposition to a re-establishment of the constitutional government of these provinces, have disavowed every purpose of reconciliation not consonant with their extravagant and inadmissible claim of Independency, the King's Commissioners think fit to declare that they are equally desirous to confer with his Majesty's well affected subjects, upon the means of restoring the public tranquility and establishing a permanent union with every Colony, as a part of the British Empire.

"The King being most graciously disposed to direct a revision of such of his royal instructions as may be construed to lay an improper restraint upon the freedom of legislation in any of his colonies, and to concur in the revisal of all acts by which his subjects there may think themselves aggrieved, it is recommended to the inhabitants at large to reflect seriously upon their present conduct and expectations, and to judge for themselves whether it be more consistent with their honour and happiness to offer up their lives as a sacrifice to the unjust and precarious cause in which they are engaged, or to return to the allegiance, accept the blessings of peace, and be secured in a free enjoyment of their liberty and properties, upon the principles of the constitution."

Given at New York, the 19th Sept. 1776.

By command of their   HOWE
    Excellencies,   W. HOWE[18]

The Army: Vast Expansion

Why Congress was in committee of the whole so much of last week is now clear: it was debating and acting upon a Board of War report that asked for a vast expansion of the Continental Army. Apparently approving that recommendation, Congress voted to direct the states to provide eighty-eight new battalions—nearly 60,000 men—as soon as possible.

The states were set these quotas: New Hampshire, three battalions; Massachusetts, fifteen; Rhode Island, two; Connecticut, eight; New York, four; New Jersey, four; Pennsylvania, twelve; Delaware, one; Maryland, eight; Virginia, fifteen; North Carolina, nine; South Carolina, six; and Georgia, one.

Perhaps more important than the size of this recruitment is the fact that these forces will fall more directly under the control of Congress. Congress, rather than the states, will formally commission all officers, and select as well as commission all generals. The states are to provide arms and clothing, deducting the cost of the clothing from each soldier's pay in accordance with the usual practice.

In order to encourage enlistments, Congress directed that a twenty-dollar bounty be given to each noncommissioned officer or private soldier who agrees to serve for the duration of the war, and not for the usual enlistment term of one year as in the past. It also promised land in the west at the conclusion of hostilities, the amount depending on rank. Colonels will receive 500 acres each; lieutenant colonels, 450; majors, 400; captains, 300; lieutenants, 200; and ensigns, noncommissioned officers and privates, 150. Should a man be killed, his heirs will be entitled to the land.

The quotas were nowhere near all filled.[19]

"If We Succeed . . . "

An American general, otherwise unidentified, is reported in the *Pennsylvania Evening Post* to be optimistic about an expected encounter with the British at Lake Champlain. Said he, in a letter from Ticonderoga: "The enemy must come on; and I think they will be severely drubbed, for we are in a good posture to receive them. General Arnold has got down with the fleet, having on board about 100 pieces of cannon, who, it is very probable, will take the fiery edge off the enemy before they reach us. If we succeed at New York, the game is up, and Great Britain undone. What sudden mischief a few designing men can bring upon a nation! But Britain was lost before. And should America ever reach the same pitch of luxury and corruption, she too will fall. Liberty can only subsist with virtue."[20]

Congress

Revising and Reaffirming

The "Rules and Regulations of the Continental Army," that it adopted in June, 1775, Congress this week revised. Now called the "Articles of War," and running to a total of one hundred two articles in eighteen sections, the revised code of military justice does away with such incongruities as fines set in shillings (they are now in dollars), and makes the United States (and not simply the Continental Army) the ultimate object of allegiance.

The new code, like the old, limits courts-martial to applying the death penalty only to those offenses specified (such as running away in the face of enemy fire, abandoning a fort, giving a false alarm of an enemy attack or making known the watchword to an unauthorized person). But it increases—from thirty-nine to one hundred—the maximum number of lashes that may be meted out for a single offense. The Articles of War are to be read at least once every two months at the head of every regiment, troop or company throughout the army, and to be duly observed by officers and soldiers alike.

Congress this week welcomed representatives of the Shawnees to Philadelphia and reaffirmed its policy of encouraging friendly relations with the Indians. It did so:

—By reversing a position it took last spring and by now granting assistance to the extent of five hundred dollars to Dartmouth College for the maintenance of Indian youths there;

—And by assuring the often barefoot redmen that their visits to Philadelphia will always be welcome since "we keep our roads clear of thorns and briars."[21]

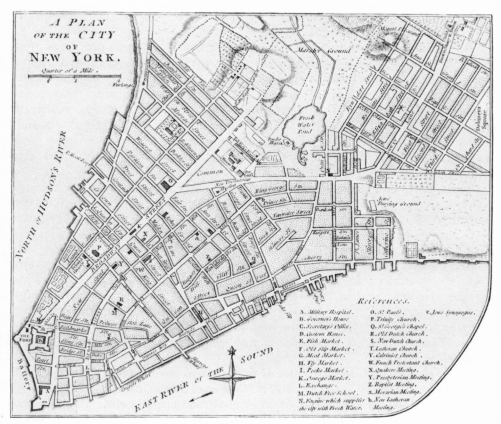

THE CITY OF NEW YORK (Thomas Jefferys, London, 1776). New York was
the second largest city in the United States of 1776, with a population of somewhere around 25,000. (Philadelphia was the largest, with a population in the
30,000s, and perhaps as many as 40,000 if some contemporary estimates are to
be believed; Boston had about 16,000, not adding British troops and not subtracting residents who temporarily left during the siege; Charleston, South
Carolina, had perhaps 11,000.) The City of New York was then only the tip
of the island of Manhattan, and was a couple of miles from the nearest village—
Greenwich. City Hall was then located in "mid-town," the intersection of Broad
and Wall Streets. What is shown here as the Common is the site of the present
City Hall. Not shown in the index accompanying this map is Bowling Green,
which is the roughly triangular plot not otherwise marked just above the fort.

Map Division—New York Public Library—
Astor, Lenox and Tilden Foundations

The States

New York: A Fourth in Ashes

As America's second largest city, New York has those problems that go with bigness. Not the least is fire prevention, which necessarily takes on a higher priority whenever population is concentrated in one spot. Like Philadelphia, Boston, Newport and Charleston—the other major cities of America—New York has hundreds of homes and shops, many of them wood, nestled one upon another, and so there is that always haunting fear that one spark may burst into an inferno that will envelop and lay waste to block after block, as happened in Boston sixteen years ago and as happened in New York in its earliest days.

New York has grappled with that fear through a number of regulations, some of which go back to the administration of Peter Stuyvesant more than a century ago. For example, each citizen is required to register his house with the city at a cost of a shilling a year, and to keep his chimney vents clean at all times. Inspectors paid in part through the registration fee make sure he does. Should fire break out, there are pumps sunk at convenient locations throughout the city to provide water. Fire engines are kept within convenient distances. To each is assigned a captain and a crew of men. As an incentive to promptness in answering an alarm, a reward is given to the first crew to arrive and get water onto a fire. Thus it has been rare for a fire ever to get beyond the building in which it broke out.

Such precautions were to no avail late this week as British-occupied New York suffered the worst fire in the history of America.

The first flames broke out at Whitehall sometime before one o'clock in the morning on Saturday. Fanned by a strong wind blowing in from the harbor at the south, they leaped to adjoining structures and it was soon evident that this was a fire going out of anyone's control. Before long flames extended to the Exchange, then swept along the west side of Broad Street as far as Verlattenberg Hill. On it raged with violence— the pitiful shrieks of burning victims sometimes audible above the roar of the flames, sometimes inaudible in the crash of falling stone and timber. Still the inferno spread, up the Broadway, claiming the seventy-eight-year-old Trinity Church and turning its steeple into a 140-foot pyramid of flame. On north, all the way to Barclay Street, it wreaked its destruction.

British Major General Robertson ordered two regiments from their encampments near the city. Lord Howe sent officers and seamen. What at last stopped the onrush of destruction late the next morning was pulling down wooden houses to form a firebreak; an inferno of this sort was beyond the scope of pumps and buckets.

What let this fire get out of hand, despite New York's many precautions? For one thing, weather is always an imponderable beyond the best of man's plans. A long dry spell had turned New York to tinder, and the wind that blew in from the south sped the destruction into, not away from, the most populous parts of the city. For another, many of New York's able-bodied men with firefighting experience are in the Army or otherwise had evacuated the city before British occupation. But there is still another factor: the possibility the fire was deliberately set. There is speculation the fire did not spread but was the result of separate fires set in five or six locations. According to one report, several persons were discovered with bundles of rosin-and-brimstone matches; a New England man, found to have a captain's commission and 500 l in his pocket, was reportedly arrested by the British. A carpenter was said to have been observed cutting the leather buckets used to carry water. It is thought these may be misguided patriots avenging the loss of the city to the British—if such accounts are true. There were reports, prior to the fire, that some New Yorkers wanted to burn the city before abandoning it to the British.

Whatever the cause, the fire has destroyed one-fourth of the city. It swept to ashes virtually all the buildings between Broad Street and the North River, as far north as City Hall, at Broad and Wall Streets, and between the Broadway and the North River as far as New York College. Laid in ashes are perhaps a thousand homes, Trinity Church, a Lutheran chapel, the public charity school—block after block now no more than smouldering rubble. The loss in houses and other buildings owned by the corporation of Trinity Church alone is estimated at 30,000 l. Miraculously the conflagration spared a number of buildings along the way—John Cortlandt's sugar house, Hull's tavern and several residences on the west side of the Broadway, and most notably, St. Paul's Church and the college.[22]

What was then called a fire engine was a portable, hand-operated pump with a reservoir for water. It was hauled to the scene by a bucket brigade.

The Fire: "Infernal Scheme?"

The stench of charred destruction still hung low over New York as British officers and New Yorkers who survived Saturday's disastrous fire gathered for Sunday services at one of the few major buildings along the Broadway that escaped damage. Ironically, for St. Paul's Church, the occasion also marked an official reopening after weeks of disuse. The church had been closed by the former clergy when countless patriot New Yorkers abandoned the city.

Now, leaving no doubt the city, and church, had changed hands, parishioners were bid to pray for "the divine favour and protection for our sovereign lord, King George," by the new minister, the Rev. Thomas Lewis O'Beirne, chaplain to General William Howe. The latter was in attendance with many of his officers.

Chaplain O'Beirne, in his sermon, laid the blame for the fire squarely on retreating colonials, telling the congregation, "your destroyers were secretly among you, spreading the ruin, and exulting in the success of their infernal scheme," while the British forces exerted "every nerve to preserve your dwellings and possessions. . . . May He [God] correct the hearts, and enlighten the understandings of your infatuated brethren, who still refuse to contribute their endeavours towards healing these unhappy disputes."[23]

Boston, 1760: Not as Bad

The worst recent fire in America prior to that in New York was in Boston March 20, 1760. Starting on Washington Street and extending to Long Wharf and Fort Hill, that fire destroyed 133 homes, 66 shops, 63 stores, 36 barns and 10 ships as well as the Quaker Meeting House. Damage was estimated at nearly 75,000 l.[24]

And Now Delaware

As New Hampshire, South Carolina, Virginia and New Jersey before it, Delaware now has a constitution and a government of its own.

Delaware will have a two-house legislature: a House of Assembly made up of seven representatives of each county; and a Council, with three from each. A State President—not Governor—will be elected jointly by the two houses.

Noteworthy features of the new government:

—A well-defined court system, made up of courts of common pleas in each county: a supreme court with statewide jurisdiction; and a last-resort Court of Appeals made up of the State President and six members appointed by the Assembly and the Council.

—A strong freedom of religion clause that goes so far as to bar from any civil office in the state a clergyman or preacher of the gospel while he continues to exercise his pastoral function. That notwithstanding, newly elected members of the state legislature, and other major office holders, before assuming office will have to swear not only an oath of allegiance to the state but an oath specifying: "I [name], do profess faith in God the Father, and in Jesus Christ, his only Son, and in the Holy Ghost, one God blessed evermore; and I do acknowledge the Holy Scriptures of the Old and New Testament to be given by divine inspiration."[25]

Foreign News

Europe's Land Forces

An account of the land forces of Europe, described as "pretty accurate," has been published by London's *St. James's Chronicle*. It shows more than 1,700,000 men (excluding Great Britain) under arms. By country, these are the totals, divided into foot soldiers and cavalrymen:

Country	Foot	Horse	Total
Russia	270,000	60,000	330,000
Prussia	170,000	70,000	240,000
Austria	160,000	65,000	225,000
Electorate and other German states	160,000	55,000	215,000
France	160,000	48,000	208,000
Spain	86,000	35,000	121,000
Sweden	86,000	20,000	106,000
Sardinia	67,000	24,000	91,000
Holland	34,000	16,000	50,000
Denmark	38,000	11,000	49,000
Portugal	27,000	11,000	38,000
Naples	18,000	16,000	34,000[26]

Medicine

Rattlesnake Remedy

A man is expected to have more sense than to grab a rattlesnake by the tail; if he does, the snake is expected to bite him. And so it happened to a soldier at Skeensboro, New Hampshire, where he and others had rendezvoused to march to Ticonderoga.

Within a few moments of the bite, his arm began to swell and develop great pain; in half an hour, the arm was swollen to twice its normal size, and the skin took on a deep orange color. The discoloration spread throughout the entire side of his body. Nausea set in.

Faced with those classic signs of severe rattlesnake poisoning, a team of medical men headed by army surgeon James Thacher set to work at once. They forced the stricken soldier to drink doses of olive oil until he had consumed one quart. At the same time they continually rubbed a large quantity of mercurial ointment on the man's arm. After two hours, said Thacher, favorable results were beginning to show. In two days, the soldier was restored to health and returned to his duties.[27]

Religion

Old Story

"But they cried, Peace, peace, when there was no peace."

The Rev. Thomas Lewis O'Beirne
Chaplain to Gen. Howe, at St.
Paul's Church, New York, on
Sept. 22, 1776

"Gentlemen may cry, peace, peace—but there is no peace."

> Patrick Henry, at St. John's
> Church, Richmond, Virginia, on
> March 23, 1775

A speech by a chaplain to the British army and a speech by an American patriot: a cogent comment in nearly the same words. Coincidence? Plagiarism? Or a common source?

Most likely the last, for both speeches were antedated by an Old Testament prophet nearly 2,500 years ago:

"They have healed also the hurt of the daughter of my people slightly, saying Peace, peace, when there is no peace."

> —*Jeremiah*, 6:14 and 8:11[28]

Books

Sailing

Robinson Crusoe, that marooned mariner who remained alive on a tropical island by using his wits, remains alive as one of literature's popular heroes. The newest edition of Daniel Defoe's fifty-seven-year-old novel has been published in Amsterdam. Still another new edition was published earlier this year in Philadelphia.[29]

Press

Three Down, One Still Going

After the Battle of Long Island, three of New York's four newspapers —the *Packet*, the *Journal* and the *Constitutional Gazette*—suspended publication. Now the fourth publisher has abandoned the British-held city, in this case to keep from suspending publication.

In nearby Newark, New Jersey, this week, publisher Hugh Gaine kept the *New York Gazette and Weekly Mercury* in print without having to face restrictions from British authorities. But the British in New York are continuing to publish a newspaper of the same name at Gaine's old printing office.

> The Packet *resumed publication in February, 1777, in Fishkill, New York, and the* Journal *in July, 1777, in Kingston, New York. The* Constitutional Gazette, *one year old when it suspended publication, never again appeared. Hugh Gaine returned to New York in November, 1776, and resumed publication of the* Gazette *at his old office.*[30]

Keeping Up

Boston's *New England Chronicle,* which was established in May of last year, has taken note of America's independence by changing its name to the *Independent Chronicle.*[31]

THE WEEK OF SEPTEMBER 23RD

The War

Two Men from Connecticut

For his part in the war, the private from Connecticut was a good soldier until, in a skirmish with the British a week ago, he retreated under fire and then turned his gun upon an officer. For such, the penalty is death.

For his part, the captain from Connecticut was a good officer, a man of undoubted service to his country, until he was captured by the British as a spy. For such, the penalty is death.

So in the battle for New York this week two men, altogether unknown to one another, happened at the same time to face the supreme consequence of the rules of war: one, the justice of his compatriots, for having chosen to run from conflict; the other, the justice of his adversaries, for having accepted a perilous mission that might help speed the conflict to a victory.

In Harlem Heights on Sunday, the private stood before a court-martial for "cowardice, disobedience of orders, and daring to present his firelock to a superior officer." He was found guilty and ordered to be shot at eleven the next morning.

On Sunday, eight miles to the south in New York—already summarily judged the day before by British military authorities and found guilty of spying for the American army—the captain was taken to an orchard and, without ceremony, led to an apple tree that would serve as his gibbet.

The next day in Harlem Heights, at the appointed hour, the private— one Ebenezer Leffingwell, a once good soldier turned coward—was led to a field and fixed upon his knees while a contingent of guards prepared to execute his sentence. As they made ready, an officer arrived with new orders from General Washington. Because of Leffingwell's "former good character and upon the intercession of the adjutant general against whom he presented his firelock," the general had decided upon a pardon.

At that same time in an orchard in New York, the captain from Connecticut had been dead and buried a day. There was no reprieve for him, one Nathan Hale.[32]

The New York Historical Society places the site of Hale's execution in the Artillery Park at what is now Third Avenue and Sixty-sixth Street; most accounts have said it was the Rutgers orchard in what was then the city of New York.

Prisoner Exchange

In accordance with a late-August proclamation of General Henry Clinton for the exchange of prisoners taken during the war in Canada, the first of the Americans released there have begun arriving in Philadelphia. In the contingent are 385 privates and an undisclosed number of officers. All will be free to return to their respective states immediately.[33]

Congress

Foreign Policy: A Beginning

Now that the United States is an independent nation, it must establish at least the rudiments of a foreign policy and a foreign service. Appropriately, that question has been occupying the attention of Congress more and more of late, but so far only this much of an American foreign policy has begun to show itself:

—A plan of treaties with foreign nations has been agreed to (on September 17th) but only that much is known;

—France will be the first nation with which formal diplomatic relations are established;

—Of all the areas of government, foreign policy will probably be the least open to public scrutiny.

There have undoubtedly been many discussions, both in committee and in full session, on foreign relations since independence was declared, but no observable step was taken until this week when Congress appointed Dr. Benjamin Franklin, Silas Deane and Thomas Jefferson as commissioners to the Court of France. Franklin, already well known in Europe, is far and away the most natural of all for appointment. Deane, a former member of Congress from Connecticut, has been in France since last spring. Jefferson, who is now back in Virginia, is also in many ways a likely choice, but there may be some question about his accepting an appointment out of the country at the present time. President Hancock, in any event, directed that Jefferson be notified of the appointment by express.

It may be presumed that the first business of the commission in Paris will be to secure agreement on a formal treaty between the United States and France. And since the appointments of Franklin, Deane and Jefferson have been settled—and they will leave for France as soon as practical—it may also be presumed that the particulars of a treaty with France have been determined. Beyond that, little more is likely to become known for some time. When it voted on the appointment of the three commissioners, Congress also resolved, "that secrecy shall be observed until further order of Congress; and that, until permission be obtained from Congress to disclose the particulars of this business, no members be permitted to say anything more on this subject than that the Congress have taken such steps as they judged necessary for the purpose of obtaining foreign alliance."

Other developments in Congress this week included these:

In preparation for the wintering of the Northern Army, Congress appointed two of its members—Richard Stockton of New Jersey and George Clymer of Pennsylvania—to take personal charge of arrangements at Fort Ticonderoga. They will contract for provisions, including in particular a number of sheep and a quantity of Indian meal, rice, oatmeal and molasses, and see to the purchase of clothing and the construction of barracks. A collateral objective: encourage the re-enlistment of soldiers.

Congress also directed the publication of such parts as are ready of the Journals of Congress by Philadelphia printer R. Aitken, promising to purchase 500 copies for its own use.[34]

On December 30, 1776, Congress, without public notice, resolved to appoint commissioners to Spain, Prussia, Austria-Hungary and Tuscany. Those missions, carried out the following year, all came to naught.

The States

And Now Pennsylvania

A single-house legislature, a limitation on the number of years any man may serve in public office, and a Council of Censors to review the functioning of the government all make the constitution of Pennsylvania —newest among the United States—also the most radical and innovative.

The constitution is the product of a convention that began meeting in Philadelphia July 15th under the presidency of Dr. Benjamin Franklin, and represents a number of departures from the governments that have been established this year in other states, as well as the former government of Pennsylvania.

The single legislative body established by the new constitution is a General Assembly to be comprised of six persons "most noted for wisdom and virtue" from each county and the city of Philadelphia. They will be elected for the first time on Tuesday, November 4th, and thereafter on the second Tuesday of October, to serve terms of one year each. After 1778 the number of delegates from each county will be adjusted to reflect the results of a census taken in the meantime.

Unlike any other legislative assembly in the United States—and certainly unlike Parliament—a member of the Pennsylvania General Assembly will not be able to serve as long as he can be elected. He will be limited by the constitution to no more than four years in any seven. Other office holders will face the same restriction: delegates to the Continental Congress, to no longer than two years successively, with a wait of three

years before again becoming eligible for appointment; members of the
Supreme Executive Council, to one three-year term, with eligibility resuming after an interim of four years. The President of Pennsylvania, being chosen from within the Council, will thus be subject to the same restriction. The reason specified by the constitution: " (By) continual rota-
tion, more men will be trained to public business."

The executive branch of government will consist of a President and
the Supreme Executive Council; the judiciary, of a Supreme Court as well
as local courts.

Among the significant provisions of the new government:

—Unlike Congress, sessions of the legislature will be open to the public "except only when the welfare of this state may require the doors to
be shut"; votes and proceedings will be reprinted weekly; all bills of a
public nature will be printed and made available to the public prior to
final reading and debate in the General Assembly; the preamble to each
bill is to state the reason and motive for such legislation.

—By direction of the constitution, "a school or schools shall be established in each county by the legislature for the convenient instruction of
youth . . . and all useful learning shall be duly encouraged and promoted
in one or more universities."

—A unique Council of Censors will be elected (two from each county
and city) every seven years, beginning in 1783, "to enquire whether the
constitution has been preserved inviolate in every part, and whether the
legislative and executive branches of government have performed their
duty as guardians of the people, or assumed to themselves or exercised
other or greater powers than they are intitled to by the constitution." To
carry out that mandate, the council will have power to summon persons,
papers and records, to order impeachments, to recommend repeal of laws,
and if necessary, to call a convention for the purpose of amending the
constitution.

Incorporated into the constitution is a declaration of rights patterned
almost entirely on that adopted by Virginia in June. There are several
additions, however: among them: the right of free assembly and the right
of a citizen "conscientiously scrupulous of bearing arms" to be exempt
from military duty, provided he "will pay such equivalent" as to furnish
another in his place.[35]

DIED: September 28th, on Long Island: Cadwallader Colden, eighty-
eight-year-old former lieutenant governor of New York, whose private life
was as notable for the quiet study of medicine and botany as his public
life was for the iron-handed and sometimes boisterous execution of royal
government. Born in Scotland, he obtained a doctor of medicine degree
at the University of Edinburgh, went on to write many medical works,
including one on the cause and cure of yellow fever in New York; it was
he who introduced to America the system of botanical classification devised by Sweden's Karl Linnaeus. Meanwhile, Colden pursued a political

career with at least as much earnest, becoming surveyor-general of the colony of New York one year after his arrival in 1718 and working up to lieutenant governor in 1761; four years later it was he who so zealously enforced the stamp act, by calling out British troops, that a mob burned his coach and hanged him in effigy on New York's Bowling Green.[36]

Foreign News

Unruffled but not Unthrown

In personal manner he is often clumsy and awkward, which once led the late Charles Townshend to think of him as "great, heavy, booby-looking." But in temperament, Britain's Lord North is as unperturbable a man as there is in the House of Commons. Wit and tact have seen him through many a debate that would have broken the temper of another. Not even the exigencies of the war in America—over which he would have preferred to resign—have marred his mellifluous demeanor.

Unruffled at work, he is less agile at play. A throw from his horse this week left Britain's First Minister with a broken arm. It happened while Lord North was taking an airing in Bushy Park in southern Middlesex, not far from London.

Though it is expected that he will fully recover, it is feared the mishap will interrupt at least some of the business of government, particularly since Parliament is scheduled to reopen in a matter of weeks.[37]

King José: Somewhat Better

Although his condition—considered grave in early August—has improved noticeably, King José I of Portugal is still ailing. He has had a return of the fever occasioned by that infectious skin disease, erysipelas, in his leg. But his doctors in Lisbon administered a bleeding, and pronounced him somewhat better.[38]

Agreed, But no Agreement

The Spanish government in Madrid has disclosed a report that its representatives and those of the Portuguese in South America have agreed to a suspension of arms. Nevertheless, Spain continues preparing for the possibility of full-scale war with her neighbor. In Marseilles, meanwhile, the French navy is hiring 800 civilian workmen to add to the readiness of its fleet.[39]

DIED: Recently, in England: Robert West, eighty-six; a native of Buckinghamshire, he moved in 1715 to Pennsylvania to join three brothers who had gone to that colony earlier with William Penn, and there married and raised ten children; he returned to England in 1764 to visit his repatriate son, painter Benjamin West, and remained until his death.[40]

Religion

"Epistle of Jesus"

It is almost universally agreed that Christ, during his lifetime, wrote nothing at all, but left his Word to be written and spread by his apostles and disciples. Yet from time to time throughout the history of Christianity, spurious writings attributed to Christ himself have appeared and, either through ignorance or deceit, been passed off as genuine.

Even today, more than seventeen and a half centuries after the time of Christ, such unauthentic writings still crop up. One such, an alleged "Epistle of Jesus" that was originally published in London, has been reprinted and placed on sale in Salem, Massachusetts. No one versed in the orthodox teaching of Christianity can doubt the spurious nature of the writing after reading the subtitle: "A copy of a letter written by our Blessed Lord and Saviour Jesus Christ, and found under a great stone sixty-five years after his crucifixion."[41]

Books

Puppyism or Patriotism?

It has long been obvious that many a British soldier bound for combat in America is unhappy about his lot, failing to see in this mission that same sense of glorious purpose that has buoyed his spirit in wars past. Thus a book of verse that was published in London earlier this year echoed the sentiments of many. Some excerpts:

> I've no ambition for a civil war,
> To strut the streets, and show a Charlestown scar.
> I will not leave the maids of honour's charms,
> For sleepless nights—and all the din of arms.
> Or shall I yield Cornley's and the Park,
> For dam'd salt-beef—within a transport bark!
> Not all the fame which gallant Warren won,
> Can make me bear th' explosion of a gun!
> Let red hot patriots boast glorious flame,
> And on thy spotless tablet martial fame.
> Such vague, vain shades of honour can't invite,
> I'll rather make apologies than fight.
> I can, I can no more ye Powers Divine;
> Ye soldiers, who have better nerves than mine
> May serve the King—but I must now resign.

The book, entitled *The Tears of the Foot Guards, Upon Their Departure for America,* was written anonymously by "an ensign of the Provincial Army" and published by G. Kearsly. It so angered one old foot guard, that he sat down and wrote a reply, which has been issued by the same publisher under the title, *An Answer to the Tears of the Foot Guards, in Which that Respectable Corps Are Vindicated from the Charges of Puppyism and Cowardice.* Some excerpts:

> From vile detraction 'tis the Muse to shield,
> The glorious few, who brave the hostile field:
> Who unreluctant quit the gay Parade,
> To march the heroes of a fierce brigade,
> Who cheerful leave each dear enchanting scene,
> Exchanging life for death, for joy, chagrin.
> Should men like these, by patriot rage inspir'd,
> By more than Grecian, Roman virtue fir'd,
> Submit in silence to each envious sneer,
> Which rudely brands so brave a corps with fear?
> Forbid it, Mars! at whose supreme command,
> These valiant soldiers quit their native land.[42]

THE WEEK OF SEPTEMBER 30TH

The War

The Next Move?

Now that the British army has possession of the city of New York, what will be its next move? A correspondent in Harlem gives this report:

"Opinions are various with respect to the enemy's designs. This is the best month in the year for fighting. The enemy must be near 20,000 effective, and the taking of New York is not a sufficient compensation for the expense of so vast an armament as the British king has sent out this year. Thence it is thought General Howe will attempt to give us a defeat, at least to get complete possession of this island and the adjoining heights. General Washington has, in public orders, assured the whole army he intends, at every hazard, to defend the ground the army now occupies. The other opinion is that the enemy will wait for the disbanding of our army, which takes place the last of December [the termination of one-year enlistments], and then obtain a bloodless victory by getting possession of our present works, as there may then be nobody to defend them."

Wednesday morning at daylight, in a daring move, 1,100 Continental troops went into Harlem Plains, between the American and British camps, and brought off all the corn, hay and other crops from the fields. It was feared by many this might trigger a long expected British attack, and indeed at one point the king's forces did begin striking their tents. But the day passed without a shot being fired.[43]

Congress

Raising Money Through Loans

Early in May, Congress estimated that war with Great Britain would require expenditures of ten million dollars over and above what had already been appropriated. A few weeks later it accounted for half the amount through an emission of five million dollars in bills of credit, and in mid-August, approved arrangements for emitting the remaining five million dollars.

Now, the war only more intense, Congress has determined that another five million dollars is required immediately. This time it will raise the funds through loans.

In carrying out the first such major loan program, Congress will establish a Continental loan office in each state. This office, under the supervision of a commissioner to be named by the state and confirmed by Congress, will supervise all details of the loan program within that state. The commissioner will issue certificates covering the loans, make payment of interest—not yet established, but likely to be four percent—and repay the loans at the end of three years. For his work, the commissioner will receive one-eighth percent in commission. Each loan must be at least three hundred dollars.

In other action this week, Congress:

—Recommended to the state legislatures that they appoint gentlemen skilled in "physick and surgery" to test and certify men joining state military units as surgeons or surgeons' mates, and withhold commissions except on evidence of certification;

—Appointed a committee of three (John Witherspoon of New Jersey, James Smith of Pennsylvania and Samuel Huntington of Connecticut) to consider a plan for providing "carriages for the publick service" so that transportation will be available to all on a more equitable basis, the prices of private carriage operators sometimes being considered oppressive for the services provided.[44]

> After news of the loan reached England, the following appeared in London's St. James's Chronicle (January 9th, 1777): "The Congress's new measure of borrowing their own paper at four percent, instead of coining more for the service of the ensuing year, is a stroke of good politicks, as it will at the same time supply their wants and raise the credit of the currency greatly."

The States

The Trial of the Turtle

The notion of a boat that travels under the water instead of on the surface is hardly new. The ancients—among them, Aristotle and Archimedes—conceived of such a device, although more for the purpose of merely descending than traveling from place to place below the surface. The latter sort was finally attempted early in the last century when a Dutchman named Cornelius van Drebbel demonstrated such a vessel in the Thames for James I. Like many another invention, van Drebbel's sparked interest, then was allowed to languish and be forgotten.

It is now known that the American army is experimenting with such a device, and there are reliable reports one such vessel has been deployed against the British—without success. According to accounts which have been circulating among American forces, this is the story of that unusual machine.

The inventor is said to be a young man of twenty-four by the name of David Bushnell, of Connecticut, who recently graduated from Yale College. The machine, variously called *American Turtle* and *Torpedo*, resembles as much as anything a turtle swimming vertically; it is shaped like two turtle shells joined together and is sailed upright. It is made of oak and sealed so as to be watertight, ballasted with lead at the bottom to keep it from overturning, and fitted with glass windows. The size is sufficiently great as to permit one man to sit inside, in an upright position.

The operator obtains forward or backward motion with an oar, and direction with a rudder. He can make the machine descend by opening a valve at the bottom and taking in water, and then ascend by operating two brass pumps that force the water back out. When the craft is at the surface, air is drawn in through a flue at the top; when it is operating below the surface, there is air enough inside to remain submerged for about thirty minutes.

But what makes the *American Turtle* unlike any such vessel even contemplated before is its use: it is plainly a military machine. Its whole purpose for being is found astern, just above the rudder. It is a wooden device, held in place by a turnscrew, and capable of storing up to 150 pounds of explosive powder. Within the wooden magazine is a clockwork mechanism, which can be set to fire the powder, through a gunlock, at any time up to twelve hours after being set. The idea is to sail the *Turtle* submerged up to an enemy ship, attach the wooden magazine to the hull by means of a self-contained screw, and then—if all has gone well—depart undetected.

Bushnell and his *Turtle* came to the attention of Major General Israel Putnam, and it was decided to test the *Turtle* at once against the most strategic target of all: Admiral Howe's *Eagle* in New York Harbor. For such an important test, Bushnell, too frail himself, had trained his brother, and the latter learned the art of piloting the *Turtle* with great dexterity. Unfortunately, the brother was ill the night of the test, and a sergeant from a Connecticut regiment, who was given only brief, last-minute instruction, substituted.

The sergeant, it is understood, made contact with the *Eagle* undetected, but was unable to affix the magazine to the ship's hull, and at last abandoned his efforts and returned to shore—leaving the magazine floating aimlessly in the harbor. In a half hour, at the appointed time, the magazine exploded with a thunderous roar, but accomplished nothing more than to send a great column of water spouting into the air—perplexing, but not the least injuring Lord Howe and his officers aboard the *Eagle*.

Further tests of the Turtle *through December, 1777, were equally unsuccessful, and the project was abandoned.*[45]

Report from New York

The British occupation of New York was described in this week's *New York Gazette and Weekly Mercury* this way:

"His Majesty's forces are now in possession of the city of New York island. They are also in possession of Powle's Hook [New Jersey] and command the East River and Connecticut sound. All this has been obtained with very little difficulty and loss on the part of the troops; the rebels, after the battle, or rather rout of the twenty seventh of August, having never attempted to face the soldiers, but fled with the utmost precipitation. They quitted works which they had been laboring upon the whole summer, without scarce the conflict of a day. The King's forces are in remarkable good health and spirits, and seem resolved to convince the world that they not only bear the name but the nature of Britons. . . . So vast a fleet was never seen together in this port, or perhaps in all America before. The ships are stationed up the east river . . . and near the town the multitude of masts carries the appearance of a wood. Some are moored up the North River, others in the bay; . . . some again off Staten Island, and several off Powle's Hook, and toward the Kills. The men-of-war are moored chiefly up New York Sound, and make, with the other ships, a very magnificent and formidable appearance."

This *Gazette* is published by the British; its patriot counterpart, the *New York Gazette and Weekly Mercury* of Newark, is published by Hugh Gaine, who fled New York after the arrival of the British.[46]

Foreign News

Priority: A Mended Arm

Convalescing from a broken arm, Britain's first minister, Lord North, is not lacking for attention. The King sends an emissary once each day to inquire about his Lordship's condition, and frequently visits himself. But his Majesty never talks about business, fearing it might retard Lord North's recovery. Once, when the first minister began turning the conversation to government, his Majesty diverted him by inquiring about the breed of sheep nibbling grass out on the lawn, advising Lord North that Welsh mutton is ever the best.[47]

Awaiting News

Since news of the Declaration of Independence reached Europe, there has been little further word received about developments in America. Considering the inevitability of battle following that Declaration, it has been a time of anxious waiting for many whose hopes and spirits are on the side of America. Typical is this letter from Bilbao, Spain: "By this time we judge the capital events of the American armies are over, and from the silence observed in the Court of London, everybody imagines the King's troops have been worsted. All Europe is in expectation of what has happened on your side, and we (are) in hourly hopes of some arrival. May God Almighty bring it soon, and to our entire satisfaction."[48]

Retirement in Florida

The ceding of East and West Florida to Great Britain by Spain in 1763 may have started it, but the war in the United States to the north is what has apparently given encouragement to a substantial increase in emigration to the Floridas. Most popular areas for settlement are St. Augustine, on the Atlantic coast, and Pensacola, the capital of West Florida, on the Gulf of Mexico. The populations of the two towns have increased by a fourth in the last two years alone. Said one who has been there: "Many settlers have retired there to avoid the troubles in the more northern parts of America."[49]

Medicine

They Should Know

Within this century alone, British troops have fought in enough wars and suffered enough gunshot wounds to make their surgeons world authorities on the treatment of battlefield injuries. American military surgeons now have access to that same fund of knowledge in a book published in Philadelphia. It is a reprint of a British manual by the surgeon-general of the British Army, Dr. John Ranby.

In *The Nature and Treatment of Gun-Shot Wounds*, Ranby advises the first order of business be the removal of the musket or pistol ball and any extraneous body that may be lodged in the wound. The surgeon is advised to get at the ball or other foreign matter with as little poking and probing as possible. A finger is the best and truest probe.

If the ball is lodged near the surface, it should be taken out immediately; if it can be felt but is not that close, the surgeon should cut for it. If the surgeon has no idea where the ball is embedded, it is better to leave it than to probe extensively. There are many cases where balls left in the body eventually work their way to the surface. If the wound is so great as to require amputation (often the case when it is at a joint) this should be done immediately.

Sometimes a gun-shot wound will cause little bleeding. When this is the case, it is necessary for the surgeon to open a vein immediately and draw a large quantity of blood—and perhaps again the next day. This timely precaution will prevent a good deal of pain and inflammation. The first dressing for a gun-shot wound should be with lint, either dry or moistened with a little oil, and a very light bandage; next, a bread-and-milk poultice, mixed with a sufficient quantity of oil to keep it moist.

Ranby recommends that the body be kept relaxed during treatment and recuperation. If pain "puts it on the rack" the immediate recourse should be opium.[50]

PART IV

OCTOBER

The Sun's too quick-revolving Beam
Will soon dissolve the human Dream,
　　And bring the appointed Hour.
Too late we catch his parting Ray,
And mourn the idly-wasted Day
　　No longer in our Power.

Burlington Almanack
October, 1776

THE WEEK OF OCTOBER 7TH

The War

First Naval Engagement

After a ragged, broken American army retreated from Canada last June, it attempted to make the most of what resources it had left by waging a defense of that key to invasion from the north: Lake Champlain. During the summer a small flotilla of vessels was constructed for the purpose, and General Benedict Arnold was placed in command. Meanwhile, the British, under General Guy Carleton, were likewise preparing a naval force as the most expeditious means of proceeding south to reclaim Crown Point and Ticonderoga at the southern tip of Lake Champlain. A naval engagement was thus certain—it would be the first of the war—and it came this week midway along Lake Champlain at Valcour Island.

Reported an American observer: "On [Friday, the 11th] at eight

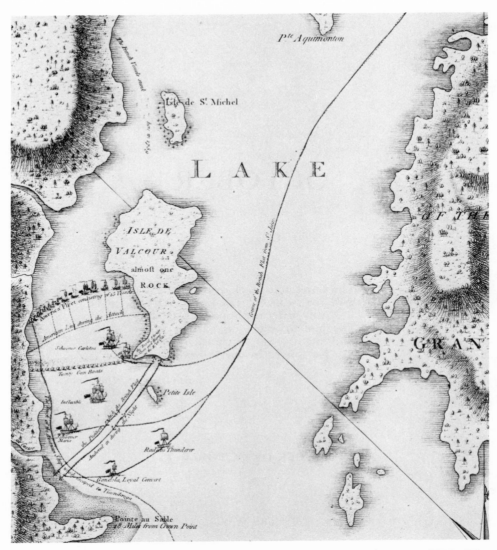

THE BATTLE OF VALCOUR ISLAND (*William Faden, London, 1776*). *The scene is mid-way along Lake Champlain. Although a defeat for a makeshift American fleet under the command of Benedict Arnold, the first naval battle of the revolutionary war was no real loss for the American cause. It briefly delayed an intended invasion of New York by the British under General Guy Carleton, and, the season being late, Carleton shortly turned around and returned to Canada for the winter (as reports in August said might be the case anyway). Valcour Island is roughly 50 miles from Crown Point, which is near the southern tip of Lake Champlain. This map, which was published in London December 3, 1776, shows the New York shore at the left and part of Grand Isle at the right.*

o'clock in the morning the enemy's fleet [of nine armed vessels and fifteen or twenty flat-bottomed gondolas] appeared off Cumberland Head [just to the north of Valcour Island]. General Arnold with his forces immediately prepared to receive them. At eleven o'clock the attack began, at half past twelve the engagement began general and very warm; some of the enemy's ships and all their gondolas beat up and rowed within musket shot of our fleet. They continued a very hot fire with round and grape shot till five o'clock, when they thought proper to retire about six or seven hundred yards distance, and continued there until dark. General Arnold and his troops conducted themselves during this action with great firmness and intrepidity, and made a better resistance than could have been expected against a force so greatly superior. The whole of our killed and wounded amounted to about sixty."

Because of the superior force of the British, Arnold elected to retreat south to Crown Point and regroup his forces. There, on Sunday, the British pursuing, another engagement took place. Arnold himself was nearly lost; his ship, the *Congress*, took a severe beating from round and grape shot. Said the same observer: "The sails, rigging and hull of the *Congress* were shattered and torn in pieces; when, to prevent her falling into the enemy's hands, General Arnold, who was on board, ran her ashore in a small creek ten miles from Crown Point, where after taking out her small arms, she was set on fire, with four other gondolas; with whose crews General Arnold reached Crown Point that evening, luckily escaping the savages who way-laid the road in two hours after he had passed it. Of our whole fleet we have saved two gallies, two schooners, one gondola and one sloop. . . . Our troops are now busily employed in completing the lines, redoubts, &c. at Crown Point, expecting the enemy to attack them with their fleet and army."

> *Arnold later abandoned Crown Point to the British and withdrew to Fort Ticonderoga. But the British—because the season was late—never pursued their advantage; they returned to Canada for the winter.*[1]

Howe: Moving at Last

Slow, methodical, deliberative as usual, General Howe has, for nearly a month, maintained his position opposite the American line at Harlem. For that same length of time there has been speculation in the American camp on his next move. Would it be a frontal attack against the Americans, seeking to overpower at once the mass of the American army, or a move to the east, somewhere along Long Island Sound, in an attempt to come about and strike from the rear?

Saturday, choosing the latter, General Howe ended the speculation. At Throgs Neck, about eight miles to the east of Harlem at the juncture of the East River and Long Island Sound, Howe landed an advance force, estimated at perhaps as many as 6,000 men, under the cover of several men of war. A witness reported: "[The British] marched with great expedition

towards the bridge leading from said Point to the Main [land], but a regiment of [American] riflemen being stationed near the spot, to keep the
bridge, which prevented their design of taking possession of a hill near it;
since which time they have been reinforced by large numbers from their
main body, so it is supposed near two-thirds of the enemy are now on the
point, where they remain under cover of their ships. Several skirmishes
have happened between our party and the enemy since they landed at
[Throgs Neck], which have terminated in favor of the Americans."

The main body of the British army is now encamped at Throgs Neck.
It remains for General Howe to deliberate—likely in his own methodical
way—about the next move.[2]

Congress

Lee: His Lot Improved

Congress showed its gratitude to the officers of the Continental army
last week by granting substantial pay increases (to all from ensign to colonel) and a handsome loan (to one general).

The loan was in the form of an advance in salary to Major General
Charles Lee, second in command of the Continental army. It totals 30,000
dollars. The reason: Lee recently bought an estate in Virginia and is long
overdue in his payment—in large measure because of difficulty in settling
his financial affairs in England. A native of England, Lee retained his commission in the British army until 1775.

The pay increases approved by Congress will bring officers up to the
following scale: colonel, 75 dollars per month (it was 50); lieutenant colonel, 60 (40) ; major, 50 (33) ; captain, 40 (20) ; lieutenant, 27 (13) ; and
ensign, 20 (10).

As added incentive for soldiers and noncommissioned officers, Congress
this week also set forth a policy of supplying each with one suit of clothes
per year. For now at least, that suit will consist of two linen hunting shirts,
two pair of overalls, a leather or woolen waistcoat with sleeves, one pair
of breeches, a hat or leather cap, two shirts, two pair of hose and two pair
of shoes. The aggregate value of that clothing Congress estimates at twenty
dollars. As an option, it said it will provide the money and let a soldier
buy his own clothing.

In other action this week, Congress appointed twenty-four men to the
rank of captain in the navy, among them the famous privateer, John Manly, now of the Continental frigate *Hancock*.[3]

*Pay of British officers and enlisted men depended on the type of regiment. The Royal
Regiment of Horse Guards was highest, and plain foot soldiers the lowest. The pay of
Dragoons (about the average) was, per day: colonel, 1 1 15 s 0 d; lieutenant colonel, 1.4.6;
major, 1.0.6; captain, 0.15.6; lieutenant, 0.9.0; serjeant, 0.2.9; corporal, 0.2.3; and private,
0.1.9. Each also received subsistence, ranging up to 1.6.6 per day for a colonel.*

Jefferson Declines

Virginia's Thomas Jefferson, a former delegate, has declined appointment by Congress as one of three commissioners to the Court of France. It was not "care for my own person, nor yet my private affairs (that) would have induced one moment's hesitation to accept," Jefferson told President Hancock in a letter from Williamsburg, but rather his family situation— his wife has been ill for some time—that compelled him to turn down a mission he would have undoubtedly liked to fill.[4]

The States

A Different Approach

While six sister states have established new governments through the adoption of constitutions, Connecticut has chosen a different approach. Its royal charter granted by King Charles II in 1662 provided for a government as freely elected as those now being established elsewhere; Connecticut has therefore merely reaffirmed what it has had for nearly a century.

As its first resolution, the state's new General Assembly this week decreed its approval of the Declaration of Independence and determined that the form of government will continue as established by royal charter "so far as adherence to the same will be consistent with an absolute independence of this state on the Crown of Great Britain." All officers, civil and military, will retain their present positions.[5]

"Also in Grammar"

Pennsylvania's new constitution—the most innovative and unusual thus far among the American states—has many admirers; it also has its share of detractors who have been taking to the columns of the Philadelphia press in recent weeks to outline their objections, primarily to a unicameral legislature. One example:

"A people who could be free and happy with one legislature might be equally free and happy without any government. Both situations suppose equal degrees of virtue in a people. The history of all countries shows us that power has done as much mischief when lodged in the hands of one assembly as it has done when lodged in the hands of one man."

Said another: "If men were wise and virtuous as angels, a single legislative assembly would be the best form of government that could be contrived for them, except a despotic one, which from being more simple would approach nearer to perfection; but as this is not the case, the inhabitants of free states, in every age, have found it necessary to secure and perpetuate their liberty by compound legislatures."

One angry writer charged that the new constitution is even "deficient in perspicuity, grammar and English."[6]

Foreign News

Close Escape

In Sweden this week, his Majesty King Gustavus III, thirty, narrowly escaped death when his carriage overturned and nearly plummeted down a mountain. His Majesty was returning from Karlskrona in the south of Sweden when the accident occurred, about midway between Norrköping and Gripsholm Castle. As the royal coach left the road and began rolling down a steep slope, it careened into a pine tree and stopped.[7]

Royal Notebook

Of the manifold and great concerns of a realm that spans the oceans of the world, none is so uppermost in the mind of Britain's King George III as the war in America. It consumes his attention as does nothing else. To help himself remember—particularly those whose gallantry or those whose incompetence has changed its course—he keeps his own personal military record in a pocket notebook. Once when General Edward Harvey, Adjutant General of the British Army, remarked in court about receiving a private letter describing a lieutenant's gallantry, his Majesty commanded the general to read it to him. When the general came to the passage about the lieutenant, the King took out his notebook and made a memorandum of it.[8]

Stern Warning

Around Naples in recent weeks there have appeared copies of a pamphlet defending that anathema of catholicism: freemasonry. Lest any Neopolitan be tempted to read such literature, Naples gave a stern warning by having the common hangman burn a copy publicly.[9]

MARRIED: October 7th, in the chapel of the Winter Palace in St. Petersburg: his Imperial Highness, the Grand Duke Paul, to Princess Sophia of Württemberg-Stuttgart; with great pomp, at a ceremony performed by the priest-confessor to her Imperial Majesty, Catherine II, herself of German birth; one day after the princess was baptized into the Orthodox Church as Maria Feodorowna. After the wedding the empress gave foreign ministers the honor of kissing her hand, then dined with the duke and the new duchess, accompanied by the four highest classes of nobility. The wedding follows by little more than five months the death of the grand duke's first wife in childbirth.[10]

Law

The Macumber Case

Can the members of a military tribunal be compelled to explain their reasons for a verdict, even when it is the Congress of the United States demanding the explanation?

Under the Articles of War, each member of a court-martial is sworn not to divulge the opinion of another. By extension of that premise, can a member be compelled to divulge his own? That question of law has proven the fundamental issue in a case that has reached all the way to Congress before coming to a final, and perhaps unexpected resolution. It is the case of Ensign Matthew Macumber.

Macumber was a junior officer in an American regiment at Harlem Heights, near the city of New York. On Tuesday, September 17, in early afternoon, he and about twenty soldiers were caught carrying a quantity of plunder—kitchen utensils, table linen, china, kettles, even furniture— from abandoned homes in the town of Harlem. The major who happened by and discovered the crime ordered Macumber and his men to halt and lay down their stolen goods. The men refused, even threatening the major with cocked weapons, as Ensign Macumber explained that the plundering was done on the orders of his regimental colonel. Outnumbered, the major and his small party left to get help, then returned and arrested the plundering soldiers. Macumber had by then escaped, but was later apprehended.

At a court-martial two days later—on charges of plunderage, robbery and mutiny—Macumber pleaded not guilty. The prosecution's case was supported by the testimony of the major and four of his men, who told of seeing the stolen property and of witnessing the plunderers' threat to "blow out the major's brains." Witnesses for the defense—two of Macumber's men—testified that the plundering was done without Macumber's knowledge, and that in fact the ensign had told them, before entering town, not to do so. Such testimony was obviously in conflict with the major's. The court, presided over by Colonel Comfort Sage, found Macumber not guilty of the specific charges, but did order him to be reprimanded for threatening the major.

The decision, higher up, was immediately unpopular. On the copy of the verdict delivered to him, General Washington added a terse comment: "It is to be observed that the men who were to share the plunder became the evidence for the prisoner." When word reached Congress in Philadelphia, some members were irate. On Monday, the 30th, the Macumber affair became the subject of a formal resolution directing Washington to call on the members of the court-martial to explain to Congress their reasons for an acquittal.

Meanwhile, Washington had already resolved his own misgivings by ordering the court-martial to reconsider its verdict. Thus, on Saturday the 21st, the case was heard again. There was one witness for the prosecution, a captain who had not previously testified. For the defense no further evidence was offered. This time the tribunal found Macumber guilty on all three original charges, ordered the original verdict annulled, and directed that Macumber be cashiered from the service. Washington, the following day, signed his approval to the sentence. In his general orders of the same day, in response to complaints of continued plundering, Washington commanded that every regiment be paraded at five o'clock that afternoon for the purpose of a surprise inspection of knapsacks and tents, and that any suspicious articles be confiscated and the offending soldiers be made to explain their possession.

Still, there was one matter left to settle. Congress had demanded an explanation of the original verdict, and that demand remained in force. The court—the nine members left in camp of the original sixteen—chose to reply, but not to answer.

"Should we consent to assign reasons for our verdict on Macumber's trial," said the court October 7th, "we think it would be establishing a precedent of the most dangerous consequences. . . . It has ever been an established maxim that judges should be free from all influence, that their opinions should proceed from the dictates of an honest and upright mind, and that no bias to any particular party, or fear of censure, should have weight in their judgments. . . . By the last articles of war, every member [of a court-martial] is to be sworn not to disclose the opinion of any particular member. Are laws to be made which are not binding on legislators?" Concluded Colonel Sage and his fellow officers: "After mature deliberation, it is the unanimous opinion of the members that we ought not to assign any reasons for the verdict of that court."

On Tuesday, General Washington forwarded the court's statement to Congress with his own verdict on the Macumber affair: ". . . that it may rest where it is."[11]

Courts-martial were common at this time for offenses ranging from plundering and insubordination to mutiny and desertion. In some measure the prevalence of these crimes was attributable to low morale and extensive periods of inactivity.

Books

The Journals of Congress

Although all sessions of Congress are held behind closed doors at the State House in Philadelphia, Congress keeps a record of the business it transacts. Recently it directed the publication of as much of that record as is ready for printing. Thus now on sale in Philadelphia is *The Journals of the Proceedings of Congress* for the period of January to May, 1776. Octavo in size, bound in boards, and totaling 240 pages, *The Journals* is priced at one dollar, making it one of the most expensive books of its size in print.

While it is a detailed record of what Congress has done, it is that and no more. Any resolution that failed to pass is not included. Nor are the votes on those resolutions that do pass. Nor are the often warm debates which, in Parliament, would be generally reported in ample detail in London's major newspapers within a few days. Except for what individual members of Congress may offer by way of amplification in their own letters and memoirs, the official, public record of Congress on even the loftiest of issues is as bland as this entry on a recent August day: "The Declaration of Independence being engrossed and compared at the table, was signed by the members."[12]

In Britain, meanwhile, the Parliamentary Register *had gone into publication in 1775. It contained detailed accounts of all debates.*

An Example to Mankind

All the difficulties between colonies and mother country might have been avoided if a certain Italian citizen three centuries ago had decided to become a priest or a physician instead of a navigator. But to Christopher Columbus, the lure of discovery exceeded any other purpose in life, and the rest is history.

A new book, *The Discovery of America by Columbus,* published in London, decides it is a good thing Columbus settled upon navigation as a career—that a lesser man, trying the same thing, might have made a shambles of it. In fact, concludes the anonymous author of *Discovery,* Columbus's zeal and integrity left behind a light not only for other discoverers to follow, but for every man in every walk of life.

An example: "Continual storms at sea, continual rebellions of a turbulent people on shore, vexations, disappointments, and cabals at court, were his lot all his life . . . [yet] his magnanimity was proof against all these, and his genius surmounted all the difficulties they threw his way. . . . His immovable fidelity to the ungrateful crown he served, the just policy of his dealing with the natives, his caution against giving them any offense, and his tender behaviour to them when conquered—which merited him the glorious title of their father—together with his zeal to have them influenced in the truths of religion, raise him to the elevated rank of those few men whom we ought to consider as examples to mankind, and ornaments of human nature."

When Columbus landed, the natives thought he was a god—especially because of the ships and the strange uniforms of the men. Columbus instructed his men to act in such a way as to perpetuate that picture, so that on their departure the natives would have the best inclinations to nurse the infant colony.

Whether settling a colony, or sailing a new course, the same kind of genius prevailed. Says *Discovery*: "Columbus had no chart to direct him, no lights from former navigators, no experience of the winds and currents of those particular seas . . . no guide but his own genius . . . in extending the boundaries which ignorance had given to the world."[13]

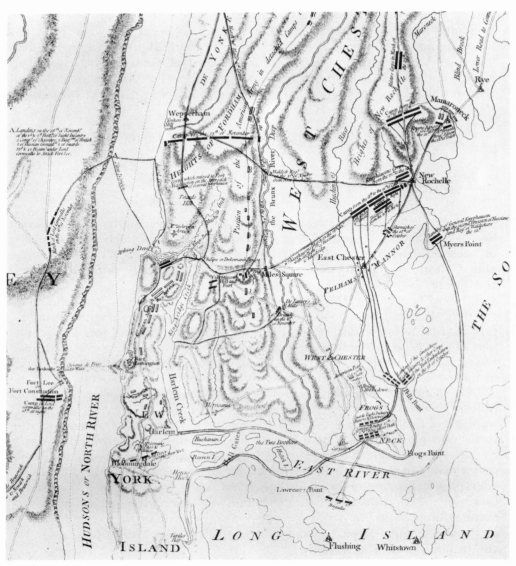

MILITARY OPERATIONS NORTH OF NEW YORK (William Faden, London, 1777). This detail of a map published in London February 25, 1777, shows military operations in Westchester County north of the city of New York in early October 1776. "Frogs Neck" (lower right) was also known (as it is today) as Throgs Neck. On the full map (the rest of which is shown with the Week of October 28th) the caption running northward along the Bronx River (upper center) reads in its entirety, "Position of the American Army in detached Camps every where entrenched from Valentines Hill [to] the White Plains from the 12th to the 27th of October."

THE WEEK OF OCTOBER 14TH

The War

"Heavy Fire" At Rodman's Point

When General Howe on the 12th made it clear that his strategy in pursuing the American army would be a flanking action through Westchester County, he chose a poor place to start. Throgs Neck, some eight miles to the east of the American line at Harlem was easily defended by two small American brigades.

Howe, typically, pondered his next move, feeling no urgency. Now, nearly a week later, has come that next move—three miles north on Long Island Sound at a place known variously as Pell's Point and Rodman's Point.

There was this report: "Under a very heavy fire from a number of ships, the enemy landed about 10,000 men at a place called Rodman's Point; . . . General Lee sent about 500 men down to attack them. . . . The 500 engaged the enemy, and retreated; the enemy followed till they came within about 50 yards of General Lee, till then undiscovered, when his party gave them three very heavy fires, which threw them into great confusion; upon which the flanking party began to play upon them so warmly that they only gave one or two fires and retreated with great precipitation, being pursued by our troops till they got under cover of their ships. The loss on our side was very small; that of the enemy's not ascertained."

The engagement, which also resulted in few casualities among the British, seems of little consequence to either side. But from the number of Americans involved—more than 6,000—it is now apparent that the main body of the Continental army has been withdrawing from its month-old encampment at Harlem Heights and is now chiefly situated in Westchester County.[14]

Congress

Intelligence: How Much is Public?

Congress is continually receiving reports on the state of the army and navy from its commanders in the field and at sea. To what extent these accounts should be made public will now be considered by a committee appointed by Congress last week for just that purpose. The committee of intelligence—Benjamin Rush of Pennsylvania, Richard Henry Lee of Virginia and Francis Hopkinson of New Jersey—will present recommendations on what the public should know.

In other action this week, Congress:

—Appointed as an engineer in the service of the United States, with the rank of colonel, thirty-year-old Thaddeus Kosciusko, a native of the Grand Duchy of Lithuania and graduate of the Royal College of Warsaw, who recently offered his services to America after studying engineering and artillery in France;

—Accepted the resignation of the Rev. Jacob Duché as chaplain of Congress because of poor health and the pressure of his other pastoral duties. Congress gave him the thanks of the House and a gift of 150 dollars for his services.[15]

Foreign News

Revision or Reprisal

Tribute from the mercantile nations of Europe to the potentates of North African countries has long been commonplace as a means of safeguarding trading ships from the pirates of the Barbary Coast. The amount of such tribute is technically subject to negotiation, but to all intent and purpose, it is the potentate who sets, and from time to time revises upward, the rate. A European nation which objects has the choice of yielding to piracy or attempting military reprisal.

The latest to face this dilemma is Holland, which was recently advised by the Emperor of Morocco that its tribute is being raised to 50,000 piastres a year. So far, Holland has refused to pay—not objecting to the principle, which is commonly accepted by most nations, but on the grounds that such an amount is more than any other nation pays. Denmark is paying 25,000 piastres. Switzerland every other year sends gifts valued at 40,000 crowns. France and England also send presents to the emperor from time to time. In addition, Morocco also makes a substantial profit by supplying provisions to the British garrison at Gibraltar. Other nations pay Morocco about 10,000 sequins yearly.

Until Holland decides about paying at the new rate, its shipping will remain at the mercy of Moroccan pirates.[16]

Until 1776, the shipping of the American colonies was protected under terms of British tribute to the Barbary nations. Once America became independent, it had to fend for itself, although for a while, it was accorded grace under France's payments.

As for Holland, it could well have afforded to pay. It was at this time the banker of Europe, and had money out on loan in almost every capital. The American agent in Paris, Silas Deane, reported in a then-secret letter to Congress: "Holland is at present the centre of money and credit for Europe, and every nation is more or less indebted to them, collectively, to such an amount that could the nations in Europe at once pay the whole of their debts to this Republick of Mammon, it would as effectually ruin it as the breaking of the sea through their dykes. Would you know the credit and situation of the affairs of the different kingdoms, consult the books of the Dutch banks. . . . Not a power in Europe, the king of Prussia excepted, can go to war without borrowing money of Holland to a greater or less amount."

Pressure on Portugal

After the battle in which it lost Montevideo to Portugal, Spain demanded restitution in the form of the death penalty for the Portuguese officers involved in the supposedly unauthorized attack. Despite diplomatic pressure from both Britain and France to do so, Portugal has still not agreed. Now, though great secrecy surrounds the matter, there is a report from Paris that France will soon send troops to the aid of Spain in the Banda Oriental and the new Viceroyalty of Rio de la Plata if restitution is not soon made.

Meanwhile, still seeing the possibility of a war with Spain, Portugal has been at work building up its army. This week it tried a new method. His Majesty, King José I, announced a general pardon of all criminals who have fled the country and will now return—provided they agree to serve in the army for five years.[17]

General Sir William

The latest general in the war in America to be knighted for his service to the King is General William Howe, commander of British military forces in North America, whose reward is the Order of the Bath. Second in distinction only to the much older Order of the Garter (c. 1346), the Order of the Bath (1725) is limited to military officers.[18]

Trade and Commerce

To Russia Instead

What is happening to all the manufactured goods Great Britain used to export to America? According to a survey by Member of Parliament Edmund Burke, the loss of the American market has been partially offset by a "prodigious" gain in exports to Russia, particularly hardware and coarse woolens. By way of Russia and the Black Sea, an additional market for British goods, especially fabrics, has been found in Persia.[19]

Theater

"New-Hatch'd, Unfledg'd"

For the past thirty years, Britain has known one Hamlet: David Garrick. Now that he has retired from the stage, what can Londoners expect? When Covent Garden introduced a new Prince of Denmark this week, Polonius, in the play itself, may have answered it:

> "Do not dull thy palm with entertainment
> of each new-hatch'd, unfledg'd comrade."

In this case, the new-hatched comrade was William Thomas Lewis, twenty-eight, who, despite his relative youth (Garrick, on retirement, was fifty-nine) has been an actor most of his life, first appearing as an infant. If not therefore wholly new-hatched, he did prove wholly unfledged. Wrote the critic for London's *St. James's Chronicle*: "Through the whole part there was a skippish lightness and inconsequence about him; the performance seemed more like that of a lively and promising boy at school than that of a first-rate actor at one of our first theatres."

Nevertheless, Lewis was well received, something with which the critic also took issue: "He was applauded from the usual misconception of the galleries, who generally take grimace for expression, and prefer extravagance to truth."

It should be noted, however, that the *Chronicle*'s critic can be rough. He once found fault with Garrick himself, allowing "there were some little circumstances which proved this great man to be mortal." For example: "On seeing his father's ghost, which he is prepared to see, Mr. Garrick throws himself into such an attitude that if Horatio did not support him, he must fall down. Allowing reasonably for stage trick, this appears to us to be extravagantly over-done; for Hamlet immediately speaks one of the most manly and most determined speeches that could have been made, and which a man knocked down with fear could not have spoken —'Be thou a spirit of health or goblin damn'd . . . I will speak to thee. . . .'"

Nor is even The Bard himself hallowed enough to have escaped the *Chronicle* critic, who once complained of "irregularities and absurdities" in the play—even as he also found "characters, scenes, and passages which have been equaled by no tragick writer, either ancient or modern."[20]

Art

More Viewed than Viewers

The son of a German painter famous in his own right, Hans Holbein, the younger, went on to become one of the most prominent artists of the German Renaissance, and also a favorite in England—especially of King Henry VIII. Among his most ambitious works was one portraying the meeting of Henry VIII and Francis I of France, a monumental work that depicts a crowd of observers totaling upwards of four thousand faces. Nowhere near four thousand have ever seen the painting, however, since it has always hung in the royal apartments at Windsor Castle. This week, his Majesty George III announced it is being placed on public view in the Royal Gallery in London.[21]

Books

Common, But Spurious, Glory

If it isn't authentic—and it appears not—it is for the most part so plausible that it could have been: a copy of a speech allegedly given by Samuel Adams at the State House in Philadelphia on Thursday, August 1st. The "speech" has now been published in London as a reprint of a pamphlet supposedly published in Philadelphia.

But three facts throw the "London edition" of publisher J. Johnson into dispute:

—On the day in question Congress, including Sam Adams, was in secret session of committee of the whole debating the Articles of Confederation;

—No trace of a Philadelphia publication of the speech has ever been seen;

—Nothing by Samuel Adams has otherwise ever been published, making it unlikely—if he had made a speech—that he would have sought out a printer to publish it.

Thus "An Oration Delivered at the State House in Philadelphia" must rank as one of the most curious publishing stories of the year. The speech wholeheartedly embraces the American patriot cause, and it does so in a way Sam Adams might have done. At the same time, the language here and there seems inconsistent with that of a New Englander, and most curious of all is the fact that the speech omits any reference at all to the Declaration of Independence—something Adams, speaking at the State House in Philadelphia four weeks to the day after its signing, would hardly have missed, and something which a spurious writer in England would not yet have known about on August 1st.

For inconsistency of language, there is this example: "The same source and resistance which are sufficient to procure us our liberties will secure us a glorious independence and support us in the dignity of free, imperial states." It is hardly conceivable Samuel Adams would have said "imperial."

And yet, there are other quotations which Adams might be proud to call his own:

"From the day on which accommodation takes place between England and America, on any other terms than as independent states, I shall date the ruin of this country."

"For my own part, I ask no greater blessing than to share with you the common danger, and the common glory."

Samuel Adams's biographer, and grandson, William V. Wells, considered the London text entirely spurious. But he gave no indication as to whether or not Adams was aware of its publication. The reason for such a book, in the first place, is a greater mystery. Adams's views were already well known in England.22

Press

Crime, and What to Do

War with the colonies has left many in Britain discontented. A London magazine recently received, and published, this letter from a reader:

"When the trade of a nation declines, it ever happens that the lower classes of people degenerate from the character of honest industry, and rather than strike into new occupations for procuring subsistence, remain in a state of inactivity.

". . . Since our unhappy dissentions in the colonies, the robberies committed in this country have been more frequent, and attended with more circumstances of horrid barbarity than we have known at any former period.

". . . To recommend vigorous exertion of the laws is an unpleasing task, and on first view, may seem to imply a want of humanity: but all partiality towards individuals must give place to considerations for the good of the community. The royal mercy having been extended to the most desperate offenders serves to defeat the intention of the laws. . . . This lenity has cooperated with the distresses of the times to encrease the number of felons; and robberies have of late been attended with such frequent and horrid acts of cruelty that it is become necessary to adopt some measures for the greater security of our lives as well as properties.

"Let every felon convicted of cruelty be immediately branded on each cheek. . . . To live in a civilized country, stigmatized with the indelible mark of shame, would be considered, even by the most hardened villains, as a punishment infinitely more severe than an ignominious death."[23]

THE WEEK OF OCTOBER 21ST

The War

A Major Engagement Near

A major battle between the American and British armies in Westchester County, New York, is being openly predicted. It must be, now that the British have made good a landing they first undertook last Friday at Rodman's Point, and the two armies have begun entrenching within a mile of each other.

The main British force is now at Eastchester, about three miles inland from the landing site, and a small engagement with minor losses was reported there. The British, meanwhile, have extended their position northeastward on Long Island Sound as far as New Rochelle, and small parties have advanced as far as Mamaroneck, about seven miles from Eastchester. It was at Mamaroneck Tuesday night that American forces claimed a small but reassuring success on the part of a Delaware regiment under Colonel John Haslet, whose men sought out a corps of Tory rangers. While Tory losses were small—thirty-six were captured—the encounter had the effect of boosting morale throughout the American ranks.

Although most of the Continental Army is now in Westchester County, the month-old line at Harlem Heights being nearly abandoned by both the British and American forces, a garrison of perhaps 1,800 American troops continues to hold Fort Washington near the northern end of New York Island. Opposite Fort Washington on the New Jersey side is Fort Lee, held by a somewhat larger American force. The two fortresses are intended to prevent northward passage of British ships on the Hudson River, though their effectiveness is still to be established.

But it is in Westchester now that any significant military action will take place, and it is from there that this report comes: "There is no dispute but what a general attack will commence very soon; I think the salvation of America depend upon our conduct in the next engagement; it will be either the destruction of the British army, or ours; the two armies are so near together that they must be both engaged at one time."[24]

Nor Last, Nor Least

With most of the American army departed to the north, Fort Washington, two hundred thirty feet high above the Hudson River at the northern end of the island on which New York is located, looms as a bigger and bigger target for the British, even though its usefulness is open to question. It is a fort, for the most part, in name only, consisting of little more than a rudimentary, open earthwork. Its only apparent reason for being is its conjunction with Fort Lee, across the river in New Jersey: to set up a cross-fire of artillery and prevent British ships from proceeding up the river. It is a strategic value that remains to be proved.

Still, as an American garrison in a region that is increasingly British, it must be considered a prime target for his Majesty's forces. Sunday—not unexpectedly—several British ships anchored opposite Fort Washington in the Hudson River and opened a furious attack. The garrison returned the fire. At length the British ships pulled back and departed. A simultaneous British advance by land against the remnants of the American line at Harlem also ended in a withdrawal. But no one thinks those advances will be the last.[25]

Tories, Whigs Alike

The Hessians, according to a report in Boston's *Independent Chronicle*, plunder indiscriminately; if they see anything they want, they take it. A Tory recently complained to General Howe that he was plundered by Hessian troops. The general is said to have replied that he could not help it; it is their way of making war.[26]

Anniversary

From British ships in New York's East River and Long Island Sound on Friday there was more firing than usual. It was the British navy's way of saluting the anniversary of the coronation of his Majesty, George III, on October 25, 1760.[27]

Congress

Oath of Allegiance

In a week of otherwise wholly routine business, Congress this week took note of the fact that there has been no formal oath for officers of the army and navy, and it established one. Henceforth all officers who already hold a commission as well as all those entering the service will be required to affirm the thirteen states as being free and independent; to renounce their allegiance to George III; to promise to defend the United States against him; and to swear to carry out their responsibilities "with fidelity and honour, and to the best of (their) skill and understanding."[28]

Welcome and Farewell

Since Congress meets every day, and has no fixed time to recess, members must choose whatever time seems most prudent, or most convenient, to leave Philadelphia and return to their constituencies for consultation, state business, personal affairs and reunion with families. At any given point in time there is someone leaving and someone else returning.

This week Boston welcomed back for a brief visit one of its most distinguished delegates in Congress—the Honorable John Adams. Three weeks ago it bid farewell, as he returned to Philadelphia, to one of its most distinguished delegates in Congress—the Honorable Samuel Adams.[29]

Larger, No Greater

The State of Connecticut has enlarged its delegation to the Continental Congress, adding Richard Law while retaining Roger Sherman, Samuel Huntington, William Williams and Oliver Wolcott. Connecticut's delegation will thus be exceeded in size only by Pennsylvania's while equaled by several others. Regardless of size, each delegation is equal in the number of votes it casts: one.[30]

Foreign News

North Is Back

For the first time since he broke his arm in September, Lord North is back at his duties as first minister, and is now reported to be able to preside at a meeting of the Board of Treasury. It is scheduled for next Tuesday, and will be a sure sign he is ready for the opening of Parliament on the 31st.[31]

American Aid: "Positive"

British Secretary of State for the Colonies Lord George Germaine, according to a report from London, has laid before the King "positive intelligence" that America received assurances of support from both France and Spain before declaring independence.

It is said America was told by both nations that some form of material assistance will come by March or April of next year. The report indicates that America wanted such aid much sooner, was told "it was impossible, as the preparations of France were not in sufficient readiness."

Assuming its authenticity, this report may have been based on the British government uncovering in full detail the real purpose of Hortelez & Cie, a supposed trading company established in France in May by Pierre Augustin Caron de Beaumarchais, but secretly financed by the French and Spanish governments for the purpose of supplying arms to America. Beaumarchais was otherwise distinguished as the author of Le Barbier de Séville *(1775) and* Le Mariage de Figaro *(1784).* [32]

New Minister in France

For the second time this year, France has a change in its Finance Ministry, this occasion brought about by the death of J. E. B. Clugny, who succeeded Turgot in May. Into the office, though not with the same title, will go Jacques Necker, Swiss-born banker and a director of the French East India Company. Because he is a foreigner, and a Protestant, Necker will not be comptroller general of finances in name as were his predecessors. But even with the lesser title of Director of the Royal Treasury, he is expected to exercise the same power. Necker last year was among those who most severely attacked Turgot's policy of free trade in grain.

Necker attempted some degree of economic reform, but not on the scale proposed by Turgot. He supported France's entry into the war in America.[33]

African Justice

In Europe and America, the most common methods of execution are hanging and the firing squad. In southern Africa, the end result may be the same, but the means are as uniquely different as the continents.

Dutch traders in the Cape of Good Hope reported the following: A Dutchman, up in the country, was killed by the Hottentots. Rather than retaliate directly, the trading company summoned the native chieftains and demanded that the offender be brought to justice by the Hottentots themselves according to their own manner for so great a crime.

When the offender was seized, a great ceremony was held. A large fire was built, and all the friends and relatives of the criminal were given the opportunity to take their leave of him one by one. Then followed not sorrowful lamenting, but feasting, dancing and drinking. When the accused was sufficiently supplied with liquor as to be insensibly drunk, he was made to dance until he was spent with fatigue. Then, to complete the ritual, he was thrown into the fire.[34]

Music

Knowing the Audience

Bombastic? Too martial? Overcharged? If so, George Frideric Handel probably knew his audience well. At least that is the conclusion reached by the late Oliver Goldsmith in his *Survey of Experimental Philosophy*, recently published in London.

Whatever Handel may or may not have been, thought Goldsmith, he correctly judged English taste in music, and became immensely popular—while not particularly concerned with how he should be greeted on the Continent.

"Foreigners," says Goldsmith, "greatly object to our [English] harmonies; they accuse them of being overcharged, so that there is never room left for occasional force of expression. . . . The fire of [Handel's] music, as they express it, is much too great, and generally unfitted to the subject and the performers." And thus not to be compared with such leading Continental composers as Hasse and Pergolesi.

Foreign critics, said the English writer, should have considered that Handel's music is in general adapted to its audience: "The English have been ever remarked for being fond of loud music. Scaliger, as early as the time of Queen Elizabeth, gives that peculiarity among the features of their national character."

Then Goldsmith turned critic himself, with uncomplimentary remarks about the music of other countries.

On the Italians: "Whatever be our defects, modern Italian music is still more defective than English. Whatever variety of expression ours may want from too much harmony, theirs actually wants from a deficiency of genius. Someone once said all modern Italian cantatas are a repetition of the same tune. They aim for simplicity, but the contrary is what one gets: a singer throws more song into his voluntary close than the composer gave him. In proportion as composers are sterile, performers are compelled to be wild and to make up in tawdry ornament what the piece wants in solidity."

On French music: "Need not be mentioned, as some will scarce allow that they have any."

Not entirely negative, Goldsmith had kind words about some favorites: Alberti, "graceful"; Tartini, "delicate"; Rameau, "though a Frenchman, often sublime"; and Corelli, "still inimitable."

And, of course, that British favorite, who died seventeen years ago: "Handel seems to have studied his audience perfectly. He knew that an English ear found less pleasure in the sound of violin than in the glorious notes of a drum."[35]

THE WEEK OF OCTOBER 28TH

The War

"The Air Groaned"

"The scene was grand and solemn; all the adjacent hills smoked as tho' on fire, and bellowed and trembled with a perpetual cannonade and fire of field pieces, hobits and mortars. The air groaned with streams of cannon and musket shot; the hills smoked and echoed terribly with the bursting of shells; the fences and walls were knocked down and torn to pieces, and men's legs, arms and bodies mangled with cannon and grape shot all around us. I was in the action, and under as good advantages as any one man, perhaps, to observe all that passed, and write these particulars of the action from my own observation."

So does an officer of the Continental army recount a general engagement at White Plains this week—an encounter which for days seemed more and more inevitable and depended only upon General Howe making up his mind.

The American army, following its retreat from Harlem Heights, had encamped in Westchester County, and by the time of the British advance, had established a line at the village of White Plains. But most of the action in Monday's engagement took place at Chatterton's Hill on the far right of the American line, across the Bronx River. It was reported this way by an officer: "We marched on to a hill about one mile & a half from our lines, with an artillery company and two field pieces, and placed ourselves behind walls and fences in the best manner we could to give the enemy trouble. About half after nine o'clock our advanced parties all came retreating in before the enemy, and the light parties of the enemy, with their advanced guard, consisting of 2 or 3,000 came in sight, and

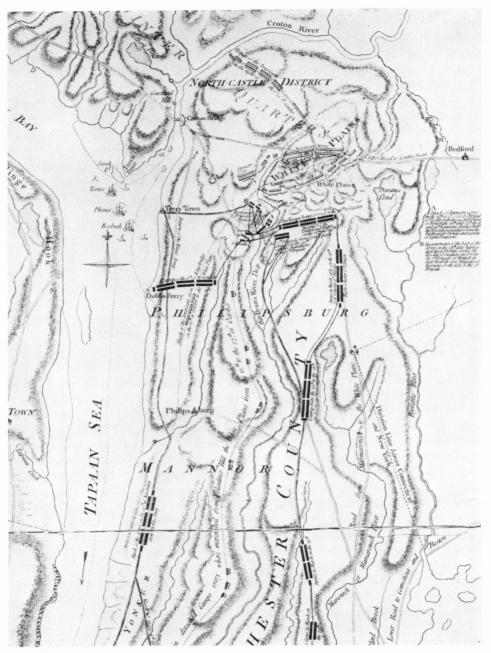

THE BATTLE OF WHITE PLAINS (William Faden, London, 1777). *This is a further detail of the map provided with the Week of October 14th and shows that portion of Westchester County, New York, which was of immediate consequence to the Battle of White Plains. The "Tappan Sea" (Tappan Zee) at left is a wide section of the Hudson River.*

Map Division—New York Public Library—
Astor, Lenox and Tilden Foundations

marched on briskly towards us, keeping the high grounds; and the light horse pranced on a little, in the rear, making a very martial appearance. As our light parties came on to the hills and discovered where we were, the enemy began to cannonade us, and to fling shells from their hobits and small mortars.

"Their light parties soon came on and we fired upon them from the walls and fences, broke and scattered them at once; but they would run from our front and get round upon our wings to flank us, and as soon as our fire discovered where we were, the enemy's artillery would at once begin to play upon us in a most furious manner. We kept the walls till the enemy were just ready to surround us, and then we would retreat from one wall and hill to another, and maintain our ground there in the same manner, till numbers were just ready to surround us.

"Once the Hessian grenadiers came up in the front of Colonel Douglas's regiment, and we fired a general volley upon them at about 20 rods distance, and scattered them like leaves in a whirlwind. And they ran out so far, that some of the regiment ran out to the ground where they were when we fired upon them, and bro't off their arms and accoutrements, and rum that the men who fell had with them, which we had time to drink round with before they came on again. They formed at a distance, and waited till their artillery and main body came on, when they advanced in solid columns upon us, and were gathering all round us, ten to our one."

At length the superiority of British numbers and an experience new to American militia, the frightful reality of a cavalry charge by those light horse who earlier made such a "martial appearance," resulted in General Washington ordering a withdrawal of all American forces—another retreat, again northward. American losses, including prisoners taken, are believed to be a couple of hundred; British losses, fewer. At the same time, General Howe has once again failed—as he has since the battle of Long Island just two months ago—to accomplish anything significantly more than making the American army retreat. For all his superior force, there is still a full-fledged American army, and a very viable one at that.[36]

Congress

All Above Any

Congress this week came face-to-face for the first time with that inevitable question of the powers of a state legislature as against those of the central government. Its position, determined quickly and clearly: the interests of the United States must prevail above those of any one of them.

That precept emerged as what may be by far more important than the issue which precipitated it: a relatively minor dispute with the State of Maryland. The state, seeking to encourage recruitment of soldiers, an-

nounced an offer of a ten-dollar cash bounty as an alternative to the promise of ten acres of land (at war's end) for both noncommissioned officers
and privates. Inasmuch as other states and Congress offer only land, Maryland's action might induce would-be soldiers to demand the same or refuse to enlist, with the result that Congress could be compelled to resort
to "an additional bounty far beyond what is reasonable."

Congress instructed President Hancock to write to the convention of
Maryland and advise the state its offer of a cash bounty will be "extremely detrimental" and that ". . . the faith which this house by virtue of the
power with which they were vested . . . must be obligatory upon their
constituents; that no one state can by its own act be released therefrom,
and that the interest of the United States would be deeply and injurious-
ly affected."

Congress this week also addressed itself anew to the matter of internal
security, appointing a committee (Samuel Adams, George Wythe, Richard Henry Lee, James Wilson and George Ross) to prepare an effectual
plan for "suppressing the internal enemies of America and preventing
communication of intelligence to our other enemies." What gave rise to
that action was the case of Timothy Dodd, an express rider from Boston,
who reported that a packet of dispatches from General Washington to
Congress was stolen from him at Bristol, Pennsylvania. A committee of
two (James Wilson and Francis Hopkinson) investigated, found the circumstances suspicious. Congress ordered Dodd imprisoned.

In other action this week, Congress:

—Accepted a decision by the Rev. Jacob Duché turning down the 150
dollars voted him on his retirement as chaplain of Congress, and honored
his wish that the money go instead to the relief of widows and children
of Pennsylvania officers killed in battle;

—Determined that the rank of officers in the Marines be the same as
officers in the land service.[37]

Next: A Lottery

A lottery will be the next way of raising revenue for the war, Congress
decided this week. It asked a committee to report back, at the earliest
possible date, with a complete plan. Congress also asked the Board of
Treasury to prepare for a new emission of five million dollars in bills of
credit—to be issued when Congress so directs—and to release "speedily"
500,000 dollars in small bills of two-thirds, one-third, one-sixth and one-
ninth of a dollar.[38]

The States

Chasing the Cherokees

Although the Continental Congress dispatched commissioners to conciliate with the Cherokee Indians in the western reaches of the southern states last spring, Indian raids continued along the frontier. A new approach —the militia—appears to be more successful.

The retaliatory strikes, the first major operations since the expedition of former Virginia Governor Dunmore two years ago, have been carried out by militia from Virginia and the Carolinas. The first result, in July, was the reported rout of three Cherokee war parties at the Holston River in western Virginia and North Carolina.

The most recent reports, dated October 14th and 15th, have come from an expedition commanded by Virginia's Colonel William Christian. He is said to have met at the French Broad River on the 12th with Cherokee representatives proposing peace, but rejected the proposals because there was no provision for delivering up white captives. The following night Christian and his force of about 1,200 marched in secret three miles down the French Broad River from the site of the meeting, crossed over, and then returned north for an attack. When he reached the Indian camp, it was abandoned. The Cherokees had retreated into the wildnerness.[39]

This was one of a number of such raids which culminated in a treaty with the Cherokees in July, 1777. But despite the treaty, Indian attacks continued.

Land Reform in Virginia

In Virginia, as in England where it has been law for centuries, property has been conveyed in one of two ways: in fee simple, which is to say, from one person to another as either shall choose; or in fee taille, which means a particular landhold may only pass by inheritance, in direct line of succession, and must do so in perpetuity. Thus—except where a special act of the legislature contravenes—all lands once established in taille can never accrue in ownership to other than an heir, even if the heir wants to sell or otherwise dispose of the land.

In Virginia, lands held in taille have created the makings of an aristocracy like that once left behind. During the course of its colonial development, much of the state was set aside in large tracts which became, through grants, the property in taille of a relatively few influential men. Such vast acreage has thus remained outside of new ownership, and has sharply restricted the degree to which a rapidly increasing population may also become a land-owning population, however modest each individual's landhold might be.

The way to change is simple enough to contemplate, but has in times past been well outside the inclination of any Virginia legislature and any royal governor. Even the General Assembly of the newly established Commonwealth—more representative than not of major landowners—might not have been thought ready so soon to consider such a far-reaching change in the law. And yet it has done more than merely consider change. A bill abolishing fee taille—chiefly through the efforts of Delegate Thomas Jefferson—was passed by the House of Delegates October 23rd. Now the Senate has given its concurrence, making fee simple hereafter the only legal way of conveying property in Virginia and eventually assuring vast tracts of land new and broader ownership.[40]

Parliament

A Sense of Urgency

On the eve of the reopening of Parliament, official London was, as it had been in the last weeks, a center of constant activity.

Preparation for the new session was temporarily halted when First Minister Lord North broke his arm in a riding accident in late September. But he recently resumed his duties, and has kept the Ministry busy of late with a series of meetings that have been far more frequent than usual. While there was no official explanation for the marked increase in activity, over and above the opening of Parliament and the war in America, many speculated that the threat of war between Spain and the British ally, Portugal, was a principal reason. Whatever the cause, there was a sense of urgency in the air. And it has been clearly noticed by British investors. In three days, India stock dropped ten percent on the London exchange.[41]

Important—But More So

Prorogued since May 23rd, Great Britain's Fourteenth Parliament reopened Thursday for its Third Session. It may be, said the *London Packet,* "the most important session of Parliament . . . perhaps, ever."

In the tradition of Parliaments past, his Majesty King George III was there—not only to make the opening official, but to remind both Commons and Lords in the most serious terms of the critical nature of business in the months ahead.

For the session that was scheduled to begin at two in the afternoon, his Majesty left St. James's Palace for the short trip to Westminster at about a quarter before two. Dressed in a relatively plain suit of deep rose color, almost scarlet, he was noticeably serene, steady, composed—giving no outward sign that the address he was about to give would be one of the most important of his reign.

But the royal procession showed clearly that the opening of Parliament is always an important occasion. There were: a military guard with drawn swords; three coaches full of gentlemen and officers of the royal household; another military escort; twelve royal footmen in new gold-colored livery trimmed in rich lace; then the yeomen of the guard, marching two by two; and a contingent of constables; and finally the State Coach, drawn by eight white horses, followed by another military guard with drawn swords.[42]

His Majesty's Message

As Parliament opened its new session Thursday, America continued to be the matter of greatest concern. But it was no longer the same America that dominated Parliament's attention last spring. And even though his Majesty continued to refer to America as "my loyal colonies," it was a bitter realty to the returning lords and gentlemen of Parliament that those same colonies had now declared themselves free and independent states—no longer to be within the province of Parliament except as the objectives of war.

His Majesty, addressing the joint opening session of Lords and Commons, dutifully reported the bad news everyone now knew, that independence had been declared; and some good news, that military operations in Canada in particular and New York as well had been successful and gave rise to hope for "the most decisive good consequences." Even so, he would rather have been able to report that all the troubles in America were over.

"Nothing could have afforded me so much satisfaction," he told Parliament, "as to have been able to inform you, at the opening of this session, that the troubles which have so long distracted my colonies in North America were at an end; and that my unhappy people, recovered from their delusion, had delivered themselves from the oppression of their leaders and returned to their duty. But so daring and desperate is the spirit of those leaders, whose object has always been dominion and power, that they have now openly renounced all allegiance to the Crown, and all political connection with this country; they have rejected, with circumstances of indignity and insult, the means of conciliation held out to them under the authority of our commission, and have presumed to set up their rebellious confederacies for independent states. If their treason be suffered to take root, much mischief must grow from it, to the safety of my loyal colonies, to the commerce of my kingdoms, and indeed to the present system of all Europe."

Other highlights of the address:

—His majesty reported "assurances of amity from the several courts of Europe," thus countering arguments by the Opposition in Parliament that France and Spain will enter the war on the side of America or that Portugal and Spain are on the verge of war;

—He predicted that adoption of the Declaration of Independence will bring about unanimity at home;

—He said another military campaign, perhaps to end the war, will have to be undertaken in America notwithstanding the recent successes in Canada and New York, and promised an estimate for military spending in 1777 to be presented to the House of Commons shortly.[43]

Not All of One Mind

The first order of business for Parliament after his Majesty's speech was to adopt a humble address of thanks. Since the speech was primarily about the situation in America, that was no easier than any other American matter this year. But what struck many observers was that the debate in the House of Commons, which went on until half past eleven at night, was both milder and more confused than usual. One who has sat through many a long session told the *St. James's Chronicle* the debate was perhaps the most ill-conceived and irregular "since the first establishment of Parliaments in this country." While others would not go that far, most agreed it was worth noting that not all the able debaters spoke at all; and those who did sometimes limited their remarks to details and not to the motion as a whole. Moreover, it was observed by no few that those who spoke for the government did so with the distinct appearance of being unprepared.

What they debated in such fashion was a motion by Mr. Neville that wholly and warmly supported his Majesty—congratulating him on the victories in Canada and New York and promising whatever financial support is needed to guarantee more like them. But what was sure to draw fire was the close: ". . . the general conviction of justice and necessity of your Majesty's measures must unite all ranks of your faithful subjects in supporting your Majesty with one mind and heart in the great national cause in which you are engaged."

Despite what observers said about the debate as a whole, those who were not of "one mind and heart" with the Administration had some remarkably incisive commentary:

—Charles James Fox: "The Americans did no more than the English did against James II. When James went out of the kingdom, the English declared the throne to be abdicated and chose another king. When the late severe laws were passed against the Americans, they were thrown into anarchy; they declared we had abdicated the government, and therefore they were at liberty to choose a government for themselves."

—John Wilkes: "Since our last meeting, sir, the scene with respect to America has totally changed. Instead of negotiations with colonies, or provincial assemblies, we have a war to carry on against the free and independent states of America; a wicked war, which has been occasioned solely by a spirit of violence, injustice and obstinacy in our ministers, unparalleled in history."

—Governour Johnstone: While not entirely approving of the American Declaration of Independence, he argued America was driven to that measure by rigorous prosecution: "We had hired foreign troops to fight against them, and they had no other way of putting themselves on a footing with us than by throwing off the yoke, declaring themselves independent, and inviting foreign aid to defend them."

Speakers in defense of the Administration included:

—Lord North, who commented in particular on the possible intervention of France and Spain: "From the present assurances of the Court of France, and stronger cannot be desired, we have every reason to be satisfied of their pacifick intentions." But to be on the safe side, said North, Britain will be prepared for the worst.

—Secretary of State for the Colonies Lord George Germaine, who talked largely of military posture: "I am further asked, what are the numbers of the armies in America? Sir, the number of that under General Howe is twenty-five thousand, and he will be reinforced by five thousand more, which are near the American coast by this time. He has besides about two thousand Provincials, and will probably have more. The army in Canada is eleven thousand and perhaps three or four hundred, which is the full complement for that department, if not a little more."

At length the House of Commons got down to a vote on the motion and, not surprisingly, approved the humble address in its original form 232 to 83.

Meanwhile in the House of Lords—where the Duke of Manchester warned that the British empire is exhibiting a remarkable parallel to ancient Rome in its decline—a similar resolution was passed by a margin of almost four to one.[44]

Press

"No Alternative"

When Philadelphia's newest paper, the thrice-a-week *Pennsylvania Evening Post,* announced a price increase last July, Philadelphia's four weekly newspapers held fast despite continually rising costs. Now they too have found no alternative, and in a joint announcement have disclosed that all four will match the *Post*'s price after the first of the year.

The four publishers—William and Thomas Bradford of the *Pennsylvania Journal,* John Dunlap of the *Pennsylvania Packet,* James Humphreys of the *Pennsylvania Ledger,* and William and David Hall and William Sellers of the *Pennsylvania Gazette*—told their readers this week: "The publishers of the several weekly newspapers in this city are under the disagreeable necessity of informing their subscribers that the extraordinary advance in the price of paper and other materials in the printing business has obliged them to raise the price to 15 shillings per annum."

The *Pennsylvania Gazette,* oldest among them, has always been sold for ten shillings per year. That was even the price in 1729, one year after its founding, when a twenty-three-year-old printer by the name of Benjamin Franklin became publisher.[45]

NOVEMBER

THE winter season now approaches near;
Provide good meat, good fires, and good strong beer;
Good clothes, a good warm house, and a good wife:
All these will help to make a happy life.

The Virginia Almanack
November, 1776

THE WEEK OF NOVEMBER 4TH

The War

No Defense

Just how effective Fort Washington and Fort Lee are in defending the Hudson River from passage of British ships north of New York is no longer in question; three of his Majesty's ships have passed unhindered.[1]

Congress

Successor to Franklin

In an otherwise largely routine week, Congress turned its attention to postal matters:

—Appointing as new Postmaster-General, to succeed Dr. Benjamin

Franklin who left for France October 30th, Richard Bache, formerly comptroller of the Post Office and Franklin's son-in-law;

—Directing the new Postmaster-General to assure frequent communication with the army camps at White Plains and Ticonderoga by hiring
additional riders, and to take the utmost pains to make sure they are "so-
ber, diligent and trusty persons";

—Requesting ferry keepers to expedite passage of riders bearing dispatches to Congress.[2]

The States

New York's Loyalists

When Lord Howe and General Howe issued a declaration of clemency
for Americans swearing allegiance to the King, most Americans paid no
attention. But in New York, which has been in British hands for nearly
two months, there are—as the declaration requires—those who do profess
to "bear true allegiance" to the King and a "warm affection to his sacred
person, crown and dignity," and who "esteem the constitutional suprem-
ecy of Great Britain over these colonies." In witness thereof, they have
jointly—all 948 of them—taken to the columns of the now-loyalist-pub-
lished *New York Gazette* to say so. Prior to British occupation, New York's
population was about 25,000.[3]

In the "Common Cause"

In establishing an additional ten-dollar bounty to encourage recruitment of soldiers, Maryland risked—in the opinion of the Continental Congress—setting a precedent unfair to other states and to the central government. But in a more important context, it presented a potential test of
the power of Congress against the power of a state.

Now, responding to a formal request of Congress that the additional
bounty be discontinued, Maryland has answered, in effect: This is not the
time to debate powers; in the interest of the "common cause," the bounty
will be withdrawn.

By resolution at its session of November 9th, the Convention of Maryland declared itself "exceedingly unhappy to find that there should have
been any the least difference of opinion" with Congress. The reason for
the bounty was simply the fact that Maryland, land-locked to the west,
does not have sufficient territory with which to make good an offer of ten
acres to every newly enlisting soldier. Thus it chose the "prudent" alternative of a cash bounty. But in deference to the wishes of Congress the
Convention will now withdraw that bounty—at the same time recording
its observation that if the offer of land "should prove a disappointment, it
cannot be imputed to this State."

On the question of states' powers, the resolution being forwarded to Congress by Convention President Matthew Tilghman declares:

"This Convention have a strong disinclination to go into any discussion of the powers with which the Congress is invested, being fully sensible that the general interest will not be promoted by either the Congress affirming or this Convention denying the existence of a fullness of power in that honorable body, the best and only proper exercise of which can be in adopting the wisest measures for equally securing the rights and liberties of each of the United States, which was the principle of their union."[4]

Parliament

Wretched or Wise?

Is the American Declaration of Independence "a wretched composition, very ill written?" Or was it "a wise political measure," successful in its purpose of "captivating the people of America?"

Both views have been heard in Parliament. The first is predominant. The second, which is not and is therefore the more interesting, was put forth recently on the floor of the House of Commons by John Wilkes, Member of Parliament for Middlesex, whose outspoken opposition to the King has already made his one of the best known names in Parliament.

Said Wilkes: "An honourable gentleman near me [the Marquis of Granby] attacks the American Declaration of Independency in a very peculiar manner, as a wretched composition, very ill written, drawn up with the view to captivate the people. That, sir, is the very reason why I approve it most as a composition, as well as a wise political measure, for the people are to decide this great controversy. If they are captivated by it, the end is attained. The polished periods, the harmonious happy expressions, with all the grace, ease and elegance of a beautiful diction, which we chiefly admire, captivate the people of America very little; but manly, nervous sense, they relish even in the most awkward and uncouth language. Whatever composition produces the effect you intend in the most forcible manner is, in my opinion, the best, and that mode should always be pursued. It has the most merit, as well as success, on the great theatre of the world, no less than on the stage, whether you mean to inspire pity, terrour or any other passion."[5]

"You Meant to Drive Them . . . "

Just after the British occupation of New York in September, Lord Howe and General Howe issued a proclamation urging the inhabitants of America "to return to their allegiance [and] accept the blessings of peace." Unlike one earlier such proclamation, this one appeared to go a step further and declared the king to be "most graciously pleased . . . to concur in the revisal of all his acts by which his subjects there may think themselves aggrieved." The declaration stirred little interest in New York, but news of it has now reached London and prompted the minority in Commons to another vigorous attack on the Administration. Their chief argument: the Howes exceeded their authority in promising a revisal of colonial laws, something which only Parliament can do.

Such a revisal, however, is something the minority has favored all along. Lord John Cavendish therefore moved that Parliament, the proper authority, so do it: "Resolve itself into a committee to consider of the revisal of all acts of Parliament by which his Majesty's subjects in America think themselves aggrieved." Explained he: such a step would be proof of a disposition to peace; it would restore the Administration to confidence; it would be the means of removing the almost universal opinion that prevails in America that every promise of the Administration is given with some insidious intention of treachery, or to divide them in order the more easily to break their strength and subdue them.

Countered Lord North: The promise contained in the Howes' declaration was by no means new; it is the principle which has pervaded the conduct of the Administration from the beginning. "One great object," said Lord North of the Howes' peace mission, "nay, the leading one, was to hear grievances, to transmit an account of them home, and to engage on the part of the Legislature that redress would be granted wherever a just cause for redress existed. That [day, September 19th] was the first opportunity the Commissioners had to discharge that part of their duty with any prospect of success."

His reasons for opposing the motion, said Lord North, should be obvious to everyone: "The Americans have declared themselves independent; why enter into deliberation about what you are willing to concede till we know first that they acknowledge our authority; and after they have returned to us. as subjects, till we know what would reasonably content them?"

Added Solicitor-General Alexander Wedderburne, only a few years ago a violent opponent of the North Administration: "Till the spirit of independency is subdued, it is idle to come to any resolutions or revisions as a means of conciliation. Take the sword out of the hand of the governing part of America, and I have not a doubt but a very considerable part of that country will return to its obedience with as much rapidity as it revolted."

To Edmund Burke, who had earlier seconded Lord Cavendish's motion, an ever more important issue was why the Howes had not been sent to America sooner, when they might have been able to do some good. "Why," he asked the Administration spokesmen, "after the act passed for them, were they delayed full seven months, and not permitted to sail till May. . . . By this delay you drove them into the declaration of independency; not as a matter of choice, but necessity; and now they have declared it, you bring it as an argument to prove that there can be no other reasoning used with them but the sword. . . . You simply tell them to lay down their arms, and then you will do just as you please. Could the most cruel conqueror say less? Had you conquered the devil himself in hell, could you be less liberal? No! Sir, you would offer no terms; you meant to drive them to the declaration of independency."

When Commons at length voted, the outcome was largely as expected. Lord Cavendish's motion to consider revisal of the colonial laws got 47 yeas and 109 noes.[6]

Foreign News

With Seeming Authority

War between Britain and France has been predicted for some time, but seldom with as much seeming authority as it was this week in the *London Packet.* Said the newspaper: "[He] has uniformly declared in his letters that he thinks war is inevitable, unless the Americans are totally routed in this campaign." *He* is Lord Stormont, Britain's ambassador to France.[7]

Why Not the Army?

The debate on the debacle of Sullivan's Island continues in Britain. Said the *London Packet* in its issue of November 8th: "We are informed from very respectable authority that three serjeants and thirty men deserted from General Clinton at Sullivan's Isle, and waded to the main. Query, if these deserters got across, what could prevent the army?"[8]

New Mayor, New Salary

Saturday being Lord Mayor's Day, London's new mayor, Sir Thomas Halifax, was sworn into office at the Guildhall to succeed John Sawbridge.

He becomes the first to take advantage of a new law raising the mayor's salary by 1,000 *l*; it was 2,372 *l.* The increase was approved by the Common Council after "warm debate" November 1st to enable mayors to fill the office in dignity and without having to expend as much in personal funds. During his term of office (1774–75), for example, Lord Mayor John Wilkes incurred expenses of 8,226 *l* while taking in receipts (including salary) of only 4,889 *l.* Lord Mayors, despite the increase, will still be left with non-reimbursable expenditures for such necessities of the office as Lord Mayor's Day, public dinners, horses, coaches, servants, liveries, lamps, candles, linen, coals, china, glass, stationery wares, newspapers, gowns for swordbearers and others in attendance, glaziers, upholsterers, music, ribands—all of which were listed in Wilkes's accounting of his year in office.[9]

DIED: Last week, at his home near Paris: M. Jean Dennis La Coffe, who, until the end, had never known a day of illness in his one hundred and two years.[10]

Religion

England's Day of Prayer

By order of his Majesty, all of England and Wales will observe a day of fasting and prayer, dedicated to supplication for an end to the conflict with the colonies, and especially that his Majesty's "deluded colonists" will see the error of their ways. The day chosen: Friday, the 13th of December.

Clergy throughout the land are already receiving a supplement to the Book of Common Prayer, outlining changes in the offices of Holy Communion, Morning Prayer and Evening Prayer on that date.

Accordingly, a priest celebrating communion will, during the second collect, petition God to "bless the arms of our gracious Sovereign, in the maintenance of his just and lawful rights, and prosper his endeavors to restore tranquility among his unhappy, deluded subjects in America, now in open rebellion against his Crown, in defiance of all subordination and legal authority."

The selection of an epistle is perhaps supreme in the invocation of scripture for a practical and patently political purpose. It is that well-known portion of the First Epistle of Peter (II:11–17) about submitting "to every ordinance of man for the Lord's sake: whether it be to the king as supreme; or unto governors . . . Honour all men. Love the brotherhood. Fear God. Honour the king."

Original prayers for the day have been carefully drafted by his Majesty's clergy. Thus, in the Prayer for our Enemies, will British subjects petition: ". . . give grace, we beseech thee, to our unhappy fellow-subjects in America, that seeing and confessing the error of their ways . . . they may again return to their duty, and make themselves worthy of thy pardon and forgiveness."[11]

And a Dissent

Not all in Britain believe the national day of prayer proclaimed for December 13th will accomplish its purpose. Said Edmund Burke in the House of Commons this week:

"In this situation, sir, shocking to say, are we called upon by another proclamation to go to the altar of the Almighty with war and vengeance in our hearts, instead of the peace of our blessed Saviour. He said, 'My peace I give you'; but we are, on this fast, to have war only in our hearts and mouths; war against our brethren. Till our churches are purified from this abominable service, I shall consider them not as the temples of the Almighty but the synagogues of Satan."[12]

Medicine

Magnetic Medicine

Vienna's Dr. Franz Anton Mesmer at forty-two has fame few other physicians will ever attain in a lifetime, but it is not from the practice of orthodox medicine. Indeed it has been some years since he has practiced traditional healing at all—ever since he discovered that magnets, applied to the body in a certain way, might produce more immediate relief than such orthodox procedures as bleedings, bed rest and the administration of various nostrums.

Mesmer's practice began to flourish, and long lines of sufferers formed outside his door, waiting the seeming magic of his magnets. It might have gone on that way indefinitely except for a strange event. One day, by accident, Mesmer discovered he could work the same remarkable cures without any magnets at all—simply with his own hands, his own will, his own "magnetic" gaze.

To his patients, ailing of this disease and suffering of that, it made no difference. But to his colleagues in the medical profession, he began seeming more and more questionable despite such impressive credentials as a degree in theology and a diploma from the Vienna School of Medicine signed by no one less than the eminent Gerard van Swieten himself.

One day recently, Dr. Mesmer addressed the Academy of Sciences in Bavaria, and complained that Vienna medical circles are becoming so increasingly hostile to him they are beginning to call him a quack.

> *Mesmer's procedure, a forerunner of hypnotism, left him a professional outsider for the rest of his life, although he was himself sincere about his work. He left to our language the word "mesmerize."*[13]

Music

New But Ancient

It was with great expectation that London's Royal Academy of Music in 1720 inaugurated a plan for patronizing Italian opera under the directorship of George Frideric Handel. Within a few years the sponsors raised the enormous sum of 50,000*l* — 1,000*l* of it from his Majesty, George I. It was an admirable beginning. But in less than a decade, it failed.

Now Londoners have a new music venture which ought to be a worthy successor to the high hopes of the Royal Academy's ambitious program of a half century ago. Called the Concerts of Ancient Music, this series is chiefly the enterprise of the Earl of Sandwich, First Lord of the Admiralty. Subscribers to the concert series pay five guineas and become entitled to hear twelve concerts. The only requirement for the selection of music is that it must be of at least twenty years standing. Thus ruled out for now will be such examples of modern music as the symphonies of Vienna's Franz Joseph Haydn, the earliest of which will not be eligible for performance for another three years. Virtually all of the music of Handel, however, may be performed at once—and likely will be.[14]

Press

Back in Boston

The *Boston Gazette,* an institution in the Massachusetts capital since 1719 but not lately published there, is back in town.

Seeking refuge from the British occupation, Publisher Benjamin Edes in June of last year moved his office to Watertown, west of Cambridge. Now with the British gone, and a further delay for smallpox over, the *Gazette* is Boston in fact as well as name once again.

Edes's edition of Monday, November 4th, announced the return routinely: "The publisher of this paper hereby informs his customers that he has removed from Watertown to the printing office opposite the Court-House in Queen-Street, Boston, where they and others may be supplied with the same as usual."[15]

THE WEEK OF NOVEMBER 11TH

The War

The Fall of Fort Washington

As it tried once before, the British army has tried again and this time succeeded in doing convincingly: brought about the fall of Fort Washington on the Hudson River, north of New York.

Although the usefulness of the fort has been open to question for some time, particularly since it has proved ineffective in blocking British ships on the river, its surrender cannot but have a dreadful effect on the morale of an American army already struggling against seemingly insurmountable odds. For while the loss in dead and wounded was not great on either side—a few hundred for each—the loss in American military power is staggering: between 2,000 and 3,000 men taken prisoner, and the loss in the materials of war—cannon, muskets, tents, and equipment of all sorts—may well be beyond calculation.

The defenders of the fort, under command of Colonel Robert Magaw, are credited with a valiant effort; but the overpowering force of the British army, more than twice the size of the defending force, and the effectiveness of British naval support, made the difference.

At the outset of fighting, it appeared things might end differently. A detachment under Lieutenant Colonel Lambert Cadwalader took the first thrust at the American out-lines about a quarter-mile from the fort. "The Hessians made the attack," according to an observer, "and marched within point-blank pistol shot of the lines, where they were kept at least two hours, and were by the intrepidity and well-placed fire of our people, cut down in whole ranks. The brave Americans kept their post until a heavy column of British troops appeared in their rear; the lines there being entirely open, obliged them to retreat and endeavour to gain the fort. but British troops being nearer the fort cut off and obliged a considerable part to surrender prisoners."

"At this time," said another, "the Hessians advanced on the north side of the fort in very large bodies; they were received by the [American] troops posted there with proper spirit, and kept back a considerable time. But at length they were also obliged to submit to a superiority of numbers, and retire under the cannon of the fort. The enemy having possessed themselves of the adjacent ground, which rendered the fort no longer tenable, the garrison surrendered." Colonel Magaw turned over his sword to the opposing commander, General Wilhelm von Knyphausen, and in so doing, left virtually all of New York Island in British hands.[16]

Congress

Fear for Philadelphia

More and more there is fear that Philadelphia will be the next objective of the British army. It was clear this week as Congress:

—Invested in the Board of War the powers of the full Congress to promote the most effectual defense of the city;

—Directed it to confer with the Philadelphia Council of Safety in preparing a plan of defense;

—Ordered the Marine Committee to deploy available American naval forces in the Delaware River so as to prevent an attack by sea (taking note of a report that the British fleet under Lord Howe was seen leaving Sandy Hook, New Jersey, and steering a southward course).

At the same time, Congress considered the possibility that the operations of the British fleet might mean a new attack in the Carolinas. It asked the state of North Carolina to station Brigadier General Moore and his regulars in such a way as to be prepared for an enemy landing in either North or South Carolina.[17]

Greater Inducement

The raising of the eighty-eight battalions ordered by Congress September 16th has not been proceeding at the pace originally hoped. In part, Congress decided this week, it is because inducements for enlistment (land and cash bounties) have been restricted to those enlisting for the duration of the war. Now soldiers volunteering for three years of duty will receive the same pay and the same bounties as those promising indefinite service; but they will not qualify for land.

Congress appears to feel that those enlisting for three years will, for the most part, be willing to remain in the service longer if the war should continue beyond 1779. Agreed the members of Congress in their resolution: ". . . the readiness of the inhabitants of these states to enter into the service for limited times in defense of the invaluable privileges on all former occasions, gives good ground to hope the same zeal for the public good will appear in the future when necessity calls for their assistance."[18]

The States

Going Home

A convoy of about two hundred British transports, accompanied by the men of war *Fowey* and *Active,* have departed America for England. Among the passengers on the voyage: former Virginia Governor Lord Dunmore, returning at last to Britain a year after abandoning his capital at Williamsburg. For Dunmore, the voyage will be one-way; for the transports, there will be a return trip, loaded with fresh troops for the war in America.[19]

No Bounds to Friendship

The *Boston Gazette* reports that a donation of five pounds and five shillings has been received from Miss Mary Braeley. It is for the poor of Boston. Miss Braeley lives in Kensington, England.[20]

Parliament

Secession in Commons

For the House of Commons, this has been a year of particularly long and bitter debate, many times into the morning hours. But it has not the least changed the course of Administration; if it has proved anything at all it is the futility of the Opposition.

Virtually all this debate, of course, has been on the Government's policy toward America and the war. That policy has produced fifteen major debates since February 15th, and fifteen votes on the side of Administration. The closest division was the beginning of March, when the Administration won by the mere difference of 93 to 44 (on a motion for providing weekly accounts of the Navy); the worst was two weeks ago when the Opposition lost its bid to amend an address to the King (242 to 87). But that was still not as bad as November 27th of last year, when the majority won 163 to 10, putting down a motion by London's Alderman Oliver to have the King explain who advised him on such measures as the one revoking the Charter of Massachusetts or the one requiring colonists to be transported to England for trial.

Despite the disheartening odds inherent in their far smaller numbers, the members of the Opposition have nevertheless showed pluck. The same was fully expected this week when the House took up preliminary appropriations for the military in 1777. Reported London's *Whitehall Evening Post*: "Great debates were expected, and a late sitting upon one or all of these motions, and the chief members in opposition being present confirmed the surmise; but instead of this, not one word of objection was stated, except by Sir Joseph Mawbey, on the large sums for the Ordnance . . . "

That large sums of money and the war in America were involved is the reason the voices of Fox and Burke and Barré and Wilkes and Johnstone and the others were expected to be heard. In committee of the whole for supply, the House had voted to employ 20,734 men (including 3,213 invalids) as land forces for 1777; to grant 648,900 *l* for maintaining them; to grant 949,720 *l* for maintaining the forces in America, Minorca, Gibraltar and elsewhere, and 93,497 *l* for maintaining the Brunswick troops in British pay. And these were understood to be only the beginning of military costs for next year. Then in regular session there were motions on expenses of the Ordnance service: 320,111 *l* 18 *s* 11 *d* for next year, and 272,705 *l* 18 *s* 1 *d* in additional expenses this year. But there was no debate; instead it became clear that the Opposition now is taking a new approach. When Lord Barrington rose to offer for Administration these latest requests for military expenditures, Edmund Burke and Sir George Savile and a number of other opponents of the war rose also— but not to speak. Instead they left their places, bowed to the chair, and departed. In so doing they confirmed what some observers have been suspecting for weeks: secession from the House as a means of dramatizing a refusal to sanction Administration policy toward America. When the new session began October 31st, some members were heard threatening such a move; and since that time—particularly after the defeat of the revisal-of-laws motion November 6th—many of them have been absenting themselves from the House except for private bills. When Opposition member Temple Luttrell last week arose to contest approval of 45,000 seamen, including 10,129 Marines, for 1777—and despite the fact no few may have agreed with his contention that "the absolute management of the Navy [is] too arduous, too solid, too important a trust to be committed to a *bon vivant* of Lord Sandwich's levity of disposition and known depravity of conduct"—he carried the Opposition banner alone. This week, no one carried it.

If this is to be an extended secession by the Opposition, it will be by no means the first. Much the same was attempted, without discernible success, against Sir Robert Walpole in 1739, and that one had ample precedent. Walking out for just the day, meanwhile, is a technique of protest almost as old as Parliament itself.

Many doubt that a secession at this time, even for an extended time, will be productive. Administration has a clear majority and can carry on the affairs of state without the least difficulty; there will be no effective disruption of government. And there is a question as to how many members of the Opposition will participate. So far the answer is obviously not all. Most of those now taking part are followers of the former First Minister, the Marquis of Rockingham, but even of this faction—as of Opposition as a whole—there is no clear leader. What then can be gained? One who has left his seat in Commons said it had simply become degrading to be a continual instrument of opposition "to the deaf insolence" of the Government. And, he suggested, passing bills without debate or inquiry may be "in some degree to leave them open for future discussion"—perhaps when some future change in membership makes for a more even match.

The partial secession lasted until mid-February, 1777, and was without effect. In part it was doomed to failure because the Opposition at this time was so badly disorganized. The final quotations are from the Annual Register *(1777) and, although not attributed, are almost certainly Burke's.*[21]

Foreign News

Celebrating

The whole town of Manchester, England, was illuminated at night. At Wakefield, said a correspondent, "every real well-wisher to the present establishment joined in wishing success to Old England." Atop Pendle Hill, on the Lancs-Yorkshire border north of Manchester, John Clayton, Esq. ordered a bonfire built, then gave out several barrels of ale to the people gathered around. In nearly every town around, noted a correspondent in Leeds, there has been great rejoicing. The reason: news that his Majesty's troops have taken New York.[22]

"Road to Popularity"

The causes that precipitated American independence are many—there were twenty-seven separate ones cited in the Declaration of Independence—but the one heard most often is taxation: "imposing taxes on us without our consent," as the authors of the Declaration summed it up.

To the British writer of *An Answer to the Declaration of the American Congress,* the issue of taxation is, in reality, a contrivance of the leaders of America for playing upon the people, a cleverly used vehicle for consolidating their own power.

The London Chronicle this week published excerpts of the recently published book, and this is what its anonymous author had to say on the issue of "taxes without consent":

"This was originally the apparent object of contest. Nor could anything have been found more proper to work upon the people. Such is the selfishness inherent in human nature that men in general are but too apt to seize any pretence for evading the obligation of paying the servants of the public. To hold forth such a pretence must be a sure road to popularity, and to all that power which popularity can give. Like the Agrarian law among the Romans, it is a standard to which the multitude would naturally flock."[23]

THE WEEK OF NOVEMBER 18TH

The War

The Fall of Fort Lee

The fate that last Saturday befell Fort Washington across the river has now signaled the end of the American possession of Fort Lee, formerly Fort Constitution, on the New Jersey side of the Hudson River. This time, there was no battle.

Following the British victory at Fort Washington, General Howe had sent Lord Cornwallis, and a force estimated at about 6,000, up the Hudson River four or five miles, with orders to cross over, double back and take Fort Lee. Their approach was discovered by an American officer on patrol. He rushed back, apprised General Nathanael Greene of imminent assault by the far larger force. Greene—who four days earlier may have been able to observe the rout across the river—wasted no time in ordering Fort Lee evacuated. But he had to leave behind all of the garrison's tents and other field equipment. Greene and his men retreated westward into Jersey.[24]

Congress

Fifty Thousand for Forty

Prizes of up to 50,000 dollars await Americans entering the first lottery of the United States, established by Congress this week. In all, 104,897 prizes are offered. However, in the fashion of past British lotteries, all but minimum prizes will be held for five years. The proceeds of the lottery, in the meantime, will finance the war and then accrue, with four percent interest, to the winner.

The lottery will consist of four classes according to the cost of the tickets. For a ten dollar ticket, an entrant has a chance of winning a grand prize of 10,000 dollars, two prizes of 5,000 dollars, thirty of 1,000 each, four hundred of 500 dollars, and 20,000 chances to win 20 dollars. The drawing for this class is to begin in Philadelphia, March 1st of next year, unless earlier subscribed in full.

In the second class, for which a drawing date has not been set, a 20 dollar ticket will provide a chance of winning anywhere from 30 to 20,000 dollars. The third class (for 30 dollars) offers up to 30,000, and the fourth class (40 dollars) up to 50,000 dollars.

The lottery will be operated by seven managers—still to be appointed —who will receive one-tenth percent of all receipts for their efforts. They must, however, first post 20,000 dollars in bond for the faithful discharge of their duties.

The British State Lottery for 1776 pays out prizes of up to 20,000 *l* on tickets selling for up to 11 *l* 17 *s* 6 *d*.

In other action this week, Congress:

—Named a committee (William Paca of Maryland, John Witherspoon of New Jersey and George Ross of Pennsylvania) to meet with General Washington on recruitment and to look into reports of grievances among Continental troops;

—Asked the states of New Hampshire, Massachusetts, Pennsylvania, Maryland and Virginia to provide a total of nine new ships for the Continental navy.[25]

Settling Accounts

The unproductive peace talks with Lord Howe and General Howe on Staten Island last September cost the government of the United States 71 and 30/90th dollars. That was the amount approved by Congress this week for payment of the expenses of its representatives, Dr. Benjamin Franklin, John Adams and Edward Rutledge.[26]

The States

Election By Electors

Perhaps the most innovative way yet devised in America for electing a legislative body is that about to come into use in Maryland, the latest in a growing number of states to adopt their own constitutions.

Maryland voters will follow the tradition now widely established only in electing their House of Delegates. In each county they will choose four delegates (in the cities of Annapolis and Baltimore, two each) as their representatives for one year. Such elections will be held on the first Monday of October.

But Maryland voters will break with tradition in electing their Senate. On the first Monday of September, every five years, they will choose electors (two in each county, one each in Annapolis and Baltimore) who will then meet in the state capital three weeks later and—either from their own number or from the state at large—elect a Senate of fifteen members, of whom nine must come from the western shore.

In other respects, Maryland's new constitution follows the same general structure of those adopted in other states this year. Likewise does its Declaration of Rights, passed at convention November 14th, except for a notable innovation: it forbids business monopolies as "odious, contrary to the spirit of a free government, and the principles of commerce."[27]

Parliament

Reluctant Benevolence

Sir Charles Whitworth, chairman of ways and means, sat kicking his heels against the empty benches as the sergeant with the mace scurried about Westminster Palace, rounding up reluctant Members of Parliament. It was only after considerable delay that the House of Commons got under way Monday. The first order of business: a vote on the land tax bill.

Once they were there, Commons' loyal majority passed it, as everyone knew they would. Then in the House of Lords Wednesday, his Majesty wasted no time in making it law, giving the time-honored royal assent: *Le roy remercie ses loyaux sujets, accepte leur benevolence, et aussi le veut.* (The King thanks his loyal subjects, accepts their benevolence, and therefore grants his consent.)

Thus is assured for Britons at least another year of a land tax of 4 *s* on the pound to help pay the cost of the war in America.[28]

Further Study

When Member of Parliament David Hartley demonstrated a fire prevention device of his design for the Lord Mayor and other city officials of London on September 2nd, there was sufficient interest shown to warrant another demonstration, on September 27th, for their Majesties, and again thereafter for members of Parliament.

In part as a result of those demonstrations, there was a bill introduced in Parliament establishing terms for the exclusive manufacture of the thin iron plates used in the prevention scheme. This week, the bill reached second reading in Commons and was duly sent to committee for further study.[29]

Foreign News

Unconfirmed

"Reports were very current yesterday," said a correspondent in London's *St. James's Chronicle,* "that advices were received of a treaty being in great forwardness between General Howe and the Congress's deputies." Apparently referring to the conference between Lord Howe and General Howe with three members of the Continental Congress in September on Staten Island, the correspondent said he understands that the basis for a compromise lies in dropping the word "Independent" from "Free and Independent States." "But," he hastened to add, "this wants confirmation." Many think the report is sheer rumor.[30]

Apparently only a rumor.

Admiral's Aviary

Lord Howe's ship, when he left for the war in America, was called the *Eagle,* but there is a report that he will return in another, now under construction. "She is already on the stocks," said the *London Packet,* "and [will be ready for his Lordship to receive] in person the thanks of both houses of Parliament for his Christian moderation in preferring the olive to the laurel." His new ship is ostensibly called the *Pigeon.*[31]

Apparently only sarcasm.

Non-Impressing Record

Britain's long-standing policy of recruiting the ranks of its army and navy through impressment—through simply taking and putting into uniform any man who did not or could not resist—has been followed to a far lesser degree in London than elsewhere in the kingdom. The reason: impressment has been vehemently opposed by the London city administration, and chiefly its last lord mayor, John Sawbridge.

Taking note of Sawbridge's recent retirement from the mayoralty, a

Court of Aldermen meeting this week in Guildhall voted him its unanimous thanks for his diligence and faithfulness to his duties. The aldermen took particular note of "the constant protection he gave to all [London's] inhabitants by refusing the sanction of his authority" to impressment.[32]

> *The tradition of impressment was not a one-way street. London's* Whitehall Evening Post, *on December 14, 1776, made a point of advising potential victims of their rights: "There is no positive law for pressing; but when the exigency of the state does absolutely require such an exertion of power, no persons are to be pressed but sailors and such as have for two years past worked upon the water. All other persons attacked by press gangs may defend themselves; and if in such defence they should happen to kill or maim any of the attackers, the laws will bear them harmless, for they do clearly justify them in making such defence."*

Young Patriots

On Sunday morning, the wife of a bricklayer in Petticoat Lane, London, was delivered of three children who were baptized Hancock, Adams and Washington.[33]

Theater

How High the Weeds?

It has been sixteen years since William Congreve's *The Old Bachelor* has had a major performance in London. The reason: it abounds too much with obscenity to be as popular with modern audiences as it was when Congreve completed it in 1693.

Now it has been revived at London's Drury Lane Theatre. And although this production has been abridged to make it more palatable, it is still too much of the old Congreve to please the critic of London's *St. James's Chronicle.* Complained he:

"We think *The Old Bachelor* a play unfit for representation before an audience who would wish to see anything like decency and honour in the commerce of the sexes. Perhaps the present managers may look further into nature and the interests of society than we do, and may have reasons we know not of for discrediting antiquated principles of confidence in the fair sex. But till those reasons are shewn, we shall think *The Old Bachelor* is an immoral and mischievous play, not from the license of particular passages, but from the general effect of the whole on the minds of the audience.

"It may serve very well for those enervated and sickly beings to whom it was addressed, but will be despised by those who wish to see our publick entertainments not as means of preparing the audience for debauchery, but as means to retard and prevent that licentiousness to which we are so inclined."

Not everyone agrees. Said the *London Packet*: "The manager of Drury Lane Theatre has undertaken, with a cautious hand, to weed this luxuriant garden and eradicate the rank-smelling plants; an office which he has very successfully executed. The play as it stands is yet sufficiently rich; the most modest may hear it without a blush, and yet even those who like relishing dishes will find it savoury enough for their palate."[34]

THE WEEK OF NOVEMBER 25TH

The War

"Our Enemies are Advancing"

"It is our duty to inform you," announced David Rittenhouse, vice president of the Council of Safety in a public notice to the citizens of Philadelphia, "that our enemies are advancing upon us and the most vigorous measures alone can save the city from falling into their hands . . . Let us defend ourselves like men determined to be free." He asked all citizens to meet next day at 10 o'clock at the State House to determine what measures to pursue. So important is it, said Rittenhouse, that "the bells will be ordered to ring, and the most public notice possible will be given of this meeting."[35]

New Offer of Clemency

In their third formal proclamation of the year, Lord Howe and General Howe have renewed their offer of clemency to Americans who will lay down their arms and swear obedience to his Majesty. The edict, issued in New York November 30th, promises "full and free pardon" to each American who appears before a royal governor, lieutenant governor, commander in chief, or military or naval commander, and swears he "will remain in a peaceable obedience to his Majesty, and will not take up arms, nor encourage others to take up arms in opposition to his authority." The offer provides for pardon of all "treasons" heretofore committed.[36]

Congress

Defense

The defense of Philadelphia against British attack and the support of the Continental Army continued paramount to Congress this week as it:
—Asked the Pennsylvania Council of Safety to have the Associators, or

militia, of Philadelphia and the surrounding counties placed under the jurisdiction of the United States during the present emergency;

—Asked the Pennsylvania Assembly to enact measures to combat trade monopolies that have slowed the supply of shoes, stockings and other necessities to the army;

—Requested delegates of the New England states to take the most effectual measures necessary for having at least 10,000 pairs of shoes and the same of stockings purchased in those states for General Washington's army;

—Asked the Pennsylvania Council of Safety to appeal to local housekeepers for as many blankets and woolen stockings as they can spare for the army, the appraised cost to be reimbursed to the housekeepers.

Congress this week also recommended to all state legislatures that they pass laws against counterfeiting and forging tickets for the new lottery.[37]

The States

"Every Able-Bodied Male"

The Continental Congress's request to Massachusetts to supply reinforcements for the Continental Army has been answered with an act of the General Court providing that every able-bodied male sixteen and up must serve as called. Accordingly: "No rank or station in life, place, employment or office (except as hereafter excepted) shall excuse or exempt any person from serving in arms for the defence of his country, either in himself or some able-bodied effective man in his stead; or in case of his neglect or refusal, from paying the fine hereinafter required." As exceptions, the act lists: Quakers, ministers of the Gospel, and the president, professors, tutors, librarian and undergraduates at Harvard College before April 19, 1775 (Lexington and Concord) as well as Indians, Negroes and mulattoes. As penalties for noncompliance: 12*l* and reduction to the ranks of the militia for officers and 12*l* or jail for soldiers.[38]

There were similar laws in other states.

Betting on the Irish

In Newport, Rhode Island, the most popular bet these days is on Ireland—that it follows America's lead and declares its own independence within eighteen months.[39]

Foreign News

He- and She-Politicians

At the Court of France, where he is now and then seen negotiating for aid to America, Commissioner Silas Deane is having little trouble distinguishing friend from adversary.

Chief among the latter is the British ambassador, Lord Stormont, who rattles his wits trying to convince France that it should not negotiate with America. In proper diplomatic fashion, Stormont saves his wily maneuvering for behind the scenes, maintaining at court the etiquette required of the occasion, even to the point of appearing an old and cordial friend of the American commissioner. But once, when he learned the American had been meeting privately with members of the French cabinet at their homes, he got so angry he upbraided Deane right in front of the King. His Majesty stopped the outburst and returned the court to its proper decorum.

Among his allies, Deane has found none other than the young Queen herself. Marie Antoinette, twenty-one, is reported to have intervened on his behalf so effectively that, without her help, he might return home to America with a different result. "It is astonishing," said one observer at the court, "the interest this she-politician bears in matters of state. She can cajole and threaten into compliance the most popular ministers about the palace."[40]

Discontent

Back in London after a trip through western England—through Cornwall, Somersetshire, Worcestershire and Cheshire—a businessman recently confessed to seeing little but dissatisfaction over the war in America. "No language can describe the discontent," said he. Only in Birmingham did people seemed pleased. An important industrial city, Birmingham has been prospering through the increased manufacture of muskets.[41]

Ominous But Not Ruinous

An earthquake on both sides of the English Channel shortly after eight o'clock Wednesday night did no real damage despite the ominous rumbling which accompanied it. In Calais, France, loaves of bread in a baker's shop plummeted to the floor; in Folkstone, England, some china on a chest of drawers moved several inches, but did not fall; in Dover, the church bell sounded all by itself.[42]

Still Remembered

As the cold of another Austrian winter approaches, there are those in Vienna who still recall this story about the late emperor, Francis I, husband of Maria Theresa: His Imperial Majesty declared that the poor people of the country could collect dead wood for their use in the Imperial Forests, but he was disturbed to find his own huntsmen stopping them. The huntsmen complained that the poor people were coming in such numbers as to block the roads and interfere with the hunting. "Ah, well," said his Majesty, reaffirming his decree, "let us consider that in traveling slower we may the longer enjoy the pleasing reflection that thousands of poor people are warming themselves comfortably with their families."[43]

Science

Conquering Scurvy

Besides enduring and surviving the hazards of uncharted seas, Captain James Cook and his crew on a voyage around the world also overcame that nemesis of seafarers past, scurvy. They did it, Captain Cook reported, in several ways: by taking along a large quantity of malt with which to make sweet-wort ("one of the best anti-scorbutic sea-medicines yet found out") ; by providing each man a weekly ration of two pounds of sour-krout ("easily stored") : by drinking plenty of soup and broth (made of fresh vegetables whenever available along the way) ; and by enjoying fresh oranges and lemons (wherever found).

This week in London, in recognition of his paper on prevention and treatment of scurvy, the Royal Society made Captain Cook guest of honor at its anniversary meeting, then presented him with its Sir Godfrey Copley Medal.

Another well-known recipient of the Copley Medal, in 1753, was America's Dr. Benjamin Franklin, so honored for his experiments with electricity. Still another: Joseph Priestley.[44]

DECEMBER

CHRISTMAS comes on this month; then let us all
Rejoice at this redeeming festival:
In acts of charity assist distress,
The *poor* will thank you, and GOD will you bless.

The Virginia Almanack
December, 1776

THE WEEK OF DECEMBER 2ND

The War

Newport: "Practical"

"Impracticable," reported Commodore Sir Peter Parker to the British Admiralty in explaining why he was not able to mount a successful invasion of Charleston, South Carolina, at the end of June. Quite a different sort of report will he file on his next major mission. It was late this week; the objective was Newport, Rhode Island; it was a complete success. New England's second largest town is now in British hands.

In part, the difference was Parker's fleet—an estimated seventy sail of ships at Newport while there were not fifty at Charleston. In larger part, it was the fact that he faced no such gallant defense as was mounted by Colonel Moultrie and his garrison on Sullivan's Island; the inhabitants of Newport, having previously decided their town was indefensible against so large a fleet, chose the wiser part of valor and retreated fifteen miles up Narragansett Bay to Bristol.

Parker's fleet arrived off Newport, from New York, on Saturday. The next day troops under Generals Henry Clinton and Hugh Percy landed and easily took possession of the town and some artillery left behind. The total military force on land and still aboard transports in the harbor is estimated at between 5,000 and 6,000, a number of them Hessians.[1]

Clinton's troops remained for three years—to no particular effect. The occupation of Newport only served to diminish British fighting strength where it would have counted.

Next: Philadelphia

Philadelphia is clearly the next objective of the British army and the danger of attack is becoming "extreme." So said the Council of Safety as it issued a warning to Philadelphia citizens: "It is the opinion of this board that all the shops in this city be shut up, that the schools be broke up, and the inhabitants engaged solely in providing for the defence of this city at this time of extreme danger." The message was signed by David Rittenhouse, vice president of the council.

Many have already left the city, particularly women, children and elderly people seeking a safer place in the countryside.[2]

"I Robbed the Poor Creature"

How the British troops were fed at White Plains was told recently by a survivor of the battle in a letter home.

The army, said he, was badly fed. Biscuits, even from a freshly opened barrel, were so infested with worms that they fell apart in the hand. But from time to time, hunger overruling more civil instincts, a meal could be found, as he recounted: "This morning I had an excellent repast. I met a mare with her foal, and I robbed the poor creature of its breakfast, for I drank the milk of the mare. We intended to have dined upon the foal next day, but were prevented."

Compared to the food, he and his comrades were "worse cloathed," said the soldier.[3]

Congress

Urgent Session

After recessing last Saturday for a normal resumption of business two days later, Congress was summoned into an extraordinary session Sunday. The reason was reported to be a communication from General Washington. No more is known.[4]

Ever More Important Chain

Military matters—over and above a still-unexplained and urgent Sunday session—continued to dominate its attention this week, but Congress also made time to meet with representatives of the Six Iroquois Nations, the Delawares and the Shawnees, whose friendship, with the advance of the British army, is more imperative than ever. Congress told them it wishes that the chain of friendship "may contract no rust"; that it will "do everything to keep it bright and strong."

The Indian leaders also heard these other assurances, couched as usual in language Congress seems to feel will best make the point:

"We take you by the hand, and bid you welcome to our great council fire."

"Our hearts are good towards all the Indians in the woods, who have a friendly disposition towards us."

"We now inform you that we wish to sit down with you under the same tree of peace; to water its roots and cherish its growth, so that it may shelter us and you, and our and your children."

Earlier in the week, before receiving the Indian representatives, Congress approved an expenditure of 13,464 and seven-and-a-half-ninetieths dollars to cover the expenses of a recent meeting in Pittsburgh for discussion of a treaty with the Indian nations. Included in the total was reimbursement for the time and transportation costs of the commissioners who were present.

As for the war—among the many such matters it acted upon—Congress:

—Asked the Pennsylvania Council of Safety to arrange to have all river craft brought over from the New Jersey side of the Delaware River to prevent their falling into the hands of the British;

—Advanced to the same Council of Safety 100,000 dollars to be used as bounty money for enlisting purposes;

—Directed President Hancock to write to the four New England governments and request their utmost influence in raising their respective quotas of troops, and to hasten their march;

—Relaxed enlistment requirements to permit the supplying of a shirt, a pair of shoes and a pair of stockings to noncommissioned officers and soldiers of the Maryland militia if they will engage to march to the immediate reinforcement of General Washington and remain at least one month (although they will still have to pay for the same) ;

—And ordered the confinement in the State Prison at Philadelphia, pending transfer to the more remote site of Frederick, Maryland, of a number of New Jersey inhabitants charged with the crime of enlisting troops for General Howe.

Congress postponed until next April 10th the first drawing in the new lottery, but specified no reason.[5]

The States

Patriotism Remembered

As a champion of the patriot cause, Boston schoolmaster James Lovell established himself early, delivering (in 1771) on the first anniversary of the Massacre at Boston a stirring oration that endeared him to those opposing British colonial measures. Accordingly, he also established himself as a target for eventual reprisal by British authorities. That reprisal came in April of last year when authorities closed down his South Grammar School; then, after the Battle of Bunker's Hill, the British went further, arresting Lovell as a spy and transporting him to Halifax for imprisonment.

Last Saturday, released in an exchange of prisoners, Lovell returned to Boston to find that neither his early militance nor his year and a half of imprisonment have been forgotten. He was named this week as one of Massachusetts's two new delegates to the Continental Congress. Lovell is thirty-nine and a graduate of Harvard College.

Also appointed: Francis Dana, thirty-three, of Cambridge, an attorney and member of the state Council. Although early a member of the Sons of Liberty, Dana at first preached reconciliation with Great Britain but changed his mind after a visit of more than a year in England, coming home convinced from what he saw and heard that independence must be the only course.

Lovell and Dana will join the present delegation in Philadelphia, serving as additional members from Massachusetts.[6]

Any or All

In Massachusetts, the counterfeiting, forging or altering of bills of credit will now carry a range of penalties sufficient to punish an offense of almost any magnitude. An act of the Council and House of Representatives provides for anyone found guilty to be: set upon a gallows with a rope around his neck for an hour of meditation upon the crime; fined up to 30 l; imprisoned up to six months; publicly whipped to a maximum of thirty-nine stripes; made ineligible to hold public office; ordered to pay treble damages to everyone defrauded; sold in service if unable to pay damages. The court, at its discretion, may mete out any or all of these punishments. Meanwhile, in New Jersey on September 20th, counterfeiting was made punishable by a much more simple penalty: death.[7]

Prices in Connecticut

Although Congress has removed nearly all price restrictions, hoping that a resulting increase in supply holds down prices, not all agree. Faced with a continuing increase in the costs of many goods, the General Assembly of Connecticut, meeting in Norwich, has established maximum prices on a wide range of goods sold in that state. Thus, among others, will these goods be held at these prices: wheat, 6s per bushel; rye, 3s6d per bushel; Indian corn, 3s per bushel; tea, 4s6d per pound; butter, 10d per pound; cheese, 6d per pound; grass-fed beef, 24s per hundred; best Muscovado sugar, 60s per hundred; West Indian rum, 6s per gallon; New England rum, 3s6d per gallon; and wool, 2s per pound. Connecticut has also acted to restrict some wages, setting a maximum of 3s per day for summer labor.[8]

EUROPE (Thomas & Andrews, Boston, c. 1780). Germany and Italy appear here, as on all maps of the period, even though in the strict sense they did not yet exist; they were still checkerboards of principalities—in Germany, most of them still nominally a part of the waning Holy Roman Empire—and did not become nations until the next century. Mapmakers used the terms Germany and Italy to denote regions with a common language—and that explains the absence of Austria, which, for cartographic purposes, was considered a part of German-speaking Europe. It might be noted that one can also turn to the maps of the Romans and find the same areas labeled "Germania" and "Italia."

Map Division—New York Public Library—
Astor, Lenox and Tilden Foundations

Franklin in France

Dr. Benjamin Franklin, designated by Congress in September as a commissioner to the Court of Paris, is now in France. He landed this week in Quiberon.

His first word to the French was on America's military position: "excellent." Not that the Continental Army hasn't had some setbacks, of course. They have had to give up some territory—New York, for example —but it has been only that which they did not think worth keeping, Franklin is reported to have said. He predicted that the United States will have 80,000 men under arms when the next campaign begins in the spring, and that this will turn the tide.

Such talk sounded like what one would expect from the *diplomate extraordinaire* that he is. And yet he seemed to be concealing his diplomatic mission. His reason for being in France, Franklin reportedly explained, is "to print some new works."[9]

John the Painter

After Edinburgh-born James Aitken, twenty-four, gave up his first profession, house painting, he kept the name but turned to another that proved more lucrative. As "John the Painter," specializing in highway robbery, shoplifting and setting fires, he has become one of Britain's best known felons.

Some say he is no more than a common criminal: others, that his goal —except for petty thefts to sustain him—is political upheaval. In support of the latter it is observed that he went to America a few years ago and is known to have helped to instigate riots in Boston and later take part in sinking some tea in the harbor.

Since his return to England last year, he has been credited with one daring robbery after another, all without being caught. But a broader goal of political sabotage—whether to help the American cause or to demonstrate his own anti-monarchial views—is beginning to look like the more important. This week John the Painter took on his most ambitious project: burning Portsmouth Naval Base. It turned out to be more than even he could handle, but he did manage to put a rope house in flames before deciding he had better get away while he could. The fire, quickly subdued, did little damage.

> *Aitken was finally taken prisoner after trying to set fire to the city of Bristol the following January, and was hanged at Portsmouth on March 10, 1777.*[10]

Expecting Again?

Her Majesty Queen Charlotte, who gave birth to her eleventh child last April 25th, is reported by London's *St. James's Chronicle* to be three months pregnant. The *Chronicle*'s report is brief and gives no source of its information. The report in its entirety: "Her Majesty, it is said, is three months advanced in her pregnancy."

The Chronicle *was premature. Princess Sophia, the twelfth child of King George III and Queen Charlotte, was not born until November 3, 1777.* 11

Books

Voltaire in English

". . . crafty and mischievous"

When a new translation of Shakespeare appeared in France earlier this year, no less an authority than Voltaire pronounced his opinion of it: *"misérable."* But it was not just that France's greatest (and thus the French would say, the world's greatest) man of letters disliked the translation; Voltaire thinks Shakespeare is generally tasteless and barbaric to begin with.

"Outrageous," was the reaction of many an Englishman to the news of Voltaire's humiliating comments to the French Academy. Said one: "The outrageous insult which Mr. de Voltaire hath committed against the memory of our immortal Shakespeare requires ample retaliation. It is but just, also, that he should be paid in his own coin."

That coin is the currency of caustic rebuke, and an anonymous author, drafting his insults in both French and English, managed to get them published in this week's *London Packet*. Said he (English version):

"Mr. Voltaire is one of those crafty and mischievous characters that should be held in detestation by all mankind. His lank and meagre visage, his dry temper, his caustic bile, and his horridly sparkling eyes, all betray in him the malice of a monkey, the cunning of a fox, and the traitorous disposition of a cat."12

Press

Only One Left

A continually growing fear that Philadelphia will suffer the same fate as New York is nowhere more clearly manifested than in the fact that four of its five newspapers have suspended publication. The *Packet*, which should have come out on Tuesday, the *Gazette* and the *Journal*, which should have appeared Wednesday, and the *Ledger*, ordinarily published on Saturday, all have not been seen this week. Only the thrice-a-week

Pennsylvania Evening Post is still going. Three of New York's four news-papers suspended publication the last week of August, and have not been published since.[13]

EDUCATION

GREEK AND SECRET

"A happy spirit and resolution of attaining the important ends of society entering [their] minds"—as they put it—five students of the College of William and Mary on December 5th joined together in what they first called a societas *philosophiae and then more simply a fraternity. Such a form of organization was not new in college life. Yale for two decades had had its Linonia Society and its Brothers in Unity; the College of New Jersey, its American Whig and Cliosophic Societies. What distinguished the fraternity established by the William and Mary students, meeting that day in secret in the Apollo Room of Williamsburg's Raleigh Tavern: it had Greek letters for a name and has lasted to this day—Phi Beta Kappa. (This brief account is here entered as a footnote, in italic, in deference to the secrecy of the occasion.)*[14]

Customs

Winters Past and Future

It is that time of year when the season becomes its own diversion; when the tingle of the cold somehow also warms the heart; when to be snowbound is to be set free, winter's own delights to enjoy the more.

What in all the year is there to compare with a sleighride through the fresh fallen snow on a moonlit night? Nothing . . . said a visitor from a foreign land a few winters ago, as he recorded these memories:

"Young ladies and gentlemen are so fond of this as a diversion that whenever the snow gives over falling, tho' it be after sunset, they will not wait till next day, but have the sleigh yoked directly and drive without the least fear of catching cold from the night air. Large parties of pleasure are often formed amongst them, when perhaps ten or twelve sleighs will drive in company (with four in each sleigh) to dine and drink tea, and return in the evening.

"About New York this sleighing is much used, and large parties of pleasure are often formed to drive to the country. Within a few miles of the city there is a little bridge, at the passing of which the young gentle-man always claims a kiss from the lady that sits along with him; this is a part of the etiquette that is never omitted. Should any of the party be a stranger to the custom, the ladies themselves will take care some way or other to have him informed."

The snow, the sleighs, and the young ladies will all be there again this winter as in the past. But a certain custom at a certain little bridge will have to await a future winter—when the young gentlemen return from war.[15]

THE WEEK OF DECEMBER 9TH

The War

"Gloomy Aspect of our Affairs"

> "Strong apprehensions are entertained
> that the British will soon have it in their
> power to vanquish the whole of the remains
> of the Continental army."

An American Officer

Retreat: It began for the Continental army with a miraculous escape from Long Island on August 29th. Then after a few weeks' respite in New York, it continued to Harlem Heights in September; then north through Westchester County to White Plains, then northward again after a general engagement there October 28th; as far north as Peekskill it went: and then Fort Washington fell, and Fort Lee; and the retreat, southward into New Jersey, went inexorably on; to Hackensack, and Newark, and across the midlands of New Jersey, to New Brunswick; now not so much retreating as staggering, limping, plodding; to Princeton, to Trenton, the Delaware River. And now the Continental army is in Pennsylvania.

The last mile is told in this report: "Boats from every quarter were collected, and our stores, together with troops remaining at Trenton, were immediately conveyed over the Delaware. On Sunday morning, having everything over, we crossed the Delaware and took our quarters about half a mile from the river. About 11 o'clock the enemy came marching down with the pomp of war, in great expectation of getting boats and immediately pursuing. But of this we took proper care, by destroying every boat, shallop, &c. we could lay our hands on. They made forced marches up and down the river, in pursuit of boats, but in vain.

"This is Thursday; the enemy are much scattered, some in Trenton, directly opposite, from that on their left to Bordentown and Burlington on the river banks. The enemy are at least 12,000 strong, determined for Philadelphia, for which purpose they are transporting flat-bottom boats from Brunswick to Trenton by land."

For the Continental army—ragged, ripped, reduced in strength to perhaps not many more than 3,500 men capable of doing any real fighting—it has been an agonizing march across the breadth of New Jersey. A soldier who has only a wretched pair of shoes and a ragged coat and a tattered blanket to dull the cold of a tentless winter night is not always a frequent sight; he is one of the lucky few. Many have not that much.

Beyond unrelenting physical hardship, there is gnawing fear. An enemy, far more powerful, is only a river's breadth away. It is indeed a dark hour, as one officer says: "Such is now the gloomy aspect of our affairs that the whole country has taken the alarm; strong apprehensions are entertained that the British will soon have it in their power to vanquish the whole of the remains of the Continental Army. The term of service of a considerable part of our troops has nearly expired, and new recruits do not arrive in sufficient numbers to supply their places."

But affairs are not yet hopeless. There is one military resource this ragged army has that the British do not. Said the same officer: "His Excellency General Washington is continually making every possible effort to produce a change of circumstances more auspicious to our country. The critical and distressing situation in which he is placed is sufficient to overwhelm the powers of any man of less wisdom and magnanimity than our commander-in-chief. He has the confidence and the affection of the officers and soldiers of the whole army; and there is not perhaps another man to be found so well calculated to discharge the duties of his important and responsible station."[16]

"Desolation and Outrage"

Until recently, the war with Britain was fought in or near a few coastal cities, leaving most of the population of America unscarred by the wounds of battle. Now that the Continental Army has retreated inland, the British in pursuit, all that has changed for people across the breadth of New Jersey.

From once tranquil towns and sleepy farms have come report after report of marauding British and Hessian troops who have broken from their organized ranks to plunder and ravage the countryside. Near Hopewell, a number of young women are said to have taken refuge on a mountain, only to be pursued by British troops and taken captive. In Woodbridge, a father shot and killed a Hessian officer ravishing his daughter, soon lay dead himself as Hessian soldiers avenged their commander's death. In Maidenhead, so many houses were stripped that the newly settled community was considered "broke up." Whatever could be carried, was taken away; what couldn't be taken away was reported destroyed. So extensive have been accounts of plundering that it is thought by many there may not be a soldier left in the British army whose horse is not loaded down with booty. That may be exaggeration. Even so, it is said that a great many families have indeed been reduced from "comfort and affluence to poverty and ruin," as one observer so described the "desolation and outrage" in New Jersey.[17]

A Warning

The high command of the Continental army has become noticeably uneasy about reports that some of its own officers and men want to burn the City of Philadelphia to keep it from falling to the use of the British army as a winter headquarters. To put down any such notion, Major General Israel Putnam has issued a terse warning: "The General will consider every attempt to burn the city of Philadelphia as a crime of the blackest dye. and will, without ceremony, punish capitally any incendiary who shall have the hardiness and cruelty to attempt it."

Putnam also made it clear that every able-bodied civilian left in Philadelphia will be expected to bear arms in its defense. Except for those "conscientiously scrupulous," all such men are to assemble at ten o'clock Saturday morning, with their arms, in the State House Yard. Said Putnam, pointedly: The General is determined that "no person shall remain in this city an idle spectator of the present contest."[18]

The Rascally Unvirtuous General

As a general he may or may not be a genius; but he is bold, often brilliant, utterly ambitious, supremely confident of his every act. His education was the digestion of nearly every treatise on military arts, and in his capacious mind are stored away the essential strategies of nearly every famous battle in history.

As a man, he may or may not be the authentic boor; he is crude, disagreeable, ill-tempered, ugly. His dogs accompany him everywhere, sometimes even occupying the next chair at the dinner table. In his captious personality are stored away nearly every known means of being offensive.

By his own estimation, Major General Charles Lee is undoubtedly the finest military man in America, and he was duly prepared to accept the designation of commander-in-chief of the Continental army last year; by the estimation of Congress Charles Lee was not the man for that job, and Congress made him second in command to General Washington. Lee has never forgotten, never missed an opportunity for a personal moment of glory to prove Congress wrong. In fact, he has probably done as much as anyone to prove Congress was right.

What gave substantial credence to his claim to highest rank was his intimate knowledge—greater than that of any other American—of the British military system. For until the outbreak of the war Cheshire-born Lee was a part of that system, retaining his commission in the British army until January, 1775. In pressing his ambitions directly with some members of Congress, he may also have pointed to the thoroughly military orientation of his life. He never really considered being anything but a soldier and, as an acquaintance recalls, "the profession of arms was his delight from infancy." He was sixteen when he became an ensign in his father's regiment. Four years later he was a lieutenant, and soon found himself with General Edward Braddock's forces at Fort Duquesne. Before he returned to Britain, he led a colorful career that included: being initiated into a Mohawk tribe with the curiously appropriate name of "Boiling Water" (Ounewaterika); taking the daughter of a Seneca chief as a bride; getting wounded severely at Fort Ticonderoga; surviving an attempted assassination by an army surgeon with whom he had had an argument.

Back in England in 1761 he became a major, then a lieutenant colonel during the British campaign in Portugal. The return of peace in 1763 left him lacking what he knew best. He settled his frustration by securing a commission as major general in the Polish Army and eventually (1769) went off to fight the Turks. Along the way he lost several fingers in a duel and twice faced death's door through illness.

Never from this time on did he see much promise in England—sensing that his own opinion of his military prowess was not everywhere shared. So like many an emigrant before him, he set out to reap the promise of new opportunities in America. And for Charles Lee—to whom "profession of arms was delight" and in whom patriotic zeal had begun to burn while allegiance to England gave way to disenchantment—no opportunity could have held so much promise as to fight against Great Britain. Last year, on the very day of the Battle of Bunker's Hill, Congress commissioned him the second major general in the Continental army. He joined Washington at Cambridge, and remained there until this spring when he was assigned first to direct the defense of New York, then to command the Southern Department.

After the American victory of Sullivan's Island, at Charleston, he wrote in his dispatches that the credit properly belonged to Colonel William Moultrie, who was already in command of the defenses of Charleston when he arrived. But such public praise as would come his own way, Lee would not refuse—the most notable of all being the decision of Congress to advance him 30,000 dollars to pay for his new Virginia plantation and indemnify him for the confiscation of his property in England.

Lee learned of the action of Congress as he rode north to rejoin Washington in October. After the battle of White Plains, Lee was ordered to take his division to Philipsburg, New York, and await further orders. As Washington began his march across New Jersey, pursued by the British, Lee's orders came: rejoin the main army. What happened since then is not altogether clear; what is known is that Lee—for whatever reason, and some would say it was intent to shine alone—did not immediately rejoin Washington. Retaining his separate command, he delayed marching for several days, in apparent disregard of orders.

This week, finally on the move, Lee's army reached Somerset County, New Jersey, following Washington's line of march. Camping near Basking Ridge, Lee himself chose to make his headquarters three miles away from his division—and for the second-ranking American general, who liked being virtually unguarded, it was perilously close to the British army of Lord Cornwallis, no more than twenty miles away.

Friday—it was the 13th of December—to the general whose nearly life-long career had spanned almost very conceivable kind of military encounter, came the one he had so far eluded. It was announced by a musket shot, then by the sudden, numbing appearance of a British colonel pushing open the door of the remote headquarters, now surrounded by British dragoons. Just like that, was it over for Charles Lee. Denied even hat and cloak to guard against the cold December weather, he was tied to a horse and taken under heavy guard to British headquarters, where he awaits an uncertain future.

For the American cause he is unquestionably a loss; for the British, a prize catch. For Lee himself, imprudent at the very least in separating his headquarters from his army, it is the sort of blunder which will indelibly mark his military record. But to Charles Lee—sometime known as "Boiling Water," always impetuous, ill-tempered, irascible, confident to a fault—prudence never was to be desired. He liked to put it down as "rascally virtue."

Lee was eventually released in April, 1778, in return for British Major General Richard Prescott, an American prisoner, and resumed a career that only became more controversial. At the Battle of Monmouth he inexplicably ordered a retreat and wound up with a court-martial for disobedience, misbehavior and disrespect of the commander-in-chief. Found guilty and suspended from command, he lived out his days largely as a recluse until his death in Philadelphia in 1782 at the age of fifty-one.[19]

Congress

Address to America

The fall of New York, the retreat of the Continental army across New Jersey, and now the very real fear that the seat of government, Philadelphia, may likewise fall to the British has indeed engulfed America in a new and greater crisis; but a look back will show the justness of the cause has inspired many a past success, and promises eventual victory.

That, basically, is the message of Congress to the people of America at a perilous moment. It is a message intended to promote unanimity of purpose and to summon up "an immediate and spirited exertion" against the advancing British army.

The message, which Congress asks to be widely published, was ordered written on the 9th and delegated to a committee of Dr. John Witherspoon, Richard Henry Lee and Samuel Adams; then it was debated paragraph by paragraph in full Congress. The result is an often eloquent document.

The text of the address of Congress to the inhabitants of America:

"The Representatives of the United States of America in Congress assembled, to the People in general, and particularly to the Inhabitants of Pennsylvania and the adjacent States.

FRIENDS AND BRETHREN:

"We think it our duty to address a few words of exhortation to you in this important crisis. You are not unacquainted with the history of the rise and progress of this war. A plan was carried on by the British Ministry for several years in a systematick manner to enslave you to that kingdom. After various attempts in an artful and insidious manner to bring into practice the laying you under tribute, they at last openly and decisively asserted their rights of making laws to bind you in all cases whatsoever.

"Opposition was made to these encroachments by earnest and humble petitions from every Legislature on the Continent, and more than once by the Congress representing the whole. These were treated with the utmost contempt. Acts of the most unjust and oppressive nature were passed and carried into execution, such as exempting the soldiers charged with murder in America from a legal trial, and ordering them to be carried to Britain for certain absolution, as also directing prisoners taken at sea to be entered on board their ships, and obliged either to kill their own friends or fall themselves by their hands. We only mention these from among the many oppressive acts of Parliament, as proofs to what horrid injustice the love of dominion will sometimes carry societies as well as men. At the same time to show how insensible they will be to the sufferings of others, you may see, by the preambles to the acts and addresses to the King, that they constantly extol their own lenity in those very proceedings which fill this whole Continent with resentment and horrour.

"To crown the whole, they have waged war with us in the most cruel and unrelenting manner, employing not only the force of the British nation, but hiring foreign mercenaries, who, without feeling, indulge themselves in rapine and bloodshed. The spirit indeed of the Army in general is but too well determined, by their inhuman treatment of those who have unhappily fallen into their hands.

"It is well known to you, that at the universal desire of the people, and with the hearty approbation of every Province, the Congress declared the United States free and independent, a measure not only just, but which had become absolutely necessary. It would have been impossible to have resisted the formidable force destined against us last spring, while we confessed ourselves the subjects of that State against which we had taken arms. Besides, after repeated trials, no terms could be obtained, but pardon upon absolute submission, which every publick body in America had rejected with disdain.

"Resistance has now been made with a spirit and resolution becoming a free people, and with a degree of success hitherto which could scarce have been expected. The enemy have been expelled from the Northern Provinces where they at first had possession, and have been repulsed in their attempt upon the Southern by the undaunted valour of the inhabitants. Our success at sea, in the capture of the enemy's ships, has been astonishing. They have been compelled to retreat before the Northern Army. Notwithstanding the difficulty and uncertainty at first of our being supplied with ammunition and military stores, those we have now in abundance, and by some late arrivals and captures there is an immediate prospect of sufficient clothing for the Army.

"What we have particularly in view in this address is not only to promote unanimity and vigour through the whole States, but to excite the inhabitants of Pennsylvania, New Jersey, and the adjacent States, to an immediate and spirited exertion in opposition to the Army that now threatens to take possession of this city. You know that during the whole campaign they have been checked in their progress, and have not till within these two weeks ventured above ten miles from their shipping. Their present advances are owing not to any capital defeat, or a want of valour in the Army that opposed them, but to a sudden diminution of its numbers from the expiration of those short inlistments which, to ease the people, were at first adopted. Many have already joined the Army to supply the deficiency, and we call, in the most earnest manner, on all the friends of liberty to exert themselves without delay in this pressing emergency. In every other part your arms have been successful, and in other respects our sacred cause is in the most promising situation. We think it proper to inform and assure you that essential services have been already rendered us by foreign States, and we have received the most positive assurances of further aid. Let us not, then, be wanting to ourselves. Even a short resistance will probably be effectual, as General Lee is advancing with a strong reinforcement, and his troops in high spirits. What a pity is it, then, that the rich and populous city of Philadelphia should fall into the enemy's hands, or that we should not lay hold of the opportunity of destroying their principal Army, now removed from the ships of war, in which their greatest strength lies.

"It is certainly needless to multiply arguments in such a situation. All that is valuable to us as men and freemen is at stake. It does not admit of a question what would be the effect of our finally failing. Even the boasted Commissioners for giving peace to America have not offered, and do not now offer, any terms but pardon on absolute submission. And though (blessed be God) even the loss of Philadelphia would not be the loss of the cause, yet while it can be saved, let us not, in the close of the campaign, afford them such ground of triumph; but give a check to their progress, and convince our friends in the distant parts that one spirit animates the whole.

"Confiding in your fidelity and zeal in a contest the most illustrious and important, and firmly trusting in the good providence of God, we wish you happiness and success."

Given at Philadelphia, December 10, 1776.

By order of the Congress:

JOHN HANCOCK, *President.*[20]

The "Seat of War" Departed

Having completed its address to America, Congress took a further agonizing look at the military situation in and around Philadelphia, decided it is too dangerous a seat of government, and adjourned to Baltimore. At the same time it also delegated extraordinary interim powers to one man—General George Washington.

The necessity of abandoning Philadelphia is beyond question, as Congress observed in its resolution to adjourn: ". . . the movements of the enemy have now rendered the neighbourhood of this city the seat of war, which will prevent that quiet and uninterrupted attention to the publick business which should ever prevail in the great Continental Council." In the hopefully more secure town of Baltimore, in Maryland, Congress will resume its daily sessions on Friday, the 20th—or sooner if a sufficient number of members be present.

This will be the first time since the outbreak of war that Congress will not be in session. And inasmuch as it has all along taken a direct, daily responsibility for the conduct of the war, a totally new question is posed: who will be in charge while Congress is not in session? It answered that as well in its adjournment resolution: ". . . until the Congress shall otherwise order, General Washington [shall] be possessed of full power to order and direct all things relative to the [military] department and to the operations of war." Such a delegation of power Washington himself appears to feel is necessary under the circumstances.

The departure from Philadelphia by no means comes as a surprise; it is only what countless citizens of Philadelphia have already done. And Congress gave rise to conjecture of such a move earlier in the week when it determined Baltimore would be the new seat of government if a move became imperative. Beyond conjecture, there have been rumors—apparently stirred by Tory sympathizers—that Congress would not merely depart the city but would disperse entirely, simply giving up, its members returning to their own constituencies. Now Congress has put to flight such rumors.

Before adjourning to Baltimore, Congress:

—Left instructions to the Continental Army to defend Philadelphia "to the utmost extremity";

—Authorized the use of all privately owned, armed vessels in the harbor for defense of the city;

—Recommended that all the states declare, at the time most appropriate to each, a day of fasting and prayer "to implore of Almighty God the forgiveness of the many sins prevailing among all ranks, and to beg the countenance and assistance of his Providence in the prosecution of the present just and necessary war."[21]

Parliament

Reverence and Recess

In recognition of the nationwide general fast and day of prayer set forth by his Majesty, Parliament Friday met only for the briefest of formalities, then broke to observe the sacred nature of the day along with most of the rest of Britain.

Members of the House of Lords went to Westminster Abbey—the Lord Chancellor by coach, in deference to the London drizzle—for a sermon by the Rt. Rev. Dr. Hurd, Bishop of Litchfield and Coventry (*See* RELIGION, p. 360). Speaker Sir Fletcher Norton, Lord North, Lord Germaine and about fourscore members of Commons, meanwhile, assembled at St. Margaret's Church, Westminster, and heard the Rev. Dr. John Butler preach the day's significance in the light of the eighth chapter of the First Book of Kings.

The religious services completed, the lords and gentlemen of Parliament returned to Westminster Palace, but only to carry out those details requisite to begin the Christmas recess, and then adjourned until January 21st, 1777—the House of Lords until January 23rd—having for the year 1776 turned 138 bills into the law of the realm.[22]

Foreign News

Can't Tell by the Cover

Londoners on the way to national day of prayer services at St. Martin's Church, Lancaster Court, were met along the way by a hawker offering purple-bound copies of the new form of prayer issued for the day. Many bought them; but on opening their copies in church, they found only a tawdry account of the execution of eight prisoners the day before at Tyburn. Apparently the hawker had been selling stories of the hanging, had a lot left over, and tucked them into purple covers for sale to unsuspecting churchgoers.[23]

Home Until Spring

There was nothing more of consequence he could do in Canada during the winter, so Lieutenant General John Burgoyne, second in command of the British army there, has returned to England, where there are things of some consequence he can do. First, he must report to the King on the status of the war. Then he will take his seat in Parliament when it resumes in January. If no reconciliation with America comes about in the meantime, he will return to Canada in the spring. He had been there since June.[24]

Cherbourg Reopened

When a ship entered the harbor of Cherbourg this week, it was worth noting. It was the first arrival at the harbor since the cleaning up of all debris left by the destruction of Cherbourg during the last war.[25]

DIED: December 12, in England: within minutes of each other, Margaret and Judith Hodges, as, within minutes of each other they were born, fifty-three years ago, twin sisters.[26]

DIED: December 15, his Grace the Hon. and Most Rev. Dr. Robert Hay Drummond, Archbishop of York. Consecrated a bishop in 1748 at St. Asaph, he was elevated to Salisbury in 1761, and later that year, on the death of Archbishop Gilbert, raised to the see of York. It was his Grace who preached the sermon at the Coronation of their Majesties in Westminster Abbey on September 22, 1761.[27]

DIED: Lately in France as extravagantly as she lived: the Duchess D'Olone; once the possessor of a magnificent fortune long since gone, she nevertheless left instructions for a funeral of considerable pomp at her estate at Montmorency, and no money to pay for it; her heirs, intent on maintaining the family honor, were left with charges of more than 150,000 livres. Wrote a correspondent to a London newspaper: "Oh Pride! Pride! thou art of all countries! But to see thee wedded to rags and beggary, one must visit these regions of vanity and emptiness."[28]

Religion

From High to Low

Ours is a time of corruption and degeneracy, of the sins of excessive luxury; what is needed, therefore, is a national reformation, beginning with each individual and extending to the body politic.

Such a message may not be new to sermons, but what made this sermon different was the preacher and his congregation. Preaching was his Lordship, the Rt. Rev. Dr. Hurd, the bishop of Litchfield and Coventry; listening was the House of Lords, convened in Westminster Abbey to observe the nationwide general fast and day of prayer.

It was on the fifty-ninth verse of Psalm cxix that the bishop spoke: "I called mine own ways to remembrance, and turned my feet unto thy testimonies." To the extent a strong interpretation of that text might offend anyone in high life, it would have to, because, said the bishop, it was his duty to speak the plain truth on such a solemn occasion . . . that only the plain truth offers the most probable means of insuring success to the measures of government for restoring peace and union to the British empire. Once Britons from high to low accept the truth about the times, he said, the way becomes clear: it is for every individual to show his zeal for his country and his public spirit by a strict regard to the moral duties and precepts of Christianity.[29]

THE WEEK OF DECEMBER 16TH

The War

Watching Each Other

A substantial British force is now reported to be in Trenton, New Jersey, but parties of horse and foot are frequently sent out around the countryside. This week five hundred Hessians entered the town of Burlington, fifteen miles down-river, but left at nightfall after American ships on the Delaware opened fire on the town. Since then, a large body of British troops is known to have advanced north along the river, to Corell's Ferry, about five miles from Trenton, and it is anticipated the British will try to cross the river at this point.

The Continental army under General Washington, meanwhile, is encamped along the western bank of the Delaware—watching every visible move of the British across the way. The army was recently joined by the Philadelphia militia; those from surrounding counties are expected soon.[30]

"You Will Hear"

This land, mourns an officer with the Continental army, is injured and bleeding; it is enough to bring tears into your eyes. But we shall not give up, he insists.

The officer, writing from headquarters in Bucks County, Pennsylvania, has reason to think it is worth holding out:

"Now, my friends, is the crisis for you in the country to exert yourselves. Use your influence and let us have an army. Every good man and well wisher to his country will exert himself. If he is a lover of this once happy land, he will exhort one and all to lend their aid to do the needful to save this injured, bleeding, distressed land. Was you to behold the Jersies, to see the distresses, it would bring tears into your eyes.

"Now is the time for us to be in earnest. As for what few troops we have, you would be amazed to see what fine spirits they are in; and the Continental troops are well disciplined, and you may depend will fight bravely, and I doubt not before one week, you will hear of an attack *somewhere,* when I trust we shall do honour to ourselves. I well know both officers and men are determined to check the pride of the redcoats. They at present are flushed with their success, which may perhaps lull them into too much security for themselves."[31]

Congress

New Home in Baltimore

A spacious three-story brick building in the center of Baltimore is the new home of the Continental Congress. On Friday, having brought along what records they could by wagon, most—though some remain absent—members reassembled there to continue, with "quiet and uninterrupted attention," the public business.

In the course of busy sessions Friday and Saturday, Congress among other things:

—Directed General Washington to pay the militia reinforcing his army on the same basis as other troops, thus hoping to promote the maximum support of militiamen who are so desperately needed at a time when existing one-year enlistments are fast running out in the regular army;

—Designated delegates Robert Morris and George Clymer of Pennsylvania and George Walton of Georgia as a committee to remain in Philadelphia and conduct such business of Congress as need be done there;

—Asked General Washington to communicate with General Howe for the purpose of determining how the recently captured General Charles Lee is being treated, and to see if permission will be granted for sending Lee such money as may be necessary to support him during his confinement in a manner suitable to his rank.[32]

Not all the members of Congress made the trip to Baltimore. Some, apparently fearful of capture by the British, stayed away until Congress resumed its sessions March 12, 1777, in Philadelphia, by then free of threat of British attack.

The States

And Now, North Carolina

A House of Commons will no longer be the exclusive fixture of British government. The State of North Carolina this week, in adopting the ninth constitution among the United States, chose that nomenclature for its lower house. It is the only state to do so, though in some cases in the past (South Carolina, for example) a colony's lower house has been informally called its commons.

North Carolina's House of Commons will have two delegates from each county, while the upper house, a Senate, will have one. Both houses will be elected annually. The constitution and an accompanying declaration of rights, adopted at Halifax, follow the general provisions of similar documents adopted elsewhere.

By the end of 1776, New Hampshire (on January 5), South Carolina (March 26), Virginia (June 29), New Jersey (July 2), Delaware (September 20), Pennsylvania (September 28), Maryland (November 21) and North Carolina (December 18) had all adopted state constitutions. Connecticut, by act of the legislature, October 10, reaffirmed the liberal form of government it had under royal charter since 1662. Rhode Island likewise continued under the provisions of its royal charter into the nineteenth century. The remaining states adopted constitutions in the years ahead: Georgia, February 5 1777; New York, April 20, 1777; and Massachusetts, March 2, 1780. Vermont, although not officially admitted to the union until 1791, declared its independence and enacted a constitution July 8, 1777.[33]

A General Hearty Wish

When Lord Howe and General Howe three weeks ago issued a proclamation renewing an offer of clemency for Americans laying down their arms, it was inevitable most Americans would only become all the more incensed. Typical was the comment Boston's *Continental Journal* appended to its announcement:

"It may suffice for the present, to observe that the proclamation in the first page of this paper, contains little in it besides a pardon to those who have been guilty of no crime. . . . There may be a comparatively small number of friends to what they [the Howes] call government who may be pleased with this proclamation; and it is the general hearty wish that they would all take the benefit of it (if there is any in it) and repair to New York to this end. The several states in America would gladly be at the expence of their transportation, as being fully satisfied they would do less mischief there, than where they now live."[34]

Foreign News

Tradition

By legend, Pope Gregory I foresaw the ending of the plague of 590 in a vision of an angel sheathing his sword atop that citadel on the banks of the Tiber River now known as the Castel Sant'Angelo. In the years since, the fortress (built by the Emperor Hadrian in the second century) has figured in the lives—and deaths—of other popes. John X was imprisoned there; Benedict VI was strangled there; John XIV died there, either from starvation or poisoning; Clement VII took refuge there when mutinous troops overran Rome.

This week the Castel Sant'Angelo figured in the life, and maybe nearly the death, of still another pope. On a parapet overlooking the street on which his Holiness, Pius VI, walks every evening from his nearby Vatican residence, someone happened to check the guns. They were loaded with powder and chain shot. Who is responsible, and why, has not been determined.[35]

Undisturbed Visitor

A popular coffeehouse called The Wits on the Rue de Comedie Française in Paris has been deserted lately; another called the Café de Conti au Descent de la Pont Neuve, has a line out front. The reason: the latter is known to be frequented by a man, lately arrived in town from America, who is as warmly regarded by the French as one of their own. He is less highly regarded among the English in town.

Hearing that the guest from America was in the coffee room of the Café de Conti, two Englishmen, obviously inebriated, denouncing America in loud voices, tried to enter. Two Frenchmen stopped them, prevailed on them to leave politely. Inside, the visitor, Dr. Benjamin Franklin, sipped his coffee undisturbed.[36]

Unacceptable Topic

Though long and widely speculated, assistance to the American states appears to be a matter the French government wants to pursue through quiet negotiation and not through public pronouncements. But over and above considerations of diplomacy, it seems equally apparent that the government is concerned about reaction within France. Many of the French people are in dire straits. They suffered through a poor harvest two years ago, staggered under the subsequent rise in prices on agricultural goods, and showed their bitterness to these immediate hardships as well as to years of adversity in the flour riots that were put down last year only by calling out the king's troops.

It may thus have come as no surprise to many a Frenchman when the proprietors of all the coffeehouses in Paris received orders from the police this week "not to suffer any conversations in their houses" relative to the assistance which, it is said, France means to send to America.[37]

Home

In London this week, accorded the honor of a conference with the King, was his Majesty's former governor in Virginia, Lord Dunmore, lately arrived from New York.[38]

No News

When his Majesty's warships *Active* and *Fowey* arrived this week from New York, the British Ministry was disappointed. There were no letters aboard from General Howe. He was with the Army in the field when the ships sailed November 13th.[39]

A Valid Excuse

A warehouse worker who fell prey to a press gang in the silk industry center of Spital Fields near London will not face military duty after all— for what may be the most unusual reason yet recorded. "He" is she.

The worker had been employed at the weaver's warehouse for more than three years with no one the wiser. It was not until the press gang took her away that she confessed her man's apparel was only a disguise adopted fifteen years ago after a disappointed love affair. In all those years, she told them, no one ever had the least suspicion.[40]

DIED: December 5th, in London, on her sixtieth birthday: her Grace, Elizabeth, the Duchess of Northumberland, patroness of literature and music, who numbered among her friends James Boswell and the late Oliver Goldsmith; mother of Major General Earl Percy, whose brigade rescued the remnants of the British army after the battle of Concord, Massachusetts, by marching thirty miles in ten hours. When she was interred this week in St. Nicholas's Chapel, Westminster Abbey, the crowd was so great that many climbed upon the oak, brick and iron facework of the adjoining St. Edmund's Chapel, causing the whole structure, built between four hundred and five hundred years ago, to crumble, seriously injuring many and halting the funeral service for two and a half hours. Even after it was resumed, the service was interrupted by the cries of sufferers who had not yet been rescued.[41]

Law

"Alienation of Affection"

Kings Arms Tavern
Cornhill, June 7

AT a special meeting this day of several members of the Constitutional Society, during an adjournment, a gentleman proposed that a subscription should be immediately entered into (by such of the members present who might approve the purpose) for raising the sum of One Hundred Pounds "to be applied to the relief of the widows, or orphans, and aged parents of our beloved American fellow subjects who, faithful to the character of Englishmen, preferring death to slavery, were, for that reason only, inhumanly murdered by the King's troops at or near Lexington and Concord in the Province of Massachusetts, on the 19th of last April." Which sum being immediately collected, it was thereupon resolved that Mr. Horne do pay tomorrow into the hands of Mess. Brownes and Collison, on account of Doctor Franklin, the said sum of One Hundred Pounds, and that Doctor Franklin be requested to apply the same to the above-mentioned purpose.

JOHN HORNE
An advertisement in
London's *Whitehall Evening Post*
June 10, 1775

It has been a year and a half since John Horne's Constitutional Society—successor to a crusade on behalf of John Wilkes—raised funds that

might be sent to America (with Dr. Benjamin Franklin) for the relief
of widows and children of the King's victims at Lexington and Concord,
whose battles were then recent news in London. Such a fund is now largely forgotten. But that British newspapers should dare to print an advertisement announcing the fact—as did four others besides the *Whitehall
Evening Post*—has been neither forgotten nor forgiven by the Government.
In the past few weeks, the publishers of all five London papers have been
brought to justice for libel against the government: on Saturday, the 7th,
T. Wright, of the *Whitehall Evening Post*; and on Wednesday, the 18th,
in separate but consecutive trials before Lord Mansfield and a special
jury at Guildhall, John Miller, of the *London Evening Post*; J. Wilkie,
of the *London Chronicle*; Mr. Randall, of the *Ledger,* and Henry Baldwin of the *St. James's Chronicle.*

A common thread of accusation and defense ran through all the trials,
the latter four of which were prosecuted by Britain's Attorney General
himself. Charged he: the advertisement was "a most scurrilous and in-
flammatory libel on Government."

Argued the defense: In all criminal prosecution it is the intention
alone that constitutes the crime, and who can say or suppose this was the
case with the printer of the newspaper? "It would be a very hard circum-
stance," argued Mr. Leigh, attorney for Mr. Miller of the *London Evening Post,* "if for every advertisement which should slip into a paper,
with the name of the author [of the advertisement] publicly at the bottom of it, as in the present case, and which in some respect presupposed
it would not have been done without its being maturely considered,
should be imputed to the printer as a malicious and libelous act."

Countered the Attorney General: the printers should have been more
careful; the advertisement contained the language of a fishwoman; it was
clearly a "scurrilous blurt, stuffed with invectives . . . composed of ribald-
ry and falsehood, with a design for blackening Administration, and alien-
ating the affections of the people from the present Government."

The presiding judge, Lord Mansfield, told the jury, when asked in
the Wilkie trial, that the publication of a libel constitutes a crime. But
even without that advice, the juries had little trouble making up their
minds, in the Miller trial not even leaving the jury box: they found all
five publishers guilty of libel. Sentencing will be after the first of the year.

Meanwhile John Horne, the author of the advertisement and apparently the chief instigator of raising funds for Lexington and Concord, has
gotten by without prosecution. Many are asking why. After all, this is the
same John Horne whose own political agitation, as well as his active support of John Wilkes, has been a thorn in the side of Government for some
years.

The Attorney General, at the conclusion of the trials, allowed himself
in a "very odd predicament." He is being censured for taking action
against the printers, and failing to take action against Horne. The reason
the printers were prosecuted, he said, is because they could clearly be

proven guilty; and against Horne, he has "not a colour of evidence." But when he has sufficient proof, he hastened to add, it will be seen whether or not he is afraid of Mr. Horne.

The five printers were subsequently fined. Horne, later more commonly known as John Horne Tooke, was brought to trial July 4, 1777, found guilty, fined 2001, and sentenced to a year in jail. The Attorney General was Edward Thurlow.[42]

Less Lenient

An English law four centuries old—it was passed in the twenty-seventh year of Edward III [1354]—provides that a foreign merchant in England shall not be suddenly subdued if his country becomes an enemy; instead he is to be given a warning to leave the country, then given forty days to sell his goods before departing. But in some cases, the law can be more lenient: "in case that for default of wind or ship, or for sickness, or for other evident cause, they cannot avoid our said realm and lands within so short a time, then they shall have another forty days, or more, if need be, within which they may pass conveniently, with selling their merchandise as afore said."

The Virginia General Assembly has adopted, in principle, the same law, making it applicable to all natives of Great Britain who were partners with or factors, agents, storekeepers or clerks for British merchants at the time trade was broken off. But Virginia's law is less lenient. "In case of default of ship" or adequate funds, such tradesmen will be placed upon a Commonwealth-owned vessel and summarily deported.[43]

THE WEEK OF DECEMBER 23RD

The War

Toward A "Becoming Fortitude"

There have been rumors in Philadelphia, apparently the work of traitors, that no more men are needed to bear arms in defense of the city. Nothing could be further from the truth; every last man is desperately needed, replied the city's Council of Safety as it issued this eloquent appeal this week:

"May Heaven, who bestowed the blessings of liberty upon you, awaken you to a sense of your danger, and rouse that manly spirit of virtuous resolution which has ever bid defiance to the efforts of tyranny. May you ever have the glorious prize of liberty in view, and bear with a becoming fortitude the fatigues and severities of a winter campaign. That, and that only, will entitle you to the superlative distinction of being deemed, under God, the deliverers of your country."[44]

Jersey's Judas

The capture of American Major General Charles Lee at Basking Ridge, New Jersey, reports the *Boston Gazette*, was neither an accident nor the result of astuteness on the part of the British forces. It was rather the result of intelligence of the general's unguarded condition supplied to the British the night before by a resident of Basking Ridge—"this Judas," the *Gazette* report calls him—who had made a pretense of friendship for the American cause.[45]

Congress

"Having Perfect Reliance"

When Congress settled on the necessity of abandoning Philadelphia for Baltimore, it recognized there would be an interim period during which an effective central government would be suspended. It reconciled that [CONGRESS—Week of December 9th] by delegating to General Washington, as commander-in-chief, substantial new powers hitherto reserved to Congress itself.

Such a decision could not have come lightly. It is known that many in Congress are manifestly opposed to placing any degree of ultimate authority in the military. In part, that is what the war is about. The last governor of Massachusetts as a royal colony was a general; and he, Thomas Gage, was despised.

Yet the power granted to General Washington little more than two weeks ago has since been viewed as not enough, rather than too much. So great is the depth of the crisis and so great the need for military success.

This week Congress chose to go further and to invest in that one man the most sweeping powers ever possessed by a single individual on this continent—greater than any royal governor, or any royal general, over whose often vast authority King and Parliament have always retained a final say.

To General Washington now go these powers, virtually dictatorial in nature:

—To take whatever he wants for the use of the Army, paying whatever he deems a fair price if the owner refuses to sell;

—To arrest and confine persons showing disaffection with the American cause or refusing to take Continental currency, and to have their names turned over to their respective states for prosecution;

—To raise, and have authority over, an additional sixteen battalions of infantry, three thousand light horse, three regiments of artillery and a corps of engineers, and to establish their pay;

—To apply directly to any state for the use of its militia, as he alone shall judge necessary;

—To stock military supplies wherever he thinks proper;

—To appoint and remove all officers under the rank of brigadier general, and otherwise fill all vacancies in the army.

Those powers Congress heretofore reserved to itself; and although it has only bestowed them for a term of six months, and although it reserves the right sooner to reclaim them, Congress has done what almost seems an utter contradiction: it has very nearly created a king. How can it be that these same representatives, who six months ago declared the independence of America by reciting the evils of one man, expressing in particular after particular that "He has" done this and "He has" done that, making not those of Parliament but the abuses of the King the grounds for separation . . . how can it be these same representatives now have delegated such awesome power to one single man?

There are two reasons, the first being the exigency of the cause. Except for as strong an army as America can muster, there may be no Congress at all. It was summed up this way in the resolution delegating to Washington his new authority: "The unjust but determined purpose of the British Court to enslave these free states, obvious through every delusive insinuation to the contrary, [has] placed things in such a situation that the very existence of civil liberty now depends on the right execution of military powers, and the vigorous, decisive conduct of these [is] impossible to distant, numerous and deliberative bodies."

The second reason is the character of George Washington himself. He is the one man most generally agreed to have the ability to use such power effectively and at the same time to have the certain judgment to use it honorably. Said Congress: it turned over such awesome authority "having perfect reliance on the wisdom, vigour and uprightness of General Washington."

The committee of Congress that transmitted the resolution to Washington wrote to him December 31st: "Happy it is for this country that the general of their forces can safely be intrusted with the most unlimited power, and neither personal security, liberty, nor property be in the least degree endangered thereby." 46

Work Schedule

In its first complete week in Baltimore, Congress wasted no time in resuming a full schedule of work. Among other things this week, Congress:

—Empowered General Washington to use every possible means—including bounties for a shorter-than-usual term—to prevail upon troops with expiring enlistments to remain beyond the end of the year and for as long as necessary;

—Asked the states of New Hampshire, Massachusetts and Connecticut to hasten the dispatch of troops to Fort Ticonderoga, since the enlistments of the troops there expire on the 31st;

—Appointed a committee of five (William Whipple of New Hampshire, James Wilson of Pennsylvania, Elbridge Gerry of Massachusetts, Thomas Nelson, Jr. of Virginia and Robert Morris of Pennsylvania) to prepare "a plan for the better conducting of the executive business of Congress by boards composed of persons who are not members of Congress";

—Named as a brigadier general of artillery Colonel Henry Knox, the former Boston bookseller who last winter led the sled-borne haul of guns from Fort George to help dislodge the British from Boston.[47]

Christmas in Baltimore

In Baltimore, members of the Continental Congress observed Christmas by taking a rare day off, and attending to the religious nature of the day in church.[48]

Foreign News

Christmas in London

In London, their Majesties observed Christmas by receiving the holy sacraments in the Chapel Royal.[49]

France: War Inevitable

The French Cabinet, according to reports in London, has virtually concluded the inevitability of war with Great Britain—thus hoping to take advantage of British preoccupation in America to avenge its defeat in the Seven Years War, restore its prestige, and make moot the costly Treaty of Paris of 1763.

What has not yet been decided, according to these reports, is at which of Britain's far-flung possessions, or at which of its allies, to strike. So far seen as the most likely: an attack against Germany. These are the reasons given:

—It is believed this would be the most agreeable, from France's point of view, with its ally of Austria, at present on the worst possible terms with George III over his dual role as Elector of Hanover;

—A land war in Europe would give French nobility their best opportunity to cultivate their love of military glory;

—The French navy is not thought to be adequate at the present time for a foreign war; some British observers say it has no more than twenty-five capital ships.

Thus are many in Great Britain convinced France will enter the war as an ally of America; how soon can only be a matter of speculation.

France declared war against Great Britain in February, 1778. 50

Blackgowns and Redcoats

To one reader at least of London's *St. James's Chronicle,* a sermon should be a means of explaining the Word of God and not the policies of the King. Signing himself "A Churchman," he complained in the *Chronicle* of December 26th: "I was much offended on Sunday last by hearing a clergyman deliver from the pulpit a political discourse, which drove several of his congregation out of church. . . . The clergy should follow the example of their Master and preach 'Peace and good will to all men' and not blow the trumpet of discord and dissention to their congregation. . . . The Red-coats and not the black-gowns are most likely to produce unanimity."[51]

Trade and Commerce

Bear Market

John Bull has had a bear market this year. Of the seventeen issues traded by stock brokers in the coffee houses of London's Exchange Alley, all but one have declined during 1776.

The worst investment by far has been in India bonds, which were selling at 64 *s* the beginning of January and were down to 38 this week. The sharpest decline was in March—a drop of 18 *s* in only a matter of weeks.

While other issues did hardly that poorly, British investors had little to cheer about in reckoning these losses for the year: Bank of England, 143$\frac{1}{8}$ *l* to 137$\frac{3}{4}$; South Sea Company, old annuities, 87 *l* to 79$\frac{5}{8}$; four per cent consolidated government securities of the 1762 issue (which helped to pay for the last war), 91$\frac{1}{2}$ *l* to 84$\frac{1}{8}$; and three per cent consolidateds, 87$\frac{1}{2}$ *l* to 82$\frac{1}{8}$. And so on.

Meanwhile, the most reliable of all British investments proved its worth. The East India Company has a reputation unequalled by any investment in Europe except the Dutch East India Company. This year—when everything else went down—the British company showed why it has that kind of reputation: a gain from 163$\frac{1}{2}$ *l* in January to 171 the beginning of December.

For the rest of the market, events of the year, and particularly the move for independence in America, have clearly had an effect. Yet in the rise and fall of British stocks over the years, the record of the last twelve months is of little significance. Compared to the South Sea Bubble of 1720—when stock in the South Sea Company plummeted from over 1,000 in July to 150 the end of September—this year's decline will be little remembered in Exchange Alley.

British stocks would decline much more in the years ahead: Bank of England, down to 111 in 1779; 3% consolidateds to 61 the same year. Stock quotations were in pounds sterling, except for India bonds, which were in shillings. The "eighth" was a well established unit of sale, and meant, except for India bonds, one-eighth of a pound. As for terminology generally, "John Bull" appears in the London Packet of November 11, 1776. The first edition of Encyclopedia Britannica (Edinburgh, 1771) has this: "In the language of Exchange Alley, the buyer in this case is called the Bull, and the seller the Bear." British stock brokers at this time, according to an advertisement for one of them, dealt in "Bank, India and South Sea stocks, with their several annuities, India bonds, Navy and Victualling bills, and all kinds of government securities bought and sold by commission." One London brokerage house had the curiously appropriate name of Hazard & Co.[52]

Press

The Denunciation of Independence

The gazettes of the loyalist provinces of Quebec and Nova Scotia in Canada have never supplied their readers with a full text of the American Declaration of Independence as have British newspapers for inhabitants of the mother country. The Canadian newspapers, however, have devoted considerable space to an essay denouncing the declaration. It was first published in the *Nova Scotia Gazette*, and now in the December 26th issue of *La Gazette de Quebec*. An extract:

"When independent states take up arms, they endeavour to impress the world with a favourable opinion of their own cause, and to lay the blame of hostilities on the injustice of their opponents. . . . This consideration, however obvious it may appear to others, seems to have totally escaped the attention of the body of men who lately sat at Philadelphia under the name of 'The General American Congress.' In a paper published under the title of 'A Declaration by the Representatives of the United Colonies of North America,' the facts are either willfully or ignorantly misrepresented and the argument deduced from premises that have no foundation in truth."[53]

YEAR'S END

The World

The Turn Against Old Ways

How the war of independence in America will affect the course of human events, one can not yet tell. Elsewhere in the world, the year near past has witnessed a record that can be told now, and it is a record in many ways noteworthy for the advance of the human spirit over the shackles of ignorance, fear, prejudice and old ways:

—The Court of Vienna took a more liberal position on Protestants, ended the use of torture in the tribunals of Austria and Hungary, and abolished villeinage in the Kingdom of Bohemia;

—It also opened Austria to trading by Turks, Armenians, Greeks, Jacobites and other subjects of the Ottoman Empire, provided such subjects agree to settle within its borders;

—The king of Sardinia forbade the imprisonment of anyone by the Inquisition until the charge is made known to his Majesty and one or more of his privy council examine the evidence;

—In Spain, though censorship of the press continues with an iron hand and the Inquisition appears to be reviving, some significance is seen in the removal of severe restrictions (such as to time and place and number of ships) on foreign trade with Mexico;

—In Morocco, the emperor was reported treating some of his captives more as prisoners of war than as slaves, a relative improvement;

—Elsewhere along the Barbary coast, a Russian sea captain, ignoring prudence and the widespread tradition of tribute, took it as a self-appointed mission to begin raiding the bases of the pirates, freeing their captives;

—And in Roman Catholic France, the king named a foreign-born Protestant to direct the nation's finances.

Particularly noteworthy was the more liberal attitude toward religion in Austria and Hungary, where mortal animosity has long existed between Roman Catholics and Protestants. By edict announced in May, Protestants are no longer forced to have Roman Catholic priests attend them at times of illness, or officiate at funerals; nor are they any longer obligated to take part in public religious processions in the cities; Catholic schoolmasters are now forbidden to issue to a Protestant pupil any book contradicting the doctrine of the pupil's religion.

Peasants in Bohemia will remember this as the year that villeinage ended throughout the Imperial domains, though not yet in those of the Bohemian nobility. The lands of the Court of Vienna were divided into lots of moderate size and made available to the villeins at easy rents. The only vestige of servitude remaining is task work, and this may be commuted for a small annual payment.

All in all, in many lands, it has been a year in which the inherent rights of man have found new meaning, even if the difference is sometimes only once removed from the theory. Where the change is cataclysmic—in the newest nation of them all—the turn against old ways has become a war that only the future will decide.[54]

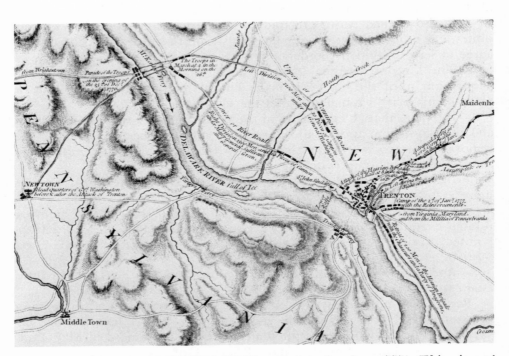

*THE BATTLE OF TRENTON (William Faden, London, 1777). This view of
the events of the last week of December 1776—Washington's crossing of the ice-
packed Delaware River and the "enterprise at Trenton," New Jersey—was published in London April 15, 1777. It is a detail of a larger map that also shows
the Battle of Princeton on January 3rd—another significant victory for the be-
draggled Continental army.*

*Map Division—New York Public Library—
Astor, Lenox and Tilden Foundations*

The War

An Enterprise at Trenton

> "Appearances are against us at present, but America will be victorious; I feel a kind of Oliverian persuasion that Heaven will soon interpose in our favour."

A correspondent with the Continental army, earlier this month

The interposition of heaven? Fortuity? Military cunning? Whatever it may have been, it is news indeed that Congress has to announce.

That announcement, dated Baltimore, December 31st, is a letter dispatched by General Washington December 27th from his headquarters at Newtown, Pennsylvania. It is already to Congress, and will be to patriots throughout America as the news spreads, the greatest cause for rejoicing since independence was declared a half-year ago.

Reported General Washington to Congress:

"I have the pleasure of congratulating you upon the success of an enterprise which I had formed against a detachment of the enemy lying in Trenton, and which was executed yesterday morning.

"The evening of the 25th, I ordered the troops intended for this service to parade back of McKonkey's Ferry, that they might begin to pass as soon as it grew dark, imagining we should be able to throw them all over, with the necessary artillery by twelve o'clock, and that we might easily arrive at Trenton by five in the morning, the distance being about nine miles. But the quantity of ice made that night [on the Delaware] impeded the passage of the boats so much that it was three o'clock before the artillery could all be got over, and near four before the troops took up their line of march."

The march from camp in Pennsylvania on Christmas night . . . the crossing of the Delaware River eight miles above Trenton . . . was thus told by General Washington himself. And the attack against the Hessians . . .

"I formed my detachment into two divisions, one to march up the lower, or river road, the other by the upper or Pennington road. As the divisions had nearly the same distance to march, I ordered each of them immediately upon forcing the out-guards to push directly into the town, that they might charge the enemy before they had time to form. The upper division arrived at the enemy's advanced post exactly at eight o'clock, and in three minutes after, I found from the fire on the lower road, that that division had also got up. The out-guards made but a small opposition, though, for their numbers, they behaved very well, keeping up a constant retreating fire from behind houses."

The attack . . . echoing the words of an American officer who, week before, predicted it would come . . . somewhere . . . and would check the pride of redcoats flushed with success and lulled into security. . . . General Washington continued:

"We presently saw their main body formed, but, from their motions, they seemed undetermined how to act. Being hard pressed by our troops, who had already got possession of part of their artillery, they attempted to file off by a road on their right leading to Princeton; but perceiving their intention, I threw a body of troops in their way, which immediately checked them. Finding, from our disposition, that they were surrounded, and they must inevitably be cut to pieces if they made any further resistance, they agreed to lay down their arms. The number that submitted in this manner was twenty-three officers and 886 men. Colonel Rohl [Rall], the commanding officer, and seven others were found wounded in the town. I do not exactly know how many they had killed, but I fancy not above twenty or thirty, as they never made any regular stand. Our loss is very trifling indeed; only two officers and one or two privates wounded."

The battle at Trenton . . . a clear victory . . . and in the opinion of the commander-in-chief, proof once and for all of the spirit of the Continental army. His letter concludes:

"In justice to the officers and men I must add that their behaviour upon this occasion reflects the highest honor upon them. The difficulty of passing the river in a very severe night, and their march through a violent storm of snow and hail, did not in the least abate their ardour; but when they came to the charge, each seemed to vie with the other in pressing forward, and were I to give a preference to any particular corps, I should do great injustice to the others."

Having made public that remarkable news, with long-awaited satisfaction, Congress completed its business for the day of December 31, 1776, and adjourned—until ten o'clock tomorrow.[55]

EPILOGUE

> "These are the times that try men's souls. . . . yet we have this consolation with us, that the harder the conflict the more glorious the triumph."

> THOMAS PAINE
> *The American Crisis*
> December . . . of this year.

SOURCES

NOTES ON SOURCES

Over and above comments included in the Preface are the following:

American Archives (Washington: Peter Force, 1837–1853). An invaluable repository of documents, legislative records, correspondence, and contemporary accounts compiled by Peter Force (archivist, journalist, historian and one-time mayor of Washington, D.C.) under contract to the U.S. Department of State and covering the years 1774 through 1776. Much of this material was not public knowledge at the time it was generated; some of it certainly was (there is a lot of material that was obviously taken from newspapers), and it is for the latter sort that the author has turned to *American Archives* for convenience.

Annual Register (London: James Dodsley, publisher in 1776). An annual record of "history, politics and literature," and virtually everything else we would call news, begun in 1759 and continued to the present, the title changing in 1954 to *Annual Register of World Events*. At the outset, and to at least a substantial degree in 1776, these yearly volumes were compiled by Edmund Burke. Nearly everything that appeared had already been in public print during the year, making this an excellent source. The *Annual Register* of that era was divided into categories—"History," "Chronicle," "State Papers," "Poetry," and so forth, and into separate numbering systems. Hence, the page references as they appear in the source notes here.

Journals of Congress (Philadelphia: R. Aitken, 1776–77). The reader's attention is called to comments in the Preface.

Thacher, James, M.D., *Military Journal During the American Revolutionary War* (1823; Hartford: Silas Andrus and Son, 1854). Thacher was a Massachusetts-born physician just shy of his 22nd birthday at the beginning of 1776. He had already been keeping notes in his journal since the summer before, when, the war breaking out, he chose to begin his medical career as a surgeon's mate in Cambridge rather than in private practice. He remained with the army throughout the war, writing almost daily accounts from Ticonderoga to Yorktown. Thacher's diary is here taken at face value; when he reports in his diary on July 18, 1776 the "hanging anecdote" about Elbridge Gerry and Benjamin Harrison on July 4th—Thacher then being in Boston—it may be supposed, if one takes the doctor at his word, that such a story, true or not, was making the rounds. The episode is duly reported here as "said to have happened." Whatever the authenticity of that particular anecdote, Thacher kept a remarkably informative record that is of unquestioned historical importance. (The 2nd edition, 1827, had a short preface by John Adams.)

Newspapers. Beyond what is offered in the Preface, it is appropriate only to note that many journalistic sources here are followed by "quoting such a place, such and such a date." These dateline references are included in the source notes—if in the original—in consideration of the time factor.

Secondary sources. Of the many used—the number prohibiting itemization —the *Dictionary of American Biography* and the *Dictionary of National Biography* should be observed as having been consulted the most often.

PRIMARY SOURCES

January

1. *Boston Gazette,* Watertown, January 1, 1776; Lossing, B. J., *Pictorial Field Book of the American Revolution* (New York, 1850), I, 577
2. *Annual Register 1776,* Chronicle, 113, Poetry, 202
3. *Annual Register 1776,* Chronicle, 113
4. *Virginia Gazette* (Purdie), Williamsburg, January 5, 1776; *New England Chronicle,* Cambridge, February 1 and 8, 1776
5. *Virginia Gazette* (Purdie), Williamsburg, January 12, 1776
6. ibid.
7. *Journals of Congress,* week cited
8. *Pennsylvania Packet,* Philadelphia, February 12, 1776, quoting Exeter, January 5, 1776; *State Papers of New Hampshire* (Concord, 1874), VIII, 2
9. *Pennsylvania Magazine,* Philadelphia, January, 1776.
10. *Gaine's Universal Register 1776,* New York
11. *New York Packet,* February 8, 1776
12. *St. James's Chronicle,* London, January 4, 1776
13. *West's New England Almanack 1776* (Providence)
14. *Massachusetts Gazette,* Boston, January 4, 1776
15. *New England Chronicle,* Cambridge, February 8, 1776
16. *Drey Vollständigen Subsidien-Tractaten* (Frankfurt and Leipzig, 1776)
17. *New England Chronicle,* Cambridge, January 11, 1776
18. *Journals of Congress,* week cited
19. *Virginia Gazette* (Purdie), Williamsburg, January 12, 1776
20. *Annual Register 1776,* Chronicle, 114

21. *St. James's Chronicle*, London, January 13, 1776
22. *St. James's Chronicle*, London, January 11, 1776
23. *London Chronicle*, January 27, 1776, quoting Paris, January 12, 1776
24. *Annual Register 1776*, Chronicle, 222
25. *Pennsylvania Gazette*, Philadelphia, January 17, 1776; *Cases Adjudged in the Supreme Court of New Jersey Relative to the Manumission of Slaves* (Burlington, 1794)
26. *Pennsylvania Evening Post*, Philadelphia, January 9, 1776; op. cit. (1st ed.)
27. *Pennsylvania Packet*, Philadelphia, May 6, 1776, quoting Cork, January 24, 1776
28. *Journals of Congress*, week cited
29. *Virginia Gazette* (Dixon & Hunter), Williamsburg, January 13, 1776
30. *St. James's Chronicle*, London, January 20 and February 22, 1776
31. *New England Chronicle*, Cambridge, January 18, 1776
32. *St. James's Chronicle*, London, March 2, 1776, quoting St. Petersburg, December 13, 1775
33. *St. James's Chronicle*, London, February 6, 1776, quoting Paris, January 20, 1776
34. op. cit. ([Philadelphia], 1776)
35. *St. James's Chronicle*, London, January 18, 1776.
36. *New Hampshire Gazette*, Exeter, January 9, 1776; *State Papers of New Hampshire* (Concord, 1874), VIII, 24
37. *Journals of Congress*, week cited
38. op. cit.
39. *Pennsylvania Evening Post*, Philadelphia, January 27, 1776
40. *Annual Register 1776*, Chronicle, 118; Thurston, H., *The Holy Year of Jubilee* (1900; Westminster, Md., 1949)
41. *Annual Register 1776*, Projects, 133
42. *New England Chronicle*, Cambridge, February 8, 1776; *Massachusetts Spy*, Worcester, February 16, 1776
43. *Journals of Congress*, week cited
44. *New England Chronicle*, Cambridge, February 8, 1776, quoting New York, February 1, 1776
45. *St. James's Chronicle*, London, February 1, 1776
46. *Pennsylvania Evening Post*, Philadelphia, January 27 and 30, February 1, 1776
47. *St. James's Chronicle*, London, January 30, 1776; op. cit.

February

1. *St. James's Chronicle*, London, February 6, 1776
2. Thacher, J., *Military Journal*, 37; *Boston Gazette*, Watertown, January 1, 1776
3. Emmet Collection, New York Public Library, 7056
4. *Journals of Congress*, week cited
5. Emmet Collection, New York Public Library, 1105
6. *Pennsylvania Packet*, Philadelphia, February 12, 1776
7. *New England Chronicle*, Cambridge, February 8, 1776

8. *Drey Vollständigen Subsidien-Tractaten* (Frankfurt and Leipzig, 1776)
9. *London Chronicle*, March 9, 1776, quoting St. Petersburg, February 6, 1776
10. op. cit. (Last known issue is February 12, 1776)
11. *St. James's Chronicle*, London, February 8, 1776
12. *St. James's Chronicle*, London, February 3, 1776
13. *New York Packet*, February 15, 1776
14. *Journals of Congress*, week cited
15. *St. James's Chronicle*, London, January 30 and February 1, 3, and 17, 1776; Curwen, S., *The Journal and Letters of Samuel Curwen, an American in England, from 1775 to 1783* (Boston, 1864)
16. Thacher, J., *Military Journal*, 37
17. Letter from Priestley to Franklin, February 13, 1776 in *Some Letters of Franklin's Correspondents* (Philadelphia, 1903)
18. op. cit., I. The preface was dated February 1, 1776
19. *Virginia Gazette* (Dixon & Hunter), Williamsburg, February 24, 1776
20. Thacher, J., *Military Journal*, 42
21. Thacher, J., *Military Journal*, 36
22. *Journals of Congress*, week cited
23. *St. James's Chronicle*, London, February 22, 1776
24. *Virginia Gazette* (Dixon & Hunter), Williamsburg, February 3, 1776
25. *London Evening Post*, February 4, 1776; Wright, L., *Clean and Decent* (New York, 1960)
26. *Virginia Gazette* (Dixon & Hunter), Williamsburg, March 2, 1776
27. *St. James's Chronicle*, London, December 22, 1775
28. *Virginia Gazette* (Purdie), Williamsburg, March 15, 1776
29. *Journals of Congress*, week cited
30. ibid.
31. *Pennsylvania Packet*, Philadelphia, June 17, 1776 quoting London, March 2, 1776
32. *St. James's Chronicle*, London, February 29, 1776
33. *St. James's Chronicle*, London, March 23, 1776 quoting Milan, March 1, 1776
34. op. cit.; Brigham, C. S., *History and Bibliography of American Newspapers, 1690–1820* (Worcester, 1947); Clayton-Torrence, W., *A Trial Bibliography of Colonial Virginia* (Richmond, 1908)

March

1. *Boston Gazette*, Watertown, March 11, 1776
2. *Boston Gazette*, Watertown, March 18, 1776; *Virginia Gazette* (Dixon & Hunter), Williamsburg, March 30, 1776
3. *Journals of Congress*, week cited
4. *New England Chronicle*, Cambridge, March 28, 1776
5. *Virginia Gazette* (Dixon & Hunter), Williamsburg, February 3, 1776
6. *St. James's Chronicle*, London, March 5 and 7, 1776
7. *Connecticut Courant*, Hartford, June 3, 1776, quoting London, February 13, 1776, and June 17, 1776, quoting Cleves, February 20, 1776
8. *St. James's Chronicle*, London, March 14, 1776
9. op. cit.; *Annual Register 1776*, Books, 241

10. *New England Chronicle,* Cambridge, March 3, 1776; *Massachusetts Spy,* Worcester, April 12, 1776
11. *Journals of Congress,* week cited
12. *London Packet,* March 15, 1776
13. *Pennsylvania Gazette,* Philadelphia, July 3, 1776, quoting Madrid, March 17, 1776
14. Curwen, S., *The Journal and Letters of Samuel Curwen, an American in England, 1775 to 1783* (Boston, 1864) —his diary notes for March 13, 1776
15. op. cit.; *Pennsylvania Evening Post,* Philadelphia, March 14, 1776
16. *Boston Gazette,* Watertown, March 18, 1776
17. *New York Journal,* April 4, 1776
18. *Journals of Congress,* week cited
19. Conway, M. D., *The Life of Thomas Paine* (New York, 1892)
20. *Virginia Gazette* (Purdie), Williamsburg, March 22, 1776
21. *Pennsylvania Packet,* Philadelphia, July 1, 1776, quoting London, March 21, 1776
22. *Pennsylvania Packet,* Philadelphia, June 17, 1776, quoting The Hague, March 22, 1776
23. *St. James's Chronicle,* London, March 23, 1776
24. Appendix to [Anon.], *Summary Observations and Facts [Regarding] a Northern Passage* (London, 1776)
25. Thacher, J., *Military Journal,* 42
26. *Connecticut Journal,* New Haven, July 24, 1776, quoting London, April 11, 1776
27. *The Autobiography of Edward Gibbon* (London, 1846)
28. *Journals of Congress,* week cited
29. *Pennsylvania Gazette,* Philadelphia, July 3, 1776, quoting London, March 29, 1776
30. *Pennsylvania Packet,* Philadelphia, April 8, 1776
31. *Constitution of South Carolina* (Charleston, 1776); *American Archives,* 4, V, 609
32. *Annual Register 1776,* Chronicle, 214
33. *St. James's Chronicle,* London, March 26, 1776
34. *Virginia Gazette* (Dunmore), off Norfolk, February 3, 1776; *Virginia Gazette* (Purdie), Williamsburg, February 23, 1776; Proceedings of the House of Lords March 14, 1776, in *American Archives* 4, VI, 338; *St. James's Chronicle,* London, December 26, 1776 (footnote)
35. op. cit. (Dublin, 1776)
36. *Virginia Gazette* (Dixon & Hunter), Williamsburg, March 30, 1776; *The Writings of George Washington* (Washington, 1931), IV, 360

April

1. *New England Chronicle,* Cambridge, April 4, 1776. (This was the last issue of the *Chronicle* published in Cambridge; it resumed publication in Boston April 25, 1776)
2. *Connecticut Courant,* Hartford, June 17, 1776, quoting London, March 28, 1776

3. *Kentish Gazette,* Canterbury, August 17, 1776
4. *Journals of Congress,* week cited
5. *Providence Gazette,* April 6, 1776; *Boston Gazette,* April 15, 1776; *Pennsylvania Packet,* Philadelphia, April 22, 1776; *Journals of Congress,* week cited
6. *Pennsylvania Packet,* Philadelphia, April 15, 1776
7. *St. James's Chronicle,* London, April 2, 1776
8. *St. James's Chronicle,* London, April 4, 1776
9. *Annual Register 1776,* Projects, 124
10. *Virginia Gazette* (Dixon & Hunter), Williamsburg, July 29, 1776, quoting London, April 9, 1776
11. *Journals of Congress,* week cited
12. *Virginia Gazette* (Dixon & Hunter), Williamsburg, June 22, 1776, quoting North Carolina, April 12, 1776
13. *New York Journal,* April 18, 1776
14. *Virginia Gazette* (Dixon & Hunter), Williamsburg, July 29, 1776, quoting London, April 9, 1776
15. *Journals of Congress,* week cited
16. *St. James's Chronicle,* London, April 13, 1776
17. *New York Packet,* April 11, 1776
18. *Pennsylvania Journal,* Philadelphia, April 10, 1776; Gimbel, R., *Thomas Paine: A Bibliographical Check List of Common Sense* (New Haven, 1956)
19. *Journals of Congress,* week cited
20. Clark, J., *The Fate of Blood-Thirsty Oppressors and God's Care of his Distressed People* (Boston, 1776)
21. *Pennsylvania Evening Post,* Philadelphia, April 20, 1776
22. *New York Packet,* April 18, 1776
23. *Connecticut Gazette,* New London, September 20, 1776
24. *Kentish Gazette,* Canterbury, May 22, 1776, quoting Vienna, May 4, 1776; *Annual Register 1776,* Chronicle, 134
25. Morgan, J., *Recommendations of Inoculation according to Baron Dimsdale's Method* (Boston, 1776)
26. *Virginia Gazette* (Dixon & Hunter), Williamsburg, February 17, 1776; *Virginia Gazette* (Purdie), Williamsburg, March 1, 1776
27. *St. James's Chronicle,* London, April 16, 1776
28. *Journals of Congress,* week cited
29. *Pennsylvania Packet,* Philadelphia, May 6, 1776
30. *Kentish Gazette,* Canterbury, April 27, 1776; *Annual Register 1776,* Chronicle, 249
31. *Parliamentary Register* (London, 1776–77), III, 499
32. *London Evening Post,* April 27, 1776
33. *London Packet,* February 16, 1776, quoting Paris, January 29, 1776; *London Chronicle,* May 4, 1776, quoting Paris, April 22, 1776
34. *Pennsylvania Magazine,* Philadelphia, April, 1776
35. ["Reprinted from the British"], *Collection of English Precedents Relating to the Office of Justice of the Peace* (New York, 1776)
36. *Pennsylvania Packet,* Philadelphia, April 22, 1776; [Adams, J.], *Thoughts*

on Government Applicable to the Present State of the American Colonies (Philadelphia, 1776)

37. *Journals of Congress,* week cited
38. *New York Journal,* May 9, 1776
39. *South Carolina and American General Gazette,* Charleston, May 22, 1776
40. *St. James's Chronicle,* London, May 2, 1776
41. *London Chronicle,* May 9, 1776
42. Barrington, D., *The Probability of Reaching the North Pole* (London, 1775–76); [Anon.], *Summary Observations and Facts [Regarding] a Northern Passage* (London, 1776) ; [Henry, D., ed.], *An Historical Account of All the Voyages around the World* (London, 1774–76) , IV
43. Thacher, J., *Military Journal,* 256

May

1. *New York Journal,* May 9, 1776; *Pennsylvania Packet,* Philadelphia, May 20, 1776
2. *Journals of Congress,* week cited
3. *Pennsylvania Packet,* Philadelphia, May 27, 1776
4. *St. James's Chronicle,* London, May 7, 1776
5. *St. James's Chronicle,* London, May 14, 1776; *Virginia Gazette* (Dixon & Hunter) , Williamsburg, August 31, 1776
6. *Gazetteer and New Daily Advertiser,* London, April 11, 1776
7. *London Chronicle,* May 28, 1776
8. Swieten, G. Van, *The Diseases Incident to Armies in the Field with the Method of Care* (Philadelphia, 1776) ; *Pennsylvania Packet,* Philadelphia, May 6, 1776
9. *St. James's Chronicle,* London, May 21, 1776; *Annual Register 1776,* Chronicle, 135
10. *Pennsylvania Packet,* Philadelphia, May 13, 1776
11. *Pennsylvania Packet,* Philadelphia, June 3, 1776; *Virginia Gazette* (Dixon & Hunter) , Williamsburg, June 8, 1776
12. *Virginia Gazette* (Dixon & Hunter) , Williamsburg, October 11, 1776, quoting London, May 19, 1776
13. *Kentish Gazette,* Canterbury, May 18, 1776
14. *Journals of Congress,* week cited
15. *New York Journal,* May 16, 1776
16. *The Proceedings of the Convention of the Delegates Held at the Capitol in the City of Williamsburg in the Colony of Virginia on Monday, the 6th of May, 1776* (Williamsburg, 1776) ; *Virginia Gazette* (Dixon & Hunter), Williamsburg, May 17, 1776
17. *Virginia Gazette* (Purdie), Williamsburg, May 17, 1776
18. *Pennsylvania Evening Post,* Philadelphia, September 28, 1776, quoting London, May 19, 1776
19. *London Packet,* May 20, 1776; *Kentish Gazette,* Canterbury, May 22, 1776
20. *London Chronicle,* May 14, 1776
21. *London Chronicle,* May 14, 1776; Curwen, S., *The Journal and Letters of*

Samuel Curwen, an American in England, from 1775 to 1783 (Boston, 1864

22. *Kentish Gazette,* Canterbury, May 18, 1776
23. *New York Journal,* May 23, 1776; *La Gazette de Quebec,* Quebec, September 5, 1776; *Annual Register 1776,* History, 151–53
24. *Journals of Congress,* week cited
25. *The Remembrancer, or Impartial Repository of Public Events for the Year 1776* (London, 1776–77), II, 234
26. *St. James's Chronicle,* London, May 23, 1776
27. *London Packet,* May 24, 1776
28. *Connecticut Courant,* Hartford, June 3, 1776
29. *Biographie Universelle, Ancienne et Moderne (Michaud)* (Paris, 1854; Graz, 1970)
30. *London Chronicle,* May 28, 1776
31. *St. James's Chronicle,* London, June 1, 1776
32. *Virginia Gazette* (Dixon & Hunter), Williamsburg, September 27, 1776, quoting London, May 21, 1776
33. *South Carolina and American General Gazette,* Charleston, August 2, 1776. (An account of the first week of June, 1776; the Gazette was not published during June and July.)
34. *Journals of Congress,* week cited
35. *Virginia Gazette* (Dixon & Hunter), Williamsburg, June 15 and 22, 1776
36. *London Chronicle,* May 28, 1776; *Virginia Gazette* (Dixon & Hunter), Williamsburg, August 31, 1776, quoting London, May 22 and 27, 1776
37. Letter of Washington dated May 31, 1776, in *American Archives,* 4, VI, 632; *Pennsylvania Packet,* Philadelphia, May 27, 1776
38. op. cit.; Brigham, C. S., *History and Bibliography of American Newspapers, 1690–1820* (American Antiquarian Society, Worcester, 1947)
39. [Anon.] *Rise and Progress, Present State and Natural Consequences of our American Disputes* (London, 1776)

June

1. *South Carolina and American General Gazette,* Charleston, August 2, 1776, quoting "the Sovereign Transport, off Charlestown," June 6, 1776. (The *Gazette* was not published during June and July.)
2. *Journals of Congress,* week cited
3. ibid.
4. *Journals of Congress,* week cited; Simes, T., *Military Guide for Young Officers* (Philadelphia, 1776—Reprinted from the British)
5. *New York Journal,* June 13, 1776
   June 4, 1776
6. *New York Packet,* June 13, 1776; *Connecticut Courant,* Hartford, June 17, 1776
7. *London Chronicle,* June 6, 1776; *Annual Register 1776,* Poetry, 203
8. *Pennsylvania Evening Post,* Philadelphia, October 8, 1776, quoting London, June 4, 1776
9. *Connecticut Courant,* Hartford, June 3, 1776, quoting London, March 5, 1776

10. *Virginia Gazette* (Dixon & Hunter), Williamsburg, October 11, 1776, quoting London, June 3, 1776

11. *Virginia Gazette* (Purdie), Williamsburg, June 7, 1776

12. *London Chronicle,* June 6, 1776

13. *Massachusetts Spy,* Worcester, February 2, 1776; *Virginia Gazette* (Purdie), Williamsburg, February 23, 1776; *Virginia Gazette* (Dixon & Hunter), Williamsburg, February 24, 1776; *Pennsylvania Packet,* Philadelphia, May 13, 1776; Thacher, J., *Military Journal,* 30

14. *Virginia Gazette* (Purdie), Williamsburg, June 21, 1776, quoting Philadelphia June 11, 1776

15. *Journals of Congress,* week cited; *Biographical Directory of the American Congress 1774–1971* (Washington, 1971)

16. *Journals of Congress,* week cited

17. ibid.

18. ibid.

19. *The Proceedings of the Convention of the Delegates Held at the Capitol in the City of Williamsburg in the Colony of Virginia on Monday, the 6th of May, 1776* (Williamsburg, 1776); *Virginia Gazette* (Dixon & Hunter), Williamsburg, June 14, 1776

20. op. cit.; *National Index of American Reprints* (American Antiquarian Society, Barre, 1969)

21. *Pennsylvania Gazette,* Philadelphia, July 3, 1776, quoting Boston, June 20, 1776

22. *Virginia Gazette* (Dixon & Hunter), Williamsburg, June 22, 1776

23. ibid.

24. *Pennsylvania Magazine,* Philadelphia, July, 1776

25. *Royal Danish American Gazette,* Christiansted, St. Croix, September 11, 1776, quoting London, June 15, 1776

26. *London Chronicle,* June 15, 1776; *Lottery Magazine,* London, July, 1776

27. *New York Journal,* June 13, 1776

28. *New England Chronicle,* Boston, June 13, 1776

29. *Pennsylvania Packet,* Philadelphia, June 24, 1776, quoting New York, June 17, 1776; *Virginia Gazette* (Purdie), Williamsburg, July 5, 1776

30. *American Archives,* 4, VI, 1143

31. *Journals of Congress,* week cited

32. *Minutes of the Provincial Congress and Council of Safety of the State of New Jersey* (Trenton, 1879)

33. ibid.

34. *New York Journal,* June 20, 1776

35. *Continental Journal,* Boston, November 21, 1776, quoting Hamburg, June 21, 1776

36. *Quarterly Musical Magazine,* London, 1818

37. *American Archives,* 4, VI, 1053–54; *South Carolina and American General Gazette,* Charleston, August 2, 1776, quoting New York, June 24, 1776

38. Transcript of Court-Martial, *American Archives,* 4, VI, 1084

39. *American Archives,* 4, VI, 1119, 1148

40. *Virginia Gazette* (Purdie), Williamsburg, July 12, 1776; *South Carolina and American General Gazette,* Charleston, August 2, 1776; *American Archives,*

5, I, 435; Simes, T., *Military Guide for Young Officers* (Philadelphia, 1776—Reprinted from the British)

41. ibid.
42. *New York Journal*, July 4, 1776
43. *Journals of Congress*, week cited
44. *Virginia Gazette* (Purdie), Williamsburg, July 12, 1776, quoting Philadelphia, June 26, 1776
45. *Pennsylvania Packet*, Philadelphia, July 1, 1776
46. *Journals of Congress*, week cited
47. *Virginia Gazette* (Purdie), Williamsburg, July 5, 1776, quoting Annapolis, June 27, 1776; *New York Journal*, July 11, 1776; Eddis, W., *Letters from America, Historical and Descriptive, Comprising Occurences from 1769 to 1777* (London, 1792). (William Eddis was Surveyor of Customs in Annapolis during that period.)
48. *American Archives*, 4, VI, 1099
49. *Virginia Gazette* (Purdie), Williamsburg, July 5, 1776
50. *Ordinances Passed at a General Convention of Delegates and Representatives, from the Several Counties and Corporations of Virginia, Held at the Capitol, in the City of Williamsburg, on Monday the 6th of May* [to the 5th of July], *Anno Dom: 1776* (Williamsburg, 1776), Chapter IX
51. *London Packet*, July 1 and 5, 1776
52. *Pennsylvania Magazine*, Philadelphia, June, 1776
53. op. cit. (Cambridge, 1776)

July

1. *Journals of Congress*, week cited; *Pennsylvania Evening Post*, Philadelphia, July 2, 1776; and for the text of the Declaration of Independence, nearly every newspaper in America
2. *Journals of Congress*, week cited
3. Thacher, J., *Military Journal*, 48
4. *Maryland Gazette*, Annapolis, July 4, 1776; *St. James's Chronicle*, London, July 4, 1776; *Gentleman's Magazine*, London, July, 1776; *Virginia Gazette* (Purdie), Williamsburg, August 2, 1776; *New York Gazette*, November 4, 1776, quoting Lisbon, July 5, 1776; *Continental Journal*, Boston, December 5, 1776, quoting London, July 4, 1776; *Annual Register 1776*, State Papers, 260
5. op. cit.
6. All 1776 editions, published late 1775: *Bickerstaff's New England Almanack*, Norwich; *Freebetter's New England Almanack*, New London; *Gaine's Universal Register*, New York; *George's Cambridge Almanack*, Salem; *Der Hoch Deutsch-Americanische Calender*, Germantown; *New York Pocket Almanack*, New York; *Poor Richard Improved*, Philadelphia; *Saunders' Pocket Almanack*, Philadelphia
7. *Pennsylvania Packet*, Philadelphia, July 8, 1776
8. *Annual Register 1776*, Chronicle, 218
9. *Virginia Gazette* (Purdie), Williamsburg, July 5, 1776
10. *New York Journal*, July 18, 1776

11. *La Gazette de Quebec,* Quebec, October 17, 1776, quoting London, July 1, 1776, in turn quoting letter from Paris

12. *St. James's Chronicle,* London, July 4 and 6, 1776

13. *New York Journal,* May 23, 1776; *Newport Mercury,* August 5, 1776

14. *Journals of Congress,* week cited

15. Thacher, J., *Military Journal,* 47

16. *St. James's Chronicle,* London, December 12, 1776; *American Archives,* 5, I, 801

17. *Journals of Congress,* week cited

18. *Journals of Congress,* week cited; *American Archives,* 4, VI, 1682

19. *Pennsylvania Evening Post,* Philadelphia, July 9, 1776

20. *New York Journal,* July 11, 1776; *New York Packet,* July 18, 1776

21. *New York Packet,* July 18, 1776

22. *Connecticut Courant,* Hartford, July 8, 1776; *Pennsylvania Magazine,* July, 1776

23. *Connecticut Courant,* Hartford, July 15, 1776; *Massachusetts Spy,* Worcester, December 4, 1776 (footnote)

24. Headley, J. T., *The Chaplains and Clergy of the Revolution* (Springfield, 1861)

25. *Virginia Gazette,* October 18, 1776, quoting London, July 11, 1776; Johnson, S., *Dictionary of the English Language* (London, 1755) (terminology)

26. *New York Gazette,* Newark, November 2, 1776, quoting London, July 11, 1776

27. *Pennsylvania Packet,* Philadelphia, July 29, 1776; *Journals of Congress,* week cited

28. *Journals of Congress,* week cited

29. ibid.

30. ibid.

31. Letter of Samuel Adams to Richard Henry Lee, dated Philadelphia, July 15, 1776, in *American Archives,* 5, I, 347

32. *Boston Gazette,* Watertown, July 22, 1776

33. *New York Journal,* July 18, 1776

34. *London Packet,* August 14, 1776, quoting Genoa, July 20, 1776

35. *Pennsylvania Evening Post,* Philadelphia, October 8, 1776, quoting London, July 20, 1776

36. *Lottery Magazine,* London, July, 1776

37. *Annual Register 1776,* Essays, 199, quoting *Westminster Magazine*

38. *Pennsylvania Gazette,* Philadelphia, July 24, 1776

39. *Newport Mercury,* July 29, 1776, quoting New York, July 22, 1776

40. *Journals of Congress,* week cited

41. *Connecticut Courant,* Hartford, July 29, 1776

42. *Virginia Gazette* (Purdie), Williamsburg, July 26, 1776

43. *Boston Gazette,* Watertown, July 22, 1776

44. *Virginia Gazette* (Purdie), Williamsburg, August 16, 1776, quoting Salem, July 23, 1776

45. *Providence Gazette,* July 27, 1776

46. *St. James's Chronicle,* London, July 25, 1776

47. op. cit. (pub. Charleston and Savannah)

48. *Virginia Gazette* (Dixon & Hunter), Williamsburg, August 31, 1776, quoting Philadelphia, August 20, 1776, in turn quoting St. Eustasius [Leeward Islands], July 28, 1776; *Continental Journal*, Boston, October 17, 1776, quoting the Journals of the Province of Over-Yessel, December 16, 1775

49. *New York Gazette*, November 18, 1776, quoting London, July 27, 1776

50. *Continental Journal*, Boston, October 10, 1776, quoting London, July 23, 1776

51. *Freebetter's New England Almanack 1776* (New London)

52. Dwight, T., *A Valedictory Address to the Young Gentlemen Who Commenced Bachelors of Arts at Yale College, July 25, 1776* (New Haven, 1776)

53. *Connecticut Journal*, New Haven, August 14, 1776, quoting Hanover, July 26, 1776

54. op. cit. (Philadelphia, 1776; reprinted from the British)

55. op. cit.

56. *Virginia Gazette* (Purdie), Williamsburg, August 16, 1776; *Virginia Gazette* (Dixon & Hunter), Williamsburg, September 14, 1776, quoting Charleston, August 2, 1776

57. *Journals of Congress*, week cited

58. ibid.

59. ibid.

60. *St. James's Chronicle*, London, August 3, 1776

61. *Boston Gazette*, Watertown, October 21, 1776, quoting London, July 29, 1776

62. *Lottery Magazine*, London, July, 1776

63. *St. James's Chronicle*, London, August 22, 1776, quoting Genoa, July 31, 1776

64. The newspapers published in the United States at the time of the Declaration of Independence, and the order in which they announced the news: July 2: Philadelphia *Pennsylvania Evening Post;* July 3: Philadelphia *Pennsylvania Gazette*, Philadelphia *Pennsylvania Journal;* July 5: Philadelphia *Pennsylvanischer Staatsbote;* July 6: New York *Constitutional Gazette;* July 8: Philadelphia *Pennsylvania Packet, New York Gazette and Weekly Mercury;* July 9: Baltimore *Dunlap's Maryland Gazette;* July 10: New Haven *Connecticut Journal*, Baltimore *Maryland Journal;* July 11: *New York Journal, New York Packet*, Boston *New England Chronicle*, Annapolis *Maryland Gazette;* July 12: New London *Connecticut Gazette*, Williamsburg *Virginia Gazette* (Purdie); July 13: Philadelphia *Pennsylvania Ledger, Providence Gazette*, Exeter *New Hampshire Gazette*, Portsmouth *Freeman's Journal;* July 15: *Norwich Packet*, Hartford *Connecticut Courant, Newport Mercury, Boston Gazette;* July 16: Salem *American Gazette;* July 17: Worcester *Massachusetts Spy;* July 18, Boston *Continental Journal;* July 19: Newburyport *Essex Journal;* July 20: Williamsburg *Virginia Gazette* (Dixon & Hunter); August 2: Charleston *South Carolina and American General Gazette.*

This list accounts for every newspaper published in the United States at the time except for the *Germantowner Zeitung*, of which no copies exist for the period following the Declaration of Indenpendence. In the case of the Annapolis *Maryland Gazette* there are no known copies of the July 11th issue, that cited here as announcing independence; but it is a virtual certainty that it did. The other two Maryland papers carried the news the preceding two days, and the Annapolis paper, judging by its other issues, was disposed to printing patriot news.

In observing the order in which newspapers announced independence, it should be kept in mind that most were published only once a week, and that the day of publication varied from paper to paper. There were no newspapers at all published in New Jersey, Delaware, North Carolina and Georgia at that time.

65. *South Carolina and American General Gazette,* Charleston, August 2, 1776
66. *Gentleman's Magazine,* London, July, 1776
67. op. cit. (Philadelphia, 1776)

August

1. *Kentish Gazette,* Canterbury, October 2, 1776
2. *Kentish Gazette,* Canterbury, August 28, 1776
3. *Continental Journal,* Boston, November 14, 1776 quoting London, August 10, 1776
4. *Journals of Congress,* week cited
5. *Pennsylvania Packet,* Philadelphia, September 17, 1776, quoting Charleston, August 5, 1776
6. *Pennsylvania Evening Post,* Philadelphia, October 8, 1776, quoting Savannah, August 10, 1776
7. *Newport Mercury,* August 19, 1776
8. *Continental Journal,* Boston, December 13, 1776, quoting Lisbon, August 7, 1776
9. *St. James's Chronicle,* London, August 10, 1776, quoting Pest, July 5, 1776
10. op. cit. (London, 1776)
11. *Pennsylvania Packet,* Philadelphia, August 5, 1776
12. *La Gazette de Quebec,* Quebec, dates cited
13. *Kentish Gazette,* Canterbury, October 10, 1776, quoting Canada, August 12, 1776; *Royal Danish American Gazette,* Christiansted, St. Croix, September 11, 1776, quoting London, June 15, 1776
14. *New York Journal,* August 29, 1776 (a dateline of Philadelphia, August 18, 1776, may or may not apply to this story) ; *Virginia Gazette* (Purdie), Williamsburg, September 6, 1776, quoting New York, August 14, 1776
15. *Journals of Congress,* week cited
16. *Pennsylvania Gazette,* Philadelphia, October 23, 1776, and November 6, 1776 quoting The Hague, August 9, 1776; *St. James's Chronicle,* London, October 31, 1776; *Maryland Journal,* Baltimore, November 27, 1776; Moses, B., *South America on the Eve of Emancipation* (New York, 1908)
17. *Kentish Gazette,* Canterbury, August 28, 1776

18. *Lottery Magazine,* London, August, 1776; *St. James's Chronicle,* London, September 7, 1776
19. op. cit. (Baltimore, 1776)
20. *Continental Journal,* Boston, September 12, 1776, quoting New York, August 26, 1776
21. *Journals of Congress,* week cited
22. *Pennsylvania Packet,* Philadelphia, July 29 and August 27, 1776
23. *Virginia Gazette* (Dixon & Hunter), Williamsburg, August 31, 1776, quoting Philadelphia, August 20, 1776
24. *St. James's Chronicle,* London, July 13, 1776, quoting Paris, July 4, 1776; *Kentish Gazette,* Canterbury, September 21, 1776, quoting Madrid, August 19, 1776
25. *Kentish Gazette,* Canterbury, August 21 and September 18, 1776
26. *Lottery Magazine,* London, August, 1776
27. *Journals of Congress,* week cited
28. *Pennsylvania Packet,* Philadelphia, September 3, 1776, quoting Williamsburg, August 24, 1776
29. newspapers cited; *Annual Register 1776,* History, 165
30. Cook, J., *Journal of the Resolution's Voyage, 1772–75* (Dublin, 1776)
31. *Annual Register 1776,* Essays, 190, quoting *London Review*
32. *Pennsylvania Packet,* Philadelphia, September 3, 1776; *Continental Journal,* Boston, September 5, and 12, 1776; *New Hampshire Gazette,* Exeter, September 7, 1776
33. *Pennsylvania Packet,* Philadelphia, September 3, 1776, quoting New York, August 31, 1776; *Continental Journal,* Boston, September 5 and October 3, 1776
34. *Continental Journal,* Boston, September 5, 1776, quoting New York, August 29, 1776
35. ibid.
36. *Pennsylvania Packet,* Philadelphia, September 3, 1776
37. *Journals of Congress,* week cited
38. ibid.
39. *New York Journal,* August 29, 1776
40. *New York Journal,* August 15, 1776
41. *Pennsylvania Evening Post,* Philadelphia, September 12, 1776
42. *St. James's Chronicle,* London, September 3, 1776, quoting Dublin, August 27, 1776
43. *St. James's Chronicle,* London, September 10, 1776, quoting Paris, August 30, 1776
44. *St. James's Chronicle,* London, August 31, 1776
45. ibid.
46. op. cit. (London, 1776)
47. *Lottery Magazine,* London, August, 1776

September

1. *Virginia Gazette* (Dixon & Hunter), Williamsburg, September 27, 1776, quoting New York, September 9, 1776

2. *Virginia Gazette* (Dixon & Hunter), Williamsburg, September 21, 1776, quoting Philadelphia, September 10, 1776

3. *Journals of Congress*, week cited; *The Writings of Thomas Jefferson* (Washington, 1903)

4. *Journals of Congress*, week cited

5. *Annual Register 1776*, Chronicle, 177; *St. James's Chronicle*, London, March 14, 1776

6. *Annual Register 1776*, Chronicle, 244

7. *St. James's Chronicle*, London, September 7, 1776

8. *Virginia Gazette* (Dixon & Hunter), Williamsburg, August 24, 1776; *Pennsylvania Evening Post*, Philadelphia, September 28, 1776

9. *Continental Journal*, Boston, October 3, 1776; Thacher, J., *Military Journal*, 58

10. *Connecticut Gazette*, New London, October 18, 1776, quoting Bergen, New Jersey, September 25, 1776

11. *Pennsylvania Packet*, Philadelphia, September 17, 1776

12. *Journals of Congress*, week cited

13. Proceedings of the Convention of the State of Delaware of September 11, 1776, in *American Archives*, 5, II, 286

14. *Kentish Gazette*, Canterbury, September 14, 1776

15. *London Packet*, September 13, 1776; *Pennsylvania Gazette*, Philadelphia, November 6, 1776

16. *Pennsylvania Gazette*, Philadelphia, September 25, 1776, quoting Boston, September 12, 1776

17. *Journals of Congress*, week cited

18. *Independent Chronicle*, Boston, October 17, 1776, quoting New York, September 19, 1776

19. *Journals of Congress*, week cited

20. *Pennsylvania Evening Post*, Philadelphia, September 21, 1776

21. *Journals of Congress*, week cited

22. *New York Gazette*, Newark, September 28, 1776; *New York Gazette*, New York, September 30, 1776; *St. James's Chronicle*, London, October 15, 1776, quoting Long Island, September 5, 1776 (regarding threats of fires); O'Beirne, T. L., *An Excellent Sermon Preached at St. Paul's Church, New York* (New York, 1776)

23. O'Beirne, ibid.

24. Dana, D. D., *The Fireman: The Fire Departments of the United States with a Full Account of All Large Fires* (Boston, 1858)

25. *Pennsylvania Packet*, Philadelphia, October 8, 1776

26. *St. James's Chronicle*, London, September 19, 1776

27. Thacher, J., *Military Journal*, 52

28. op. cit.

29. op. cit.

30. op. cit.; Lathem, E. C., *Chronological Tables of American Newspapers 1690–1820* (American Antiquarian Society, Barre, 1972)

31. *Independent Chronicle*, Boston, September 19, 1776

32. *Continental Journal*, Boston, October 3, 1776, quoting New York, September 26, 1776; *American Archives*, 5, II, 448 and 501

33. *Pennsylvania Evening Post,* Philadelphia, September 28, 1776
34. *Journals of Congress,* week cited
35. *Pennsylvania Gazette,* Philadelphia, October 16 and 23, 1776
36. Primarily *Dictionary of National Biography*
37. *Annual Register 1776,* Chronicle, 180
38. *St. James's Chronicle,* London, October 29, 1776, quoting Lisbon, September 24, 1776
39. *St. James's Chronicle,* London, October 26, 1776, quoting Madrid, September 25, 1776, and October 15, 1776, quoting Paris, October 4, 1776
40. *Annual Register 1776,* Chronicle, 181
41. op. cit. (Salem, 1776)
42. op. cit. (London, 1776)
43. *Continental Journal,* Boston, October 17, 1776, quoting Harlem, October 3, 1776
44. *Journals of Congress,* week cited
45. Thacher, J., *Military Journal,* 62
46. *New York Gazette,* New York, October 7, 1776
47. *London Packet,* November 11, 1776; *Annual Register 1776,* Chronicle, 180
48. *Continental Journal,* Boston, December 5, 1776, quoting Bilbao, October 6, 1776
49. *St. James's Chronicle,* London, November 23, 1776
50. op. cit. (Philadelphia, 1776; included with: Swieten, G. Van, *The Diseases Incident to Armies in the Field with the Method of Care)*

October

1. *New York Gazette* (Newark) November 2, 1776 quoting Philadelphia, October 23, 1776; *Boston Gazette* October 21, 1776, quoting Albany, October 14, 1776
2. *Boston Gazette,* October 28, 1776
3. *Journals of Congress,* week cited; *Gaine's Universal Register–1776* (New York)
4. *American Archives,* 5, II, 987, quoting letter of October 11, 1776
5. *Connecticut Journal,* New Haven, October 16, 1776; *Connecticut Courant,* October 14, 1776; *Connecticut: Her Constitutions* (Hartford, 1935)
6. *Pennsylvania Packet,* September 24, 1776 and October 8, 1776
7. *St. James's Chronicle,* London, November 2, 1776, quoting Stockholm, October 11, 1776
8. *Continental Journal,* Boston, December 19, 1776, quoting London, October 4, 1776
9. *Kentish Gazette,* Canterbury, November 13, 1776, quoting Naples, October 8, 1776
10. *St. James's Chronicle,* London, October 24, 1776; *Annual Register 1776,* Chronicle, 184
11. Court-martial transcript in *American Archives,* 5, II, 499; correspondence and general orders of General Washington in *American Archives,* 5, II, 447; *Journals of Congress,* week cited
12. *Pennsylvania Gazette,* Philadelphia, October 9, 1776; *Journals of Congress,* week cited

13. [Anon.], *The Discovery of America by Columbus* (London, 1776)
14. *Independent Chronicle,* Boston, October 31, 1776
15. *Journals of Congress,* week cited
16. *Kentish Gazette,* Canterbury, November 13, 1776, quoting Leghorn, October 18, 1776; Letter of Silas Deane to the Secret Committee of Congress, dated Paris, December 1, 1776, in *American Archives,* 5, III, 1019 (footnote)
17. *Pennsylvania Gazette,* Philadelphia, February 26, 1777, quoting Paris, October 14, 1776; *Pennsylvania Gazette,* March 12, 1777, quoting Lisbon, October 15, 1776
18. *St. James's Chronicle,* London, October 17, 1776
19. *Virginia Gazette* (Dixon & Hunter), Williamsburg, October 18, 1776, quoting London, July 16, 1776
20. *St. James's Chronicle,* London, October 19, 1776
21. *Annual Register 1776,* Chronicle, 185
22. *An Oration Delivered at the State House in Philadelphia* (London, 1776)
23. *Lottery Magazine,* London, October, 1776—letter signed only "A.B."
24. *Independent Chronicle,* Boston, October 31, 1776, quoting "Extract of a letter from East-Chester, October 23," 1776; *Connecticut Journal,* New Haven, November 6, 1776
25. *Independent Chronicle,* Boston, November 7, 1776
26. *Independent Chronicle,* Boston, October 24, 1776
27. *Connecticut Journal,* New Haven, November 6, 1776
28. *Journals of Congress,* week cited
29. *Independent Chronicle,* Boston, October 17 and 31, 1776
30. *Continental Journal,* Boston, October 31, 1776, quoting New Haven, October 23, 1776
31. *St. James's Chronicle,* London, October 31, 1776
32. *Pennsylvania Gazette,* Philadelphia, February 12, 1777, quoting London, October 23, 1776
33. *Annual Register 1776,* History, 185
34. *Lottery Magazine,* London, October, 1776
35. Goldsmith, O., *A Survey of Experimental Philosophy* (London, 1776), II, 160
36. *Connecticut Journal,* New Haven, November 6, 1776
37. *Journals of Congress,* week cited
38. ibid.
39. *Continental Journal,* Boston, December 13, 1776, quoting Williamsburg, November 1, 1776
40. *Pennsylvania Gazette,* Philadelphia, October 30, 1776; *Journal of the House of Delegates of Virginia, Anno Domini 1776* (Williamsburg, 1776)
41. *Kentish Gazette,* Canterbury, October 30, 1776
42. *London Packet,* November 1, 1776
43. *St. James's Chronicle,* London, October 31, 1776; Proceedings of Parliament in *American Archives,* 5, III, 961
44. *St. James's Chronicle,* London, November 2, 1776; Proceedings of Parliament in *American Archives,* 5, III, 962
45. *Pennsylvania Gazette,* Philadelphia, October 30, 1776

November

1. *Connecticut Journal,* New Haven, November 13, 1776
2. *Journals of Congress,* week cited
3. *New York Gazette,* November 4, 1776
4. *American Archives,* 5, III, 627
5. Proceedings of Parliament in *American Archives,* 5, III, 987
6. *London Packet,* November 8, 1776
7. ibid.
8. ibid.
9. *Annual Register 1776,* Chronicle, 190; Treloar, W. P., *Wilkes and the City* (London, 1917), 182
10. *Kentish Gazette,* Canterbury, October 30, 1776
11. *St. James's Chronicle,* London, November 5, 1776; *A Form of Prayer Issued by Special Command of his Majesty George III* (London, 1776)
12. Proceedings of Parliament in *American Archives,* 5, III, 1013
13. *Pennsylvania Gazette,* Philadelphia, April 9, 1777, quoting Vienna, November 10, 1776
14. *Quarterly Musical Magazine,* London, 1818
15. *Boston Gazette,* November 4, 1776
16. *Connecticut Journal,* New Haven, December 11 and 18, 1776
17. *Journals of Congress,* week cited
18. ibid.
19. *Continental Journal,* Boston, December 19, 1776, quoting New York, November 18, 1776
20. *Boston Gazette,* November 11, 1776
21. *London Packet,* November 11 and 18, 1776; *Whitehall Evening Post,* London, November 16, 1776; *Boston Gazette,* January 27, 1777; *Annual Register 1777,* History, 48; *Parliamentary Register* (London, 1776–77) VI; *Cobbett's Parliamentary History of England* (London, 1813) XVIII; *American Archives,* 5, III, 1016
22. *Kentish Gazette,* Canterbury, November 20, 1776, quoting Leeds, November 12, 1776
23. *London Chronicle,* November 14, 1776
24. *Massachusetts Spy,* Worcester, December 4, 1776
25. *Journals of Congress,* week cited; *St. James's Chronicle,* London. November 5, 1776
26. *Journals of Congress,* week cited
27. *Pennsylvania Gazette,* Philadelphia, November 20 and 27, 1776; *Maryland Journal,* Baltimore, November 27, 1776
28. *St. James's Chronicle,* London, November 19, 1776; *Whitehall Evening Post,* London, November 19, 1776; *Annual Register 1776,* Chronicle, 192; *Encyclopedia Brittanica* (1st ed., Edinburgh, 1771)
29. *Kentish Gazette,* Canterbury, November 23, 1776
30. *St. James's Chronicle,* London, November 21, 1776
31. *London Packet,* November 22, 1776
32. *Annual Register 1776,* Chronicle, 192
33. *St. James's Chronicle,* London, November 21, 1776

34. *London Packet,* November 20, 1776; *St. James's Chronicle,* London, November 21, 1776
35. *Boston Gazette,* December 16, 1776
36. *Continental Journal,* Boston, December 19, 1776, quoting New York, November 30, 1776
37. *Journals of Congress,* week cited
38. *Continental Journal,* Boston, December 5, 1776
39. *Boston Gazette,* December 2, 1776, quoting Newport, November 25, 1776
40. *Pennsylvania Gazette,* Philadelphia, April 9, 1777, quoting London, November 30, 1776, in turn quoting Paris, September 21, 1776
41. *Pennsylvania Gazette,* Philadelphia, April 9, 1777, quoting London, November 30, 1776
42. *Annual Register 1776,* Chronicle, 193
43. *St. James's Chronicle,* London, December 19, 1776, quoting Vienna, November 27, 1776
44. *Annual Register 1776,* Chronicle, 193

December

1. *Providence, Gazette,* December 14, 1776; *Continental Journal,* Boston, December 19, 1776
2. Broadside of the Council of Safety, Philadelphia, dated December 2, 1776
3. *Kentish Gazette,* Canterbury, December 28, 1776
4. *Journals of Congress,* week cited
5. ibid.
6. *Continental Journal,* Boston, December 5, 1776
7. *Massachusetts Spy,* Worcester, December 19, 1776
8. *Continental Journal,* Boston, December 26, 1776 quoting Norwich, December 2, 1776
9. *Kentish Gazette,* Canterbury, December 28, 1776, quoting France, December 6, 1776
10. *St. James's Chronicle,* London, January 28, 1777; *Annual Register 1776,* Chronicle, 198; *Annual Register 1777,* History, 30
11. *St. James's Chronicle,* London, December 3, 1776
12. *London Packet,* December 4, 1776
13. op. cit. and Lathem, E. C., *Chronological Tables of American Newspapers (1690–1820)* (American Antiquarian Society, Barre, 1972)
14. Voorhees, O. M., *The History of Phi Beta Kappa* (New York, 1945)
15. McRobert, P., *A Tour through Part of the North Provinces of America* (Edinburgh, 1776)
16. *Connecticut Journal,* New Haven, December 25, 1776; Thacher, J., *Military Journal,* 67
17. *Pennsylvania Packet,* Philadelphia, December 18, 1776,
18. ibid.
19. *Boston Gazette,* December 30, 1776; Thacher, J., *Military Journal,* 66
20. *Boston Gazette,* January 6, 1777; *Journals of Congress,* week cited
21. *Journals of Congress,* week cited
22. *London Packet,* December 16, 1776; *Pennsylvania Gazette,* Philadelphia,

April 2, 1777, quoting London, December 13, 1776; Her Majesty's Stationery Office, *Chronological Table of the Statutes* (London, 1970)

23. *Kentish Gazette,* Canterbury, December 18, 1776
24. *Pennsylvania Gazette,* Philadelphia, April 2, 1777, quoting Portsmouth, England, December 11, 1776
25. *Annual Register 1776,* Chronicle, 200
26. *Annual Register 1776,* Chronicle, 203
27. *Annual Register 1776,* Chronicle, 230
28. *St. James's Chronicle,* London, December 21, 1776
29. *St. James's Chronicle,* London, December 14, 1776
30. *Pennsylvania Packet,* Philadelphia, December 18, 1776
31. *Continental Journal,* Boston, January 9, 1777, quoting Bucks County, Pennsylvania, December 19, 1776—"Extract from a letter from an officer in the American Army"
32. *Journals of Congress,* week cited; Burnett, E. C., *The Continental Congress* (New York, 1964)
33. *Constitutions of the United States* (Philadelphia, 1791)
34. *Continental Journal,* Boston, December 19, 1776
35. *Annual Register 1776,* Chronicle, 202
36. *St. James's Chronicle,* London, December 28, 1776, quoting Paris, December 19, 1776
37. *St. James's Chronicle,* London, December 31, 1776, quoting Paris, December 16, 1776
38. *St. James's Chronicle,* London, December 21, 1776
39. ibid.
40. *St. James's Chronicle,* London, December 19, 1776
41. *Annual Register 1776,* Chronicle, 196
42. *Whitehall Evening Post,* London, June 10, 1775 and December 7 and 19, 1776; *Annual Register 1776,* Chronicle, 197 and 201
43. *Virginia Gazette* (Purdie), Williamsburg, December 20, 1776
44. *Pennsylvania Packet,* Philadelphia, December 27, 1776
45. *Boston Gazette,* December 30, 1776
46. *Journals of Congress,* week cited
47. ibid.
48. ibid.
49. *Annual Register 1776,* Chronicle, 202
50. *Kentish Gazette,* Canterbury, December 28, 1776
51. *St. James's Chronicle,* London, December 26, 1776
52. *London Chronicle, London Packet* and *St. James's Chronicle,* London, selected dates throughout 1776; *Encyclopedia Britannica* (1st ed., Edinburgh, 1771); Ashton, T. S., *An Economic History of England* (London, 1955)
53. *La Gazette de Quebec,* Quebec, December 26, 1776
54. *London Packet,* May 13, 1776; *Annual Register 1776,* Chronicle, 146, 191, History, 185–189
55. *Boston Gazette,* December 30, 1776 (introductory quotation) and January 20, 1777, quoting Baltimore, December 31, 1776

INDEX

Acteon, British man-of-war, 180

Active, British man-of-war, 180, 331, 364

Adams, John, 152, 166, 310; new term in Congress, 49; *Thoughts on Government*, 127–28; named to committee to draw up Declaration of Independence, 164; named to Board of War, 165; named to committee on treaties, 165; as representative to peace talks, 264, 267, 270, 335, 337

Adams, Samuel, 166, 211, 215, 310; new term in Congress, 49; on committee on Articles of Confederation, 165; purported speech of, 307; on internal security committee, 316

Admiralty, British, 154, 234, 343

Africa, 304, 311–12

Air: pollution in London, 230–31; effects of on human body, 62–63

Aitken, James ("John the Painter"), 348

Aitken, R., 281

Albany, 208; British strategy regarding, 239

Alberti, Domenico, 313

Alexander, William. *See* Stirling, Lord

Algiers, 91

Allen, Captain, 160

Allen, Col. Ethan, imprisonment in Ireland, 38–39, 101

Alsop, John, 55

Altonaischer Mercurius, Hamburg, 251*n*

American Turtle, submarine, 287–88

Amherst, Lord, 161

Amsterdam, 269

Amusements, 218–19, 223

Annapolis, 197, 336

Annual Register (London), 91, 251*n;* re-

view of *Wealth of Nations*, 86–87

Answer to the Declaration of the American Congress, An, 334

Apollo, British frigate, 269

Arch Street Presbyterian Church, Philadelphia, 99

Armenians, 373

Armies, of Europe, 247, 276–77

Army, British: budget, 35, 49, 110, 123, 332–33; troop treaty with Germany, 33, 56–57, 223; in Ireland, 35, 259; North American campaign, 49; recruitment of slaves, 56, 94; in New York, 60, 201–2, 239, 240, 295–96; in Virginia, 65; weapons, 65, 161, 180–81, 341; in Boston, 27–28, 72–73, 80, 82–83, 108; resistance, 85–86; battle of The Cedars, 206–7; land grants, 220; in New York, 223, 234, 240, 245–46, 262, 266–67; 285, 288, 303, 308–10; in Canada, 147–48, 239; battle of Long Island, 254–56, 266; prisoners of war, 264, 280; New York fire, 274–76; captures Nathan Hale, 279; pay, 296*n*; at Gibraltar, 304; evacuation of Boston, 87–89; public subscription, 111, 129–30; military strategy, 112–13, 129, 201–2, 239–40, 245, 246; tory enlistment, 122–23; supplies and provisions, 139–40, 147–48, 344; in South Carolina, 152, 180–81; uniforms, 161; battle of Sullivan's Island, 180–81, 219, 234, 256–57, 326; battle of White Plains, 313, 315; deserters, 326; fall of New York, 329–30; troop strength, 321, 332–33; fall of Fort Lee, 334–35; impressment, 337–38; capture of Newport, 343–44; New

Jersey advance, 352; plundering, 352; capture of Gen. Lee, 354–55; in Trenton, 361, 375–76

Army, Continental: bonuses, 34, 39, 271; enlistment, 23, 182, 331, 369, 370; pay, 44, 89, 159, 196, 296, 362; furloughs, 33; weapons, 161, 286–88; recruiting, 48, 49, 83, 271, 335, 340; provisions and supplies, 34, 54, 122, 281, 340; rules and regulations, 178, 272; sickness, 28, 137–38, 148, 226, 277; troop transports, 34; action in Canada, 34, 39, 60–61, 122, 147–48, 226, 239, 272, 293, 295; field hospitals, 62, 286; fortifications at Dorchester Heights, 80, 82; regains Boston, 87–89; ordered to New York, 107, 114; prisoners of war, 148–49, 262–63, 264, 280, 346; preparations in New York, 173, 239–40, 246; uniforms, 174, 271, 296; plot against Washington, 177–78; battle of Sullivan's Island, 180–81, 219, 234; officer vacancies, 182; bounties, 182, 271, 315–16, 323–24, 331, 345; surrender at The Cedars, 206–7; chaplains, 211–12; exemptions, 208, 216, 241, 258, 340; British defectors, 219–20; battle of Long Island, 254–56, 262–63, 266; retreat from New York, 266–67, 285; pensions, 257; commissions, 271, 370; land grants, 271; Indian raids, 316–17; from New York to Westchester, 295–96, 303, 308–9; courts-martial, 298–300; battle of White Plains, 313, 315; fall of Fort Washington, 329–30; fall of Fort Lee, 334, 335; retreat to Pennsylvania, 351–52; battle of Trenton, 361, 375–76; morale, 361

Army, French, 247, 277; pardons, 27

Arnold, Benedict, 147, 208, 272; action at Lake Champlain, 293, 295, 295n

Art, 145–46, 306

Articles of Association, 108, 128

Articles of Confederation, 207–8, 220, 226, 234, 246

Articles of War, 272, 299; translation into French, 44

d'Artois, Comte, 216

Askew, Thomas, 227

Athletics, 62, 212, 212n

Atlee, Colonel, 254–55

Austria-Hungary, 236, 277, 281n, 341–42, 370, 373

Bache, Richard, 322–23

Baldwin, Henry, 366

Baltimore, 336, 357–58, 362

Banda Oriental, 241, 243, 305

Bank of England, 371, 372n

Baptists, 99, 245, 249

Barbary pirates, 91, 304, 373

Barber, Esther, 36

Barré, Col. Isaac, 70, 85, 95, 135–36; debate on official secrecy, 150

Barrington, Daines, 133

Barrington, William (2nd Viscount), 332

Barry, Lt. Colonel, 255

Bartlett, Josiah, 74, 165

Basking Ridge, 354–55; 368

Bath, Order of the, 202, 305

Beacon Hill, 65

Beaumarchais, Pierre Augustin Caron de, 311n

Bedel, Colonel, 207, 207n

Bell, Robert, 45; publication of Common Sense, 37–38, 49–50; publication of Plain Truth, 92

Bickerstaff's New England Almanack, 201

Bilbao, 289

Bill of Rights (1689), 167–68

Birmingham, 341

Bissel, Joseph, 227

Blackstone, Sir William, 32

Blackwell's Island, 262

Blais, Monsieur, 260–61

Blockade of Boston, a farce, 54

Board of War, American, 165, 267–68, 271, 330

Bohemia, Kingdom of, 373

Bomb, in use at Sullivan's Island, 180–81; definition of, 181n

Book of Common Prayer, 204–5, 327

Books, 45, 102–3, 127–28, 152, 155–56, 172, 251–52, 254, 278, 284–85, 300–301, 307, 349; Decline and Fall of the Roman Empire, 63–64, 97–98; Wealth of Nations, 86–87 (see also Common Sense)

Bordentown, 351

Boston, 220; British evacuation of, 87–89; defense of, 134; reopening of port, 169–70; smallpox epidemic, 210–11, 211n; hardship, 23; rumors of British evacuation, 82–83; siege of, 23, 26, 27–28, 72–73; celebration of Declaration of Independence, 215–16

Boston Gazette, 92, 155, 329, 331, 368

Boston News-Letter, 155

Botetourt, Lord, 55

Bounties, British army, 32; Continental army, 39, 182, 271, 315–16, 323–24, 345

Boxing, 212
Braddock, Gen. Edward, 353
Bradford, William and Thomas, 50, 321
Braeley, Miss Mary, 331
Braidwood, Thomas, 111–12
Braxton, Carter, 66, 143
Brazil, Viceroyalty of, 241, 243
Brest, 247
Bristol, British man-of-war, 180–81, 234
British empire, 123, 321
Bronx River, 313
Brooklyn, 202, 255
Brown, William, 238–39
Brunswick and Lunenburg, duke of, 56–57, 84–85
Brunswick, Germany, troop treaty, 33, 56–57, 84–85, 332
Buchan, Dr. W., 244–45
Buckner, John, 76
Bucks County, 361
Buenos Aires, 241, 243
Bull, Colonel, 54
Bunker Hill, 70, 211, 346; British garrison at, 88
Burgoyne, Major Gen. John, 70, 95; promotion of, 100; sails to Canada, 112; warned about treatment of prisoners, 207; military strategy, 239; returns to England, 359
Burke, Edmund, 95, 150, 305; debate on peace terms, 325–26; on day of prayer, 327–28; affiliation with *Annual Register*, 91*n*
Burlington, 174, 202, 351
Bushnell, David, 286–88
Bushy Park, 283
Butler, Rev. Dr. John, 359
Butterfield, Major, 207, 207*n*

Cadiz, 247
Cadwalader, Lt. Col. Lambert, 330
Calais, 341
Calvert, Caroline, 183
Cambridge, 163, 187; Continental army encampment, 21, 28, 34, 54, 62, 65
Camden, Lord, 101; views on retribution, 100–101
Cameron, Allan, 153
Campbell, Lord William, 99
Canada, war in, 34, 39, 60–61, 122, 239; American diplomatic mission to, 61, 93
Canterbury, 62
Canterbury, archbishop of, 36, 76, 125, 145
Cape of Good Hope, 130, 312

Capitol, in Williamsburg, first use of term in America, 185*n*
Carleton, Gen. Guy, promotion of, 100; in Canada, 147–48, 239, 293–95; knight of the Bath, 202
Carlos III, king of Spain, 243
Carnes, Thomas, 258
Carpenters, of London, threaten to strike, 185–86
Carroll, Charles, 61, 93, 208
Castel Sant' Angelo, 363
Castle William, 82, 216
Caswell, Col. Richard, 74
Catalogus . . . Harvardino, 187
Catherine II (The Great), empress of Russia, 41, 57, 139, 145, 298
Catholicism, 61, 228, 373; Holy Year of Jubilee, 45–46
Cato, pseudonym. *See* Smith, Rev. William
Cavendish, Lord, 325–26
Cedars, The, 206–7
Cevallos, Lt. Gen. Don Pedro de, 243
Champlain, Lake, 112, 148, 196, 272, 293, 295, 370
Chance, American ship, 160
Charades, 218–19
Charcas, 243
Charles River, 23
Charleston, 152, 157, 180, 225; celebrates independence, 235
Charlestown, 257–58
Charlotte, queen of England, 125, 144–45, 160, 265, 337, 348–49, 370
Chase, Samuel, 61
Chatham, earl of. *See* Pitt, William
Chatham, England, 61–62
Chatterton's Hill, 313
Cherbourg, 359
Cherokee Indians. *See* Indians, Cherokee
Cheshire, 341, 353
Christian, Col. William, 317
Church of England, 75–76, 130, 204–5, 275–76, 327, 360
Churches: destruction in Boston, 88; closed in New York, 256, 275; destruction in New York, 274–75
Clark, Abraham, 175
Clark, Rev. Jonas, 118
Clayton, John, 333
Clinton, Major Gen. Sir Henry, 60, 65; promotion, 100; sails to America, 112; attack on South Carolina, 157–58, 180, 181, 234; war in New York, 254–55, 266; capture of Newport, 344

Clugny, J. E. B., 137, 154, 311

Clymer, George, 214, 281, 362

Coffee, medicinal use of, 46–47

Colden, Cadwallader, 282–83

Columbus, Christopher, 301

Committees of Safety, Massachusetts, 121; Virginia, 121; New York, 115–16; Pennsylvania, 135

Common Sense, publication of, 37–38, 117*n;* second edition announced, 49; controversy over, 50–51, 116; authorship of, 45, 49–50, 152; success, 92, 116-17; rebuttal, 115–17, 162; effect in South Carolina, 93–94

Concerts of Ancient Music, 329

Congress, American ship, 160, 295

Congress, Continental. *See* Continental Congress

Congreve, William, 338–39

Connecticut, 220, 370; as place of exile for Gov. Franklin, 182, 210; General Assembly, 297; reaffirms royal charter, 297; delegates to Continental Congress, 310

Connecticut Courant, 210, 228

Connolly, John, 153

Constitutional Gazette (New York), 229

Constitutional Society, 365–67

Constitution, Fort. *See* Lee, Fort

Constitutions, 141–42, 363*n;* New Hampshire, 29–30; South Carolina, 99–100; Virginia, 141, 142–43, 184–85; New Jersey, 202–3; Delaware, 268, 276; Pennsylvania, 281–82, 297; Maryland, 336; North Carolina, 362–63; Connecticut, 297; Rhode Island, 221; Georgia, 363*n;* New York, 363*n;* Massachusetts, 363*n;* Vermont, 363*n;* summary of constitutional development, 363*n*

Continental Army. *See* Army, Continental

Continental Congress: action against Queens County tories, 28–29, 39, 49; currency emissions, 29, 61, 66, 135, 148, 241; declaration against currency depreciation, 34; provisions for war, 34, 122, 174, 281, 335, 340, 345; appropriations, 34, 39, 54, 61, 286; franking privilege, 34; orders additional troops, 34, 39, 60, 89, 98, 159, 196, 271, 316, 317, 345, 370; Indian relations, 43–44, 83, 113, 166, 196, 272, 331, 344–45; army recruitment of minors, 48; supplementary note on, 51–52; cost of being a delegate, 55; sets day of prayer, 89; Canadian relations, 60–61, 93, 208, 226; attends funeral of Samuel Ward, 99;

trade restrictions, 108–9, 128–29, 152–53, 346; opening of ports, 108; honors Gen. Washington, 109; aid to Dartmouth College, 114, 272; asks arrest of Gov. Eden, 117–18, 129; formation of new colonial governments, 141–42; prisoner of war policy, 148–49, 206, 207, 214, 234, 264; debate on independence, 158–59, 163–64, 191–92; committee to draw up Declaration of Independence, 164–65, 191–93; committee to explore new form of government, 165; committee to study foreign relations, 165; establishes board of war and ordnance, 165; threat of invasion in New York, 173; civil law, 173–74; orders confinement of Gov. Franklin, 181–82; army bounties, 182, 271, 331, 345, 369; Declaration of Independence, 192, 193–96, 225, 226; reaction to surrender at The Cedars, 206–7; Articles of Confederation, 207–8, 220, 234, 246; postal service, 208, 257, 322–23; chaplain to Congress, 208, 304, 316; chaplains for army, 211–12; British peace proposals, 213–14, 263–64, 267, 269–71, 355; salaries, 214; rules of order, 215; censures Esek Hopkins, 234, 240–41; military exemptions, 208, 216, 241; requirement for allegiance, 248–49, 310; military pensions, 257; term "United States" officially used, 268; Articles of War, 272; appoints commissioners to France, 280–81; public transportation, 286, 323; increases army pay, 296; army clothing, 271, 296; naval commissions, 296; loan to Gen. Lee, 296; court-martial of Matthew Macumber, 298–300; *Journals of*, 281, 300–301; military intelligence, 303; voting, 310; Maryland bounty dispute, 315–16, 323–24; orders imprisonment of Timothy Dodd, 316; internal security committee appointed, 316; marine ranks determined, 316; lottery, 316, 335, 340, 345; defense of Philadelphia, 330, 339–40, 345, 357–58; grievance committee appointed, 335; address to inhabitants of America, 355–57; moves to Baltimore, 357–58, 362; grants Gen. Washington interim powers, 358, 368–69; army pay, 362; executive business committee, 370; observation of Christmas, 370; battle of Trenton, 375–76

Continental Journal and Weekly Advertiser (Boston), 363

Continental Navy. *See* Navy, Continental

Conway, Gen. H. S., 149–50
Cook, James, report on voyage around the world, 101–2, 251, 342
Cooper, John, 67
Copley Medal, 63, 342
Coquataginta. *See* White Eyes, Capt.
Corelli, Arcangelo, 313
Corell's Ferry, 361
Cork, Ireland, 39, 112
Cornwall, 341
Cornwallis, Major Gen., Lord, 36; promotion, 100; sails to America, 112; battle of Sullivan's Island, 181; battle of Long Island, 254–55; fall of Fort Lee, 334–35
Cornwallis, Lt. Gen. Edward, dies, 36
Cornwallis, Dr. Frederick, archbishop of Canterbury, 36
Counterfeit money. *See* Currency, Continental, counterfeit
Courts-martial, 272, 298–300
Covent-Garden, theater, 59, 91–92, 305–6
Cricket, 62
Crime, 86, 115, 159, 227–28, 236, 264, 300n, 308, 311–12, 346, 348
Croatia, 119
Crops, garden and agricultural, 84, 246
Crown Point, 293, 295
Culpeper, Lord, 77
Currency, British, 79, 208n
Currency, Continental: supplementary note on, 78–79; emissions of, 29, 61, 66, 135, 148, 241; depreciation of, 34, denominations of, 66, 208n; signing of, 83–84; value relative to gold and silver coin, 84; counterfeit, 119, 151, 346
Customs, 58, 110, 244–45, 251, 350; development of the water closet, 71–72; latest Paris fashions, 244; last night of summer at Vauxhall Gardens, 259–60

Daily Advertiser (London), 250
Dana, Francis, 346
Dartmouth College, 114, 224, 272
Dartmouth, earl of, 90
Davis, Dr., 255
Deafness, 111–12
Deane, Silas, 280, 304n, 340–41
Declaration of Independence. *See* Independence, American
Decline and Fall of the Roman Empire, The. See Gibbon, Edward
Defoe, Daniel, 278
DeHart, John, 67
De Laponne, Monsieur, 260–61

Delaware, adopts constitution, 268, 276
Delaware Indians. *See* Indians, Delaware
Delaware River, 345, 351, 361
Denmark, 277, 304
Desaguliers, Major Gen. Thomas, 161
Diario de Madrid, 251n
Dickinson, John, 165, 214, 214n
Dionaea muscipula, 186–87
Discovery of America by Columbus, The, 301
Dixon, John. *See* Dixon and Hunter
Dixon and Hunter, 76–77
Dodd, Timothy, 316
Dollar, Continental. *See* Currency, Continental
D'Olone, Duchess, 360
Domestic Medicine, 244–45
Dorchester Heights, 80, 82
Dorchester Neck, 216
Douglas, Colonel, 315
Douglas, Rev. William, 121
Dover, 341
Drummond, Dr. Robert Hay, 360
Drury-Lane, theater, 42, 59, 122, 171, 338–39; retirement of David Garrick, 171–72
Duane, James, 61
Dublin, 26, 152, 269
Duché, Rev. Jacob, 208, 211, 304, 316
Dunlap, John, 238, 321
Dunmore, Lord, governor of Virginia, 143; orders destruction of Norfolk, 27; correspondence of with British, 40, 215; declaration of martial law (1775), 55–56; effects of freeing slaves for recruitment purposes, 56, 94; publishes newspaper, 76–77, 100; views on retribution, 100–101; at Gwynn's Island, 210; at Staten Island, 246–47; Indian raids (1774), 317; returns to Britain, 331, 364
Duquesne, Fort, 353
Duyckink, Christopher, 115–16
Dwight, Timothy, 223–24

Eagle, British flagship, 213, 287–88, 337
Earthquake, 341
Eastchester, 308–9
East India Company, British, 370
East India Company, Dutch, 371
East River, 255, 266, 288, 310
Eclipses, 32, 223
Eden, Robert, governor of Maryland, 117–18, 129, 183–84, 215
Edes, Benjamin, 329
Edinburgh, 111, 247

Education, 111–12, 113, 114, 187, 197, 223–24, 231–32, 265–66, 350n, 373
Electricity, 236–37
Elizabeth, N. J., 235
Ellery, William, 135
Ellis, John, 186–87
Elmer, Ebenezer, 58
England. *See* Great Britain
Episcopal Church. *See* Church of England
Epistle of Jesus, 284
Exchange, London stock. *See* Stock market, London
Exeter, 30
Experiment, British man-of-war, 180, 181
Exploration, 96, 101–2, 130, 132–33; Columbus, 301

Falconer, William, 256–57
Faneuil Hall, 88
Fashion, 59, 170, 244
Faucitt, Sir William, 56
Fee taille, abolished in Virginia, 316–17
Ferguson, Capt. Patrick, 161
Fire: prevention, 265, 336–37; of New York, 274–76; in Boston (1760), 276; scientific discussion of, 237–38; great fire of London, 264–65
Firemen, 216, 275
Fisk, Capt. John, 221
Flag: Continental, of thirteen stripes (also known as Grand Union Flag; Continental Colors), 26, 144; British ensign, 26; pine-tree, 47, 48; "In Union There's Strength," 55; rattlesnake, 221; "Don't Tread on Me," 221; of truce, 262–63
Flatbush, 254
Flintlock. *See* Musket
Florida, East and West, 170, 289
Flying camp, 215, 241; defined, 159n
Folkstone, 341
Forbes, Gilbert, 177–78
Foreign relations, American, 130, 165, 176, 280–81, 281n; with Portugal, 197, 200; with Holland, 222; with France, 280, 311, 340–41, 348, 364; with Spain, 281n, 311; with Austria-Hungary, 281n; with Tuscany, 281 n; with Prussia, 281n
Forrester, The, pseudonym, 117 (*see also* Paine, Thomas)
Fort Hill, 216
Fowey, British man-of-war, 331, 364
Fowle, Daniel, 43
Fox, Charles James: debate on enquiry into war, 67, 70–71; homage to Gen. Mont-gomery, 95; debate on official secrecy, 150; debate on war, 320
France: pardon for Army deserters, 26–27; price controls, 36; possible war with Britain, 90; economy, 125–26, 137, 203, 311, 373; possible intervention in American war, 154, 311; aid to America, 154, 311, 340–41, 348, 364; relations with Spain, 243, 247, 305; relations with Portugal, 243, 305; relations with Great Britain, 243, 305, 326, 341, 370–71; military build-up, 247, 283; tribute to Barbary pirates, 304; earthquake, 341; relations with Austria-Hungary, 370; navy, 370 (*see also* Army, French)
Francis I, Holy Roman emperor, 341–42
Franklin, American schooner, 139–40
Franklin, Benjamin, 63, 210, 281; delegation to Canada, 61, 93, 208; on committee to draw up Declaration of Independence, 164; reelected to Congress from Pennsylvania, 214; experiments with electricity, 237; as representative to peace talks, 264, 267, 270, 335; commissioner to France, 280–81, 348, 364; as printer, 321; as postmaster general, 322–23; as recipient of Copley Medal, 342
Franklin, Franky, 120
Franklin, William, 184, 215; declared enemy, 174–75; ordered confined, 182; in custody in Wallingford, 210
Frederick II (The Great), king of Prussia, 176
Freebetter's New England Alamanack, 44–45, 201
Freeman's Journal (Dublin), 251n
Freemasonry, 298
French Academy, 252, 349
French Broad River, 317
Friendship, British warship, 181
Frogs Neck. *See* Throgs Neck
Fund for the Support of Decayed Musicians and their Families, 176

Gadsden, Col. Christopher, 93
Gage, Gen. Thomas, 52, 65, 368
Gaine, Hugh, 126, 278, 288
Gaine's Universal Register, 201
Garrick, David: production of *Blackamoor Whitewashed*, 59; retirement of, 171–72; as Hamlet, 305–6
Garter, Order of the, 305
Gates, Gen. Horatio, 33; in New York, 114
Gazette de Quebec, La, 238–39, 372

Gazette D'Utrecht, 251n

Gentleman's Magazine (London), 230

George II, king of England, 45, 92, 259

George III, king of England, 26, 100, 125, 133, 145, 259, 265, 288, 306, 310, 336, 337, 370; address to Parliament, 150–51, 318–19; celebrates birthday, 160; grievances against, 141, 193–95, 235; statue of, in New York, 209; keeps military notebook, 298; orders day of prayer, 327, 358–59; conference with Gov. Dunmore, 364; as Elector of Hanover, 370

George's Cambridge Almanack, 201

Georgia, delegates to Continental Congress, 170

Germaine, Lord George, 52n, 359; opinions on military strategy, 40, 75, 140; supplementary note on, 51; correspondence with Gov. Eden, 117–18, 129, 183, 215; debate on war, 321

German mercenaries, *See* Hessian soldiers; Hesse-Cassel; Brunswick

German states (Germany), 277, 370

Gerry, Elbridge, 61, 165n, 196, 370

Gibbon, Edward: publication of *Decline and Fall of the Roman Empire*, 63–64; review of, 97–98

Gibraltar, 243, 304, 332

Gilbert, Archbishop, 360

Gill, John, 155

Girdwood, Archibald, 227–28

Goldsmith, Oliver: as classicist of the Royal Academy, 64; posthumous publication of *Survey of Experimental Philosophy*, 236–38; on music, 260, 312–13

Goodman's Fields, theater, 171

Grafton, duke of, 89–91

Granby, marquis of, 324

Grant, Brig. Gen. James, 255, 256

s'Gravenhaagse Courant, 250

Gravesend, 246, 254

Great Britain: effect of war, 30, 140, 305, 308; budget, 35, 110, 123–24; public debt, 95–96; cabinet, 112; public subscriptions, 111, 129–30; military strategy, 112–13, 129; new taxes, 123–25, 203–4; request for Cossack troops, 176; peace proposals, 213–14, 263–64, 269–71, 324–26, 337, 339; relations with Holland, 222; relations with Portugal, 243, 305; relations with Spain, 243, 259; relations with France, 154, 243, 305, 326, 341, 370, 371; ship building, 268–69; tribute to emperor of Morocco, 304; exports, 305; economy,

318, 371–72; foreign policy, 319; debate on battle of Sullivan's Island, 326; day of prayer, 327, 358–59; celebration of victory in New York, 333; earthquake, 341 (*see also* Army, British; Navy, British)

Greeks, 373

Greene, Gen. Nathanael, 234, 334–35

Greenwich, England, 32

Green, William, 177–78

Grenville, George, 136–37

Greville, Madame, 115

Gunpowder, 222

Gunshot wounds, treatment of, 289–90

Gustavus III, king of Sweden, 298

Gwinnett, Button, 165

Gwynn's Island, 210

Hackensack, 351

Haines, Caleb, 36

Hale, Nathan, 279, 279n

Halifax, N. C., 114

Halifax, N. S., 83, 123, 202, 240, 346

Halifax, Sir Thomas, 326

Hall, William and David, 321

Hamburg, 176

Hamlet, 252, 253, 305–6

Hancock, American frigate, 197, 296

Hancock, Ebenezer, 181

Hancock, John, 44, 73, 129, 211, 316, 357; new term in Congress, 49; home in Boston, 73, 88; made honorary chieftain, 166; message to New York, 173; signing of Declaration of Independence, 196, 225

Hancock, Lydia Henchman, 129

Hancock, Thomas, 129

Handel, George Frideric, 91, 176, 260n, 312, 313, 328–29

Hanover, Elector of (George III), 370

Harlem, 266, 267, 285, 309

Harrison, Benjamin, 143, 158–59, 163–64, 192, 193, 196, 220; named to treaty committee, 165; named to Board of War and Ordnance, 165

Hart, John, 175

Hartley, David, 110, 136, 265, 336–37

Harvard College, 129, 187, 224, 340; honorary degree for Gen. Washington, 109–10

Harvey, Gen. Edward, 298

Haslett, Col. John, 309

Hasse, Johann, 312

Hatch, Colonel, 254–55

Haydn, Joseph, 329

Heath, Brig. Gen. William, 234

Heister, Gen. Philipp von, 233, 255

Henry, Patrick, 278; colonel-in-charge of Virginia forces, 61; governor of Virginia, 202, 249

Herdman, Rev. James, 121

Hesse-Cassel, hereditary prince of, 56–57

Hesse-Cassel, landgrave of, 56–57, 85; reaction in Vienna, 95

Hessian soldiers, 56–57; final approval of treaty for, 84–86; as emigrants, 107–8; in New York, 112, 223, 240, 245–46, 330; additional forces, 134, 141; plundering by, 309–10, 352; battle of White Plains, 315; at Newport, 344; in New Jersey, 352; at battle of Trenton, 361, 375–76

Hewes, Joseph, 165

Heyward, Thomas, Jr., 165n

Hickey, Pvt. Thomas, 177–78

Highlanders, 240; battle of Moore's Creek, 73–74, 93; capture of, 225

Hobbes, Thomas, 167

Hoboken, 267

Hoch Deutsch-Americanische Calendar, Der, 201

Hodges, Margaret and Judith, 360

Holbein, Hans, the younger, 306

Holidays, 30, 145n; New Year's Day in London, 26; "St. Yankey's Day," 119; birthday of George III, 160; feast of St. Louis, 259; anniversary of coronation of George III, 310; Lord Mayor's Day, 326; Christmas, 370

Holland, 304n; army, 277; relations with America, 222; relations with Great Britain, 222; tributes to Barbary pirates, 304

Hollandsche Historische Courant, 250–51n

Holston River, 317

Holt, John H., 76–77, 229

Holy Roman Empire, 95

Hope, British warship, 139–40

Hopewell, 352

Hopkins, Commodore Esek, 234, 240–41

Hopkinson, Francis, 175, 303, 316

Hopkins, Stephen, 165, 240

Horne, John, 365–67

Hottentots, 311–12

Household hints, 221–22

House of Commons. *See* Parliament

House of Lords (Peers). *See* Parliament

Howe, Col. Robert, 27, 73, 74

Howe, Admiral, Lord Richard, 287–88, 337; appointment as commander-in-chief, 53; debate on war, 70; peace talks and terms, 149–50, 213–14, 263–64, 267, 269–71, 323, 324–26, 337, 339, 363; named viscount, 162; battle of Long Island, 254–56; fire of New York, 274

Howe, Major Gen. Sir William, 53, 54, 364; preparation for attack at Dorchester Heights, 82; rumors of evacuation of Boston, 82–83; promotion, 100; military strategy, 112, 201–2, 239, 285; Tory enlistments, 122–23; peace talks and terms, 149–50, 213–14, 263–64, 267, 269–71, 323, 324–26, 337, 339, 363; fall of The Cedars, 208; in New York, 240, 245–46, 254–56, 266–67, 295–96, 303; fire of New York, 275; knighted, 305; reaction to Hessian plundering, 309–10; battle of White Plains, 313–15

Hudson River, 267, 309, 322

Hume, David, 97–98, 247–48

Humphreys, James, 227

Humphreys, James, publisher, 321

Hungary. *See* Austria-Hungary

Hunter, Dr. John, 222–23

Hunter, William. *See* Dixon and Hunter

Huntington, Samuel, 196, 286, 310

Hurd, Rt. Rev. Dr., 359, 360

Hutchinson, Thomas, 197

Hydraulics, 237

Hypnotism, 328

Impressment, 337–38n, 364–65

Independence, American: resolved for in North Carolina, 113–14; talked about in America, 118–19, 149, 170, 172; talked about in Britain, 144, 247–48, 324, 334; support for, in Maryland, 153, 182–83; support for, in Massachusetts, 153; proposed by Virginia, 143, 158, 191; reports of debates on, 158–59, 163–64, 191–93; Declaration of, 164–65, 193–96, 196n, 225–26; support for, in Georgia, 170; support for, in Pennsylvania, 170, 182; Portugal, reaction to, in principle, 197, 200; reported in press, in America, 200, 228–29; approved by New York, 206; celebrated throughout America, 208–9, 215–16, 220, 235; comment on by Samuel Adams, 215; a child, so baptized, 220; approved by Rhode Island, 221; reported in press, in Europe, 249–51n; reported by press, in Canada, 269, 372; talked about in Europe, 289; approved by Connecticut, 297

India bonds, 318

Indians: agitation of by British, 43–44,

206–07; Proclamation of 1763, 43; Cayugas, 44; Mohawks, 44; Oneidas, 44; Onondagas, 44; Senecas, 44; Six Nations of the Iroquois, 43, 166, 231, 344–45; Tuscaroras, 44; Delawares, 113, 231–32, 344–45; education of, 113, 114, 272; Indian Affairs Committee, 113, 196; Shawnees, 272, 344–45; Cherokees, 316–17; military raids against, 316-17; treaties, 345

Inoculation, smallpox. *See* Smallpox

Inquisition, 373

Ireland, 152; British troops in, 35, 259; confinement of Col. Ethan Allen in, 39; troops of, 85–86; question of independence, 35, 259; war shortages, 269

Iroquois Indians. *See* Indians, Six Nations of the Iroquois

Italy. *See* Milan; Naples; Rome; Sardinia; Tuscany

Jacobites, 73, 373

Jamaica, New York, 254

James River, 112

Janus, pseudonym, 155–56

Jay, John, 55

Jefferson, Thomas, 143; committee to draft Declaration of Independence, 164; committees of Congress, 196, 214–15; resignation from Congress, 263; selected for and declines acceptance to commission to France, 280, 297; Virginia land reform bill, 317–18

Jenkinson, Charles, 227

Jeremiah, Book of, 278

"John the Painter." *See* Aitken, James

Johnson, Samuel, 111–12

Johnstone, Governour, 320

Jonson, Ben, *Epicoene*, 42

José I, king of Portugal: bans American shipping, 197, 200; illness, 235–36, 236n, 283; announces pardons, 305

Journal of the Resolution's Voyage. See Cook, James

Journals of Congress, 196n, 225, 281, 300–301

Jubilee, Holy Year of, 45–46

Judaism, 46

Julius Caesar, 252

Karlskrona, 298

Kearsly, G. 284–85

Kellum, Curtis, 121

Kent, 62, 108

Kentish Gazette, 146–47, 247–48, 250

Ketchum, Isaac, 178

Kip's Bay, 266

Kirkland, Moses, 135, 142

Knox, Col. Henry, 370

Knyphausen, Lt. Gen. Wilhelm von, 330

Kosciusko, Thaddeus, 304

Labor: threatened strike of London carpenters, 185–86; military-exempt jobs, 208, 216, 241, 258, 340

La Coffe, Jean Dennis, 327

Lagoa dos Patos, 243

Lake George, 34, 112, 267

Lancaster County, Va., 33

Land reform, in Virginia, 317–18

Langdon, John, 74

Laurens, Henry, 100

Lavoisier, Antoine, 63

Law, 32–33, 100–101, 121, 126, 151, 248–49, 298–300, 365–67, 373; *King vs. Barber*, 36–37; land reform in Virginia, 317–18

Law, Richard, 310

Ledger, The (London), 366

Lee, American cruiser, 47–48

Lee, Major Gen. Charles: report on New York, 60; assignment to Canada, 60–61, 74; new command in Southern Department, 74; battle of Sullivan's Island, 180–81, 219; loan from Congress, 296; defense of Rodman's Point, 303; military career, 353–54; capture of, 354–55, 363, 368

Lee, Fort, 309, 322; fall of, 334–35

Lee, Francis Lightfoot, 143

Lee, Richard Henry, 55, 143, 303, 316

Leffingwell, Ebenezer, 279

Leigh, Mr., attorney, 366

Leonard, Rev. Mr., 88–89

Lespinasse, Julie de, 151

Le Tourneur, Pierre, 252

Lewis, Brig. Gen. Andrew, 210

Lewis, William Thomas, 305–6

Lexington, and Concord, 23, 119, 211, 365; commemoration of, 118

Liberty tree, 88

Linnaeus, Carl, 186–87, 282

Lisbon, 197, 241

Livingston, Philip, 55, 164, 196

Livingston, Robert R., 164–65, 165n

Locke, John, 166–67, 169

London, 197, 264; threatened strike of carpenters, 185–86; lord mayor of, 197, 265, 326, 336–37; air pollution, 230–31; great fire of, 264–65; reopening of Parliament, 318; Lord Mayor's Day, 326; impressment in, 337–38, 364–65

London Chronicle, 146, 154, 250, 334, 366

London Evening Post, 366

London Gazette, 135, 136–37, 249–50

London Packet, 97, 125, 250, 269, 318, 326, 337, 339, 349

Long Island, N. Y., 177, 202, 246; battle of, 254–56, 262–63

Lottery, American, 316, 335, 340, 345; British, 124, 335

Lottery Magazine, 217, 227, 248

Loudon, Samuel, 115–16

Louis XVI, king of France, 126, 154, 341; dismisses Turgot, 137; down with measles, 216

Lovell, James, 345–46

Luttrell, Temple, 333

Lynch, Thomas, Jr., 165*n*

Lyttelton, Lord, 90

McDonald, Brig. Gen. Donald, 73–74, 264

McDougall, Alexander, 55

McElroy, Captain, 160

McKean, Thomas, 165

McKonkey's Ferry, 375

Macumber, Ensign Matthew, 299–300

Madrid, 91, 96, 216, 247

Magaw, Col. Robert, 320

Magna Charta, 167

Maidenhead, N. J., 352

Malden, Mass., 149

Malsbourg, Frederic de, 56

Mamaroneck, 309

Manchester, duke of, 90, 321

Manchester, England, 333

Manly, Capt. John, 40; escape from British, 47–48; promotion in navy, 296

Mansfield, Lord, 366

Maria Feodorowna, grand duchess of Russia, 298

Maria Josephena Anna Augusta, daughter of Emperor Charles VII, 139

Maria Theresa, archduchess of Austria and queen of Hungary, 130, 341

Marie Antoinette, queen of France, 259, 341

Marines, British, 112, 333

Marines, Continental, 316

Marseilles, 283

Martin, Josiah, governor of North Carolina, 73, 215

Maryland, 335, 345; Convention of, 153, 182–84, 197; Council of Safety of, 183–84; bounty dispute with Congress, 315–16, 323–24; constitution, 335

Maryland Gazette, 197

Mary, princess of England, 144–45, 160

Mason, George, 185

Massachusetts, 335, 346; honors Gen. Washington, 109; General Assembly of, 153–54, 173, 211; army reinforcements, 340, 370; additional delegates to Congress, 345–46

Massachusetts Gazette, 32

Matthews, David, mayor of New York, 177–78

Maurepas, Comte de, 126

Mawbey, Sir Joseph, 332

Mayo, John, 227

Mechanics' Committee, New York, 115–16

Medicine, 46–47, 62, 120, 137–38, 154–55, 210–11, 216–17, 230–31, 244–45, 260–61, 277, 282, 289–90, 328, 342

Medway, River, 62

Melchior, Isaac, 83

Mendoza, 243

Mercer, Hugh, 159

Mercure de France, 251*n*

Mercury, British frigate, 60, 65

Mermaid, British frigate, 269

Mesmer, Dr. Franz Anton, 328

Messiah, of Handel, 91–92

Mexico, 373

Milan, burning of ducal playhouse in, 76

Miles, Colonel, 254–55

Miller, Heinrich, 229

Miller, John, 366

Minorca, 243, 332

Modena, duke of, 228

Mohawk Indians. *See* Indians, Mohawks

Montevideo, 243, 305

Montgomery, Brig. Gen. Richard, 44, 94–95

Montreal, 206

Moore, Col. James, 73–74; as brig. general, 330–31

Moore's Creek, battle of, 73–74

Moravian missionaries, 231–32

Morgan, Dr. John, 62, 120

Morning Post (London), 250

Morocco, 304, 373

Morris, Capt. John, 181

Morris, Robert, 165, 214, 362, 370

Morton, John, 214, 220

Moulder, the sailmaker, 54

Moultrie, Fort, 225

Moultrie, Col. William, 157, 180, 219, 225

Moylan, Stephen, 159
Mugford, Capt. James, 139–140
Murray, Mrs. Robert, 267n
Music, 91–92, 133, 176, 245, 260, 312–13, 328–29
Musket, 160–61, 341
Muskingum River, 323

Nantasket, 216
Naples, 277, 298
Narrows, The, 246, 254
Narragansett Bay, 343
Navy, British: enlistments, 32; budget, 35, 100, 110, 123; military strategy, 112–13, 129, 201–2; battle of Sullivan's Island, 180–81, 225; weapons, 180, 181; prisoners of war, 234; in New York, 322; in North Carolina, 330–31; additional forces, 331, 333; impressment, 336–37; capture of Newport, 343–44; in South Carolina, 154
Navy, Continental, 195, 330, 335; pensions, 257; prisoners of war, 234; censure of Commodore Esek Hopkins, 234, 240–41; commissions, 296
Necker, Jacques, 311
Negroes, 94, 340; the poet, Phillis Wheatley, 102–3 (see also Slavery)
Nelson, Thomas, Jr., 61, 165, 370
Netherlands, Austrian, 130
Neville, Mr., 320
Newark, 266, 351
New Brunswick, 351
Newburyport, 197
New Castle, 268
New England Chronicle (Cambridge and Boston; later Independent Chronicle), 40–41, 229, 279
Newgate Prison, 151
New Granada, 243
New Hampshire, 335, 370; adopts constitution, 29–30, 141, 142, 184; Provincial Congress, 29–30; House of Representatives, 43, 74; elections, 184
New Hampshire Gazette, 43
New Jersey, 346; manumission of slaves, 36–37; Provincial Congress, 67, 174–75, 184; General Assembly, 184; delegates to Continental Congress, 66–67, 165, 175; adopts constitution, 202–3; British forces in, 201–2; declares Gov. Franklin enemy, 174–75, 181–82; fall of Fort Lee, 334–35; tories, 345, 368; Continental army retreat, 351, 352; capture of Gen. Charles Lee, 354–55; College of, 224, 241, 350n

Newport, 340, 343–44
Newport Mercury, 229
New Rochelle, 309
New Spain, 243
Newtown, 375
New Utrecht, 246, 254
New York: Provincial Assembly of, 175–76; Convention of, 206, 258. See also Long Island; New York City; Westchester County
New York City: election of representatives, 55, 119n; threat of British invasion, 60; reassignment of Continental army to, 107, 114; alert in, 173; as military objective, 201–2, 233, 246; evacuation of, 239–40; British occupation of, 266–67, 288; celebration of independence, 209; fire of, 274–76; tory allegiance, 323
New York, College of, 224
New York Gazette and Weekly Mercury, 278, 288, 323
New York General Hospital, 258
New York Journal, 172, 209, 229, 278
New York Packet, 115–16, 209, 228, 278
New York Pocket Almanack, 201
Nicholas, Elizabeth (Betsey), 258–59
Nicholas, Robert Carter, 259
Norfolk: destruction by British, 27; aid from colony, 35
North Carolina: battle of Moore's Creek, 73–74; British strategy, 112, 129; delegates to vote for independence, 113–14; defense of, 330–31; adopts constitution, 362–63
North Church, Boston, 88, 97
North, Lord, 52n, 95, 197, 359; rumors of resignation, 40; military budget, 49, 110, 123–24; supplementary note on, 51; debate on enquiry into war, 70–71; new taxes, 124–25; suffers broken arm, 283, 288; reopening of Parliament, 311, 318; debate on war, 320–21; debate on peace terms, 325
North Pole, 130, 132–33
Northumberland, duchess of, 365
Norton, Sir Fletcher, 78n, 162, 359
Norwich, 346
Nova Scotia, 269, 372
Nova Scotia Gazette, 372
Nurses, 258

O'Beirne, Rev. Thomas Lewis, 275–76, 277
Ohio River, 219
Old Bachelor, The. See Congreve, William

Old Bailey, 151
Old South Church, Boston, 96–97
Oliver, Peter, 197
Oliver, Richard, 136
Onondago, Chief, 166
Opium, 47, 138, 290
Oration Delivered At The State House In
   Philadelphia, An, 307
Orlov, Aleksey, 57
Ottoman Empire, 373
Over-Yessel, Dutch Province of, 222
Oxford, University, 197; lord bishop of,
   197

Paca, William, 335
Paine, Robert Treat, new term in Con-
   gress, 49
Paine, Thomas, 376; as anonymous author
   of Common Sense, 37–38, 45, 117n, 152;
   controversy over profits of Common
   Sense, 49–50, 50–51
Paraguay, 243
Paris, 26–27, 348, 364, 370; prices of goods,
   36
Parker, Commodore Sir Peter: sails to
   America, 112, 147; in South Carolina,
   152; battle of Sullivan's Island, 180–81,
   206, 225, 234; at Newport, 343–44
Parks, William, 77
Parlement, French, 125–26
Parliament, British: preliminary military
   budget, 35; debate on enquiry into war,
   67–71; supplementary notes on, 77, 151n;
   debate on Hessian treaties, 84–85; debate on suspension of arms, 89–91; homage to Gen. Montgomery, 94–95; debate
   on pickles and vinegar for troops in
   Boston, 95; British budget for year, 123–
   24; new taxes, 124–25n; debates on
   secrecy in government, 135–36, 149–50;
   debate on taxation of colonies, 136; debate on peace negotiations, 149–50;
   address of George III, 150–51; proroga-
   gation, 151; further prorogation, 226;
   peace discussions, 263, 267, 324–26; Parliamentary Register, 301n; preparation
   for reopening, 318; opening of 3rd session of 14th Parliament, 318; address of
   George III, 319; debates on war, 319–
   21, 331–33; views on Declaration of Independence, 324; day of prayer criticized,
   327–28; secession in House of Commons,
   331–33; preliminary military spending
   estimates for 1777, 332–33; continuation
   of land tax, 336; fire prevention bill,
   336–37; observance of day of prayer,
   358–59; Christmas recess, 359; number
   of bills passed into law during year, 359
Parrot, James, 212
Parsons, Col. (later Brig. Gen.) Samuel H.,
   177, 255
Patterson, Col. James, 214
Paul, grand duke of Russia, son of Catherine II, 139, 298
Paulus Hook (Jersey City), 267, 288
Peace talks, Britain and America, 149–50,
   213–14, 263–64, 267, 269–71, 323, 324–
   26, 337, 339, 363
Peerages, 162, 202, 259, 305
Pell's Point. See Rodman's Point
Pendleton, Edmund, 142
Penn, John, governor of Pennsylvania, 215
Pennsylvania, 335; college of, 224; adopts
   constitution, 281–82, 297; General Assem-
   bly of, 99, 281; Council of Safety, 135;
   Provincial Congress, 182, 214; delegates,
   214
Pennsylvania Evening Post, 45, 118–19,
   192, 224–25, 228, 272, 321, 350; first
   announcement of Declaration of Inde-
   pendence, 200
Pennsylvania Gazette, 98, 225, 321, 350
Pennsylvania Ledger, 225, 228, 321, 350
Pennsylvania Packet, 139, 225, 238, 246,
   321, 350
Pennsylvanischer Staatsbote, 229
Pensacola, 289
Percival, Dr. Thomas, 46–47
Percy, Brig. Gen. Earl, 65, 82, 365; pro-
   motion, 100; capture of Newport, 344
Pergolesi, Giovanni Battista, 312
Persia, 305
Peru, 243
Petersborough, bishop of, 90
Petrowna Alexiewna (nee Princess Wilhel-
   mina of Hesse-Darmstadt), wife of
   Grand Duke Paul of Russia, 139, 298
Phi Beta Kappa, 350n
Philadelphia, 99, 307, 335; celebration of
   independence, 208–9; defense of, 330, 339,
   340, 344, 352–53, 367–68
Philipsburg, N. Y., 354
Phoenix Park, Dublin, 152
Pigeon, purported (and apparently spur-
   ious) British flagship, 337
Pimlico, royal menagerie at, 222–23
Pinkney, John, 76–77
Pipe, Captain, 113

Piper, Colonel, 255
Pirates. *See* Barbary Pirates
Pittsburg, 345
Pitt, William, 90, 97
Pius VI, pope, 45–46, 363
Plain Dealer (Bridgeton), 57–58
Plain Truth, 115–16n, 162; publication of, 92
Plundering, 299–300, 309–10, 352
Plymouth, England, 269
Poetry, 102–3, 139, 160, 206; "Ode for the New Year," 26; patriotic, 139, 284–85
Point Alderton, 216
Point-de-Chambeau, 148
Poland, army of, 354
Poor Richard Improved, 201
Pope, Alexander, 128
Population, 248; American and British in 1976, compared, 248; in East and West Florida, 289
Portsmouth, England, 348
Portugal, 197, 200; relations with Spain, 216, 241, 243; dispute over South America, 241, 243, 283, 305; army, 277; relations with Great Britain, 243, 305, 354; relations with France, 305; pardons announced, 305
Postal service, 181, 196, 208, 257, 316, 322–23
Potemkin, Grigory Aleksandrovich, 57
Potosi, 243
Powle's Hook. *See* Paulus Hook
Prescott, Major Gen. Richard, 264, 355n
Press, 57–58, 71, 76, 97, 139, 146–47, 155, 162, 172, 213, 217, 238–39, 278, 308, 329, 349–350; *Gazette* publisher ordered to appear before New Hampshire House of Representatives, 42–43; *New York Packet* publisher's reply on freedom of the press, 115–16; reporting of independence, in America, 200, 228–29; newspaper tax in Britain, 203–4; newspaper price increases, 204, 224–25, 321; reporting of independence, in Europe, 249–51n; reporting of independence, in Canada, 269, 372; trial of London publishers for "scurrilous" advertisement on behalf of victims of Lexington and Concord, 365–67n
Price, Richard: *Observations on the Nature of Civil Liberty*, 50–51, 51n, 172
Prices of goods, 36, 128–29, 152–53, 346
Priestley, Joseph, 62–63, 342
Princeton, 209, 351
Prindle, William, 159

Privateers, American, 47–48, 139–40, 160, 221; rules for, from Continental Congress, 48n
Protestantism, 373
Providence Gazette, 228
Provincial Congresses and Conventions, supplementary note on, 51–52
Prussia, 86, 176, 281n; treaty with Great Britain, 227; army, 277
Publick Occurrences, 155
Purdie, Alexander, 76–77, 144, 162
Putnam, Major Gen. Israel, 254–55, 267, 267n, 287; defense of Philadelphia, 352–53

Quakers, 340; yearly meeting, 41–42
Quebec, 147–48, 238, 372
Queens College, 224
Queens County, tory resistance in, 28–29, 49
Quiberon, 348

Rabies, purported cure, 260–61
Racing: boat, 212n; horse, 212n
Rall, Col. Johann Gottlieb, 376
Rameau, Jean Philippe, 313
Ranby, Dr. John, 289–90
Randall, Mr., printer, 366
Randolph, Edmund, 258–59
Rationing, 28
Rattlesnake bite, purported cure, 277
Reed, John, 159
Religion, 41–42, 45–46, 75–76, 96–97, 204–5, 211–12, 228, 231–32, 245, 249, 277–78, 284, 327–28, 360, 371. (*see also* Churches)
Rhode Island: General Assembly of, 135, 221; proclaims statehood, 221; ratifies Declaration of Independence, 221; college of, 224
Richardson, Samuel, 252
Richmond, duke of, 85, 90
Rifle, British military development of, 160–61
Rio de la Plata, Viceroyalty of, 243, 305
Rio Grande (Banda Oriental), 243
Rise and Progress of the Contest in America. *See* Janus, pseudonym
Rittenhouse, David, 339, 344
Robertson, Major Gen. Archibald, 274
Robinson Crusoe. *See* Defoe, Daniel
Rochefort, 247
Rockingham, marquis of, 333
Rodman's Point, 303, 308
Rome, 363

Root, Jesse, 119
Ross, Col. George, 214, 316, 335
Rotterdamsche Courant, 250
Rowney, George, 227–28
Rowney, Thomas, 228
Royal Gallery, 306
Royal Academy, 145–46; of Music, 328–29
Royal Society, 63, 133, 186–87, 342
Rural Economy, 224
Rush, Dr. Benjamin, 214, 303
Russia, 145, 227, 373; polar exploration, 132; new British request for Cossacks, 176; army, 277; British imports, 305
Rutledge, Edward, 165, 165n
Rutledge, John, 100; as representative to peace talks, 264, 267, 270, 335, 337

Sage, Col. Comfort, 299
St. Augustine, 289
St. Eustasia, 269
St. James's Chronicle (London), 40, 59, 97, 121–22, 221, 250, 286n, 306, 319, 337, 338, 366, 371; price increase, 204
St. James's Palace, 26, 53, 145, 318
St. John, Fort, 206
St. Lawrence River, 148, 207
St. Margaret's Church, London, 359
St. Paul's Cathedral, London, 265
St. Paul's Church, New York, 275
St. Peter's, Rome, 44–45
St. Petersburg, Russia, 298
Salem, 284
Sandwich, earl of, 90, 329, 333
Sandy Hook, 201–2
San Francisco, 96
San Juan del Pico, 243
Santa Cruz de la Sierra, 243
Santa Teresa, Fort, 243
Sardinia, 273, 277
Saunders' Pocket Almanack, 201
Savannah, 235
Savile, Sir George, 332
Sawbridge, John, 136, 264, 326, 336–37
Scaliger, Joseph Justus (Renaissance scholar), 312
Schlieffen, Martin Erneste de, 56
School books, 265–66
Schuyler, General Philip, 34; report on Indian relations, 43–44; in Canada, 122
Science, 32, 62–63, 101–2, 130–33, 151–52, 186–87, 223, 236–38, 342
Scituate, 48
Scotch Regiments. *See* Highlanders
Scottish Gazette, 213

Scurvy, 342
Sellers, William, 321
Senate, of Virginia, first use of term in modern times, 184
Sergeant, Jonathan Dickinson, 67, 165n
Seven Years War, 137n, 359
Shakespeare, William, 251–52, 253, 305–6, 349
Shawnees. *See* Indians, Shawnee
Shelburne, earl of, 90
Sherman, Roger, 164, 165, 310
Shuldham, Rear Admiral Molyneux, 80, 234
Six Nations of the Iroquois. *See* Indians, Six Iroquois Nations
Slavery: military enlistments, 40, 56, 94; New Jersey Supreme Court decision, 36–37; restrictions on importation, 108–9
Smallpox, 28, 98–99, 120; epidemic in Boston, 210–11, 211n
Smallwood, Colonel, 254–55
Smith, Adam, 247–48; publication of *Wealth of Nations*, 86–87
Smith, Col. James, 214, 286
Smith, John, 153
Smith, Richard, 61, 67
Smith, Rev. William, 116–17
Smolensk, 145
Snuff, 269
Solebay, British man-of-war, 39, 180
Somerset County, 354
Somersetshire, 341
Sophia, princess of Württemberg-Stuttgart. *See* Maria Feodorowna
South America, 241, 243, 283, 305
South Carolina: Provincial Congress, 93–94, 99; constitution, 99–100, 141, 142, 184; invasion strategy, 112, 129, 152, 157–58; battle of Sullivan's Island, 180–81; defense of, 330–31
South Carolina and American General Gazette, 229–30
South Carolina and Georgia Almanack, 221–22
South Sea Company, British, 371–72
Southwark, 185
Southwick, Solomon, 229
Spain, 281n; possibility of war with Britain, 90; expedition against Algiers, 91; exploration of northwest America, 96; relations with Portugal, 216, 241, 243; hostilities in South America, 241, 243, 305; relations with Britain, 243, 305; relations with France, 243, 247, 305; military buildup, 247, 283; army, 277; reaction to

Declaration of Independence, 289; aid to America, 311; censorship, 373; inquisition, 373
Spencer, Major Gen. Joseph, 234
Sphinx, British man-of-war, 180
Sports. *See* Athletics
Standish, James, 227
Stanley, Hans, 227
Staten Island, 112, 240, 245, 247, 254, 263, 267, 288
Stirling, Major Gen., Lord, 74–75, 264; battle of Long Island, 254–55
Stock market, London, 140, 318, 371–73
Stockton, Richard, 175, 281
Stone, Thomas, 165, 165n
Stormont, Lord, 326
Strike, threat of by London carpenters, 185–86
Submarine, attempted development of, 286–88
Sullivan, Major Gen. John, 234, 255, 255n, 263, 264
Sullivan's Island, battle of, 157–58, 180–81, 225, 230, 234, 256–57; deserters, 326
Survey of Experimental Philosophy, A. See Goldsmith, Oliver
Sweden, 277, 298
Swieten, Dr. Gerard Van, 137–38, 328
Switzerland, 304
Sydenham, Dr. Thomas, 120, 216-17
Syren, British man-of-war, 180

Talbot, earl of, 85
Tappan, 246
Tartini, Giuseppe, 313
Taxes: new British, 123–24, 124–25, 336; on British newspapers, 203–4; as issue relative to American independence, 136, 194, 334
Taylor, George, 214
Tea, price restrictions on continued, 128, 152
Temple, Harriot, 257–58
Thacher, Dr. James, 133
Thames, River, 62, 223
Theater, 42, 76, 115, 121–22; survey of London theater season, 59; Garrick's retirement, 171–72; *Hamlet*, 305–6; the question of obscenity, 338–39
Thirteen Hymns Suited to the Present Times, 245
Thomas, Major Gen. John, 82; promotion, 83; military action in Canada, 147–48
Thomson, Charles, 166, 196, 208, 225

Thoughts on Government, 127–28
Throgs Neck, 295–96, 303
Thurlow, Edward, 367n
Thunder, British bomb vessel, 180, 181
Ticonderoga, Fort, 34, 148, 196, 272, 281, 293, 295; dispatches from, 323; additional troops, 370
Tilghman, Matthew, 324
Tooke, John Horne. *See* Horne, John
Tories, 159, 266; in Queens County, 28–29; arrest of leaders, 49, 142; in North Carolina, 73–74, 93; in Boston, 87–88, 122–23; and Committees of Safety, 121; plot against Gen. Washington, 177–78; in British army, 309; in New Jersey, 345, 368
Torpedo, experimental American submarine, 287
Toulon, 247
Towne, Benjamin, 200 (*see also Pennsylvania Evening Post*)
Townshend, George, 4th viscount, 85, 161
Townshend, Thomas, 67, 70–71
Trade and commerce, 224, 305, 367, 373; effect of war in Britain, 30, 140, 305, 341, 371–72; Barbary pirates, 91, 304, 373; price restrictions generally, 108–9, 128–29; 373; London stock market, 140, 318, 371–72; reopening of Boston port, 169–70; Portuguese ban on American ships, 197, 200, 216; British ship building, 268–69; war shortages, 269; reopening of Cherbourg harbor, 359
Transportation, 41, 286, 323
Treason, 248–49, 339; definition of by Britain, 32–33
Trenton, 209, 351; battle of, 361, 375–76
Trinity Church, New York, 204–205, 274, 275
Tryon, William, governor of New York, 177
Tucuman, 243
Tuffnal, George Foster, 95
Turgot, A. R. J., 125–26, 203, 311; dismissed as comptroller general of finances in France, 137; British assessment of result on world affairs, 154
Tuscany, 281n
Tyburn, 227, 359
Tyrannicide, American privateer, 221

United Colonies (term superseded by *United States* after Declaration of Independence). *See* Continental Congress; Army, Continental; Navy, Continental;

respective colonies (*see also* United States)

United Provinces. *See* Holland

United States (term popularly used in July, 1776, and officially adopted by Congress Sept. 9, 1776) : term first used, 143–44; allegiance to, 248–49, 310; population prediction, 248; first official usage of term, 268 (*see also* Independence, American; Continental Congress; Army, Continental; Navy, Continental; Foreign relations, American; respective states)

Valcour Island, 293, 295

Vander Capellen, Johan Theodor, 222

Vauxhall Gardens, 259–60

Venus's-flytrap, 186–87

Vertiz, Gen. Juan José de——y Salcedo, 241, 243

Vienna, 328; reaction to British-Hessian troop treaties, 95; Court of, 373

Virginia, 335; aid for Norfolk, 35; Convention of, 61, 142–43, 144, 168–69, 185, 202, 263; British forces in, 65, 72, 112, 129; adopts constitution, 141, 142–43, 184–85; declaration of rights, 143, 168–69; proposes independence, 158, 191; elects Patrick Henry governor, 202; land reform through abolition of fee taille, 317–18; deportation of British merchants, 367

Virginia Gazette, 221n, 228–29; history and status of newspapers with that title, 76–77; motto of, 162

Voltaire, François Marie Arouet: denunciation of Shakespeare, 251–52, 254; British reply to, 349

Walpole, Sir Robert, 333

Walton, George, 362

Warasdin, 119

Ward, Gen. Artemas, 173

Ward, Samuel, 98–99, 120, 135

War Office, American, 165

Washington, Fort, 309, 322, 334–35; fall of, 329–30

Washington, Gen. George, 34, 72–73, 148, 196, 335, 362; at Cambridge, 26; at Dorchester Heights, 82; reply to poem by Phillis Wheatley, 103; army to New York, 107, 114, 122; honored by Massachusetts General Court, 109; recipient of gold medal from Congress, 109; awarded honorary degree by Harvard, 109–10; in New York, 155, 175–76, 285; effect on public morale, 162–63; Tory plot against, 176–77; request for chaplains, 211–12; British peace proposals, 214; orders evacuation of New York, 239–40; battle of Long Island, 254–56, 266; retreat in New York, 266–67; pardons convicted soldier, 279; court-martial of Matthew Macumber, 299–300; battle of White Plains, 315; retreat through New Jersey, 352; granted interim powers by Congress, 358, 368–69n; in Pennsylvania, 361; powers regarding enlistments, 369; battle of Trenton, 375–76

Washington, Lawrence, 155

Washington, Martha, 163; inoculated against smallpox, 154–55

Water closet, development of, 71–72

Watertown, 92, 173, 329

Wealth of Nations, The. See Smith, Adam

Weather: in America, 23, 26, 246; in Britain, 35, 61–62, 146–47, 359; predictions for Fourth of July in various almanacs, 201; as a factor in the battle of Trenton, 375–76

Wedderburn (e), Alexander, 325

Welch, William, 178

Wells, R, and son, 229–30

Wentworth, Benning, governor of New Hampshire, 29

West, Benjamin, 145–46, 283

West, Robert, 283

West Church, Boston, 88

Westchester County, 30, 303, 308–9, 313

Westminster Abbey, 365

Westminster Magazine, 218

Westminster Palace, 77n, 359

Wheatley, Phillis, 102–3

Whigs, 41n, 94

Whipple, William, 74, 370

Whitecomb, Brig. Gen. John, 159

White Eyes, Capt., 113

Whitehall Evening Post (London), 250, 365–66

Whitehead, William, 160

White Plains, 206, 323, 344; battle of, 313, 315

Whitworth, Sir Charles, 336

Wigs, 59, 244

Wilkes, John, 264, 320, 365–66; comment on Declaration of Independence, 324; as lord mayor of London, 326

Wilkie, J., 366

William, British flagship, 55, 210

William and Mary, College of, 142, 187, 224; founding of *Phi Beta Kappa*, 350

Williamsburg, 35, 168, 202, 297; Convention of Virginia proposes independence, 142; "capitol" and "senate," first uses of terms in modern times, 184–85n; celebration of independence, 220

Williams, William, 310

Willing, Thomas, 61

Wilson, James, 165, 214, 316, 370

Wimbledon, 265

Winchester, Rev. Elhanan, 245

Windsor Castle, 306

Witherspoon, John, 175, 286, 335

Wolcott, Oliver, 310

Women: the poet, Phillis Wheatley, 102. emulation of Martha Washington, 163, substituting for men at the harvest. 246: as nurses, 258

Woodbridge, 351

Woodcock, 151–52

Wood, William, 212

Worcestershire, 341

Wright, Sir James, governor of Georgia, 215

Wright, T., 366

Wythe, George, 143, 316

Yale College, 51n, 164, 350n; valedictory address at commencement exercises, 223–24

York, archbishop of, 76

Young, Edward, 252

Zeisberger, David, 231–32